HERMAN MELVILLE

an annotated bibliography

Volume I: 1846 - 1930

A
Reference
Publication
in
Literature

Hershel Parker
Editor

HERMAN MELVILLE,
an annotated bibliography .

Volume I: 1846 - 1930

BRIAN HIGGINS

G.K.HALL&CO.
70 LINCOLN STREET, BOSTON, MASS.

Library of Congress Cataloging in Publication Data

Higgins, Brian, 1943-
  Herman Melville, an annotated bibliography.

(A Reference publication in literature)
  Includes index.
  CONTENTS: v. 1. 1846 - 1930.
  1. Melville, Herman, 1819 - 1891--Bibliography.
I. Title. II. Series.
Z8562.58.H53 [PS2387] 016.813'3 78-23446
ISBN 0-8161-7843-7

This publication is printed on permanent/durable acid-free paper
MANUFACTURED IN THE UNITED STATES OF AMERICA

For Harrison Hayford and Hershel Parker

Contents

Acknowledgments

This bibliography was prepared at the Newberry Library Melville Collection and without its resources would not have been possible. Grateful acknowledgment is made to all friends and members of the Northwestern-Newberry Melville Edition project who have helped build up the collection. Thanks are also due to Richard Colles Johnson for his ready assistance; to William Thrasher, Vonciel Gaines, Zoe-Ann Colin, and Stephen Wiberly for their patient help at the University of Illinois at Chicago Circle Library; and to Merton M. Sealts, Jr., who provided the review of The Piazza Tales printed in the Daily Wisconsin and the Weekly Wisconsin, and George Monteiro, who provided the review of Clarel from the International Review. The transcriptions and photocopies of the newspaper reviews of Melville's lectures which Professor Sealts has deposited in the Newberry Melville Collection were a valuable aid. A faculty summer fellowship and a sabbatical leave from the University of Illinois at Chicago Circle greatly helped completion of the volume.

Finally, a very large debt, happily acknowledged, is to Harrison Hayford and Hershel Parker, who have made great personal contributions to the Newberry Melville Collection and have generously encouraged and aided this project.

Introduction

The first volume of this bibliography of writings on Herman
Melville covers the years 1846-1930. During that time Melville's
reputation underwent two major revolutions. Typee (1846, published
in England as Narrative of a Four Months' Residence Among the Natives
of a Valley of the Marquesas Islands) and Omoo (1847), his first two
books, were popular successes, though they enraged Protestant missionaries and their supporters by their portrayal of the South Sea island
missions. Mardi (1849) baffled and irritated most of its readers by
its mixture of South Sea romance, allegory, and satire, but Redburn
(1849) and White-Jacket (1850) enhanced Melville's reputation as a
modern Defoe. Though it sold poorly and was assailed by some critics
for its "mad" English, transcendental "ravings," and violation of
narrative "rules" Moby-Dick (1851, published in England as The Whale)
brought Melville his highest critical acclaim, many reviewers hailing
it as a work of remarkable originality and power. His next work,
Pierre (1852), an experimental psychological novel, was roundly abused
by almost all reviewers, and even led some to speculate that Melville
was mad. Thereafter, Israel Potter (1855) and The Piazza Tales (1856),
though favorably received in general, were not as widely noticed as
Melville's books prior to Pierre; reviewers of The Confidence-Man
(1857) were often hostile, usually perplexed. Melville's volumes of
verse, Battle-Pieces (1866), Clarel (1876), and the privately published John Marr and Other Sailors (1888) and Timoleon (1891) in no
way salvaged his reputation. His last work of fiction, Billy Budd,
Sailor, was unfinished at his death in 1891. After the publication
of The Confidence-Man and his brief career as a lecturer in 1857-
1860, Melville received during the remaining 30 years of his life
only occasional mentions in the literary columns of newspapers and
magazines, apart from the few reviews of his poems, and only cursory
treatment in literary histories and encyclopaedias. He was remem-
bered primarily, as he had feared, for having "lived among the cannibals," and written Typee and Omoo, travel books to be ranked with
Mayo's. In 1889, an English admirer, Henry S. Salt, published the
lengthiest assessment of Melville since the 1850s: his best work,
Salt judged, was Typee; Moby-Dick was only perhaps more successful
than Mardi.

By the time of Melville's death, however, the first stirrings of
a new appraisal of his work had begun to appear. During the later

part of the nineteenth century, Moby-Dick was apparently something of
a cult-book among a number of English literary men. The novelist
W. Clark Russell was exceptional nonetheless in publishing his claim
in 1884 that Moby-Dick was actually Melville's finest book; but by
1892 Salt had revised his earlier opinion, now finding Moby-Dick less
shapely and artistic than Typee, but still Melville's supreme work.
Americans, too, paid occasional brief tributes to Moby-Dick in the
late 1880s and early 1890s; and Arthur Stedman's editions of Typee,
Omoo, White-Jacket, and Moby-Dick (1892) led to a certain amount of
acknowledgment during the rest of the 1890s that Moby-Dick ranked with
the best of Melville's work, if it were not, in fact, his best. By
the last year of the century, in the most penetrating analysis of
Moby-Dick since some of the English reviews and the New York Literary
World review of 1851, Archibald MacMechan was claiming that Melville
was, in fact, a man of one book. The same year the New York Times
reported a "conspicuous revival of interest" in Melville in England,
brought about by Clark Russell's "repeated glowing tributes" to his
genius; and a columnist for the same newspaper, William Livingston
Alden, who wrote about Melville on a number of occasions in the late
1890s and early 1900s, declared Melville "far and away the most original genius" America had produced. The following year, Arthur Stedman
claimed, somewhat prematurely, that Melville now held "his station" in
Britain and America as one of his country's most original romancers.

   In the early part of the new century, Moby-Dick continued slowly
to gain recognition as part of Melville's finest work, or his finest,
and was published in "Everyman's Library" in 1907. Primarily the book
was valued as a powerful sea novel, accurate in its descriptions and
its accounts of whalingmen and for its vivid portrayal of character.
After MacMechan, who had commented on the atmosphere, structure, theme,
and style of Moby-Dick, further critical advances were slow in coming.
Some admirers still echoed complaints raised about the book in 1851-
1852: Louis Becke found its brilliant description too often marred
by Melville's "weird and fantastic metaphysical imagination," and
even Clark Russell found parts too obscure and objected that the reader
was frequently "harassed" by "a transcendental mysticism" out of
place in the mouths of sailors. As in the 1890s Melville's later
works were seldom mentioned, but were occasionally dismissed as incomprehensible or unreadable.

   Despite admiration for Typee, Omoo, and Moby-Dick in the early
1900s, no one appears to have seconded Alden's high claim for Melville;
certainly most academic writers of the time did not share his enthusiasm. In 1900 Walter C. Bronson labelled Melville one of the minor
writers of New York (A Short History of American Literature), while
Barrett Wendell dismissed his career in one sentence as one of "literary promise, which never came to fruition" (A Literary History of
America); for Julian W. Abernethy, Melville was just another forgotten
New York novelist (American Literature, 1902). A decade later Melville
still did not deserve to be classed with Cooper or above Paulding,
according to William B. Cairns (A History of American Literature,
1912); and according to W. P. Trent and John Erskine, except for

Moby-Dick, Melville was less important than Simms, while Cooper was superior to them both (Great Writers of America, 1912). Two years later, John Calvin Metcalf (American Literature, 1914) noted nonetheless that Melville was again widely read at home and abroad; Moby-Dick, Metcalf judged, put Melville in the company of "other masters of the sea story" from Defoe to Conrad. Carl Van Doren's lengthier assessment of Melville in The Cambridge History of American Literature (1917) was probably more influential in the "Melville revival" which Percy H. Boynton noted was taking place in 1919 (A History of American Literature). Boynton followed Van Doren in seeing Moby-Dick as Melville's greatest work, after which his preoccupation with metaphysics destroyed him as a novelist. Later critics were slow to revise this estimate.

After the laudatory essays of the centennial year, excitement about Melville escalated rapidly. Boynton attributed the "revival" partly to the vogue of South Sea literature, partly to post-war skepticism, but more to the fact that "in Melville has been rediscovered one of the immensely energetic and original personalities of the last hundred years." Boynton's assessment and two essays of 1920 were prophetic of the estimate and treatment of Melville and Moby-Dick in the following decade. Viola Meynell, in her introduction to the English "World's Classics" edition, declared Moby-Dick "the crown of one's reading life"; and E. L. Grant Watson found in it an analysis of the stages of Melville's own mentality, the story of his "fiercely vivid life-consciousness." For many other critics of the 1920s, Moby-Dick was not simply Melville's major book (or as some, reminiscent of MacMechan, would have it, his only book), but one of the supreme works of world literature, to be ranked with the best of Shakespeare, Dostoievsky, Balzac, Tolstoy, Gorky, Conrad, and Hardy. Critics and (slowly joining the ranks) scholars now examined the meaning, symbolism, or "prophecy" of the book, focusing mainly on Ahab and the Whale and frequently relating their interpretations to what they saw as Melville's own inner struggles. Reflecting the new psychological interests of the time, critics offered confident accounts of Melville's unconscious impulses and "suppressions," and in the fascinatingly tortured personality now revealed to them discovered an heroic giant, a maimed Titan at odds with a complacent and crippling age.

The three biographies published in the 1920s were instrumental in promoting this new interest in Melville's personality. Raymond M. Weaver's Herman Melville: Mariner and Mystic (1921), the first book-length study, was valuable in bringing together hitherto unpublished material by and about Melville, but focused almost entirely on his first 33 years and further distorted the picture of Melville by treating his fiction as autobiography. In addition to brilliant critical insights, Lewis Mumford (1929) offered a fuller account of Melville's later years, but both John Freeman (1926) and Mumford were dependent on Weaver for details of his earlier years and followed Weaver in taking the fiction as autobiography.

Writers in the 1920s tended to see Melville as a powerful rather than an artistic author, but occasional tributes to his craftsmanship appeared. One of the notable personal revaluations of individual works by Melville which took place in the 1920s was that of Van Wyck Brooks, who in 1921 found "strange lapses" in Moby-Dick that showed Melville's insecure artistic control: he simply forgot his story and lost himself in the details of cetology, Brooks considered; he was powerful only in a phrase or paragraph or episode, not in a larger composition. Two years later, Brooks was surprised at a third reading of Moby-Dick to discover how conscious Melville was of what he was doing; stressing the "careful disorderliness" of Melville's method, his "cunning" craftsmanship throughout Moby-Dick, Brooks, like others after him, now defended the cetological matter as the ballast necessary for an epic.

In the finest of the centenary essays, Frank Jewett Mather, Jr. championed Melville's later works, finding them great in human interest, and two years later Weaver judged Pierre a "high achievement as a work of art." Their enthusiasm was not shared by most critics in the 1920s, who were slow to appreciate the merits of works other than Typee, Omoo, Redburn, White-Jacket, and Moby-Dick. A few, nonetheless, found value in Mardi, Pierre, some of The Piazza Tales, and Billy Budd, after it was first published in 1924. Two major personal revaluations of the short fiction took place in the 1920s. In his biography, Weaver devoted only one sentence to The Piazza Tales and on the basis of the manuscript, which he had not yet transcribed and studied, dismissed Billy Budd as "not distinguished"; in his 1928 edition of "Benito Cereno," "Bartleby," "The Encantadas," and Billy Budd (Shorter Novels of Herman Melville), Weaver found all four works of "prime importance" as works of art and for their "peculiar position" in Melville's development as artist and man; "Benito Cereno" and "The Encantadas" he now saw as Melville's supreme technical achievements, while in Billy Budd he discovered a "remarkably detached, subtle, and profound" study in abnormal psychology. Reviewing Weaver's edition, Carl Van Doren, who in 1917 had dismissed The Piazza Tales, with Israel Potter and The Confidence-Man, as "not markedly original," now ranked all four stories with "the most original and distinguished fiction" yet produced in America.

While writing on most of Melville's less popular works was mainly remarkable for the claims critics made, Pierre attracted a number of thoughtful analytical commentaries. In 1930 E. L. Grant Watson offered the most sustained psychological analysis of any single one of Melville's works yet made and concluded that Pierre was his greatest book, a more profound work and better artistic whole than Moby-Dick. Robert Forsythe's introduction to his edition of Pierre the same year provided a necessary corrective to the biographical methods of the 1920s by showing the book's unreliability as a record of Melville's own experience and psychological tendencies. Forsythe's essay was of further value in indicating the need for study of Melville's literary sources.

Throughout the 1920s The Confidence-Man was generally held, as earlier, to be a total failure. In 1922 Carl Van Vechten made a major breakthrough in seeing Emerson as the "Confidence Man" and his essay on friendship as required reading for the book. But critics in the rest of the 1920s made little further advance in understanding, though Mumford spoke of its "dangerous and exhilarating satire." Freeman and Mumford were alone in the 1920s in giving extended treatment to Melville's verse.

Considerable progress had been made in other areas, however. Though by no means textually impeccable, the Constable Standard Edition (1922-1924), together with the Princeton edition of The Apple-Tree Table and Other Sketches (1922) and John Marr and Other Poems (1922), made available most of Melville's work; and most of his fiction was also available in inexpensive single editions. A number of his important letters were collected in book form, and parts of his journals were in print; work towards a bibliography had commenced. Obviously much still remained for later editors, biographers, bibliographers, and critics to perform. But by 1930 a student of Melville was in a far better position than one in 1920; and though his works were still missing from reading lists for most university literature courses, Melville's position as a major American author had been virtually secured.

Note: Entries in the bibliography are arranged in chronological order. Asterisks indicate items referred to in other works which I have not been able to locate. My aim in this volume has been to list and annotate all the known writings on Melville in the years 1846-1930. Readers should bear in mind, however, that scholars are still discovering hitherto unknown items about Melville from this period. The Melville Society Newsletter (formerly Extracts), in particular, should be consulted for their most recent finds.

References Abbreviated in the Text

Aaron   Aaron, Daniel. "Melville and the Missionaries." New England Quarterly, 8 (September 1935), 404–408.

Anderson (1937)   Anderson, Charles Roberts. "Contemporary American Opinions of Typee and Omoo." American Literature, 9 (March 1937), 1–25.

Anderson (1939)   Anderson, Charles Roberts. Melville in the South Seas. New York: Columbia University Press, 1939; rpt. New York: Dover Publishers, 1966.

Anderson (March 1939)   Anderson, Charles Roberts. "Melville's English Debut." American Literature, 11 (March 1939), 23–38.

A.S.P.   P., A. S. "Toward the Whole Evidence on Melville as a Lecturer." American Notes and Queries, 2 (October 1942), 111–112.

Birss (February 1934)   Birss, John Howard. "Herman Melville Lectures in Yonkers." American Book Collector, 5 (February 1934), 50–52.

Birss (1932)   Birss, John Howard. "Melville's Marquesas." Saturday Review of Literature, 8 (2 January 1932), 429.

Birss (December 1933)   Birss, John Howard. "A Satire on Melville in Verse." Notes and Queries, 165 (9 December 1933), 402.

Birss (1943)   Birss, John Howard. "Toward the Whole Evidence on Melville as a Lecturer." American Notes and Queries, 3 (April 1943), 11–12.

Birss (December 1934)   Birss, John Howard. "'Travelling': A New Lecture by Herman Melville." New England Quarterly, 7 (December 1934), 725–728.

Birss (April 1933)   Birss, John Howard. "Whitman and Herman Melville." Notes and Queries, 164 (22 April 1933), 280.

Branch   Branch, Watson G., ed. Melville: The Critical Heritage. London and Boston: Routledge & Kegan Paul, 1974.

Burgert — Burgert, Hans. "William Faulkner on Moby-Dick: An Early Letter." Studi Americani, 9 (1963), 371-375.

Cameron — Cameron, Kenneth Walter. "Emerson and Melville Lecture in New Haven (1856-1857)." Emerson Society Quarterly, No. 19 (Second Quarter 1960), 85-96.

Chase — Chase, Richard, ed. Melville: A Collection of Critical Essays. Englewood Cliffs, N. J.: Prentice-Hall, Inc., 1962.

Colum — Colum, Padraic. "Epic of the Sea and Epic of the Desert," in A Half-Day's Ride. New York: Macmillan & Co., 1932, pp. 175-180.

Davis (1952) — Davis, Merrell R. Melville's MARDI: A Chartless Voyage. New Haven: Yale University Press, 1952.

Davis (1941) — Davis, Merrell R. "Melville's Midwestern Lecture Tour, 1859." Philological Quarterly, 20 (January 1941), 46-57.

Doubloon — Parker, Hershel, and Harrison Hayford, eds. MOBY-DICK As Doubloon. New York: W. W. Norton & Co., 1970.

Duffy — Duffy, Charles. "Toward the Whole Evidence on Melville as a Lecturer." American Notes and Queries, 2 (July 1942), 58.

Duncan — Duncan, Robert W. "The London Literary Gazette and American Writers." Papers on English Language and Literature, 1 (Spring 1965), 153-166.

Edel — Edel, Leon, ed. Henry James: The American Essays. New York: Vintage Books, 1956.

Ellis — Ellis, Theodore. "Another Broadside into Mardi." American Literature, 41 (November 1969), 419-422.

Falk (Grove) — Falk, Robert P., ed. The Antic Muse: American Writers in Parody. New York: Grove Press, 1955.

Falk (Twayne) — Falk, Robert P., ed. "The Mysterious, Ambiguous Mr. Melville." American Literature in Parody. New York: Twayne Publishers, 1955.

Flanagan — Flanagan, John T. "The Spirit of the Times Reviews Melville." JEGP, 64 (January 1965), 57-64.

Fracchia — Fracchia, Charles A. "Melville in San Francisco." Extracts, No. 25 (February 1976), pp. 2-3.

Gifford — Gifford, George E., Jr. "Melville in Baltimore." Maryland Historical Magazine, 51 (September 1956), 245-246.

Gohdes (1937)

Gohdes, Clarence. "Gossip About Melville in the South Seas." New England Quarterly, 10 (September 1937), 526–531.

Gohdes (1944)

Gohdes, Clarence. "Melville's Friend 'Toby.'" Modern Language Notes, 59 (January 1944), 52–55.

Haraszti

Haraszti, Zoltan. "Melville Defends Typee." More Books: The Bulletin of the Boston Public Library, 22 (June 1947), 203–208.

Heflin

Heflin, Wilson. "An Indignant Contemporary Editorial on White-Jacket." Extracts, No. 25 (February 1976), pp. 8–9.

Hetherington (1961)

Hetherington, Hugh W. Melville's Reviewers: British and American 1846–1891. Chapel Hill: University of North Carolina Press, 1961.

Hetherington (1955)

Hetherington, Hugh W. "A Tribute to the Late Hiram Melville." Modern Language Quarterly, 16 (December 1955), 325–331.

Hillway

Hillway, Tyrus. "A Note on Melville's Lecture in New Haven." Modern Language Notes, 60 (January 1945), 55–57.

Hubbell

Hubbell, Jay B. Who Are the Major American Writers? Durham: Duke University Press, 1972.

Kaplan (1972)

Kaplan, Sidney, ed. "Contemporary Reviews," in Battle-Pieces and Aspects of the War. Amherst: University of Massachusetts Press, 1972, pp. xxix–xliv.

Kaplan (1975)

Kaplan, Sidney. "Moby-Dick in New Bedford." Extracts, No. 21 (February 1975), p. 9.

Kennedy

Kennedy, Frederick James. "Herman Melville's Lecture in Montreal." New England Quarterly, 50 (March 1977), 125–137.

Kummer

Kummer, George. "Herman Melville and the Ohio Press." Ohio State Archaeological and Historical Quarterly, 45 (January 1936), 34–36.

Lawrence

Lawrence, D. H. The Symbolic Meaning. Edited by Armin Arnold with a Preface by Harry T. Moore. Fontwell, Arundel, England: Centaur Press, 1962.

Letters

Davis, Merrell R., and William H. Gilman, eds. The Letters of Herman Melville. New Haven and London: Yale University Press, 1960.

Leyda (1954)

Leyda, Jay. "Another Friendly Critic for Melville." New England Quarterly, 27 (June 1954), 243–249.

Lloyd

Lloyd, Francis V., Jr. "Melville's First Lectures." American Literature, 13 (January 1942), 391–395.

Log

Leyda, Jay, ed. The Melville Log. New York: Harcourt, Brace and Co., 1951; rpt. (with supplement) New York: Gordian Press, 1969.

McElderry

McElderry, B. R. "The National Era Review of White Jacket." Melville Society Newsletter, 15 (Winter 1960), n.p.

McNeilly

McNeilly, Dorothy V. B. D. R. "The Melvilles and Mrs. Ferris." Extracts, No. 28 (November 1976), pp. 1-9.

Mailloux and Parker

Mailloux, Steve, and Hershel Parker. Checklist of Melville Reviews. The Melville Society, 1975.

Mead

Mead, David. "Herman Melville: Solemn Mariner." Yankee Eloquence in the Middle West: The Ohio Lyceum 1850-1870. East Lansing: Michigan State College Press, 1951, pp. 74-77.

Minnigerode

Minnigerode, Meade. Some Personal Letters of Herman Melville and a Bibliography. New York: Brick Row Book Shop, 1922.

Monteiro (Spring 1975)

Monteiro, George. "'Far and Away the Most Original Genius That America Has Produced': Notations on the New York Times and Melville's Literary Reputation at the Turn of the Century." Resources for American Literary Study, 5 (Spring 1975), 69-80.

Monteiro (Third Quarter 1975)

Monteiro, George. "A Half Hour with Melville, 1887." Papers of the Bibliographical Society of America, 69 (Third Quarter 1975), 406-407.

Monteiro (Fourth Quarter 1976)

Monteiro, George. "Herman Melville in the 1890s." Papers of the Bibliographical Society of America, 70 (Fourth Quarter 1976), 530-536.

Monteiro (June 1976)

Monteiro, George. "Melville: A Reference in 1897." Extracts, No. 26 (June 1976), p. 13.

Monteiro (Fourth Quarter 1974)

Monteiro, George. "Melville Reviews in The Independent." Papers of the Bibliographical Society of America, 68 (Fourth Quarter 1974), 434-439.

Monteiro (May 1977)

Monteiro, George. "More on Herman Melville in the 1890s." Extracts, No. 30 (May 1977), pp. 12-14.

Monteiro (September 1974)

Monteiro, George. "Mrs. Melville and The New York Times." Extracts, No. 19 (September 1974), pp. 11-12.

Monteiro (November 1977)

Monteiro, George. "'Not a Novel....a Most Astounding Epic': Moby-Dick in 1900." Extracts, No. 32 (November 1977), p. 9.

Monteiro   Monteiro, George. "References to Typee and Pierre,
(September 1973)   1884." Extracts, No. 15 (September 1973), p. 9.

Monteiro   Monteiro, George. "An Unnoticed Contemporary
(September 1977)   Review of Battle-Pieces." Extracts, No. 31
                      (September 1977), pp. 11-12.

Murry   Murry, John Middleton. "The End of Herman
                      Melville," in John Clare and Other Studies.
                      London and New York: Nevill, 1950, pp. 208-212.

Norton The   Parker, Hershel, ed. The Confidence-Man: His
Confidence-Man   Masquerade. New York: W. W. Norton & Co., 1971.

Norton   Hayford, Harrison, and Hershel Parker, eds. Moby-
Moby-Dick   Dick. New York: W. W. Norton & Co., 1967.

Orth   Orth, Ralph. "An Early Review of The Confidence-
                      Man." Emerson Society Quarterly, No. 43
                      (Second Quarter 1966), p. 48.

Parker   Parker, Hershel. "Five Reviews Not in MOBY-DICK
(March 1972)   As Doubloon." English Language Notes, 9
                      (March 1972), 182-185.

Parker   Parker, Hershel. "Further Notices of Pierre."
(October 1972)   Extracts, No. 12 (October 1972), pp. 4-5.

Parker   Parker, Hershel. "New Cross-Lights on Melville
(1965)   in the 1870's." Emerson Society Quarterly, No. 39
                      (Second Quarter 1965), pp. 24-25.

Parker   Parker, Hershel, ed. Shorter Works of Hawthorne
Shorter Works   and Melville. Columbus, Ohio: Charles E. Merrill
                      Publishing Co., 1972.

Parker   Parker, Hershel. "Three Melville Reviews in the
(January 1970)   London Weekly Chronicle." American Literature, 41
                      (January 1970), 584-589.

Pilkington and   Pilkington, Walter, and B. Alsterlund. "Melville
Alsterlund   and His Public: 1858." American Notes and Queries,
                      2 (August 1942), 67-71.

Pollin   Pollin, Burton R. "Additional Unrecorded Reviews
(April 1975)   of Melville's Books." Journal of American Studies,
                      9 (April 1975), 55-68.

Pollin   Pollin, Burton R. "An Unnoticed Contemporary
(May 1975)   Review of Moby-Dick." Extracts, No. 22 (May 1975),
                      pp. 3-4.

Pollin   Pollin, Burton R. "Unreported American Reviews
(October 1975)   of Melville, 1849-1855." Extracts, No. 23
                      (October 1975), pp. 7-8.

Potter   Potter, David. "Reviews of <u>Moby-Dick</u>." <u>Journal of the Rutgers University Library</u>, 3 (June 1940), 62-65.

<u>Recognition</u>   Parker, Hershel, ed. <u>The Recognition of Herman Melville: Selected Criticism Since 1846</u>. Ann Arbor: University of Michigan Press, 1967.

Ricks and Adams   Ricks, Beatrice, and Joseph D. Adams. <u>Herman Melville: A Reference Bibliography 1900-1972</u>. Boston: G. K. Hall & Co., 1973.

Rountree   Rountree, Thomas J., ed. <u>Critics on Melville</u>. Coral Gables: University of Miami Press, 1972.

Scholnick   Scholnick, Robert J. "Politics and Poetics: The Reception of Melville's <u>Battle-Pieces and Aspects of the War</u>. <u>American Literature</u>, 49 (November 1977), 422-430.

Sealts (1950)   Sealts, Merton M., Jr. "Did Melville Write 'October Mountain'?" <u>American Literature</u>, 22 (May 1950), 178-182.

Sealts (1974)   Sealts, Merton M., Jr. <u>The Early Lives of Melville</u>. Madison: University of Wisconsin Press, 1974.

Sealts (1976)   Sealts, Merton M., Jr. "Mary L. D. Ferris and the Melvilles." <u>Extracts</u>, No. 28 (November 1976), 10-11.

Sealts (1971)   Sealts, Merton M., Jr. "Melville and Richard Henry Stoddard." <u>American Literature</u>, 43 (November 1971), 359-370.

Sealts (1957)   Sealts, Merton M., Jr. <u>Melville as Lecturer</u>. Cambridge: Harvard University Press, 1957.

Smith   Smith, Nelson. "Eight British Reviews and Notices of Melville, 1846-1891." <u>Extracts</u>, No. 23 (October 1975), 6-7.

Stern   Stern, Milton R. "A Checklist of Melville Studies," in <u>The Fine Hammered Steel of Herman Melville</u>. Urbana: University of Illinois Press, 1957, pp. 251-291.

Stewart   Stewart, Randall. "Hawthorne's Contributions to <u>The Salem Advertiser</u>." <u>American Literature</u>, 5 (January 1934), 327-341.

Tanselle   Tanselle, G. Thomas. "The First Review of <u>Typee</u>." <u>American Literature</u>, 34 (January 1963), 567-571.

Thorp (1942)   Thorp, Willard. "Did Melville Review <u>The Scarlet Letter</u>?" <u>American Literature</u>, 14 (November 1942), 302-305.

References Abbreviated in the Text

Thorp
(1938)

Thorp, Willard. "'Grace Greenwood' Parodies
Typee." American Literature, 9 (January 1938),
455–457.

Thorp
(1968)

Thorp, Willard, ed. Great Short Works of the
American Renaissance. Perennial Classics. New
York: Harper & Row, 1968.

Vincent

Vincent, Howard P., ed. The Merrill Studies in
MOBY-DICK. Charles E. Merrill Studies. Columbus,
Ohio: Charles E. Merrill Publishing Co., 1969,
pp. 2–20.

Walser

Walser, Richard. "Another Early Review of Typee."
American Literature, 36 (January 1965), 515–516.

Willett

Willett, Ralph. The Merrill Studies in PIERRE.
Charles E. Merrill Studies. Columbus, Ohio:
Charles E. Merrill Publishing Co., 1971.

Williams
(1948)

Williams, Mentor L. "Horace Greeley Reviews
Omoo." Philological Quarterly, 27 (January 1948),
94–96.

Williams
(1950)

Williams, Mentor L. "Some Notices and Reviews of
Melville's Novels in American Religious Period-
icals, 1846–1849." American Literature, 22
(May 1950), 119–127.

Yannella
(1976)

Y[annella], D[onald]. "Respectability, 1852" and
"Melville and American Humor, 1852." Extracts,
No. 26 (June 1976), pp. 14–15.

Yannella
(1975)

Yannella, Donald J. "'Seeing the Elephant' in
Mardi," in Artful Thunder: Versions of the Roman-
tic Tradition in American Literature In Honor of
Howard P. Vincent. Ed. Robert J. Demott and
Sanford E. Marovitz. Kent, Ohio: Kent State
University Press, 1975, pp. 105–117.

Zimmerman

Zimmerman, Michael. "Herman Melville in the
1920's: An Annotated Bibliography." Bulletin
of Bibliography, 24 (September–December 1964),
117–120, 106; (January–April 1965), 139–144.

Writings about Herman Melville, 1846 - 1930

1846 A BOOKS — NONE

1846 B SHORTER WRITINGS

1   ANON. Review of <u>Narrative of a Four Months' Residence Among</u>
     <u>the Natives of a Valley of the Marquesas Islands</u>. London
     <u>Athenaeum</u>, No. 956 (21 February), 189–191.
          Mainly summary, with extracts from chapters 3, 4, 6, 7,
     and 10. The book is full of rich and freshly-colored mat-
     ter. Melville's manner is New World all over. Continued
     in 1846.B2. Reprinted in 1846.B37 and 1846.B43.

2   ANON. Review of <u>Narrative of a Four Months' Residence Among</u>
     <u>the Natives of a Valley of the Marquesas Islands</u>. London
     <u>Athenaeum</u>, No. 957 (28 February), 218–220. Continued from
     1846.B1. Mainly summary, with extracts from chapters 23,
     24, 29, and 32 selected as adding "to the store of enter-
     taining or useful knowledge"; also extracts from chapters
     11 and 12. Identifies Melville as "our journalist." Re-
     printed in 1846.B43 and 1846.B44.

3   ANON. Review of <u>Narrative of a Four Months' Residence Among</u>
     <u>the Natives of a Valley of the Marquesas Islands</u>. London
     <u>Spectator</u>, 19 (28 February), 209–210.
          Summary, with extracts from chapters 9, 18, and 26. The
     book is very interesting, though the American fluency be-
     comes rather uninteresting where there is no action to re-
     lieve it, especially as Melville's mind, though vigorous
     enough, has not been trained in those studies which enable
     men to observe with profit, and Melville did not master the
     Typee language sufficiently to understand any but the com-
     monest subjects of communication. The book is a great
     curiosity in being the first published account of living
     among Polynesian natives by someone who has lived with them
     in their own fashion. As the work of an English common
     sailor, its authority would be questionable; but in the
     United States, young men of respectability serve as common
     seamen and the American system of popular education gives

1

1846

them a greater familiarity with popular literature and a
readier use of the pen than is usual with their English
counterparts. Much of the book is not beyond the range of
invention, especially by someone acquainted with the Islands
and the fictions of Defoe, and several things seem to have
been heightened for effect. But many of the incidents seem
too natural to have been invented. Certain sea freedoms
should have been removed before the book was issued for
family reading. Reprinted in 1846.B43; reprinted in part
in Anderson (March 1939), p. 28, and Branch, pp. 53-55.

4   ANON. Review of <u>Narrative of a Four Months' Residence Among
     the Natives of a Valley of the Marquesas Islands</u>. London
     <u>Critic</u>, NS 3 (7 March), 219-222.
         A most entertaining and refreshing book. The picture
     Melville has drawn of Polynesian life and scenery is incom-
     parably the most vivid and forceful ever published. The
     incidents are sometimes exaggerated and the coloring over-
     charged, yet in the narrative generally there is a
     <u>vraisemblance</u> that cannot be feigned; the minuteness and
     novelty of the details could only have been given by some-
     one who had nature for his model. Melville's clear, lively,
     pointed style, the skillful management of his descriptive,
     his philosophical reflections and sentimental apostrophes
     at first suggest the book was the joint work of an American
     sailor and man of letters. The book does not abound in
     stirring incident or action; and its suspenseful episodes
     are the least welcome parts, "so strongly do they bear the
     impress of exaggeration." Summary, with extracts from chap-
     ters 2, 4, 6, 7, and 9. Continued in 1846.B8. Reprinted
     in part in Branch, pp. 56-57.

5   ANON. Review of <u>Narrative of a Four Months' Residence Among
     the Natives of a Valley of the Marquesas Islands</u>. London
     <u>Examiner</u> (7 March), pp. 147-148.
         Accepts the authenticity of this "really curious book."
     There may be a little "colouring" here and there, but the
     result is a thorough impression of reality. The book is a
     mixture of grace, license, and oddity. It does not have
     such unaffected vigor and straightforward simplicity of
     description as Dana's <u>Two Years Before the Mast</u>. But few
     narratives of escape have a more sustained interest or more
     dramatic close. Summary, emphasizing Melville's life among
     the Typees; he is probably the only man who has described
     them "from this very social and familiar point of view."
     Extracts from chapters 2, 26, 23, and 30. Reprinted in
     Branch, pp. 60-64.

6   ANON. Review of <u>Narrative of a Four Months' Residence Among</u>
    <u>the Natives of a Valley of the Marquesas Islands</u>. London
    <u>John Bull</u> (7 March), p. 156.
        Reviewer has not met with such a bewitching work since
    <u>Robinson Crusoe</u> and suspects that if there really is a
    Herman Melville he has employed a Daniel Defoe to describe
    his adventures. The easy, graceful, and graphic "style of
    composition" does not suggest the work of a common sailor.
    Melville has produced a narrative of singular interest in
    his exciting and romantic adventures and in his powerful
    delineation of the manners and customs of the Typees. Re-
    printed in part in Anderson (March 1939), p. 29; reprinted
    in Branch, pp. 64–65.

7   ANON. Review of <u>Narrative of a Four Months' Residence Among</u>
    <u>the Natives of a Valley of the Marquesas Islands</u>. London
    <u>Mirror</u>, 47 (7 March), 154–157.
        Melville's and Toby's adventures, though true, are not
    less striking than the fictitious incidents reported by
    Crusoe and Quarll. Summary, mainly of adventures before
    the Typee valley is reached, with extracts from chapters 6,
    7, and 10.

8   ANON. Review of <u>Narrative of a Four Months' Residence Among</u>
    <u>the Natives of a Valley of the Marquesas Islands</u>. London
    <u>Critic</u>, NS 3 (14 March), 251–254.
        Continued from 1846.B4. "The predominant and most objec-
    tionable characteristic of this book is the obtrusive ear-
    nestness with which its author supports a favourite notion
    that savage is preferable to civilised life." Seldom have
    savages found so zealous a vindicator of their morals;
    rarely has Christianity owned so ungrateful a son. Melville
    gives charming descriptions of savage life, but the social
    condition is neither sufficiently scrutinized nor described,
    "while the isolated facts he offers are so tinged with the
    colouring through which he perversely beholds them as to be
    little better than worthless." Melville never speaks of the
    missionaries but in terms of downright disrespect or ridi-
    cule and the tone of mock respect in his preface is the more
    despicable and mischievous because it may lead the unthink-
    ing to believe he has the real interest of Christianity
    seriously at heart. Yet Melville's description of life,
    manners, and scenery are always interesting, his pages often
    amusing. Extracts from chapters 11, 14, 18, and 19. Con-
    tinued in 1846.B23. Reprinted in part in Branch,
    pp. 57–59.

1846

*9   ANON. Review of <u>Typee</u>. New York <u>Evening Mirror</u> (17 March).
      Cited in Mailloux and Parker, p. 1.

10   ANON. Review of <u>Typee</u>. New York <u>Morning News</u> (18 March).
      "For the most part the book is a rose colored account
      of a tropical race which seems pictured to us cold north-
      erners, like the performers in some rich ballet...." <u>Typee</u>
      "is a happy hit which ever way you look at it, whether as
      travels, romance, poetry or humor. It has a sufficiency of
      all of these to be one of the most agreeable, readable books
      of the day. Curiosity is piqued, good sense flattered;
      there is a dash of romantic Rousseauism, with now and then
      a shadow of the Cannibal as a corrective. The peculiarity
      of the book...is the familiar and town life of the author
      among a race of naked savages.... The <u>bonhommie</u> of the
      book is remarkable." Extract from chapter 24. Continued
      in 1846.B13. Reprinted in 1846.B15.

11   ANON. Review of <u>Narrative of a Four Months' Residence Among</u>
      <u>the Natives of a Valley of the Marquesas Islands</u>. London
      <u>Atlas</u> (21 March), pp. 185-186.
      Melville's book is one of the most singular and best
      told in its class (of striking episodes and the adventurous
      lives of seamen). His hint of acquaintance with a more re-
      fined grade of society obviates certain doubts which would
      otherwise be apt to mar the readers' enjoyment, for no
      illiterate man could have written anything like such a book;
      and the pleasure derived from Melville's narrative would be
      much diminished if we supposed its contents reached us at
      second-hand, after being largely modified by a professional
      <u>littérateur</u>. The book is as remarkable for the distinctive
      character of its lively style as for the novelty of its
      facts. Summary, with extracts from chapters 2, 7, 10, and
      27. Continued in 1846.B22.

12   ANON. Review of <u>Typee</u>. New York <u>Anglo American</u>, 6 (21 March),
      523.
      All of the details of the islands are delightful, inter-
      esting, and new.

13   ANON. Review of <u>Typee</u>. New York <u>Morning News</u> (21 March).
      Continued from 1846.B10. Innumerable anecdotes of the
      pleasant Typee life are told with great good humor. The
      book is full of entertainment and enjoyment in spite of the
      cannibalism. Undoubtedly the missionaries have had a dif-
      ficult task in the Sandwich Islands, but it would be well
      to inquire, at Melville's suggestion, whether the best and
      wisest men have always been sent there. Summary, with

extracts from chapters 4, 2, 3, 6, and 11. Reprinted in
1846.B24.

14 ANON. Review of <u>Typee</u>. New York <u>Spirit of the Times</u>, 16
(21 March), 48.
Melville's name looks a little like a <u>nom de plume</u>. His
style is not only agreeable but delightful, and his descriptions give a better idea of the Marquesas than any previously encountered. Reprinted in Flanagan, pp. 58-59, and
Walser, pp. 515-516.

15 ANON. Review of <u>Typee</u>. New York <u>Weekly News</u> (21 March).
Reprint of 1846.B10. Reprinted in part in <u>Log</u>, p. 914;
reprinted in Tanselle, pp. 567-571.

16 ANON. Review of <u>Typee.</u> Boston <u>Daily Advertiser</u> (23 March),
p. 2.
<u>Typee</u> is quite an interesting narrative and gives a
pleasant and detailed description of the manners and customs, the climate, fruits, etc. of the islands.

17 ANON. Review of <u>Typee</u>. New Bedford <u>Daily Mercury</u> (23 March),
p. 1.
<u>Typee</u> is a singularly attractive and delightful work.
The careless elegance of style suits admirably with the
luxurious and tropical tone of the narrative, bespeaking
the practised and accomplished writer rather than the
inmate of the forecastle. But such instances of unusual
talent and superior literary acquirements are not rare
among the crews of our whaleships. Extracts from chapters
10 and 17. Reprinted in 1846.B21; 1846.B97; Branch, p. 66.

18 ANON. Notice of <u>Typee</u>. Philadelphia <u>Dollar Newspaper</u>
(25 March).
<u>Typee</u> is an exceedingly agreeable and pleasant work.
Reprinted in Pollin (April 1975), p. 56.

19 [Hawthorne, Nathaniel]. Review of <u>Typee</u>. Salem <u>Advertiser</u>
(25 March).
<u>Typee</u> is a very remarkable work. "The book is lightly
but vigorously written; and we are acquainted with no work
that gives a freer and more effective picture of barbarian
life.... The author's descriptions of the native girls are
voluptuously colored, yet not more so than the exigencies
of the subject appear to require. He has that freedom of
view--it would be too harsh to call it laxity of principle--
which renders him tolerant of codes of morals that may be
little in accordance with our own; a spirit proper enough

1846

to a young and adventurous sailor, and which makes his book
the more wholesome to our staid landsmen. The narrative is
skillfully managed, and in a literary point of view, the
execution of the work is worthy of the novelty and interest
of its subject." Reprinted in Stewart, pp. 328-329; Thorp
(1968), p. 721; Parker, Shorter Works, p. 161; Rountree,
p. 13; Branch, pp. 67-68.

20   ANON. Review of Typee. Albany Argus (26 March).
        After cursory examination it seems that Melville has
written a decidedly interesting book--embodying valuable
information and amusing narrative. There is a tinge of
romance throughout, which gives it the charm of a beautiful
novel. Melville has stores of observation and information
combined with a piquant style.

21   ANON. Review of Typee. New Bedford Mercury (27 March), p. 4.
        Reprint of 1846.B17.

22   ANON. Review of Narrative of a Four Months' Residence Among
        the Natives of a Valley of the Marquesas Islands. London
        Atlas (28 March), pp. 202-203.
        Continued from 1846.B11. Summary, with extracts from
chapters 26, 31, 29, and 18. "...were we to extract all
the amusing things that tempt in almost every page, we
should go nigh to copy the whole book."

23   ANON. Review of Narrative of a Four Months' Residence Among
        the Natives of a Valley of the Marquesas Islands. London
        Critic, NS 3 (28 March), 315-320.
        Continued from 1846.B8. Melville's descriptions of the
physical aspect of the country and of the customs and amuse-
ments of the natives are remarkably corroborated by Dr. John
Coulter in Adventures in the Pacific. The most obvious
difference is in their respective estimates of the morals
and condition of the people, Melville finding the natives
happier in the primitive state, Coulter pitying and deplor-
ing their abject condition and finding them to be "grovel-
ling, sensual, indolent, and brutish." Coulter's is the
most accordant with the commonsense view. Deformed with
some blemishes, Melville's book is nonetheless "one of the
most brilliantly coloured and entertaining that has for a
long while past issued from the press." Extracts from chapters 20, 23, 24, 26, 29, 31, and 34. Reprinted in part in
Branch, pp. 59-60.

24   ANON. Review of Typee. New York Weekly News (28 March).
        Reprint of 1846.B13.

25   ANON. Review of <u>Typee</u>. New York <u>Gazette and Times</u> (30 March),
     pp. 1-2.
     <u>Typee</u> "is one of the most delightful and well written
     narratives that ever came from an American pen," with a
     fresh, graceful and animated style well suited to its theme.
     Melville "has made the subject of the Typee henceforth
     wholly his own by his felicitous mode of showing off its
     wild and novel charms." Reprinted in Branch, pp. 68-70.

26   ANON. Review of <u>Narrative of a Four Months' Residence Among</u>
     <u>the Natives of a Valley of the Marquesas Islands</u>. <u>Tait's</u>
     <u>Edinburgh Magazine</u>, NS 13 (April), 268.
     "The adventures are very entertaining; so much so, in-
     deed, as to beget a flitting notion that they may sometimes
     be a little embellished. The style is evidently touched up,
     or, as masons say, 'pointed' by some literary artist, which
     also confirms the notion that the story may have been a
     little coloured."

27   ANON. Review of <u>Narrative of a Four Months' Residence Among</u>
     <u>the Natives of a Valley of the Marquesas Islands</u>. London
     <u>Douglas Jerrold's Shilling Magazine</u>, 3 (April), 380-383.
     Mainly on the delights of life in the Typee valley, a
     "garden of Eden, from which man is not yet an exile." It
     "is impossible to read this pleasant volume without being
     startled at the oft-recurring doubt, has civilization made
     man better, and therefore happier? If she has brought much
     to him, she has taken much away; and wherever she has trod,
     disease, misery and crime have tracked her footsteps." This
     is one of the most captivating of books, with a <u>real</u>
     Robinson Crusoe and a <u>real</u> man Friday. The early part is
     full of vivid excitement, the hair-breadth escapes in vivid
     contrast to the voluptuous ease and tranquil enjoyments of
     the happy valley. With "little pretension to author-craft,"
     there is a life and truth in the descriptions, and a fresh-
     ness in the style which is in perfect keeping with the
     scenes and adventures. Reprinted in Branch, pp. 70-73.

28   ANON. Review of <u>Narrative of a Four Months' Residence Among</u>
     <u>the Natives of a Valley of the Marquesas Islands</u>. London
     <u>Eclectic Review</u>, NS 19 (April), 448-459.
     Admires the book for its novel scenes and hazardous ad-
     ventures and for the impression it leaves of "increased
     knowledge arising from introduction to a new and singularly
     interesting race." But mocks Melville's favorable views of
     savage man. Defends the missionaries and advises Melville
     to learn the worth of their morality before he criticizes
     their motives or disparages their work. Extracts from

1846

chapters 2, 3, 6, 9, 10, 12, and 24. Reprinted in part in
Anderson (March 1939), pp. 24-25, and Log, p. 212.

29   ANON. Review of Narrative of a Four Months' Residence Among
the Natives of a Valley of the Marquesas Islands. London
Simmonds' Colonial Magazine and Foreign Miscellany, 7
(April), 499-501.
     One of the most interesting works that has yet appeared
in Murray's Colonial Library, owing to the novelty of its
scenes and the freshness of its descriptions. It is full
of marvelous adventure and has a charm calculated to rivet
the reader's attention as strongly as Defoe's Robinson
Crusoe. But some of the descriptions seem to have been
wrought up for effect, and the reality of many is doubtful.
One or two voluptuous scenes might well have been expunged,
and the high strain of admiration for savage life and un-
civilized customs somewhat moderated, before the book was
sent forth for circulation in families to fascinate the
minds of inexperienced youth. Extracts from chapters 4,
2, 3, 14, and 17.

30   ANON. Review of Typee. New York American Review: A Whig
Journal, 3 (April), 415-424.
     The style of Typee is plain and unpretending, but racy
and pointed, and the romantic interest "thrown around" the
adventures will be highly charming to most readers. Many of
Melville's conclusions and inferences cannot be assented to
and his remarks on the missionaries are prejudiced and un-
founded; but his own adventures carry an air of truthfulness
and fidelity. Extracts from chapters 2, 4, 9, 10, 11, 12,
18, 31, 17, and 28. Reprinted in part in Log, p. 212.

*31   ANON. Review of Typee. New York Illustrated Magazine, 1
(April), 380.
     Cited in Potter, p. 62.

32   ANON. Review of Typee. Richmond Southern Literary Messenger,
12 (April), 256.
     Typee contains many curious and interesting matters.
Polynesia is destined to a rapid rise in historical and
geographical importance.

33   B. Review of Typee. New York National Anti-Slavery Standard,
6 (2 April), 175.
     Melville's account of the natives exactly corresponds
with Captain Porter's, which he says he has never seen.
Typee is very pleasantly written and apparently faithful.
The adventures are highly wrought and exciting and the whole

narrative more entertaining than Robinson Crusoe, not so much for the style as the facts. It is curiously charming and charmingly instructive.

34   ANON. Review of Typee. Cincinnati Morning Herald (3 April).
        The narrative is worthy of the author of Robinson Crusoe in style and in interest, with the additional advantage of being a simple record of facts.

*35   ANON. Review of Typee. Cincinnati Morning Herald (4 April).
        Cited in Hetherington (1961), p. 34.

36   ANON. Review of Typee. New York Albion, NS 5 (4 April), 168.
        Two volumes of interesting and curious matter, with a description of a little-known country and people; written in a very easy familiar style.

37   ANON. "Adventures in the Marquesas Islands." New York Anglo American, 6 (4 April), 555-557.
        Reprint of 1846.B1.

38   ANON. Review of Typee. New York Daily Tribune (4 April).
        Typee seems to be the record of imaginary adventures by someone who has visited the region. "But it is a very entertaining and pleasing narrative, and the Happy Valley of the gentle cannibals compares very well with the best contrivances of the learned Dr. Johnson to produce similar impressions." Melville has the power to make pretty and spirited pictures and a quick and arch manner. His account of the Sandwich Island missionary enterprises corresponds with other reports. Reprinted in Recognition, p. 3, and Branch, pp. 77-78.

*39   ANON. Review of Typee. New York Evening Mirror (4 April), p. 416.
        Cited in Anderson (1937), p. 11, and Log, p. 210.

40   ANON. Review of Typee. West Roxbury (Mass.) Harbinger, 2 (4 April), 263-266.
        Reviewer is most interested by Melville's account of the "social state" of the Typees and the lessons it teaches. The peace and goodwill of the Typee Valley can be achieved in civilized societies through the production of universal abundance. Since Dana's Two Years Before the Mast there has been nothing to compare with Typee for fresh and natural interest; the whole book is the work of an artist. Extracts from chapters 25, 18, 27, and 26. Reprinted in part in Branch, pp. 74-77.

1846

41 ANON. Review of <u>Narrative of a Four Months' Residence Among</u>
   <u>the Natives of a Valley of the Marquesas Islands</u>. London
   <u>Times</u> (6 April), p. 3.
       Murray's <u>Home and Colonial Library</u> does not contain a
   more interesting book and hardly a cleverer one. It is
   full of captivating matter and has freshness and originality. But it is by no means authentic. Melville is a very
   uncommon common sailor, even for America. His reading has
   been extensive, and his style throughout is rather that of
   an educated literary man than that of "a poor outcast working as a seaman." The narrative contains improbabilities
   and inconsistencies. Extract from chapter 4. Reprinted
   in part in Branch, pp. 78-80.

42 C., H. Review of <u>Typee</u>. New York <u>Evangelist</u> (9 April).
       <u>Typee</u> is racily-written, with an attractive vivacity and
   great good humor, but is extremely exaggerated, if not sheer
   romance. It "abounds in praises of the life of nature,
   <u>alias</u> savageism, and in slurs and flings against missionaries and civilization." When Melville touches matters of
   fact at the Sandwich Islands, he shows the sheerest ignorance and utter disregard of truth. The work was made for
   London, not America. Reprinted in Branch, p. 81.

43 ANON. "Herman Melville's Residence in the Marquesas." Boston
   <u>Littell's Living Age</u>, 9 (11 April), 82-93.
       Reprint of 1846.B3, 1846.B1, and 1846.B2.

44 ANON. "Adventures in the Marquesas Islands." New York <u>Anglo</u>
   <u>American</u>, 6 (11 April), 580-582.
       Reprint of 1846.B2.

45 ANON. Review of <u>Typee</u>. New York <u>Golden Rule and Odd-Fellows'</u>
   <u>Companion</u>, 4 (11 April), 246.
       <u>Typee</u> conveys much information about the Marquesas
   Islands, is written in an agreeable style, and abounds with
   incidents. Reprinted in Pollin (April 1975), p. 59.

46 ANON. Review of <u>Typee</u>. Brooklyn <u>Eagle</u> (15 April).
       A strange, graceful, most readable book. <u>Typee</u> seems
   to be "a compound of the 'Seward's Narrative,' and
   'Guidentio de Lucca,' style and reading."

*47 ANON. Review of <u>Narrative of a Four Months' Residence Among</u>
   <u>the Natives of a Valley of the Marquesas Islands</u>. London
   <u>John Bull</u> (17 April).
       Cited in Davis (1952), p. 16.

48   ANON.   Review of <u>Typee</u>.   <u>Morning Courier and New-York Enquirer</u>.
     (17 April).
          <u>Typee</u> is written in a racy and readable style, and
     abounds in anecdote and narrative of unusual interest.   In
     all essential respects it is a fiction, a piece of
     Munchausenism, from beginning to end.   Melville may have
     visited the Marquesas Islands, and there may be foundation
     for some parts of the narrative, but many of the incidents
     are utterly incredible.   As a book of travels, as a state-
     ment of facts, it has no merit whatever.   The accounts of
     missionary labors and the French are not reliable, owing
     to the spirit of fiction in which the whole book is written.
     Reprinted in part in <u>Log</u>, p. 211; reprinted in Haraszti,
     pp. 204-205.

49   ANON.   "Herman Melville's Book."   Albany <u>Argus</u> (21 April).
          Reports that Melville "desires to state to the public,
     that <u>Typee</u> is a true narrative of events which actually
     occurred to him."   Yet his description of life in the South
     Seas is more novel and romantic than any book of travels in
     many years.   Quotes from 1846.B4.   Reprinted in 1846.B50.

50   ANON.   "Herman Melville's Book."   Albany <u>Argus</u> (24 April).
          Reprint of 1846.B49.

51   ANON.   Review of <u>Typee</u>.   Charleston (S.C.) <u>Southern Patriot</u>
     (25 April).
          <u>Typee</u> is a very curious and interesting narrative of
     savage life reminiscent of the voyages of Cook, Carteret,
     Byron, and Anson.

52   ANON.   "Adventure of Herman Melville."   <u>Chambers's Edinburgh
     Journal</u>, NS 5 (25 April), 265-269.
          Summary of <u>Narrative of a Four Months' Residence Among
     the Natives of a Valley of the Marquesas Islands</u>.   Reprinted
     in 1846.B64 and 1849.B68.

*53 ANON.   Boston <u>Illustrated Family Magazine</u>, 3 (May), 277-283.
          Reprint of 1846.B52.   Cited in Mailloux and Parker, p. 5.
     [See 1846.B64.]

54   ANON.   Review of <u>Typee</u>.   New York <u>Knickerbocker</u>, 27 (May), 450.
          <u>Typee</u> is a very entertaining work with an easy, gossiping
     style and constant and infectious <u>bonhommie</u>.   Melville seems
     occasionally to be romancing, however.   Quotes from 1846.B48.
     Reprinted in part in <u>Log</u>, p. 216.

55   ANON.   Review of <u>Typee</u>.   New York <u>Merchants' Magazine and
     Commercial Review</u>, 14 (May), 491.

1846

Typee has all the elements of a popular book--novelty,
originality of style and matter, and deep interest from
first to last. Melville's perfect sang froid in his intercourse with the cannibals and the ease with which he seemed
to regard his Polynesian life give a particular richness to
the book. The faithfulness of the descriptions and narrative give it a peculiar charm.

56 ANON. Review of Typee. New York National Magazine and
Industrial Record, 2 (May), 1172.
A very curious account of what Melville saw and felt.
He describes, in simple and plain narrative, the native's
"manners, customs, and mode of life, which, though not very
full of incident, are, nevertheless, far from being devoid
of interest." Reprinted in Pollin (April 1975), pp. 58-59.

57 ANON. Review of Typee. New York United States Magazine and
Democratic Review, NS 18 (May), 399.
The scenes in Typee are described with peculiar animation
and vivacity. Though taxing credulity, they are without
doubt faithfully sketched. The volumes are most amusing
and interesting. Reprinted in Anderson (1937), p. 17, and
Branch, p. 83.

58 ANON. Review of Typee. Philadelphia Godey's Magazine and
Lady's Book, 32 (May), 238.
Typee is extremely interesting, treating "untrodden
ground"; its scenes are novel and striking to an unusual
degree. American travelers surpass all others in the liveliness and freedom of their descriptions and narratives.

59 ANON. Review of Typee. Philadelphia Graham's Magazine, 28
(May), 240.
An entertaining work. Melville's pen riots in describing
the felicity of the Typees. His book is full of strange
things, but his descriptions are doubtless transcripts of
facts, not imagination, sounding as they do, "as bad as
truth." Reprinted in Branch, p. 82.

60 ANON. "The Marquesas and the Marquesans." Chambers's
Edinburgh Magazine, NS 5 (2 May), 282-284.
A description of the islands is offered as a "sequel to
the Adventure of Herman Melville, which appeared in our last
number."

*61 ANON. Review of Typee. New York Evangelist (9 May).
Cited in Hetherington (1961), p. 44.

62   ANON. "Typee, a Veritable Narrative." New York <u>Evening</u>
    <u>Mirror</u> (9 May).
      "We are requested to state, on the authority of the
    writer himself of this universally read, though suspected
    book, that the work is a genuine history of actual occur-
    rences, and not by any means the fiction it has been repre-
    sented. The misbelief in the story arises from the actual
    poverty of most persons' imaginations...." Reprinted in
    1846.B63.

63   ANON. New York <u>Morning News</u> (19 May).
    Reprint of 1846.B62.

64   ANON. "Adventure of Herman Melville." Boston <u>Illustrated</u>
    <u>Family Magazine</u>, 3 (June), 277-283.
    Reprint of 1846.B52.

65   ANON. "Alleged Forgery." London <u>Almanack of the Month</u>, 1
    (June), 368-369.
      Comic item, reporting that Melville had been "brought up"
    on a charge of having forged several valuable documents
    concerning the Marquesas. "A good deal of conflicting evi-
    dence was brought forward on both sides, and it was obvious
    that whether the papers were forgeries or not, the talent
    and ingenuity of Herman Melville were of themselves suffi-
    cient to recommend him very favourably to a literary tri-
    bunal." Reprinted in part in <u>Log</u>, p. 220; reprinted in
    Anderson (March 1939), pp. 37-38, and Branch, p. 84.

66   ANON. Albany <u>Argus</u> (5 June).
    Obituary of Gansevoort Melville.

67   [CHASLES, PHILARÈTE]. "Séjour de deux Américains chez les
    Taïpies, dans L'île de Noukahiva." Paris <u>Journal des Débats</u>
    (22 June).
      Summary of <u>Typee</u>, with commentary. Melville's style is
    so ornate, and he has so strong a predilection for dramatic
    effects that one does not know how much to rely on his nar-
    rative. But the violence of his coloring is natural in a
    sailor and derives from the force and variety of his
    impressions.

68   [CHASLES, PHILARÈTE]. "Séjour de deux Américains chez les
    Taïpies, dans L'île de Noukahiva." Paris <u>Journal des Débats</u>
    (25 June).
      In Melville's personal adventures one sees clearly a very
    truthful man, one who desires sensation and excitement at

any cost; he is as curious as a child, as adventurous as a savage. His is the American spirit of violence, enterprise, and disregard of consequences.

69   ANON. "Ingenious Notice of 'Typee.'" New York <u>Morning News</u> (29 June).

Reprints 1846.B65, with introductory note: Melville's "story is substantially the same with that of the other travellers who have visited the islands, but they have had the art, the cunning rogues, to cover over all the romance of the region which is the natural element, with a layer of dullness." Melville "passed through the city a day or two since" and maintained the "perfect genuineness of the narrative."

70   ANON. Review of <u>Typee</u>. Boston <u>Universalist Quarterly and General Review</u>, 3 (July), 326-327.

<u>Typee</u> is very interesting and would be very instructive, but for the apparent "strong coloring of the romantic" in the descriptions and "an evident attempt at effect in the management of the narrative." It is unclear what is simple matter of fact and what is imaginative recollection. But the pictures of natural scenery and the voluptuous life of the natives are vivid. At times, Melville's taste appears to have been affected by this voluptuousness; if so, he would be apt to regard as evils many of the changes introduced by the missionaries which others would regard as improvements. The standard of moral and social excellence by which he judges the missionaries is unclear.

71   ANON. Review of <u>Narrative of a Four Months' Residence Among the Natives of a Valley of the Marquesas Islands</u>. London <u>Gentleman's Magazine</u>, NS 26 (July), 66.

The whole narrative is most interesting, most affecting, and most romantic.

72   ANON. Review of <u>Typee</u>. New Haven <u>New Englander</u>, 4 (July), 449-450.

<u>Typee</u> is not without literary merit and is a very companionable book. But it is difficult to believe that Melville "was not actuated, either by a perverse spirit of intentional misrepresentation, or that he is not utterly incapable, from moral obtuseness, of an accurate statement." The moral obtuseness appears in the glowing descriptions of savage life and the small anathemas against civilization. Wherever civilization comes in contact with savage life, the savage wastes away; but Melville, apparently ignorant of "truths of general history," crudely attributes the

depopulation of the Sandwich Islands to the efforts of
missionaries. Melville's course of life has not been calculated greatly to improve his "moral eye sight." Reprinted
in Recognition, pp. 4-5.

73   ANON. "Typee: The Traducer of Missions." New York Christian
Parlor Magazine, 3 (July), 74-83.
        Typee is an "apotheosis of barbarism," a "panegyric on
cannibal delights," an "apostrophe to the spirit of savage
felicity." Melville assails the cause of missions "with a
pertinacity of misrepresentation and degree of hatred" which
can only entitle him "to the just claim of traducer." He
seems to possess a cultivated taste and a fair education,
but his deficient reading causes many of his errors of
general fact, as well as gross misstatements about the
missionaries. With his lively imagination and often graceful description, he has written an attractive history of
personal adventure. But the book is filled with the most
palpable and absurd contradictions, even in consecutive
paragraphs. Reviewer doubts whether Melville ever saw the
Marquesas; or, if he did, whether he ever lived among the
Typees. Reprinted in part in Log, p. 224, and Branch,
pp. 85-89.

74   ANON. "How strangely things turn up!" Buffalo Commercial
Advertiser (1 July).
        Reports that "Toby" of Typee is living in Buffalo, work-
ing as a house and sign painter. His turning up is a
strange verification of a very strange and almost incredible
book. Prints letter from Richard Tobias Greene, stating "I
am the true and veritable 'Toby,' yet living, and I am
happy to testify to the entire accuracy of the work so long
as I was with Melville...." Reprinted in 1846.B75; 1846.B77;
Minnigerode, pp. 16-19; reprinted in part in 1846.B82 and
1846.B91; Haraszti, p. 207; Log, p. 220.

75   ANON. "'Toby' Identified!" Albany Evening Journal (3 July).
        Reprint of 1846.B74, with introduction: "Toby" authen-
ticates the book, yet his "testimony tends to increase
rather than to resolve our doubts."

*76   GREENE, RICHARD T. Albany Argus (3 July).
        Reprint of "Toby's" letter in 1846.B74. Cited in Log,
p. 221.

77   ANON. "A Veritable Witness." Albany Argus (4 July). Reprints
editorial comments and letter of 1846.B74, with brief introduction. Reprinted in 1846.B81.

1846

78   ANON. Albany Evening Journal (6 July).
      Report that Melville "has no doubt but that the Buffalo
Sign Painter is his veritable Ship-Mate and Companion
'Toby.'" [See 1846.B74.] Reprinted in 1846.B81 and
Haraszti, p. 207.

79   ANON. "Toby." Buffalo Commercial Advertiser (6 July).
      Reprints part of 1847.B75. "Our friend of the Journal
may dismiss his doubts. There is no mistake whatever. The
father of 'Toby' called upon us last Saturday, and confirmed
his son's story in every essential particular." As a proof
of his regard for his friend, "Toby" induced a married sis-
ter to name her boy Melville. Reprinted in part in 1846.B82.

80   ANON. Albany Argus (7 July).
      Reports receiving note from Melville saying that the
"Toby" of the Buffalo Commercial Advertiser is all that he
claims to be. [See 1846.B74.] Reprinted in 1846.B82.

81   ANON. Morning Courier and New-York Enquirer (9 July).
      Notes the "difference of opinion" about Typee: in
England general opinion seems to favor its accuracy; in
the United States it has not received "such ready and general credence." Some "collateral evidence" in support of
Melville's fidelity to truth is afforded by the appearance
of his companion. Reprints 1846.B77 and 1846.B78.

82   ANON. New York Morning News (9 July).
      Reprints in part 1846.B74 and 1846.B79; reprints 1846.B80.
Defoe is rendered next to immortal by his familiar work,
and Melville in Typee has all the material of a lasting
and an enviable reputation.

*83   GREENE, RICHARD T. "Toby's Own Story." Buffalo Commercial
      Advertiser (11 July).
      Cited in Log, p. 222.

*84   ANON. Review of Typee. Boston Recorder (12 July).
      Cited in Hetherington (1961), p. 44.

*85   GREENE, RICHARD T. "Toby's Own Story." Albany Evening
      Journal (13 July).
      Reprint of 1846.B83. Cited in Log, p. 222.

86   ANON. "Typee: the Traducer of Missions." New York Evangelist
      (16 July), p. 114.
      An approving summary of 1846.B73, with frequent quotation.
Typee is handled with the severity it deserves.

87   ANON. "Singular Development/Typee--Mr. Melville--Toby."
      New York National Press (25 July).
           Few people regarded Typee as other than a very agreeable
      work of fiction with the slightest possible foundation in
      fact. The promise of Toby's reappearance is not likely to
      increase the story's credibility until the identity of the
      Toby of the book and Richard Greene is fully established.
      Reprints 1846.B82.

88   ANON. "Adventure in the Pacific--Dr. Coulter and Herman
      Melville." Dublin University Magazine, 28 (August), 127-139.
           Melville's lively and easy style is sure to make him a
      favorite with the public. His book's main interest hangs
      on his personal narrative; its value as a contribution to
      knowledge arises from his minute account of the Typees.
      Summary, with extracts from chapters 2, 6, 10, and 29.

*89   ANON. New York Evening Mirror (1 August).
           Reprint of 1846.B74. Cited in Anderson (1937), p. 11.

90   ANON. "Typee; A Residence in the Marquesas." Albany Argus
      (4 August).
           Announcement of forthcoming revised edition of Typee.
      "It will be improved under the author's revisal, by the
      omission of some portions of it, not connected with the
      narrative; and will contain some interesting additions."
      If anything, Typee has been read with even greater avidity
      and more enthusiastic commendation in England than in the
      United States.

91   ANON. London Athenaeum, No. 980 (8 August), p. 819.
           Melville's "clever work on the Marquesas" has received
      "a somewhat unexpected testimony to its authenticity, the
      value of which every reader must decide for himself."
      Quotes from the editorial comments and reprints the letter
      of 1846.B74.

92   ANON. Review of Revised Edition of Typee. New York Christian
      Parlor Magazine, 3 (September), 160.
           The most objectionable parts of the first edition are
      omitted in the revised edition, an evidence that, for some
      reason, the counsels of truth and decency have been regarded.

93   ANON. Review of Narrative of a Four Months' Residence Among
      the Natives of a Valley of the Marquesas Islands. London
      New Quarterly Review, 8 (October), 18-35.
           The parts of the book in which the whole system of
      colonization is attacked without discrimination and contrasts

are drawn between the blessings of barbarism and the
pernicious effects of civilization might better have been
omitted. But its literary merits are undeniable. (The
opening is reminiscent of parts of Tennyson's "Lotos-
Eaters.") Melville is an acute rather than a profound
observer. Summary, with extracts from chapters 32, 33, 34,
18, 20, 2, 6, 10, 11, and 17.

94 ANON. "Ladies, Attention!" Honolulu Polynesian (3 October).
    Exhorts ladies to read what Melville says of their
"mongrel cart and carriage equipages, which are so vastly
comfortable to the occupants." Extract from chapter 26 of
Narrative of a Four Months' Residence Among the Natives of
a Valley of the Marquesas Islands.

95 ANON. Review of The Story of Toby; a Sequel to "Typee."
    London Athenaeum, No. 988 (3 October), pp. 1014-1015.
    Continues to doubt Typee's authenticity; vouches for its
verisimilitude, but not its verity. Summarizes Sequel and
prints extracts.

96 ANON. Honolulu Friend, 4 (15 October), 157.
    Melville's talent for observation and description is
evident from extracts of Typee appearing in papers which
have reached the Islands. But his account of the Typees is
evidently overdrawn, too beautiful. He neglects to mention
that the Typee warriors file their teeth to resemble a saw,
which gives their mouths the appearance of "toothed steel
traps." The Friend is in possession of a letter addressed
to Melville on board the Acushnet.

97 ANON. Review of Typee. Honolulu Polynesian (17 October).
    Notes the doubt of some reviewers whether Typee is "the
genuine production of the reputed author." Reprints
1846.B17. Reprinted in 1847.B4 and 1847.B5.

98 ANON. Review of Narrative of a Four Months' Residence Among
    the Natives of a Valley of the Marquesas Islands. London
    Literary Gazette, No. 1560 (12 December), p. 1042.
    Contemporary reviewers have dwelt at length on the book's
"wonderful adventures and extraordinary revelations" and
considered them real and authentic. But "we happened to
fancy the name of Melville to be equivalent to that of
Sinbad the Sailor" and so "abstained from noticing this
clever and entertaining production."

1847 A BOOKS - NONE

1847 B SHORTER WRITINGS

*1   BINGHAM, HIRAM. <u>A Residence of Twenty Years in the Sandwich</u>
       <u>Islands</u>. New York: S. Converse, p. 446.
          Cited in Aaron, pp. 405-406.

2   CHANNING, WILLIAM ELLERY. "The Island Nukuheva," in <u>Poems,</u>
       <u>Second Series</u>. Boston: James Munroe and Co., pp. 144-152.
          Inspired by <u>Typee</u>, the poem includes lines on "the bold/
       Adventurous Melville" and accounts of Mehevi and Fayaway.

3   ANON. "Beauty and Deformity." Cincinnati <u>Herald of Truth</u>,
       1 (January), 23-25.
          Quotes from <u>Typee</u> to support thesis that "every thing
       in nature is beautiful."

4   ANON. "A Residence on the Marquesas." Monterey <u>Californian</u>,
       1 (2 January), 1.
          Reprint of 1846.B97. Continued in 1847.B5.

5   ANON. "A Residence on the Marquesas." Monterey <u>Californian</u>,
       1 (9 January), 1.
          Reprint of 1846.B97. Continued from 1847.B4.

6   ANON. "The Library of Choice Reading." New York <u>United</u>
       <u>States Magazine and Democratic Review</u>, 20 (March), 239.
          Article on the Wiley and Putnam series of foreign and
       domestic works. Melville's "lively and picturesque" <u>Typee</u>
       included in a short list of American works equal to the
       foreign works.

7   ANON. Review of <u>The Prose Writers of America</u> by Rufus Wilmot
       Griswold. New York <u>Literary World</u>, No. 7 (20 March), p. 151.
          Mention: "Melville should have had a place for his
       <u>Typee</u>."

8   ANON. "American Literary Intelligence." New York <u>Literary</u>
       <u>World</u>, No. 8 (27 March), p. 185.
          The forthcoming publications of the Harpers include
       Melville's "new series of Adventures in the South Seas, to
       be issued under the title of Onevo [sic], as soon as the
       London copyright has been secured."

9   ANON. Review of <u>Omoo</u>. London <u>Athenaeum</u>, No. 1015 (10 April),
       pp. 382-384.
          The incidents of the early chapters are depicted with
       force and humor. But Melville has nothing new to tell about

1847

an island so frequently described as Tahiti. Many "sailor-
like tricks and humours" follow in arbitrary succession,
not sustaining any connected interest, and at times growing
even wearisome and dull. In the style and narrative indica-
tions of romance suggest a power of prolonging these adventures for as long as a public demands them. Extracts from
chapters 7, 8, 10, 33, and 42.

10   ANON. Review of Omoo. London Britannia (10 April).
        Without being a copyist, Melville has caught the spirit
     of Cooper's nautical style, and by a free bold style of
     description, and perhaps some romantic license in dealing
     with facts, gives great animation to his pages. Reprinted
     in Branch, p. 90.

11   ANON. Review of Omoo. London Critic, NS 5 (10 April),
        286-287.
        Summary, with extracts from chapters 2, 6, 5, 10, 18,
     and 33. Continued in 1847.B15.

12   ANON. "Herman Melville's Omoo." London Spectator, 20
        (10 April), 351-352.
        Unlike most sequels, Omoo is equal to its predecessor.
     Without the same novelty of subject as Typee, it still has
     sufficient freshness, deriving from Melville's fluent viva-
     cious style and natural aptitude for describing a scene or
     telling a story. The book's true characteristic is its
     nautical pictures and the glimpses it gives of the strange
     characters that are to be found scattered over the South
     Seas. The "composition" is clear, vivacious, and full of
     matter. As in Typee, there are a few free passages that
     might as well have been omitted. Summary, with extracts
     from chapters 19, 28, and 29. Reprinted in 1847.B57;
     reprinted in part in Branch, pp. 91-92.

13   ANON. Notice of Omoo. New York Yankee Doodle, 2 (10 April),
        2.
        "Important If True--Mr. Herman Melville's forthcoming
     work, Omoo." (Complete item.)

14   ANON. Review of Omoo. London Bell's Weekly Messenger
        (12 April).
        Readers will experience intense delight in following
     Melville through his various scenes, which he describes
     with a truthfulness almost worthy of Defoe. It would have
     been better if he had spoken with more respect of the mis-
     sionaries and not mentioned so openly the names of indi-
     viduals, such as that of the acting British consul at

Tahiti. But <u>Omoo</u>, on the whole, will be a rich treat to
those who delight in stirring adventures graphically and
pleasantly narrated and will probably have an even greater
popularity than <u>Typee</u>.

15 ANON. Review of <u>Omoo</u>. London <u>Critic</u>, NS 5 (17 April), 308-311.
     Continued from 1847.B11. Notes Melville's lively manner
     of description. Summary, with extracts illustrative of life
     in Tahiti from chapters 43, 45, 46, 68, 69, 73, and 81.

16 ANON. Review of <u>Omoo</u>. London <u>John Bull</u> (17 April), p. 248.
     Readers coming to <u>Omoo</u> with high expectations after
     <u>Typee</u> will not be disappointed. Nothing can exceed the
     interest of the narrative, which arises mainly from the
     clearness and simplicity of the style and the absence of
     prolixity. Melville's accounts of Tahiti, the natives, the
     French, and the missionaries form by far the most valuable
     and interesting parts of the work. Reprints chapter 45.
     Reprinted in Branch, p. 93.

17 ANON. Review of <u>Omoo</u>. London <u>People's Journal</u>, 3 (17 April),
     223-224.
     It would be difficult to imagine a man better qualified
     than Hermann Melville (if that is his real name) to describe
     the impressions such a life and such scenes (as related in
     <u>Omoo</u>) are calculated to call forth. Every variety of
     character, scene, and incident he studies and describes
     with equal gusto. Extracts from chapters 2, 10, 69, 68,
     and 81. Reprinted in part in Branch, pp. 94-95.

18 ANON. "Passages from Mr. Melville's 'Omoo.'" New York
     <u>Literary World</u>, No. 12 (24 April), pp. 274-275.
     One paragraph summary, mentioning Melville's attractive
     style. Reprints chapters 37 and 68 from the proof sheets.

19 ANON. "The New Work by the Author of Typee." New York <u>Spirit
     of the Times</u>, 17 (24 April), 99.
     Announcement of publication of <u>Omoo</u>; notes that readers
     are well aware of "the peculiar characteristic power and
     brilliancy" of <u>Typee</u>. Reprints all of chapter 16 from
     <u>Omoo</u>.

20 ANON. Review of <u>Typee</u>. Boston <u>Christian Observatory</u>, 1
     (May), 230-234.
     The literary merit, candor, and truth of <u>Typee</u> are mea-
     ger. It has a vivacity designed to gain readers, but its
     attempts at wit are so constant and so laborious that they
     are far from pleasing to a chaste mind. Reviewer mocks

1847

Melville's "depreciation of Christian communities" and concludes that he has little knowledge of Christianity and
still less love for its doctrines and precepts. Melville
ascribes the wasting away of the Hawaii population to the
influence of the missionaries, but the success of the missions is widely acknowledged. Melville has only retailed
the "old scandals" without any of the "old wit" or "old
industry or research" of earlier opponents of the missions.

21   ANON. "Mr. Melville's New Work." Albany Evening Journal
     (1 May).
         Typee "was among the most delightful books we have ever
     read." Confidently expects to find Omoo interesting and
     instructive and predicts good sales.

22   ANON. Review of Omoo. London Douglas Jerrold's Weekly News-
     paper (1 May).
         Omoo is a stirring narrative of very pleasant reading,
     possessing "much of the charm that has made Robinson Crusoe
     immortal--life-like description." Melville's account of
     the natives of Tahiti corresponds with that of Kotzebue
     and others. Extract from chapter 8.

23   ANON. Review of Omoo. New York Evening Mirror (1 May).
         Omoo is a very spirited and highly entertaining work.
     Melville has lost nothing of the freshness and vigor of
     style which, as much as the novelty of subject, made Typee
     so popular. Reprints chapters 16 and 18 from Omoo.

24   ANON. Review of Omoo. New York Atlas (2 May).
         Omoo will be more popular than Typee. Melville seeks to
     amuse more than to instruct; he makes no pretension to
     philosophic research. In a familiar way he describes what
     he has seen, and his reflections are spontaneous.

25   ANON. Review of Omoo. New York Sunday Times and Noah's
     Weekly Messenger (2 May).
         Marvelous as some of the stories are, Omoo is evidently
     a narrative of important facts. Some of the anecdotes are
     very entertaining, and throughout the interest never flags;
     the style is charming. Melville is the greatest writer of
     the age, in his way, and has deservedly been styled the
     "De Foe of America."

26   ANON. Review of Omoo. Albany Evening Journal (3 May), p. 2.
         Omoo fully justifies the expectations raised by Typee.
     Melville's talents and genius impart life and spirit to
     even commonplace occurrences. In his truthful and graphic

descriptions of sea life he excels most other nautical
writers; he makes the sailor talk and act naturally. If
the South Sea missionaries are less faithful and devoted
than those in other parts of the world, it is well the
fact be known. Extracts from chapters 2, 12, and 13.

27 ANON. Notice of Omoo. New York Evening Mirror (3 May).
      Has learned that Omoo is characterized by "even more
    astonishing recitals" than Typee and so predicts immense
    popularity. Typee was said to resemble Robinson Crusoe
    more than any work of modern times.

28 ANON. Review of Omoo. Boston Daily Advertiser (4 May).
      Melville's style is very good, the narrative amusing,
    and the popularity of Typee will recommend this new work
    to the public.

29 ANON. Review of Omoo. Boston Daily Bee (5 May).
      Omoo has all the attractiveness of a book of travels,
    abounding in wit, humor, romance, and poetry, and is
    written with all the mellow elegance of style that charac-
    terized Typee. In some respects it resembles Dana's Two
    Years Before the Mast, but is much more racy and captivating.
    Many good stories are told of sailor life. Extract from
    chapter 11.

30 ANON. Review of Omoo. Boston Post (5 May), p. 1.
      If Melville has not visited the places he describes, his
    books are worthy a place with Robinson Crusoe and Gulliver's
    Travels; if he has visited them he has a greater descriptive
    power than any traveler of the age. It is hard to believe
    that everything in his book is true, but he imparts a great
    deal of information tallying with the reports of former
    voyagers; he also gives an array of characters as inter-
    esting as those of romance, stirring incident, and here and
    there a touch of the genuine comic. Reprinted in Branch,
    p. 96.

31 ANON. Review of Omoo. Brooklyn Daily Eagle (5 May).
      Omoo is the most readable sort of reading, thorough
    entertainment. The question whether the stories are authen-
    tic or not does not have much to do with their interest.
    One can revel in such richly good-natured style, if nothing
    else. Reprinted [and attributed to Walt Whitman] in Birss
    (April 1933), p. 280; Anderson (1937), p. 21; Branch, p. 95.

32 ANON. Review of Omoo. New York Evening Post (5 May).
      Omoo seems to have all the liveliness of Typee.

1847

33   ANON. Review of <u>Omoo</u>. Baltimore <u>American and Commercial</u>
      <u>Daily Advertiser</u> (6 May), p. 2.
          Melville's style is agreeable and without affectation;
      the scenes described, on sea or land, are instructive as to
      Polynesian character.

34   ANON. Review of <u>Omoo</u>. Boston <u>Evening Transcript</u> (6 May),
      p. 2.
          Few books give greater delight and in a sufficiently
      instructive and innocuous way than <u>Omoo</u>. Melville has not
      been content with merely repeating himself. <u>Omoo</u> has every-
      where the marks of an originality which could only arise
      from a personal acquaintance with the scenes he so happily
      depicts. His easy and natural style enhances the book's
      pleasing impression.

35   ANON. Nantucket <u>Inquirer</u> (7 May).
          Summary of <u>Omoo</u> (a "very amusing book"), with extracts
      from chapters 1 and 7.

36   ANON. Review of <u>Omoo</u>. New York <u>Albion</u>, NS 6 (8 May), 228.
          Melville has more than sustained his widely spread repu-
      tation with <u>Omoo</u>. Though he treats familiar topics, <u>Omoo</u>
      contains so much that is positively new. There is a fresh-
      ness and novelty in the graphic sketches of society in the
      islands. <u>Omoo</u> and <u>Typee</u> are delightful romances of real
      life, embellished with powers of description, and a graphic
      skill of hitting off characters little inferior to the
      highest order of novelist and romance writers. Reprinted
      in Branch, p. 97.

37   ANON. Review of <u>Omoo</u>. New York <u>Anglo American</u>, 9 (8 May), 69.
          <u>Omoo</u> abounds in all attractive things; not a chapter but
      is replete with interest; not a sentence but glistens. The
      direct, straightforward air about the narrative parts pre-
      cludes the conclusion that any of the incidents are mere
      fictions. <u>Typee</u> was something rare; <u>Omoo</u> is still rarer.
      Reprinted in Anderson (1937), p. 13.

38   ANON. Review of <u>Omoo</u>. New York <u>Literary World</u>, No. 14 (8 May),
      pp. 319-321.
          The adventures in <u>Omoo</u> are related with all the animation,
      picturesqueness, and felicity of style which make <u>Typee</u>
      worth a second reading. Dr. Long Ghost and other characters
      are drawn with vigor; the ship scenes are made full of inter-
      est and attraction by their graphic humor; the descriptions
      of nature are vivid and refreshing. Extracts from chapters
      2, 11, 7, 44, and 49. Reprinted in part in Branch, pp. 97-99.

39   ANON. "To Correspondents." New York <u>Yankee Doodle</u>, 2
      (8 May), 44.
          "Omboog, or three months residence in the Moon," by
      Herman Melville, included in a comic list of papers sub-
      mitted to <u>Yankee Doodle</u> for "judgment upon their merits."

*40   ANON. Review of <u>Omoo</u>. Springfield (Mass.) <u>Republican</u>
      (8 May).
          Cited in Leyda (1954), p. 243.

41   ANON. Review of <u>Omoo</u>. New York <u>Sunday Times and Noah's
      Weekly Messenger</u> (9 May).
          In <u>Omoo</u> "one may find food for laughter and sterling
      information into the bargain." This "remarkable and unsur-
      passable work" is written in "a pleasant, off-hand style"
      and abounds in interesting sketches, "infinitely superior
      to anything of the kind we ever before read."

42   ANON. Review of <u>Omoo</u>. Newark <u>Daily Advertiser</u> (10 May), p. 2.
          On the basis of his own similar "career of nautical
      vagabondism," reviewer testifies to Melville's perfect
      credibility in his "bewitching yarns," especially in his
      account of the Tahitian character as developed under the
      influence of sailors and missionaries.

43   ANON. Review of <u>Omoo</u>. New York <u>Gazette and Times</u> (11 May).
          The style of <u>Omoo</u> is exceedingly felicitous; the inci-
      dents it relates, the scenery it describes, the aboriginal
      race it treats, all awaken and retain the interest of the
      reader. It has a sufficiency of original characters, dash-
      ingly and concisely hit off, to set up a score of modern
      novelists. On shore or at sea Melville is equally happy
      and amusing. As the testimony of an unbiased intelligent
      witness, the results he reports of missionary labors must
      make a deep impression.

44   ANON. "'Who Reads an American Book?'" Albany <u>Evening Journal</u>
      (12 May), p. 2.
          Such questions are no longer asked in English reviews.
      American books have not only readers but admirers in Eng-
      land. Quotes from 1847.B12.

*45   ANON. Review of <u>A Summer in the Wilderness</u> by Charles Lanman.
      New York <u>Evening Mirror</u> (12 May).
          Comparisons with Melville's "incomparable" <u>Typee</u>. Cited
      in <u>Log</u>, p. 244.

1847

46   ANON. Review of <u>Omoo</u>. Boston <u>Recorder</u> (13 May), p. 74.
      "This is a very entertaining sketch of his wanderings by
      a wild rover of the seas."

47   ANON. Review of <u>Omoo</u>. Boston <u>Massachusetts Ploughman</u>
      (15 May).
          <u>Omoo</u> is full of marvelous adventures and entertaining
      descriptions of savage life.

48   ANON. Review of <u>Omoo</u>. Schenectady (N.Y.) <u>Parthenon; a Semi-</u>
      <u>Monthly Magazine, conducted by the Students of Union College</u>,
      NS 1 (15 May), 31.
          Like <u>Typee</u>, <u>Omoo</u> "will be pleasure-giving and attractive
      to lazy voluptuaries, who are found in college as elsewhere."
      Melville's "descriptions are vigorous and life-like, his
      fancy rich, and his style in simplicity and elegance reminds
      one of Irving's."

49   ANON. "Polynesian Life.--'Typee' and 'Omoo.' By Herman
      Melville." New York <u>Evening Mirror</u> (21 May).
          The adventures of <u>Typee</u> and <u>Omoo</u> have raised doubts
      about their authenticity only because of their novelty;
      they are verified by incidents in the career of almost
      every sailor who has spent a few years in the Pacific.
      <u>Typee</u> is an extraordinary book only because it is written
      in a most brilliant and captivating style. Visitors to the
      Marquesas and Society Islands have testified that Melville's
      descriptions of the natives and the progress of civiliza-
      tion there are strictly and vividly accurate. But the
      genial flow of Melville's humor and good nature and a
      thousand nameless beauties of tone and sentiment are the
      captivating ingredients of <u>Omoo</u>. Melville's remarks on
      missionaries deserve serious consideration as the testimony
      of a candid and impartial witness; he has given a greater
      amount of reliable information on the subject than all the
      missionary works palmed off on the credulity of the public.
      <u>Typee</u> and <u>Omoo</u> are the best works on Polynesian life yet
      published in the United States or in England; no nautical
      work can compare with them in the spirit and vividness of
      their forecastle revelations. Reprinted in 1847.B51 and
      Branch, pp. 99-104; reprinted in part in <u>Log</u>, pp. 244-245.

50   ANON. "Literary Gossip." <u>American Literary Gazette and New</u>
      <u>York Weekly Mirror</u>, NS 6 (22 May), 11.
          Report that <u>Omoo</u> is selling rapidly and "carrying off
      with it" large quantities of <u>Typee</u>.

51 ANON. "Polynesian Life.--'Typee' and 'Omoo.' By Herman
    Melville." American Literary Gazette and New York Weekly
    Mirror, NS 6 (22 May), 1-2.
        Reprint of 1847.B49.

52 ANON. Review of Omoo. New York Golden Rule and Odd-Fellows'
    Family Companion, 6 (22 May), 350.
        "We have seldom taken up two more interesting volumes....
    They are full of incident, which is narrated in the most
    racy and off-hand style...." Reprinted in Pollin
    (April 1975), p. 68.

53 ANON. Review of Omoo. New York Evangelist (27 May), p. 4.
        The lively, graphic sketches of Omoo and its scenes of
    strange and surpassing interest steal one's favor and
    approbation. But at the end it is clear that the book is
    little else than romance. Melville's mendacity is some-
    times flagrantly visible, as is his spite against religion
    and its missionaries.

54 B. Review of Omoo. New York National Anti-Slavery Standard,
    7 (27 May), 207.
        Typee was entirely new and fresh, not made up of pickings
    from other books. It opened to the reading world views of
    a new existence, proving that men could be happier and more
    humane without the excrescences of civilization. Omoo is
    written in the same free and jocular style but contains
    nothing so purely novel as some of the scenes in Typee. Its
    sketches of sea life and character are very lively and
    accurate; its insight into the state of society in the
    Islands is entertaining and instructive. Nothing in it
    contradicts the many accounts of travelers in that part of
    the world. Reprinted in Branch, pp. 112-113.

55 ANON. Review of Omoo. Washington National Era (27 May).
        Typee and Omoo are both simple narratives of strange
    adventures in the South Seas, without any connecting link
    except the connection of the author with them all; they are
    interspersed with frequent observations on the manners and
    customs of the South Sea Islands, and singularly beautiful
    descriptions of natural scenery. Like Defoe, Melville has
    the faculty of telling a peculiarly captivating story in
    the simplest style; of multiplying adventures and incidents
    capable of interesting the feelings even more than the most
    ingeniously complicated plot could do. Summary of early
    chapters, with extracts from chapters 6, 7, 23, and 24.

1847

56 ANON. Review of <u>Typee</u> and <u>Omoo</u>. Washington <u>National Intel-</u>
    <u>ligencer</u> (27 May).
        <u>Typee</u> unites the imaginative cast of Borrow's <u>Bible in</u>
    <u>Spain</u> with the adventurous air of Warburton's <u>Eothen</u> and
    has the advantage over both in presenting scenes even re-
    moter from everyday life. It is written to please, not
    instruct: to please by a general conformity to fact, but
    to please chiefly and with the license of some suppression
    and some embellishment. It seems quite as true in its
    particulars as Sterne's <u>Sentimental Journey</u>. English
    critics who debated the reality of the facts in <u>Typee</u>
    should have seen that it is one of those works in which
    the writer creates and sustains the illusion of truth, but
    by no means tells it. Certain adventures of Melville and
    Toby are poetically exaggerated. Typee life is presented
    with the shadowy indistinctness which is used to present
    distant times in MacPherson's <u>Ossian</u> and which proved it
    unauthentic. The residence among the Typees is probably
    imaginary, drawing upon a vague account Melville had heard
    of that part of the island and what he had seen of the rest.
    Toby's testimony proves nothing. [<u>See</u> 1846.B74.] <u>Omoo</u> in
    general shows the same talents as <u>Typee</u>, but applied to
    incidents less congenial to them. Why Melville chooses to
    present himself as little better than the rest of the crew
    is puzzling; his elegance of mind bespeaks refinement of
    morals and feeling. Dr. Long Ghost is hardly less witless
    than worthless; as a principal character he is a complete
    failure. Continued in 1847.B60. Reprinted in Branch,
    pp. 105-111 [dated 26 May].

57 ANON. "Herman Melville's Omoo." Boston <u>Littell's Living Age</u>,
    No. 159 (29 May), pp. 426-427.
        Reprint of 1847.B12.

58 ANON. "Life in the Pacific." <u>Chambers's Edinburgh Journal</u>, 7
    (29 May), 338-341.
        The part of <u>Omoo</u> where Melville is aboard ship will
    likely be found more interesting than the part where he
    becomes a wanderer among the Islands. Details of life and
    provisions in the <u>Julia's</u> forecastle and extract from
    chapter 11. Summary, with extracts from chapters 62, 65,
    67, 68, 73, 74, and 82. Reprinted in part in Anderson
    (March 1939), p. 30.

59 ANON. Review of <u>Omoo</u>. London <u>Literary Gazette</u>, No. 1584
    (29 May), pp. 396-397.
        <u>Omoo</u> carries on Melville's imaginary adventures in the
    Pacific in the same Crusoe-ish vein as <u>Typee</u>. He dashes

off his feats and exploits by sea and land in a style
worthy of Philip Quarles or Robinson Crusoe. Some of the
sketches of character are very happy; and the descriptions
of the islands and their inhabitants graphic, truth-like,
and effective. Extracts from chapters 7, 12, 18, 33, 79,
and 69.

60 ANON. Review of Omoo. Washington National Intelligencer
    (29 May).
         Continued from 1847.B56. Extracts, with short introduc-
    tions, from chapters 8, 39, 63, and 68. [Dated 28 May in
    Mailloux and Parker, p. 20.]

61 ANON. "Pacific Rovings." Blackwood's Edinburgh Magazine, 61
    (June), 754-767.
         Omoo is excellent, quite first-rate, a skillfully con-
    cocted Robinsonade, where fictitious incident is ingeniously
    blended with genuine information. Melville has visited the
    countries he describes, but not in the capacity he states.
    He is no Munchausen; there is nothing improbable in his
    adventures, "save their occurrence to himself, and that he
    should have been a man before the mast" on board South Sea
    whalers or any ship whatever. His tone is refined and well-
    bred; he writes like one accustomed to good European society,
    who has read books and collected information other than
    could be read or gathered in the places and among the rude
    associates he describes. Herman Melville sounds "like the
    harmonious and carefully selected appellation of an imagi-
    nary hero of romance." There is a world of wild romance
    and thrilling adventure in the occasional glimpses of the
    whale fishery in Omoo and a picturesque portrait gallery
    of characters. The adventures ashore are as pleasant and
    original as the seafaring ones; Melville excels at terse
    description. Notes "occasional slight yankeeisms" in
    Melville's style which prove him an American. Summary,
    with extracts from chapters 10, 66, and 80. Reprinted in
    1847.B72 and 1847.B79; reprinted in part in Anderson
    (March 1939), pp. 33-34, and Branch, pp. 114-119.

62 ANON. Review of Omoo. New Orleans Commercial Review of the
    South and West, 3 (June), 586.
         Favorably known to the world by his brilliant and
    spirited Typee, Melville has now continued in a similar
    vein those sketches.

63 ANON. Review of Omoo. New York Columbian Magazine, 7 (June),
    283.
         Omoo has greater apparent credibility than Typee, the story
    seeming not to draw so extensively on the faith of the

reader. The delineations of the whaler's crew are full of
spirit and none the less amusing for being perhaps overdrawn. Melville's account of the Society Islands and their
native and foreign inhabitants seems worthy of full belief.
It plays havoc with the romance long attached to the preva-
lent conception of the islands, leaving a much reduced estimate of the islanders in their original character and as
converts to Christianity; they appear not only worthless,
profligate, and corrupt but ridiculous and absurd. Reprinted
in part in Rountree, pp. 14-15.

64   ANON. Review of Omoo. New York Knickerbocker, 29 (June), 562.
     Without being equal in spirit and interest to Typee,
Omoo is a very clever and entertaining work, full of incident. Melville's simple, unpretending style is one of its
highest recommendations. He professes to describe merely
what he has seen; his pages are so evidently natural we
are bound to take him at his word. Reprinted in Branch,
pp. 119-120.

65   ANON. Review of Omoo. New York Merchants' Magazine and
     Commercial Review, 16 (June), 641.
     "The author, as a roving sailor, spent three months upon
the islands of Tahiti and Omoo, and we have the result of
his experience conveyed in a characteristic style."

66   ANON. Review of Omoo. Richmond Southern and Western Literary
     Messenger and Review, 13 (June), 383.
     Notes Melville's new and interesting field of adventure,
his animated and vivid style, humorous vein and sailor-like
spirit. There appears at times rather a license in the tone
and spirit of Omoo; but from a sailor, under such circumstances, this might be expected.

67   ANON. Review of Revised Edition of Typee. Honolulu Friend,
     5 (1 June), 86.
     In addition to the omissions of the revised edition,
Melville ought to have suppressed some of the "glaring
facts respecting his habits of gross and shameless familiarity not to say unblushing licentiousness, with a tribe
of debased and filthy savages of Marquesas." Hundreds of
passages might be quoted, showing that he sank "lower than
the debased people among whom he took up his temporary
abode." It is not strange that such a man could find little to praise and much to blame in the efforts of his missionary countrymen. Reprinted in part in Log, p. 246.

68 ANON. Review of The Monk's Revenge by Samuel Spring. New
    York Literary World, No. 19 (12 June), p. 441.
        Reviewer suggests that a "Typee novel, in which some
    Fayaway of Marquesas sentiment, whose mind is first opening
    to Christianity, balancing similarly between her old and
    her new law of conjugal affection, would make a good meta-
    physical pendant" to one part of Spring's work.

69 ANON. "Blackwood's Review of 'Omoo.'" Albany Evening Journal
    (25 June).
        Reply to 1847.B61. Melville was actually a man before
    the mast on South Sea whalers and Herman Melville is his
    actual name. But it is impossible to decide how much the
    delightful Omoo owes to Melville's imagination. Reviewer
    did not believe in the existence of Toby of Typee until the
    appearance of Richard Tobias Greene. [See 1846.B74.]

70 G[REELEY], H[ORACE]. "Editorial Correspondence." New York
    Weekly Tribune (26 June).
        Omoo is replete with the merits and faults of Typee.
    Everyone was mistaken who thought the fascination of Typee
    was due mainly to its novel subject. Omoo proves Melville
    "a born genius, with few superiors either as a narrator, a
    describer, or a humorist." Typee and Omoo, "doubtless in
    the main true narratives," rank in interest with Robinson
    Crusoe and in vivacity with the best of Stephens's Travels.
    Yet they are "unmistakably defective if not positively dis-
    eased in moral tone" and will be dangerous reading for those
    of immature intellects and unsettled principles. A "pen-
    chant for bad liquors is everywhere boldly proclaimed, while
    a hankering after loose company not always of the masculine
    order, is but thinly disguised and perpetually protruding
    itself throughout the work." These tendencies will prevent
    Melville's apparently candid account of the missionaries
    from having its due weight with the friends of missions.
    Reprinted in Williams (1948), pp. 94-95, and Branch, pp.
    121-122 [dated 23 June]; reprinted in part in Log, p. 248.

71 P[ECK], G[EORGE] W[ASHINGTON]. "Omoo." New York American
    Review, 6 (July), 36-46.
        Peck read Omoo with interest but "with a perpetual re-
    coil." Melville shows on almost every page his ability to
    be an imaginative writer of the highest order; some of his
    descriptions are very fine, in the highest and most poetic
    way. But the "reckless spirit which betrays itself on
    every page of the book--the cool, sneering wit, and the
    perfect want of heart everywhere manifested in it, make it
    repel, almost as much as its voluptuous scenery-painting

1847

and its sketchy outlines of stories attract." Melville's
smartness and impudence, continued through two volumes,
become wearisome. Typee and Omoo lack vraisemblance;
Melville does not seem to care to be true; he constantly
defies the reader's faith by his cool superciliousness.
Dr. Long Ghost lacks consistency and credibility; the
book's details disregard naturalness and congruity.
Melville spices his books with accounts and dark hints
of "innumerable amours" with the half-naked damsels of
Nukuheva and Tahiti; he "gets up voluptuous pictures, and
with cool, deliberate art breaks off always at the right
point, so as without offending decency, he may stimulate
curiosity and excite unchaste desire"; but the stories of
his voluptuous adventures are unbelievable. As one who did
nothing to the islanders "but amuse himself with their peculiarities and use them for his appetites," Melville is not
a credible witness against the missionaries. Contrary to
1847.B29, Omoo is inferior to Dana's Two Year's Before the
Mast in truthfulness, eloquence, and poetic effects.
Melville has all the confidence of genius, all its reckless abandonment, but little of its power. Reprinted in
part in Branch, pp. 123-132.

72   ANON. "Pacific Rovings." New York Eclectic Magazine, 11
      (July), 408-419.
          Reprint of 1847.B61.

73   ANON. Review of Omoo. Philadelphia Godey's Magazine and
      Lady's Book, 35 (July), 56.
          There are some vivid descriptions of natural scenery in
      Omoo, but Melville's great talent is in his sketches of
      character, some of which are exquisite. Dickens has noth-
      ing more amusing in The Pickwick Papers than the portraits
      of Zeke and Shorty. Reprinted in Log, p. 254.

74   ANON. Review of Omoo. Philadelphia Ladies' National Magazine,
      12 (July), 40.
          Melville's adventures are real; everything seems truth-
      ful, his style is full of spirit, and his descriptions are
      full of beauty. Omoo also induces much laughter. Reprinted
      in Pollin (April 1975), pp. 65-66.

*75   ANON. "American Authors." Milwaukee Daily Wisconsin (1 July).
          Cited in Log, p. 249.

76   ANON. Review of Adventures in the Pacific by John Coulter,
      M.D. London Examiner (10 July), p. 435.

First paragraph notes that Coulter's book "goes far to
prove the reality" of Melville's "adventures in the same
extravagant scenes" and has some of the same literary qualities Melville has shown.

77   ANON. Morning Courier and New-York Enquirer (14 July).
Notes that Typee and Omoo, two books which have attracted
a great deal more attention and comment than they deserve,
are reviewed in "a just and highly interesting paper" by
G. W. Peck [see 1847.B71], an article envincing "uncommon
critical acumen and a clear-sighted, discriminating sympathy
with what is sound and healthy in literature and morals."

78   A[ULD], J[EBEDIAH] B. "Notes on New Books." New York
Evening Mirror (21 July).
Reply to 1847.B71, a "disgusting and spiteful review,"
an "affected jumble of smuttey morality and personal abuse."
Melville is innocent of pandering to a depraved taste but
the reviewer for the American Review is not. For Auld the
"illusion" in Omoo was perfect, "and the incidents and
scenes were as vivid and natural as ever words painted."
Reprinted in part in Log, p. 251; reprinted in Branch,
pp. 133-134.

79   ANON. "Pacific Rovings." Boston Littell's Living Age, 14
(24 July), 145-153.
Reprint of 1847.B61.

80   ANON. "One of its Assistant Editors 'Reflects Credit' on the
Courier and Enquirer." New York Yankee Doodle, 2 (24 July),
160.
Critical of G. W. P., an assistant editor at the Courier
and Enquirer, for his "high parsonical style in 1847.B71.
Reprinted in part in Log, p. 253.

81   ANON. "De Tocqueville." New York United States Magazine and
Democratic Review, 21 (August), 117-120.
Quotes from 1847.B61 to show that, being "firmly con-
vinced that under any circumstances he cannot be 'humbugged,'
your genuine Englishman is a perfect specimen of gullibility."
In Blackwood's review of Omoo, the book's improbabilities
are cheerfully swallowed, but the plain matter-of-fact ex-
cites suspicion. Young seamen in the merchant vessels of
America are to a considerable extent well-educated young
men of good families. Herman Melville is brother to
Gansevoort Melville, U.S. Secretary of Legation to the
Court of St. James.

1847

*82   ANON. Albany <u>Daily Knickerbocker</u> (4 August).
        Report of Melville's marriage, used as reply to 1847.B61.
        Cited in Hetherington (1961), p. 89.

*83   ANON. "Breach of Promise Suit Expected." New York <u>Daily
     Tribune</u> (7 August).
        Reports Melville's marriage; anticipates breach of
     promise suit by the "fair forsaken Fayaway." Cited in <u>Log</u>,
     p. 256.

*84   ANON. "Married." Albany <u>Daily Knickerbocker</u> (10 August).
        Report of Melville's marriage, proof for "friend
     Blackwood" that Herman Melville is real flesh and blood.
     [<u>See</u> 1847.B61]. Cited in <u>Log</u>, p. 256.

 85   ANON. "Coulter's Cruise." <u>Blackwood's Edinburgh Magazine</u>,
     62 (September), 323-324.
        A review of Dr. John Coulter's <u>Adventures on the Western
     Coast of South America</u>. After Melville's pungent and admir-
     ably written <u>Omoo</u>, most books of the same class must appear
     flat and unprofitable, as to a large extent Coulter's does.
     Reminiscences of Dr. Long Ghost, who would have written a
     far spicier book than Coulter's.

 86   CHASLES, PHILARÈTE. "Littérature pseudo-populaire en
     Angleterre et en Amérique." Paris <u>Revue des Deux Mondes</u>,
     19 (15 September), 1109-1110.
        Two paragraphs on <u>Typee</u>, which Chasles finds the most
     amusing of the fictions he is writing about. There is
     warmth, movement, show, and interest in its rapid narra-
     tive; the author seems to be laughing at the public quite
     ingenuously. Chasles likes Melville's effrontery and
     swaggering style of lying.

 87   ANON. "Omoo.--By the Author of Typee." London <u>Times</u>
     (24 September), p. 7.
        Melville is no common sailor. "If he be an American, he
     is quite as familiar with English literature and London
     streets as he is with Bryant and Longfellow, Broadway and
     Long Island. If he needs an illustration, Regent-street
     occurs to him as it would to Mr. Dickens; the cockney, not
     the Kentuckian, is the subject of his satire, and King John
     and George IV. supply matter for discussion which Washington
     and Jackson fail to furnish." <u>Omoo</u> is no less charming than
     the fiction <u>Typee</u> and appears no more authentic; quite as
     fascinating as <u>Robinson Crusoe</u>, it is 20 times less probable.
     In <u>Typee</u> and <u>Omoo</u> the illusion is not perfect: the "artifi-
     cial is mixed with the natural; the <u>vraisemblable</u> with the
     utterly improbable; the craftsman peeps out where the un-

tutored traveller should alone be visible...." Melville's
delightful books are unquestionably founded on facts, and
he has undoubtedly visited the spots they describe, but on
the whole they are untrue. Melville has a rare pen for the
delineation of character and an eye for the humorous and
grotesque "worth a Jew's"; he is not to be beaten in description of natural scenery; in invention he will bear
comparison with the most cunning of the modern French
school; no satirist is more quiet and stinging. Melville's
account of missionary doings agrees with that of trustworthy
travelers. Reviewer gives his own account of missionary
follies. Extracts from chapters 2, 18, and 45. Reprinted
in part in Branch, pp. 134-138.

88   ANON. Review of Omoo. Boston Mother's Assistant and Young
      Lady's Friend, 11 (October), 95.
            Readers will find Omoo exceedingly interesting.

89   ANON. "Typee." New York Robert Merry's Museum, 14 (October),
      109-114, 135-139, 173-178.
            Summary of Typee, a "very amusing book." Continued in
      1847.B96.

*90   B[OURNE], W[ILLIAM] O. "To the Editor of the Tribune." New
      York Daily Tribune (2 October).
            Letter, alleging "the most palpable errors, if not will-
      ful misrepresentations" in Omoo. [See 1847.B92.] Cited
      in Log, pp. 260-261.

*91   ANON. Editorial. New York Daily Tribune (6 October).
            On the favorable British reception of Omoo. Cited in
      Hetherington (1961), p. 74.

92   ANON. New York Evening Mirror (6 October).
            Reply to 1847.B90, "a very ill-natured and bigoted
      notice." Omoo is daily becoming more widely known and its
      author more universally admired. Its reception was even
      more favorable in England than in the U.S. The merits of
      Melville's books "consist in their pleasant narrative style,
      and the vividness with which he produced impressions of
      scenes that more learned, grave, and pious men had not been
      able to do with all their correctness and respectability....
      Such books are just as necessary to give us correct notions
      of distant countries, as are the reports of statistical com-
      pilers and topographical engineers. They are to such works
      what landscape paintings are to maps."

93   [LIPPINCOTT, SARA JANE]. "Letter from the Author of 'Typee.'"
      Philadelphia Saturday Evening Post (9 October).

1847

        Letter, purportedly from Melville, stating "it is my belief that poets are not properly esteemed and recompensed in our country" and giving a comic account of a poet and his treatment in Typee. Reprinted in 1850.B2.

*94   P. New York Daily Tribune (30 October).
        Quotes praise of Omoo in 1847.B87. Cited in Log, p. 264.

95   ANON. "Protestant Missions in the Sandwich Islands."
        Baltimore United States Catholic Magazine and Monthly Review, 6 (November), 580-583.
        Typee is a sprightly, well written, entertaining book. The one fatal objection to it is its voluptuousness. Doubts were cast on the authenticity of Typee by those who believed all testimony against the missions must be fictitious. But the publication of Omoo "has decided" that Melville "deals in truth." His accounts are corroborated by the uniform evidence of disinterested travelers and by the admissions of the missionaries themselves. Extracts from chapter 26 and "Appendix." Reprinted in Anderson (1937), pp. 16-17.

96   ANON. "Typee." New York Robert Merry's Museum, 14
        (November), 135-139.
        Continues summary from 1847.B89. Continued in 1847.B100.

97   ANON. Review of Fresh Gleanings by Ik Marvel. Philadelphia
        Ladies' National Magazine, 12 (November), 184.
        Mention: "What the author of Omoo is in the isles of the ocean, Ik Marvel has proved himself in the fields of continental Europe."

98   ANON. "An American Author in England." Milwaukee Daily
        Wisconsin (18 November).
        Gratified to see that Omoo is received with "the highest encomiums" in England. Quotes praise from 1847.B87. Probably no author has ever acquired so wide a name in so brief a time. Melville has "peculiarly a popular style," something like that of Paley, "and therefore whatever he writes is agreeable, and will take with the people." Reprinted in part in Log, p. 264.

99   ANON. Review of Typee and Omoo. London Dublin Review, 23
        (December), 341-363.
        Questions the authenticity of Melville's adventures and wonders "how such a book came to be written by one 'before the mast'...or how one capable of so thinking, reflecting, recollecting, and inditing, could have gone before the mast," and in a whaler, too. Melville claims to be American but it is very difficult to identify him by his tone, habits,

or thoughts, with any of the "peculiar classes" into which
America is divided. But throughout the book there runs a
vein of humor and irony, combined with great powers of
observation and expression, which renders it highly interesting and engrossing; Melville has the power to make his
adventures palatable to the most fastidious readers. The
social conditions of the Tahitians show that the all-
powerful, sacred cause of the missionaries is impotent before the evils which accompnay or precede it. Extracts from
Typee, chapters 5 and 3; Omoo, chapters 39, 53, 63, 81, 46,
44, and 45.

100   ANON. "Typee." New York Robert Merry's Museum, 14 (December),
      173-178.
            Continues summary from 1847.B96.

1848 A BOOKS - NONE

1848 B SHORTER WRITINGS

  1   [SANDERS, ELIZABETH ELKINS.] Remarks on the "Tour Around
      Hawaii," by the Missionaries, Messrs. Ellis, Thurston,
      Bishop, and Goodrich. Salem, pp. 34, 36.
            Brief references to Melville's justifiable criticism of
      missionaries (in Typee), which the "missionary party"
      strenuously tried to suppress.

  2   ANON. "Protestantism in the Society Islands." Baltimore
      United States Catholic Magazine and Monthly Review, 7
      (January), 1-10.
            Summarizes past arguments over the authenticity of Typee,
      quoting from English and American reviews; concludes that
      there is no valid reason for suspecting the truth of
      Melville's narrative of adventures. The style of Omoo is
      equally graphic and classical as that of Typee, but more
      sober and so more in keeping with a truthful narrative.
      "The vraisemblance is so perfect, the details are so minute,
      the incidents are so natural, the portraitures of character
      and life so very graphic, that fiction seems out of the
      question." As a Protestant, Melville can have no motive
      for underrating the labors of Protestant missionaries. He
      cites the testimonies of other Protestant travelers; and
      what he tells of the missionaries may be fully and implic-
      itly relied on as the truth. The failure of the Tahitian
      mission is additional evidence of the falsity of Protestant-
      ism and the truth of Catholicity. Extracts from "Preface"
      and chapters 48, 49, 45, and 46.

1848

3   WARREN, J. E. Para; Or, Scenes and Adventures on the Banks of
    the Amazon, Chapter 3. London Bentley's Miscellany, 23
    (January), 18.
        "We then began to attend to domestic affairs, and much
    did we feel the want of a nice little Fayaway to take charge
    of these important matters for us." (Complete allusion.)

4   ANON. "Missionary Operations in Polynesia." New Haven New
    Englander, 6 (January), 41-58.
        A defense of missionary labors. Omoo is full of state-
    ments calculated to mislead; the missionaries have done
    much toward the islanders' regeneration and redemption. The
    presence of Tommos and Long Ghosts on the islands is an
    additional hindrance to the establishment of pure religion
    among the natives. The "unfinished records of the love
    scenes of our modern Boccaccio...leave the reader in a
    state of not very uncertain surmise as to the secret inci-
    dents...." Extracts from chapter 48.

5   DUYCKINCK, EVERT A. "Wrinkles." New York Union Magazine, 2
    (February), 58.
        "The conversion of the Sandwich Islanders, according to
    Herman Melville, is a magnificent wrinkle.... Typee is a
    wrinkle, but it is as charming as a smile, and lovely as a
    dimple itself."

6   ANON. "Cannibalism." New York Elephant (12 February).
        Comic item; gives brief extract from a new work, entitled
    "Travels in the Cannibal Islands, by the author of Omoo."
    Reprinted in Yannella (1975), p. 111.

7   ANON. "Polynesia." London English Review, 9 (March), 51-84.
        Typee and Omoo unfavorably compared with John Coulter's
    Adventures in the Pacific (1845) and Adventures on the West-
    ern Coast of South America, and the Interior of California
    (1847). There is a laxity of moral feeling, an absence of
    religious principle throughout Typee and Omoo, "and the
    jesting tone, or the unoffensive expression which accompany
    or veil the most objectionable passages, make them yet more
    pernicious." In these respects Omoo is worse than Typee.
    Melville's strange mixture of genuine licentiousness and
    affected morality is painful and ludicrous. Melville seems
    never to have reflected that he might have attempted to
    enlighten the minds of the Typees on "temperance, righteous-
    ness, and judgment to come." Lengthy account of the Poly-
    nesians and their relations with Europeans, with extracts
    from Typee, chapters 2, 3, 32, 4, 6, 17, 26, 23, and 21;
    Omoo, chapters 62 and 63.

*8   ANON. "The Valentine Party." New York Home Journal
        (4 March).
            Article includes verse "valentine" by Bayard Taylor in
        honor of Melville's South Sea tales. Cited by Anderson
        (1937), p. 23.

 9   ANON. "Breach of Promise." Honolulu Polynesian (18 March),
        p. 174.
            Notes Melville's marriage; suggests he is guilty of
        breach of promise to Fayaway; wonders at the apparent
        inconsistency of his "exchanging his delightful fairy for
        one who has been nurtured amid the odious distinctions of
        civilization."

10   ANON. "Typee and Omoo." Honolulu Polynesian (18 March),
        p. 174.
            Typee and Omoo are unequalled as works of fiction, writ-
        ten in a brilliant and captivating style, full of graphic
        sketches of sea life and genial humor. But as narratives
        of facts they are a tissue of falsehood and misrepresenta-
        tion. Melville's contempt for constituted authorities, his
        choice of low society, his frequent draughts of Pisco, his
        "gentle associations with Tahitian and Marquesan damsels,"
        all prove that he was "utterly unqualified to act as an
        intelligent observer." He scorns the missionaries because
        they attempt to restrain the licentiousness of adventurers
        like himself. Reviewer met Melville in New York before
        leaving for Honolulu in the spring of 1845.

*11   ANON. Honolulu Sandwich Islands News (23 March).
            Claims that 1848.B10 is plagiarized from the New York
        Tribune. Cited in Log, p. 274.

12   ANON. Review of Omoo. London Gentleman's Magazine, NS 29
        (April), 399.
            "We do not know how much of this narrative is authentic
        and how much embellished; but it is very entertaining and
        very pleasingly written." [Complete review.]

13   ANON. "Missions Commercially Considered." Honolulu Friend,
        6 (1 April), 27-28.
            Article on the benefits to commerce from missionary
        activity. Notes that "many readers have been found to
        credit every word Melville has written in praise of the
        Marquesan savages, and discreditable to his missionary
        countrymen, while they will not read the truthful testimony
        of old and veteran missionaries, who have spent twenty or
        thirty years in doing the people good."

1848

14 H., E. B. "Catholic and Protestant Missions." Boston <u>Christ-ian Examiner and Religious Miscellany</u>, 44 (May), 417, 437-438.
Reply to 1847.B95 and 1848.B2. Melville is their most important authority in asserting the failure of Protestant missions in the South Sea islands. But not all his assertions are against the missionaries; some are strongly in their favor. He dropped charges against the missionaries from the second edition of <u>Typee</u>.

15 ANON. "Tempting Titles." London <u>Puppet-Show</u>, 1 (2 September), 201.
While formerly the object of a title was to give some idea of a work's character and contents, now it is merely a bait to procure a purchaser. Startling titles such as <u>Omoo</u> and <u>Typee</u> are just about as intelligible as <u>Row-de-dow</u> or <u>Fol-de-rol</u>.

16 ANON. "What is Talked About." New York <u>Literary World</u>, No. 94 (18 November), p. 834.
Announces that Melville "is about putting to press a new work, which, it is expected, from peculiar sources of interest, will transcend the unique reputation of his former books."

17 ANON. "Literary Intelligence." New York <u>Literary World</u>, No. 99 (23 December), p. 953.
Announces that <u>Mardi</u> is to be ready early in the spring.

<u>1849 A BOOKS - NONE</u>

<u>1849 B SHORTER WRITINGS</u>

1 WALPOLE, FRED. <u>Four Years in the Pacific</u>. Vol. 2. London: Richard Bentley, p. 111.
Reference to Queen Pomare's "own large garden with the <u>carabouse</u>, or State-prison of former times, where Omo [sic] passed, according to his own account, a most disagreeable captivity."

2 WISE, LIEUT. HENRY A. <u>Los Gringos: or, An Inside View of Mexico and California, with Wanderings in Peru, Chili, and Polynesia</u>. New York: Baker and Scribner, pp. 398-399.
Testifies that "the delineations of Island life and scenery" in <u>Typee</u> and <u>Omoo</u> "are most correctly and faithfully drawn." At Nukuheva Wise saw a girl from Typee named Fayaway "who apparently was maid of all work to a French

Commissary of the garrison" and who appeared to have a young
child. At Tahiti he saw Dr. Johnstone, who was "excessive
wroth" and "resolving shortly to prosecute the English publishers for libel"; also learned of other Omoo characters.
Reprinted in Birss (1932), p. 429.

3   ANON. Review of Mardi. London Athenaeum, No. 1117 (24 March),
     pp. 296-298.
        In Mardi, the reader "will be at once struck by the
     affectation of its style, in which are mingled many mad-
     nesses." Melville has been influenced by Carlyle, Emerson,
     and Southey's The Doctor. Mardi fails as pleasantry, alle-
     gory, romance, and prose-poem, if intended as any of these.
     There are good early pages; but as the story develops at
     Mardi improbability deepens; Melville becomes more and more
     outrageous in his incidents and language. Matters become
     crazier and crazier. Extracts from chapters 13 and 19.
     Reprinted in part in Log, p. 293, and Branch, pp. 139-141.

4   ANON. Review of Mardi. London Atlas (24 March), pp. 185-186.
        Mardi is a compound of Robinson Crusoe and Gulliver's
     Travels, seasoned throughout with German metaphysics of the
     most transcendental school. The great questions of natural
     religion, necessity, and free will are discussed here by
     tattooed and feathered skeptics. Melville's richness of
     imagination frequently disguises the triteness of his lead-
     ing ideas. Politics are sometimes most absurdly illustrated.
     The great merit of the work is its fanciful descriptions of
     nature amid all her variations. The style is that of the
     true German metaphysician--"full of tender thoughts and
     false images--generally entertaining--often ridiculous--
     attaining sometimes the brightest colourings of fancy, and
     at others talking the most inaffable [sic] bombast."
     Reprinted in part in Branch, pp. 141-142.

5   ANON. Review of Mardi. London Literary Gazette, No. 1679
     (24 March), pp. 202-203.
        Mardi is "a 3 vol. metaphor," the applications of which
     the reviewer can only now and then glimpse; he has no idea
     of what the book is about, but occasionally thought of
     Laputa in getting through Melville's "vagaries." The
     images are brilliant, and "you wonder how aught so luminous
     can be so dark"; the book is like a kaleidoscope. The ad-
     ventures are superb. The sharks and other fish are described
     in the style of Coleridge's "Ancient Mariner." The ocean
     scenery is painted with great spirit. Extracts from chap-
     ters 13, 1, 3, 60, 68, 89, 91. Reprinted in part in Log,
     p. 293; Duncan, p. 159; Recognition, p. 8.

1849

6   ANON. Review of <u>Mardi</u>. London <u>Examiner</u> (31 March),
        pp. 195-196.
        <u>Mardi</u> is "a transcendental <u>Gulliver</u>, or <u>Robinson Crusoe</u>
        run mad"; a heap of fanciful speculations, vivid descrip-
        tions, satirical insinuations, and allegorical typifica-
        tions, flung together with little order or connection, so
        that interest is curiously disproportioned to the amount of
        cleverness and ability employed in the book. Not always
        seeing clearly the intention, the reader gets tired of the
        allegory. Melville, as before, shows his chief powers on
        the waters of the Pacific; the book's natural descriptions
        are always good and pleasing. There are sly hits at many
        mortal absurdities, and Melville talks sensibly in his sa-
        tirical discussion of socialism, republicanism, and monarchy.
        <u>Mardi</u> contains chapters of "thoughtful writing, and very
        extensive reading, much in the manner of Sir Thomas Browne,
        and with a dash of old Burton and Sterne." Reprinted in
        part in <u>Log</u>, p. 295; reprinted in Branch, pp. 143-146.

7   ANON. Review of <u>Mardi</u>. London <u>Bentley's Miscellany</u>, 25
        (April), 439-442.
        <u>Mardi</u> is a "gorgeous dream" of rapidly changing and con-
        trasting scenes. The story is the least part of the work,
        which "consists of an infinite number of episodes and di-
        gressions, descriptions and speculations, theories and com-
        mentaries sometimes immeasurably fantastical." Rabelais is
        scarcely more discursive. Melville habitually operates
        through a medium which is neither verse nor prose, "but a
        singular compound of both, which tolerates the bold licenses
        of the former and the minuteness and voluminousness of the
        latter." It would be hard to find a style better suited to
        Melville's subject. He appropriately gives a strange utter-
        ance to strange thoughts and ideas, "churning up language,"
        to create in the reader a sense of bewilderment and dizzi-
        ness, "which must put to flight all wish to revert to a
        simple phraseology." Melville is wild and fabulous and full
        of Utopian fantasies, but with him we escape the ordinary
        novelist's familiar vapid pictures of society. Readers will
        like or detest <u>Mardi</u> according to the measure of their imag-
        ination. With a good deal that might be objected to, the
        book excited, on the whole, very pleasurable sensations.
        Reprinted in part in <u>Log</u>, p. 295, and Branch, pp. 146-149.

8   ANON. Review of <u>Mardi</u>. London <u>New Monthly Magazine and</u>
        <u>Humorist</u>, 85 (April), 510-512.
        The <u>Gesta Romanorum</u> story of a garden of paradise where
        a magician persuades his victims that death in his service
        leads to a more beautiful paradise is the basis of <u>Mardi</u>,

with the modification that the traveler kills the magician
and saves the victim. The wanderings among the islands are
delightful. But Babbalanja's philosophy becomes at times
too mystical, and his theology is even more objectionable.
The style is too frequently objectionable; and there is a
lack of consecutiveness in the narrative and of decided
purpose at the end. But there is "a misture of quaintness
and shrewdness, and of learning and fancy, which imparts a
charm to every page, however desultory." Extracts from
chapters 37, 94, and 132.

9   ANON. Review of Mardi. London Critic, NS 8 (1 April), 156-158.
    Melville's fancy, imagination, and pictorial power are
    as strong as before, but as an admitted romance Mardi lacks
    his previous books' charm of mystery. It is not purely a
    romance, but an extraordinary mixture of all kinds of com-
    position and the strangest variety of themes, strung to-
    gether by the slight thread of a not very intelligible
    story. Mardi will be read, not for the tale, but for the
    interspersed passages of beauty and interest. Those who
    look to be instructed by their reading will learn much; a
    lesson and a moral are conveyed in every incident. Melville
    satirizes men, manners, and institutions at home somewhat
    after the plan of Gulliver's Travels, which Mardi resembles.
    Beyond question a work of extraordinary talent. Extracts
    from chapters 13, 60, and 19. Reprinted in part in Log,
    p. 295.

10 ANON. Review of Mardi. London Weekly Chronicle (1 April).
    Reviewer has turned the book over, "like a dog might a
    jellyfish," without being able to make it out, though the
    first volume opens intelligibly enough and the description
    of the flight across the Pacific in the small boat is in-
    tensely interesting. After the arrival at Mardi, all is
    the most marvellous, bright, and picturesque confusion;
    Taji talks in the most incoherent manner. The last two
    volumes are "downright lunatic"; but they exhibit the most
    extraordinary power and fancy--every line is original,
    strange, and outlandish. The reader is led on in spite of
    himself by Melville's artistic power. Reviewer has never
    read a stranger book. Extracts from chapters 12 and 93.
    Reprinted in Parker (January 1970), pp. 585-586.

*11 ANON. Review of Omoo. New York Picayune (before 4 April).
    Quoted in advertisement for Mardi in New York Evening
    Mirror (4 April 1849). Cited in Mailloux and Parker, p. 24.

1849

*12   ANON. Review of <u>Mardi</u>. Boston <u>Times</u> (before 7 April).
        Quoted in advertisement for <u>Mardi</u> in New York <u>Literary
        World</u>, No. 114 (7 April), p. 328.

13   ANON. "Melville's New Book--Mardi." New York <u>Literary World</u>,
        No. 114 (7 April), pp. 309-310.
        <u>Mardi</u> is an onward development, with new traits, of all
        the fine literary qualities of <u>Typee</u> and <u>Omoo</u>; the inven-
        tion is bolder, the humor as strong, sometimes more subtle,
        the descriptive power felicitous. Reprints chapter 84.
        Reprinted in 1849.B39 and 1849.B42.

14   'COM.' Review of <u>Mardi</u>. New York <u>Evening Mirror</u> (13 April).
        <u>Mardi</u>, "with all its fascinations, its unique style, its
        beautiful language, its genial humor, its original thoughts,
        its graphic descriptions, its poetic flights, its profound
        reasonings, its philosophic reflections, its gentle reli-
        gious teachings, its inimitable whole, stretches before us
        like a new world, and the mental eye can never weary of
        gazing upon its strangely beautiful landscape. Here are
        points of interest for every mind."

*15   ANON. Review of <u>Mardi</u>. <u>Morning Courier and New-York Enquirer</u>
        (13 April).
        Cited in <u>Log</u>, p. 298.

*16   ANON. Review of <u>Mardi</u>. London <u>Britannia</u> (14 April).
        Cited in Hetherington (1961), p. 104.

17   ANON. Review of <u>Mardi</u>. New York <u>Literary World</u>, No. 115
        (14 April), pp. 333-336.
        <u>Mardi</u> is "not only a very happy genial production, but a
        book of thought, curious thought and reflection." It is
        "the romance of real life, human nature in a new setting,
        the romance of Rasselas, Gaudentio di Lucca, the Voyage of
        Panurge." It is suggestive of Rabelais. The early chapters
        are remarkable for picturesque narration and vivid descrip-
        tion. Yillah is a beautiful conception; Fayaway "is mere
        earthiness before her spirituality." Extracts from chapters
        1, 2, 31, 19, 30, 36, 40, 43, and 54. Reprinted in part in
        <u>Recognition</u>, pp. 9-11, and Branch, pp. 150-152.

18   ANON. Review of <u>Mardi</u>. New York <u>Spirit of the Times</u>, 19
        (14 April), 85.
        <u>Mardi</u> is a work of great genius and deep interest, a far
        advance beyond Melville's previous works, characterized by
        the same attractive style and striking originality of thought.
        <u>Mardi</u> is one of the most valuable productions of this or any
        other age. Reprinted in 1849.B27 and Flanagan, p. 60.

19 ANON. Notice of Mardi. New York Atlas (15 April).
    Announces publication of "a very beautiful edition of
    this work," to be noticed more fully the following week.
    [See 1849.B36.]

20 ANON. Notice of Mardi. New York Sunday Times and Noah's
    Weekly Messenger (15 April).
        Mardi opens spiritedly, more so than Omoo. A friend who
    has read the whole book reports that Mardi is equal to
    Typee in style, while the incidents are even more
    interesting.

21 ANON. Review of Mardi. Boston Daily Evening Transcript
    (16 April), p. 2.
        Quotes part of Melville's preface to Mardi and adds:
    "Our correspondent, who found fault with us for comparing
    Melville to De Foe, will see that the parallel holds good
    in this work. We commend it to the favor of our readers."

22 ANON. Notice of Mardi. New York Commercial Advertiser
    (16 April).
        Reviewer has barely glanced over Mardi; but anticipates
    from such portions as he has read the same liveliness of
    style, with quite as much romance of circumstances as in
    Omoo.

*23 ANON. Review of Mardi. Washington National Intelligencer
    (16 April).
        Reprint of 1849.B13. Cited in Hetherington (1961),
    p. 115.

*24 ANON. Review of Mardi. Hartford Daily Courant (17 April).
    Cited in Hetherington (1961), p. 114.

25 ANON. Review of Mardi. Boston Post (18 April), p. 1.
        Melville's reputation as a writer of commingled fact and
    fiction is deservedly high, but not as high as it should be.
    For his unpretending, homely, real delineation of character
    in the midst of so much that is wild, light, fanciful, and
    gorgeous, for his tact and knowledge of human nature, he
    has not received sufficient praise. In Typee and Omoo he
    is worthy of being called a modernised Defoe. Mardi is not
    only inferior to Typee and Omoo but a really poor perform-
    ance. Even the first volume is almost spoiled by the ever-
    lasting assumption of the brilliant, jocose, and witty in
    the style. After the arrival at Mardi, the book becomes
    mere hodgepodge, reminiscent of the talk in Rabelais without
    its coarseness, and without all its wit and humor. Mardi

1849

lacks truth and naturalness. The conversations are like
nothing one ever read or heard; their significance, if they
have any, is too recondite for the reviewer to fathom. The
characters are "legion" and uninteresting. The whole book
is not only tedious but unreadable. Reprinted in part in
Log, p. 298; reprinted in Recognition, pp. 14-15, and
Branch, pp. 155-156.

26   ANON. Review of Mardi. Philadelphia Dollar Newspaper,
     (18 April), 2.
         Mardi is a graphically written and highly interesting
     fiction. Quotes approving sentence from 1849.B13. Re-
     printed in Pollin (April 1975), p. 56.

27   ANON. Review of Mardi. Philadelphia Spirit of the Times, 20
     (18 April).
         Reprint of 1849.B18. Reprinted in Pollin (April 1975),
     p. 67.

28   ANON. Review of Mardi. New Bedford Mercury (20 April), p. 2.
         Mardi offers "adventures of all sorts by sea and land,
     through some 700 or 800 pages of unique but graphic descrip-
     tion, mingled with a genial humor, philosophy and original-
     ity of thought, altogether inimitable." Extract from
     chapter 1.

29   ANON. Review of Mardi. Springfield (Mass.) Republican
     (20 April).
         The success of Typee and Omoo presages a wide popularity
     for Melville's latest and more elaborate production.

30   ANON. Review of Mardi. London John Bull (21 April), p. 247.
         Melville "indulges in much keen satire, and in great
     license of discussion on topics of every description, chiefly
     political and religious." It is impossible not to admire
     the brilliant coloring of the whole tale and "the striking
     truth of many of the allegorical remarks and frequent home-
     thrusts"; but regrettable that Mardi is used for the dissem-
     ination of skeptical notions, introducing the saviour of
     mankind under a fabulous name and talking down the verities
     of the Christian faith by sophistry. Melville should not
     have introduced crude metaphysics and unsound notions of
     divinity into such a light craft. Reprinted in part in Log,
     p. 299, and Branch, pp. 158-159.

31   ANON. Review of Mardi. London Spectator, 22 (21 April),
     374-375.
         In Mardi, Melville's nautical knowledge is overwhelmed by
     a mass of verbiage, his acquaintance with South Sea islanders

turned to no account. He employs "the most vulgar and
obvious tricks of <u>writing</u>." His hero's adventures at
Mardi defy description in their absurdity and total lack
of interest. Melville appears to be imitating <u>The Arabian</u>
<u>Nights</u> and <u>Gulliver's Travels</u>. He has neither the mind nor
mental training for fiction; in aiming to become what he is
not, he has spoiled what he is. He "cannot rise beyond
colouring matter-of-fact."

32   ANON. Review of <u>Mardi</u>. New York <u>Albion</u>, NS 8 (21 April), 189.
      <u>Mardi</u> contains an infinite fund of wit, humor, pathos,
and philosophy, and the same charming powers of description
as <u>Typee</u> and <u>Omoo</u>, but Melville's abilities are still further developed. He offers delicate satire, sound political
hints, and a pungent, instructive bundle of his thoughts
and imaginings. Too much inversion and an overstraining
after antithesis and Carlyle-isms mar his style. Parts of
<u>Mardi</u> require the wide-awake application of <u>Gulliver's</u>
<u>Travels</u>. Reprinted in Branch, pp. 157-158.

33   ANON. "Melville's Mardi." New York <u>Home Journal</u> (21 April).
      <u>Mardi</u> is in a higher vein than <u>Typee</u> or <u>Omoo</u>, still
richer in description, fuller of incident, with more humor,
wit, and character. Yillah will prove to be the favorite
character, "<u>the pet little Nell</u>" of the book. Extract from
chapter 50.

34   ANON. Review of <u>Mardi</u>. New York <u>Literary World</u>, No. 116
      (21 April), pp. 351-353.
      Gives details of the characters and allegory in <u>Mardi</u>,
but despairs of giving in any way an account of all its
"multifold contents." <u>Mardi</u> "is a species of Utopia--or
rather a satiric voyage in which we discover--human nature.
There is a world of poetical, thoughtful, ingenious moral
writing in it which Emerson would not disclaim--gleams of
high-raised fancy, quaint assemblages of facts in the learned
spirit of Burton and the Doctor." Certain episodes are in
the highest style of invention, oriental richness, and moral
truthfulness. The Vivenza section (chapter 146) is a "sign
of true manhood, when an American author lifts his voice
boldly to tell the truth to his country people." The discourse of the narrator's party "is generally very poetical,
at times quite edifying, excepting when they get into the
clouds, attempting to handle the problem of the universe."
<u>Mardi</u> reveals Melville as the capital essayist as well as
the fascinating novelist and painter of sea life. Extracts
from chapters 63, 87, 147, 145, and 146. Reprinted in part
in <u>Recognition</u>, pp. 11-13, and Branch, pp. 152-154.

1849

35   ANON. Review of <u>Mardi</u>. Syracuse <u>Literary Union</u>, 1
        (21 April), 42.
             As in <u>Typee</u> and <u>Omoo</u>, the chief interest of <u>Mardi</u> is the
        freshness and peculiarity of its style. The sentences can
        be easily "transposed into an irregular versification, re-
        taining a measure as perfect as that of 'Thalaba' or any
        similar effort." Sets out two prose passages from chapters
        192 and 195 in verse form. Reprinted in Pollin (April 1975),
        pp. 62-64.

36   ANON. Review of <u>Mardi</u>. New York <u>Atlas</u> (22 April).
             <u>Mardi</u> is a work of signally intrinsic value, a wonder of
        Polynesian adventure, equalling in its characteristics the
        merits of Ellis and the beauties of Sir John Singleton.
        Melville possesses a lively imagination and is wonderfully
        felicitous in description.

*37   ANON. Review of <u>Mardi</u>. Newark <u>Daily Advertiser</u> (24 April).
             Cited in Hetherington (1961), p. 117.

38   ANON. Review of <u>Mardi</u>. Worcester (Mass.) <u>Palladium</u> (25 April).
             Melville's indistinctness of expression mars his per-
        formance: he does not draw the line vividly between truth
        and fiction, so that there is no chance to mistake one for
        the other. He has many attractive qualities, but <u>Mardi</u>
        will not improve his reputation.

39   ANON. Review of <u>Mardi</u>. Washington <u>National Intelligencer</u>
        (26 April).
             Reprint of 1849.B13.

*40   ANON. Review of <u>Mardi</u>. Richmond <u>Republican and General
        Advertiser</u> (27 April).
             Cited in Hetherington (1961), p. 117.

41   ANON. Notice of <u>Mardi</u>. Boston <u>Daily Bee</u> (28 April).
             <u>Mardi</u>, "which we are now reading, is thrillingly
        interesting."

42   ANON. "Melville's New Book--Mardi." Boston <u>Littell's Living
        Age</u>, 21 (28 April), 184-186.
             Reprint of 1849.B13.

43   ANON. Review of <u>Mardi</u>. New York <u>Literary American</u>, 2
        (28 April), 402.
             Finds very little difference between Melville's three
        books. <u>Typee</u>, <u>Omoo</u>, and <u>Mardi</u> are all marked by the same
        offhand, facile style, the same engrossing marvelous

incidents, and the same knowledge of the sea. Mardi contains, no doubt, a faithful portraiture of the manners of
the Polynesian people.

*44   ANON. Review of Mardi. Washington National Intelligencer
      (28 April).
           Reprint of 1849.B13. Cited in Hetherington (1961),
      p. 115.

*45   ANON. Review of Mardi. Baltimore American (before 30 April).
           "A mind well stored with various reading, originality of
      thought and expression without affectation, and masterly
      descriptions of scenery, impart a high interest to these
      descriptions or pictures of oceanic life." Quoted in ad-
      vertisement for Mardi in Morning Courier and New-York
      Enquirer (30 April 1849).

46   ANON. Review of Mardi. London Morning Post (30 April).
           In Mardi Melville communicates extraordinary ideas in a
      still more extraordinary and extravagant style. On every
      fitting occasion hits are made at the foolish importance
      attached in society to mere conventionalities. Melville
      has something to say on every subject and uses every means
      to accomplish his main object of awakening interest and
      exciting admiration, conducting us through a gorgeous dream
      of rapidly changing scenes in which "the most stupendous of
      the known phenomena of nature are exaggerated beyond limit
      by the insatiable appetite of human fancy." Everything is
      treated in a new way. The commingling of learning and
      imagination makes Mardi useful as well as entertaining.

47   ANON. "A Page By the Author of Mardi." London Man in the
      Moon, 5 (May), 284-285.
           A burlesque of Mardi. Reprinted in Ellis, pp. 419-422,
      and Branch, pp. 159-161.

48   ANON. Review of Mardi. New York Eclectic Magazine, 17 (May),
      144.
           Quotes first paragraph of 1849.B3.

49   ANON. "Honolulu." New York Holden's Dollar Magazine, 3 (May),
      259.
           Hopes, for the honor of the missionaries, that Melville's
      account of them in Omoo was made from hearsay rather than
      actual observation. Omoo passage reprinted in Log, p. 302.

50   ANON. Review of Mardi. New York Merchants' Magazine and
      Commercial Review, 20 (May), 572.

1849

Mardi will more than repay careful reading. The style
is unique and cannot be described. The language possesses
all the polish of an Irving with all the spirit of a Scott.
The matter is truly poetical--philosophical as Plato, yet
beautifully imaginative as Moore. As a whole, it is a
master stroke of genius.

51   ANON. "Letters from New-York." Richmond Southern Literary
     Messenger, 15 (May), 309.
         Typee is good, Omoo less good, Mardi least good--a fail-
     ure. All readers will discern the grossness and utter im-
     probabilities of its fabrications. There is a continual
     straining after effect, an effort constantly at fine writing,
     a sacrifice of natural ease to artificial witticism.
     Melville has been overfed with praise; he has a reputation
     to lose and is attempting to write up to it. Reprinted in
     part in Log, p. 305.

52   ANON. Review of Mardi. Boston Daily Bee (2 May), p. 2.
         Despite Melville's preface, reviewer can scarcely realize
     that the characters portrayed in the pages he has had time
     to read are not real. Jarl, Samoa, Anatoo, Yillah,
     Borabolla, and Babbalanja must have been real personages
     or Melville could never have given such lifelike portrayals
     of them. Extract from chapter 58.

53   ANON. Review of Mardi. New York Gazette of the Union, Golden
     Rule and Odd-Fellows' Family Companion, 20 (5 May), 288-289.
         Mardi is written in Melville's peculiar style, and al-
     though it does not possess the highest literary merit it is
     a very readable book. Melville's thought is not deep but
     graceful; Mardi amuses but does not instruct. Extract from
     chapter 50. Reprinted in Pollin (April 1975), p. 68, and
     Pollin (October 1975), p. 7.

54   ANON. Review of Mardi. New York Home Journal (5 May).
         Mardi is characterized by the same adventurous spirit
     and freshness of description as Typee. The large class who
     delight in records of travel and graphic narrative will
     enjoy it in the highest degree.

55   ANON. Review of Mardi. New York Daily Tribune (10 May), p. 1.
         After Typee and Omoo, Mardi is a constant disappointment,
     "a monstrous compound of Carlyle, Jean-Paul, and Sterne,
     with now and then a touch of Ossian thrown in." Early pas-
     sages display unrivaled beauty and power, the same unaffected
     grace and easy command of language as the previous books.
     But after the arrival at Mardi, we are presented with a

tissue of conceits in language equally intolerable for its
affectation and its obscurity. The story has no movement,
no proportions, no ultimate end; and unless it is a huge
allegory, no significance or point. Melville has failed by
leaving his sphere. Reprinted in part in Log, p. 303; reprinted in Recognition, pp. 16-17, and Branch, pp. 161-163.

56 ANON. Review of Mardi. Richmond Enquirer (11 May).
        Mardi "abounds in very spirited and graceful sketches of
    land and ocean, of the pursuit of the whale, &c."

57 ANON. Review of Mardi. Richmond Watchman and Observer
        (before 12 May).
        Mardi is a most extraordinary production that evinces
    unusual strength of thinking. It is "a sort of cross be-
    tween the Pilgrim's Progress, Gulliver's Travels, Sartor
    Resartus, and the Doctor; having something in common with
    them all, and something peculiar to itself." It hits off
    "with much truth, pleasantry, and delicate satire," the
    peculiarities of all the countries of Europe and America
    in their customs, religion, and politics. Quoted in adver-
    tisement for Mardi in the New York Literary World, No. 119
    (12 May), p. 422.

58 ANON. Review of Mardi. Sharpe's London Journal, 9 (15 May),
        192.
        Mardi is difficult to describe because it aims at many
    things and achieves none satisfactorily. Its main intention
    "is to be a mild satire on the whole world and its ways, and
    a preaching of certain transcendental nonsense which is
    meant for bona fide transcendental philosophy." There is
    little or no story, and after the first volume the labor of
    reading is "perfectly Herculean" and "remarkably
    unprofitable."

59 CHASLES, PHILARÈTE. "Voyages Réels et Fantastiques d'Hermann
        Melville." Paris Revue des Deux Mondes, 2 (15 May), 541-570.
        Commentary on Typee (with extracts) and Mardi. Biograph-
    ical details of Melville, provided by "one of the most hon-
    orable citizens of the United States," who vouched for the
    authenticity of Typee and claimed that Melville enjoyed his
    reputation as an imaginative novelist and was somewhat vexed
    when the reappearance of Richard Tobias Greene (Toby) re-
    duced his stature to that of a mere narrator. [See 1846.B74.]
    Contrary to the opinion of English and American critics,
    Typee is a work of recollection rather than imagination,
    though its colors are somewhat heightened for effect. The
    book provides a model in the art of communicating vividly-

felt sensations; its pages are full of movement, dramatic
interest, and life. Mardi is unique, the dream of an ill-
educated cabin boy intoxicated with hashish; a book worthy
of a Rabelais without gaiety, a Cervantes without grace, a
Voltaire without taste; an extraordinary and vulgar book,
original and incoherent, full of sense and nonsense, full
of interesting facts and repetition, profound instruction,
and indifferent epigrams. Melville's attempt to be perfectly original resulted in an awkward mixture of grotesque
comedy and fantastic grandeur, a mingling of the pompous
and the vulgar, the commonplace and the unintelligible.
Originality comes late and belongs only to ripe minds with
a perfect knowledge of their depth and extent. Sterne,
Jean Paul, and Cervantes alone have been able to accomplish
a "humoristic" book, the rarest product of art; Melville
has certainly not succeeded. Except for his continual
effort to be eloquent and original, the first part of Mardi
is charming and full of life, but when the narrator and
Jarl reach the islands Melville renounces reality for fairy-
land and somnambulism, commencing a symbolic Odyssey very
clumsily imitated from Rabelais. Includes interpretations
by Chasles of the "symbolic signification" of various characters and islands. Melville misuses vocabulary and creates
new words contrary to all the Anglo-Germanic laws. Trans-
lated in part in 1849.B89 and 1849.B90; followed by commentary in 1849.B90.

60   ANON. "Mardi, and a Voyage Thither." London Morning Chronicle
      (19 May), p. 6.
          Melville is not a genius, perhaps, but a superlatively
      clever and highly-read man with very considerable powers of
      fancy and a very rare talent for writing that is at once
      enthusiastic and epigrammatic, full of both poetic ardor
      and artful rhetoric. But after the first excellent volume
      of Mardi he riots in a chaos of incoherent poetry (or prose
      run mad) and vague satire. He lashes the vices and follies
      of the nations of the earth, but makes no attempt at con-
      sistent, natural satire. Mardi is a wonderful and unread-
      able compound of Ossian and Rabelais, More's Utopia,
      Harrington's Oceana, Gulliver's Travels, and Cook's Voyages,
      "spiced with rhetoric from Mr. Macaulay's essays, and sar-
      casm from Mr. Disraeli's perorations." Continuous interest
      must necessarily be shattered by Melville's reckless fan-
      tasticality. Mardi is full of evidence of great imaginative
      strength and wonderful graphic power, but totally lacks
      method, order, purpose, intelligibility, and commonsense.
      Reprinted in part in Log, p. 304.

61   ANON. "Literature of the Past Year: Romances." <u>Illustrated
      London News</u> (Supplement), 14 (26 May), 358.
          <u>Mardi</u> is one of the most grotesque volumes encountered
      in a long time. The early description of the passage
      across the ocean in an open boat contains some of the
      finest nautical description that the world has ever seen;
      Melville's language is elegant and expressive, sometimes
      even beautiful to the last degree. The conversations after
      Mardi is reached are often highly quaint and ingenious,
      still more often absurd and ridiculous. The latter are
      readily forgiven for the former.

62   ANON. Review of <u>Kavanagh, a Tale</u> by Henry Wadsworth Longfellow.
      New York <u>Literary World</u>, No. 121 (26 May), p. 452.
          Refers to the character Churchill's "theory of poetical
      mathematics, involving a puzzle of flowery propositions in
      the unforgivable perplexity of Herman Melville's Queen
      Hautia."

63   ANON. Review of <u>Adventures in Borneo</u>. London <u>Gentlemen's
      Magazine</u>, NS 31 (June), 625-626.
          <u>Typee</u> and <u>Omoo</u> cited as examples of a regrettable current
      trend of "dressing up works of fiction in the disguise of
      truth." They are "told so exceedingly like truth as to
      impose on the unsuspecting reader, and, were it not for a
      reckless flight of imagination which the author every here
      and there indulges, in spite of his habitual caution, are
      apt to deceive even the more watchful critic." Passage on
      <u>Typee</u> and <u>Omoo</u> reprinted in Smith, p. 6.

64   ANON. Review of <u>Mardi</u>. New York <u>Holden's Dollar Magazine</u>,
      3 (June), 370-373.
          If Melville had not been a poet he could never have
      worked up the slight and commonplace materials of <u>Typee</u>
      and <u>Omoo</u> so as to create the impression they were purely
      works of the imagination. <u>Mardi</u> shows a marked difference
      of style and has been written with more care and ambition.
      The volumes are most entertaining. Their great defect is
      "the apparent want of motive in the composition." It is
      difficult to guess at Melville's aims; if he had any satir-
      ical intentions, they are cunningly covered up. There is
      no story to interest. A "dreamy kind of voluptuousness,
      and an ecstatic outbreak of animal impulse" seem to be the
      book's "pervading peculiarities." Affectations of style
      and rhapsodical episodes puzzle the reader, whose bewildered
      feeling of having been in a dream was perhaps Melville's
      object. Extracts from chapters 31, 32, and 84.

1849

65   ANON. Review of <u>Mardi</u>. Philadelphia <u>Godey's Magazine and Lady's Book</u>, 38 (June), 436.
      <u>Mardi</u> is one of the most interesting books of travel the reviewer has ever seen, giving more knowledge of Polynesian life and customs than any work extant.

66   ANON. Review of <u>Mardi</u>. Philadelphia <u>Graham's Magazine</u>, 34 (June), 385.
      The best evidence of the truthfulness of Melville's former books is the decidedly romantic character of much of <u>Mardi</u>, the most striking work he has produced, "exhibiting a range of learning, a fluency of fancy, and an originality of thought and diction," of which <u>Typee</u>, "with all its distinctness and luxuriance of description, gave little evidence." But its rich materials are not sufficiently harmonized to produce unity of effect; confusion, rather than fusion, characterizes the book as a whole. The first volume is by far the best, but both contain abundant evidence of the richness, strength, and independence of Melville's mind. Reprinted in Rountree, p. 16.

67   ANON. Review of <u>Mardi</u>. Philadelphia <u>Peterson's Magazine</u>, 15 (June), 219.
      The skimmer will find <u>Mardi</u> a book of interest, novelty, and peculiar imagination. The reader who ploughs deeper will discover "gems of thought, delicate sarcasms and sly allusions, to say nothing of quaint words and oddly termed expressions." <u>Mardi</u> shows Melville to be a man of thought and high principle, "not wedded to any form of bigotry, but one capable of seeing the good and beautiful in any guise." Reprinted in Pollin (April 1975), p. 66.

68   ANON. "Adventures of Herman Melville." <u>Adelaide Miscellany of Useful and Entertaining Knowledge</u>, 2 (9 June), 295-302.
      Reprint of 1846.B52.

*69   ANON. New York <u>Journal of Commerce</u> (13 June).
      Quotes from 1849.B59 and 1849.B60. Reports that the French critic and British reviewers are pleased with volume 1 of <u>Mardi</u> and that they all regard volumes 2 and 3 as "monstrous vagaries." Reprinted in 1849.B75.

70   CHASLES, PHILARÈTE. "Herman Melville's Voyages." Boston <u>Daily Advertiser</u> (15 June), p. 2.
      Translation of part of 1849.B59. Reprinted in 1849.B71 and 1849.B72.

71   CHASLES, PHILARÈTE. "Herman Melville's Voyages." Albany
      Argus (18 June), p. 2.
           Reprint of 1849.B70.

72   CHASLES, PHILARÈTE. "Herman Melville's Voyages." Albany
      Weekly Argus (23 June), p. 4.
           Reprint of 1849.B70.

73   ANON. Review of _Kaloolah_ by W. S. Mayo. New York _Literary
      World_, No. 125 (23 June), p. 533.
           "Not so imaginative as Typee, Mr. Romer is more inventive
      and ingenious; his fancy is more 'forgetive,' though less
      full of delectable shapes...."

74   ANON. Review of 1849 edition of _Typee_. Philadelphia _Dollar
      Newspaper_ (27 June).
           "With few superiors as a narrator, a describer and a
      humorist," Melville "is unsurpassed in invention, fancy,
      and brilliant imagination." Reprinted in Pollin (April
      1975), p. 57.

75   ANON. "Correspondence of the Journal of Commerce." New York
      Literary World, No. 126 (30 June), p. 556.
           Reprint of 1849.B69.

76   ANON. Review of 1849 edition of _Typee_. New York _Spirit of
      the Times_, 19 (30 June), 228.
           Typee is one of the most popular and fascinating books
      ever written. On its first publication, all the journals
      of the United States and Europe united in the warmest com-
      mendations of its novelty, power, and beauty.

77   ANON. "Melville's _Mardi_." New York _United States Magazine
      and Democratic Review_, 25 (July), 44-50.
           Typee and _Omoo_ were to _Mardi_ "as a seven-by-nine sketch
      of a sylvan lake, with a lone hunter, or a boy fishing,
      compared with the cartoons of Raphael," flute-like music
      compared with a magnificent orchestra. The fact that _Mardi_
      is an allegory that mirrors the world has so far escaped
      the critics, who seem to have forgotten _Pilgrim's Progress_
      and _Gulliver's Travels_. But the manner of _Mardi_ is unique,
      "and like all new things must take the chance of being con-
      sidered ugly, because it is uncommon." The veil of mystery
      thrown over _Mardi_ "enhances its beauty to those who have
      sympathy with the author, and can finish his creation with
      a corresponding or heightened sublimity." The reader who
      "wishes to see the spirit of philosophy and humanity, love
      and wisdom, showing man to himself as he is, that he may

know his evil and folly, and be saved from them, will be
reverently thankful" for the book. Parts of it are written under the divine impulse in which "God's <u>must</u>" is upon
the author, "and he does his work in his own and other's
spite." <u>Mardi</u> contains majestic poetry, "which reminds us
of the Hebrew" and passages of sweet and gentle beauty.
But Melville seems to lack the absolute faith that God had
a purpose in creating the world. He must emerge from this
evil state. Extracts from chapters 119 and 63. Reprinted
in part in <u>Recognition</u>, pp. 18-19, and Branch, pp. 177-183.

78   ANON. Review of 1849 edition of <u>Typee</u>. New York <u>Evangelist</u>
      (5 July), p. 4.
          The virtues and vices of <u>Typee</u> both conspire to give it
      notoriety. It exhibits a spirit and grace irresistible to
      most readers and depicts the loveliest scenery in the world
      with true poetic genius. Its degraded moral tone, slander-
      ous attacks on missionaries, and unquestionable falsehood
      from beginning to end are equally undeniable. Melville
      might have added to our information, opened our sympathy
      for the Marquesans, and secured a permanent fame; instead
      he must be content with the brief notoriety from a splendid
      piece of fiction.

79   ANON. Review of 1849 edition of <u>Typee</u>. New York <u>Literary</u>
      <u>American</u>, 3 (7 July), 15.
          Critics in the United States have thus far treated
      Melville with considerable respect. Quotes from 1849.B60
      and 1849.B59 to show that "he does not fare so well beyond
      the ocean."

80   ANON. New York <u>Literary World</u>, No. 127 (7 July), p. 8.
          Note that the Harpers "have published a new edition of
      'Typee,' the stereotype plates of which have just passed
      into their hands, rendering their series of Mr. Melville's
      works complete."

81   ANON. Review of 1849 edition of <u>Typee</u>. Springfield (Mass.)
      <u>Republican</u> (7 July).
          Criticism of <u>Typee</u> has been very generally favorable.
      It is no small merit to have written a book so consistent
      in its details, and so plausible in its plot, that the
      reading world is wholly undecided whether it is entirely
      true or entirely false.

82   ANON. Notice of <u>Typee</u>. New York <u>Christian Intelligencer</u>
      (12 July).

Announces publication of the 1849 Harper edition and
recalls that the first edition "was thought to do great
injustice" to missionaries in the Pacific. Has not yet
had time to learn how the topic is treated in the new
edition.

83 ANON. "What is Talked About." New York Literary World,
No. 128 (14 July), p. 32.
Introduction to description of the island of Taboga:
the writer has caught "a glimpse of 'Typee'" there.

84 ANON. Review of 1849 edition of Typee. New York Independent
(19 July), p. 132.
Notes Melville's "extensive reputation as a vivacious
if not altogether a veracious author." Pleased that he has
"so far profited by criticism" as to omit passages "which
had given just offense to the friends of missions." Reprinted in Monteiro (Fourth Quarter 1974), p. 435.

85 ANON. "Jonathan in Africa." Blackwood's Edinburgh Magazine,
66 (August), 172-173.
Melville is the pioneer of a new school of novelists
whose style seems a "compound imitation of Gulliver,
Munchausen, The Arabian Nights, and Robinson Crusoe." He
has most completely disappointed with Mardi, a rubbishing
rhapsody, trash mingled with attempts at a Rabelaisian vein
and with strainings at smartness; the style of the whole is
affected, pedantic, and wearisome exceedingly. Mardi is
unfavorably compared with W. S. Mayo's Kaloolah. Reprinted
in part in Log, p. 311.

86 ANON. Notice of Typee. New York American Review: A Whig
Journal, NS 4 (August), 218.
Notes publication of the 1849 Harper edition, with
Melville's "own revisal and improvements."

87 HAYWARDE, RICHARD. Review of Mardi. Philadelphia Graham's
Magazine, 35 (August), 130.
There are "such beautiful Aurora-flashes of light" in
Mardi that you can almost forgive the puerilities; it is a
great network of affectation, with some genuine gold shining
through the interstices. Ridicules a number of passages in
Mardi and illustrates Melville's tendency to write hexameters
in his prose. Reprinted in part in Log, p. 311.

88 ANON. Review of Mardi. Philadelphia Sartain's Union Magazine
5 (August), 126.

1849

        Melville has either been happy in his choice of subject
or has the still higher merit of having produced a very
entertaining work from an indifferent subject.

89   CHASLES, PHILARÈTE. "The Actual and Fantastic Voyages of
       Herman Melville." New York <u>Literary World</u>, No. 131
       (4 August), pp. 89–90.
          First part of partial translation of 1849.B59. Continued
       in 1849.B90. Reprinted in part in Rountree, pp. 17–18, and
       Branch, pp. 164–169.

90   CHASLES, PHILARÈTE. "The Actual and Fantastic Voyages of
       Herman Melville." New York <u>Literary World</u>, No. 132
       (11 August), pp. 101–103.
          Continued from 1849.B89. Second part of partial trans-
       lation of 1849.B59, followed by commentary. Acknowledges
       the general acuteness of Chasles's criticism; his account
       of <u>Mardi</u> is the nearest approach to a full and fair estima-
       tion of the work by a foreigner. Notes errors in the bio-
       graphical information Chasles provides. Reprinted in part
       in Rountree, pp. 18–21, and Branch, pp. 169–177.

91   ANON. "Literary Novelties." London <u>Literary Gazette</u>,
       No. 1701 (25 August), p. 630.
          Announcement of <u>Redburn</u>. Claims there is general puzzle-
       ment as to whether Melville's works are all fiction, or
       fiction founded on actual adventure, or "composition from
       published voyages dressed up with imagination." Does not
       know whether to believe biographical information given in
       1849.B89 or even that Herman Melville is the author's real
       name.

92   ANON. Review of <u>Mardi</u>. New York <u>American Review: A Whig
       Journal</u>, NS 4 (September), 329.
          Melville has been too ambitious and failed in <u>Mardi</u>.
       Every page of the book undoubtedly exhibits the man of
       genius, and facile writer, but exhibits also pedantry and
       affectation. The faults are attributable to the astonish-
       ment of reviewers of <u>Typee</u> and <u>Omoo</u> that a common sailor
       should exhibit so much reading and knowledge of literature.

*93   ANON. Review of <u>Four Years in the Pacific</u> by Lieut. the Hon.
       Fred Walpole, R. N. London <u>Examiner</u> (before 22 September).
          Notes that a passage by Walpole "if not suggested by
       Herman Melville, bears out his description wonderfully."
       Quoted in 1849.B94.

94   ANON. Review of <u>Four Years in the Pacific</u> by Lieut. the Hon.
      Fred Walpole, R. N. New York <u>Literary World</u>, No. 138
      (22 September), pp. 248-249.
          Quotes from 1849.B93 and notes other coincidences.
      Walpole became lame and disabled in the Sandwich Islands
      "and found similar careful nurture in a domestic household
      with a gentle Fayaway in the person of the graceful little
      Elekeke."

95   ANON. Review of <u>Mardi</u>. New York <u>Saroni's Musical Times</u>, 1
      (29 September), 6.
          Complains of having been "flattered with the promise of
      an account of travel, amusing, though fictitious" but then
      "compelled to pore over an undigested mass of rambling
      metaphysics" and immersed in a "fathomless sea of Allegory,"
      full of "monstrous Types, Myths, Symbols and such like fan-
      tastic weeds." Style is <u>Mardi's</u> sole redeeming feature.
      So poetic in his prose, Melville is remarkably unfortunate
      in his verse. Reprinted in Branch, pp. 184-186.

96   ANON. Review of 1849 edition of <u>Typee</u>. Andover (Maine)
      <u>Biblical Repository and Classical Review</u>, Third Series, 5
      (October), 754.
          Melville is a very racy and entertaining writer. His
      picture of Polynesian life is strongly drawn and a remark-
      able one if true. But a deep romantic feeling and a fertile
      imagination seem to have given coloring to the picture.
      Melville's good sense and the moral sentiments of the world
      have constrained him to omit the reckless assertions and
      false charges against the missionaries. Reprinted in
      Williams (1950), pp. 124-125.

97   ANON. Review of <u>Mardi</u>. Charleston (S.C.) <u>Southern Quarterly
      Review</u>, 16 (October), 260-261.
          <u>Mardi</u> takes the form of allegory rather than action or
      adventure, being a fanciful voyage about the world in search
      of happiness. Melville satirizes the deeds of the more
      prominent nations and in his somewhat monotonous progress
      gives many glowing rhapsodies, much epigrammatic thought,
      and many sweet and attractive fancies. But he spoils every-
      thing for the Southern reader when he paints a loathsome
      picture of Calhoun as a slavedriver. Reprinted in Branch,
      p. 187.

98   ANON. Review of 1849 edition of <u>Typee</u>. New York <u>Methodist
      Quarterly Review</u>, Fourth Series, 1 (October), 679.
          Without the offensive and unjust observations on the
      missions, the fascinating <u>Typee</u> can now be recommended
      almost without reserve.

1849

*99   [WILLIS, N. P.]. Review of Los Gringos by Lieut. Henry A.
       Wise. New York Home Journal (13 October).
           Complimentary to Typee and Omoo. Cited in Log, p. 320.

100   ANON. "What is Talked About." New York Literary World,
       No. 141 (13 October), p. 319.
           Notes that Melville is among the passengers on the London
       packet ship Southampton, to sail that week, and carries with
       him to London proofsheets of a new work "to appear the
       coming season."

101   ANON. "Omoo and Realities." London Literary Gazette, No. 1709
       (20 October), pp. 776-778.
           Not impressed with Melville's earlier books but pleased
       with Redburn, which deals with common and real life and is
       "as perfect a specimen of the naval yarn as we ever read,"
       awakening new interest by being the narrative of a mere
       lad rather than an old hand. The second volume is more
       desultory than the first, but "both display much various
       talent and power, though the first is the most peculiar and
       novel." Redburn's adventures, sufferings, and portraits of
       his companions appear to be altogether free from fiction and
       hardly dressed up beyond the simple truth. Melville's use
       of certain Yankee words show him to be really an American.
       Reprinted in part in Branch, pp. 188-189.

102   ANON. Review of Redburn. London Britannia (27 October),
       pp. 683-684.
           The fierce and swaggering exaggeration of the genuine
       Yankee style is unpleasantly conspicuous in Redburn.
       Melville's faculty of representation is similar to that of
       a bad glass: he distorts whatever he reflects, making nearly
       every object appear monstrous and unnatural. There are some
       saltwater passages of great power, but the staple of the
       book is coarse and horrible, mingled with much that is
       tediously minute. Melville's talent seems to be running to
       seed from want of careful pruning. Extracts from chapters
       48 and 59. Reprinted in Branch, p. 190.

103   ANON. Review of Redburn. London John Bull (27 October).
           As time passes, Melville's faults grow less conspicuous,
       while his excellencies remain undiminished. Redburn is
       equal to any of his previous works in interest, diversity
       of narrative, liveliness of tone, and graphic power of
       delineation, and avoids their tendency to exhibit vice
       scarcely veiled for the amusement of readers.

104   ANON. "Herman Melville's Redburn." London Spectator,
       No. 1113 (27 October), pp. 1020-1021.
           Redburn is even more remarkable than Typee and Omoo.
       Lacking their novelty of subject, variety, and adventure,
       it is still, except for some chapters describing common-
       place things, a very readable and attractive book. It
       does not have the veracity of Dana's Two Years Before the
       Mast or the comprehensiveness and truthfulness of delinea-
       tion of some of Cooper's sea novels, but it is a book of
       information and interest, though merely the narrative of a
       voyage, containing nothing beyond the common probabilities
       of the merchant service. The interest of Redburn arises
       from its quiet naturalness. The book reads like a true
       story--"as if it had all taken place." The innocent lad
       amidst the roughness and novelty of a ship can be found in
       Peter Simple; but Redburn's circumstances and the nautical
       incidents and characters are so different that the story
       has the effect of originality. Redburn's reputed character
       as "the son of a gentleman" is not always consistently
       maintained. Extracts from chapters 6, 16, and 48. Re-
       printed in 1849.B152 and Branch, pp. 191-193.

105   ANON. New York Literary American, 3 (27 October), 341.
           Report that Melville "has forwarded to Bentley, the
       London publisher, the manuscript of a new work, under the
       title of 'Red Horn'" and has sailed for London, intending
       to spend a year abroad.

106   ANON. Review of Los Gringos by Lieut. Henry A. Wise. New York
       Literary World, No. 143 (27 October), pp. 355-356.
           Prints Wise's passage on Melville [see 1849.B2]. Regards
       the Fayaway that Wise saw as "a pretender to the character."

107   ANON. Review of Redburn. London Daily News (29 October).
           Redburn is as pleasant as Two Years Before the Mast in
       its earnestness of purpose and simplicity, but does not
       have the holiday look or joyous blitheness of Dana.
       Melville imparts sea matters in a clear, simple style; one
       is reminded of Defoe by the way in which ship and crew are
       depicted and artfully made subservient to the development
       of character and story. Melville gives an account of
       Liverpool with daguerreotype fidelity and freshness, but
       is "not at home" in London. Reviewer has seldom met with
       a book from which more striking or more powerfully written
       extracts could be taken. Reprinted in Branch, pp. 195-196.

108   ANON. Review of Redburn. London Morning Post (29 October).
           Melville has the art of making old material look fresh.
       Redburn is not a novel "for there is neither plot nor love

1849

in it; it is simply what it professes to be, the narrative
of a voyage." But it is full of interest and contains many
bold portraits of striking individual sea characters, many
graphic pictures of ship life, and some clever sketches of
men and manners and scenes in Liverpool (though some of
these scenes are rather apocryphal). The details of the
horrors of the return voyage particularly deserve notice.
Mardi gave high promise, which has been fully borne out in
Redburn. Extracts from chapters 18, 26, 42, and 34. Reprinted in part in Branch, pp. 193-194.

109   ANON. Review of Redburn. London Morning Herald (30 October).
Redburn develops a story of maritime life somewhat in
the style and spirit of Marryat. The details of ship life,
though familiar to most novel readers, are sketched with a
faithful pencil, and the characters of the crew and passengers are drawn with nature and truth. Some of Redburn's
adventures are exceedingly diverting. His observations at
Liverpool tell strongly against the liberality of Americans
and the personal freedom they boast so much of. Extracts
from chapters 41 and 61.

110   ANON. "Across the Atlantic." Blackwood's Edinburgh Magazine,
66 (November), 567-580.
Redburn does not have the spontaneous flow and racy
originality of Typee and Omoo, but it also lacks much of
the obscurity and nonsense of Mardi. Its style is more
natural and manly. Some incidents and reflections are
dwelt upon too long. Absurdities, improbabilities, and
inconsistencies mar the characterization of Redburn and
Harry Bolton, but the portrayal of other characters is
generally effective. Melville's straining for striking
similes at the expense of truth and good taste is deplorable,
as are his exaggerated exhibitions of the horrible, such as
the "utterly absurd" Launcelott's-Hey episode. The London
expedition is in the very stalest style of minor theater
melodrama. Melville should "stick to the ship," where he
is at home; he is most effective when most simple and unpretending. If he will put away affectation and curb the ec-
centricities of his fancy, he can become "a very agreeable
writer of nautical fictions. He will never have the power
of a Cringle, or the sustained humour and vivacity of a
Marryat, but he may do very well without aspiring to rival
the masters of the art." Detailed summary, with extracts
from chapters 3, 5, 14, 50, and 59. Reprinted in part in
Branch, pp. 196-201.

111   ANON. Review of Redburn. London Bentley's Miscellany, 26
       (November), 528-530.
          Values Redburn, a sort of Robinson Crusoe on shipboard,
       more highly than any of Melville's previous works. With
       occasional snatches of their wild and visionary spirit,
       Redburn is a narrative of palpable life, related with broad
       simplicity, depending on closeness and truthfulness of por-
       traiture for influence over the reader's sympathies. Its
       interest consists in the detail of the process by which
       Redburn is disenchanted of his pleasant delusions. The
       sailors are individuals to a man. The Harry Bolton episode
       is perhaps a little in excess but makes "a strong opposition
       of colour" to the rest of the story. The American idiomatic
       peculiarities greatly increase the work's sense of reality,
       its paramount merit.

112   ANON. Review of 1849 edition of Typee. New Orleans De Bow's
       Commercial Review of the South and West, 7 (November), 465.
          "With all the attractiveness of elevated romance, it
       gives truthful views of life in the far distant isles of
       the sea."

113   ANON. Review of 1849 edition of Typee. Philadelphia Sartain's
       Union Magazine, 5 (November), 320.
          Among the improvements is the omission of parts relating
       to Tahiti and the Sandwich Islands, which gave much discon-
       tent without being necessary to the narrative. Typee is one
       of the choicest collections of adventures extant.

*114   ANON. Review of Los Gringos by Lieut. Henry A. Wise. New York
       Evangelist (8 November).
          The "performances" of Melville were Wise's "model."
       Cited in Mailloux and Parker, p. 13.

*115   ANON. "Brevities." New York Home Journal (8 November).
          Reports that Melville sailed a few days previously for
       England and predicts that he will be admitted through "the
       most difficult portals of English society" by his genius,
       the popularity of his books, and "the extraordinary charm
       of his narrative powers in conversation." Cited in Log,
       p. 328.

116   ANON. Review of Redburn. London Athenaeum, No. 1150
       (10 November), pp. 1131-1133.
          The Peter Simple-ism of Redburn looks "a little pale" in
       Melville's imitation of Marryat. Redburn lacks the novelty
       of interest and subject of Typee and Omoo but on the whole
       is better written than either. The improvement on Mardi is

1849

striking in some respects. Apart from the chapter "A
Mysterious Night in London" there is little extravagance.
Extracts from chapters 2, 7, 8, 5, 6, 9, and 22.

117 ANON. "Passages from New Books." New York Literary World,
No. 145 (10 November), pp. 395-397.
Brief introduction to extracts. Redburn is eminently
attractive throughout--a piece of fresh natural composition.
Melville proves himself "the De Foe of the Ocean." Reprints
chapters 14 and 48. Reprinted in 1849.B125.

118 ANON. Notice of Redburn. Boston Daily Evening Transcript
(14 November).
A "glance" through Redburn suggests that, after the
failure of Mardi, Melville will now have retrieved his
popularity.

119 ANON. Review of Redburn. Philadelphia Public Ledger and
Daily Transcript (15 November).
Redburn "will repay any person for the time spent in its
perusal, being a lively and entertaining volume."

120 ANON. Notice of Redburn. Albany Evening Journal (17 November),
p. 2.
Predicts that Redburn will be interesting and find numerous readers. Melville is a graceful, happy, beautiful
writer.

*121 ANON. Review of Redburn. Hartford Daily Courant (17 November).
Cited in Hetherington (1961), p. 144.

122 ANON. Review of Redburn. New Bedford Mercury (17 November),
p. 2.
In Redburn Melville has taken new ground. After many
adventures his hero goes to London, "where of course we find
him making all sorts of odd comparisons between the hospital-
ities of civilized and savage life." Extract from chapter
41.

123 ANON. Review of Redburn. New York Literary World, No. 146
(17 November), pp. 418-420.
Melville deserves to be called the Defoe of the Ocean
"by the life-like portraiture of his characters at sea, the
strong relishing style in which his observations are conveyed, the fidelity to nature, and, in the combination of
all these, the thorough impression and conviction of reality." The book has no verbosity, no artificiality, no
languor. The sailors are not stage sailors but actual men;

their talk is plain, direct, straightforward. This "sailor's use of language, the most in the shortest compass," may be "the literary school" which has rescued Melville from the dull verbosity of many of his contemporaries. The Liverpool scenes are "all reeking with life." The death of Jackson is one of the most striking scenes in nautical fiction. Extracts from chapters 3, 12, 59, and 27. Reprinted in part in Recognition, p. 21, and Branch, pp. 201-202.

124 ANON. Review of Redburn. New York Spirit of the Times, 19 (17 November), 468.
Redburn is quite worthy of Melville's genius. Reprinted in Flanagan, p. 60.

125 ANON. Review of Redburn. Washington National Intelligencer (17 November).
Reprint of 1849.B117.

126 ANON. Review of Redburn. New York Sunday Times and Noah's Weekly Messenger (18 November).
Mardi is the book on which Melville "would probably choose to rest his fame--a work of great thought and wonderful power." Redburn is in the old vein of Typee and Omoo--written for the million, who will doubtless be delighted with its racy descriptions of a young sailor's life. Melville took with him to England the proofsheets of Redburn and "letters which will introduce him to the most exclusive set of the British aristocracy." He will represent there "a very fair type of the energetic self-reliant American."

127 ANON. Review of Redburn. Springfield (Mass.) Republican (19 November).
Redburn has more the air of reality than Melville's previous books and possibly may be less interesting in consequence. But, as the admirers of Melville are legion, it will doubtless have a large sale.

128 ANON. Review of Redburn. Boston Post (20 November), p. 1.
A "Crusoe-like naturalness," the "first of all qualities in fiction" is the distinguishing excellence of Redburn. There is "no glimmer of the levity, coxcombry, affectation, inconsistency and hodge-podge" of Mardi. The book's great charm is its realness. It "seems to be fact word for word," except for a little that is melodramatic and exaggerated in the hero at the outset; with that exception, the tale is told simply and without pretension. Yet within its narrow bounds there are flashes of genuine humor, strokes of pure

pathos, and real and original characters. The hero is a sort of American Peter Simple. Redburn is a Robinson Crusoe modernized. Reprinted in Branch, pp. 203-204.

*129   ANON. Review of Redburn. Norwich Evening Courier (20 November).
      Cited in Hetherington (1961), p. 145.

130   W. Notice of Redburn. Albany Argus (21 November).
      Reviewer has looked into Redburn sufficiently to see that it has the characteristic marks of Melville's genius and many bright and beautiful passages.

*131   ANON. Review of Redburn. Baltimore American (21 November).
      Cited in Hetherington (1961), p. 146.

132   ANON. Review of Redburn. Philadelphia Dollar Newspaper (21 November).
      Some of the scenes on shipboard in Redburn are depicted with graphic power; the whole book contains a life and sprightliness few authors can rival. Melville has a rare pen for the delineation of character and an eye for the humorous and grotesque; in description of natural scenery he is not to be beaten. For invention "he will bear comparison with the most cunning of the modern French school." [Cf. 1847.B87.] Reprinted in Pollin (April 1975), p. 57.

133   ANON. Review of Redburn. Worcester (Mass.) Palladium (21 November), p. 3.
      No writer plans better than Melville; no one uses better materials or gives them better workmanship. In description of natural scenery or delineation of character there is an attractive vividness, freshness, and variety. The story of Redburn is simple but not lacking in that multiplicity of incidents that gives attraction to this species of writing.

134   ANON. Review of Redburn. Washington National Era (22 November).
      Except for a little verbosity and an occasional imitation of Dickens's particularities of description, Melville is himself again. As an account of a boy's first shipboard experience Redburn is unequalled for fidelity, humor, and interest. Reprinted in Pollin (October 1975), p. 8.

135   ANON. Review of Redburn. Washington National Intelligencer (22 November).
      Redburn is unquestionably a work of genius and quite as interesting as it is unique. Reviewer does not know where a better idea of sailor life can be found.

136   ANON. Review of Redburn. Lansingburgh (N.Y.) Gazette
      (23 November).
         The style of Melville's writings is not beautiful, nor
      eloquent, nor always in good taste; but it has an air of
      simplicity, ease, and originality that inspires confidence
      and holds attention spellbound to the end. Reviewer has
      read Redburn only cursorily, but with interest.

137   ANON. Review of Redburn. New York Albion, NS 8 (24 November),
      561.
         Earlier sea writers have generally chosen the picturesque
      side of nautical life. Melville "often selects those views
      of it which, apart from his clever treatment, would be un-
      interesting, if not repulsive." He paints his pictures so
      truthfully and vividly "that one forgets the unpromising
      nature of his subjects in consideration of his skill in
      treating them. The Oliver Twists of ocean life are his
      best dramatis personae--not the Pelhams." The exceeding
      gravity of the book is unusual for a nautical tale.
      Melville sees evil with an observant eye, without having
      cut and dried remedies. The visit to a London gambling
      house only shows Melville's inability to paint scenes of
      this sort. Extracts from chapters 25 and 28. Reprinted
      in part in Branch, pp. 204-206.

138   ANON. Review of Redburn. New York Home Journal (24 November).
         Rousseau, Lamartine, and Melville have all written their
      "Confessions," and Melville's will not be found the least
      interesting of these "partial autobiographies," nor inferior
      in "amplicity" of style, warmth of heart, and general truth-
      fulness of manner. Mardi is still read and re-read with
      interest and with doubt as to its purpose. Its author
      might have been expected to write a Tale of a Tub or
      Pantagruel, but not Redburn. The lifelike manner in which
      every event is brought to the reader is most astonishing.
      Redburn will be more popular than Melville's previous works
      but will not perhaps raise his literary reputation "from
      the pinnacle where Mardi placed it." Reprints chapter 14
      from Redburn. Reprinted in part in Branch, pp. 207-208.

139   ANON. Review of Redburn. New York Literary American, 3
      (24 November), 419.
         If not as fresh and imaginative as Melville's former
      works, Redburn is at least more interesting in its plot
      and more nervous in its style. There are no monstrosities
      or artificialities in it. The dialogues are natural;
      Melville is a sailor and writes like one. Redburn shows a
      power he has not previously displayed of drawing the darker

1849

pictures of life, with a somber reality. His reputation
will be fully sustained, even increased, by Redburn. Extract from chapter 59.

140   ANON. Review of Redburn. New York Saroni's Musical Times,
       1 (24 November), 97.
         With little plot and a "nowise novel theme," Melville
has still succeeded in making Redburn interesting. Redburn's
circumstances furnish opportunities for racy anecdote which
Melville has used with much wit and humor. He never lapses
into sentimentalism when he has something tragic to relate.
Melville is so completely at home on ship that Redburn is
as instructive as amusing. Reprinted in Branch, pp. 209-210.

141   ANON. Review of Redburn. Richmond Whig (24 November).
         Enjoys Melville's unromantic treatment of ocean life.
Redburn is written in his usual natural style. Queries:
does Melville mean it is such an extraordinary thing for
the "son of a gentleman" to go to sea as a sailor boy that
special mention has to be made of it on the title page?

142   ANON. Review of Redburn. New York Evening Mirror (27 November).
         Redburn is very well told, and not deficient in graceful
humor and vivid description, but is not a book to make a
sensation or deserve one.

143   ANON. Philadelphia Dollar Newspaper (28 November).
         Brief introduction to extract from chapter 3 of Redburn,
which some of "our sea-crazy young friends" may read with
as much profit as pleasure.

144   ANON. Review of Redburn. New York Christian Union and Reli-
       gious Memorial, 2 (December), 759-760.
         Redburn happily shows few traces of the anti-religious
temper of Typee and Omoo. It has the merits of naturalness
and simplicity and will be read with interest and pleasure.

145   ANON. Review of Redburn. New York United States Magazine and
       Democratic Review, 25 (December), 575.
         Redburn, written in Melville's own peculiar vein, has
reawakened the ardor of the public after the disappointment
with Mardi. Its pictures are drawn with a power and skill
seldom reached, and the humor is of the most contagious
nature.

146   ANON. Review of Redburn. Richmond Southern Literary Messenger,
       15 (December), 760-762.

Melville has made ample amends in Redburn for the grotesqueness and prolixity of Mardi. If it is an imaginary
narrative, it is the most lifelike and natural fiction
since Robinson Crusoe. Every incident has the air of strict
probability. The descriptions of life before the mast and
in Liverpool are well-drawn and sometimes reminiscent of
Smollett. Melville should leave Polynesia alone, as a subject he has exhausted. Summary, with extracts from chapters
14, 31, 40, and 59. Reprinted in part in Log, p. 355.

147   R[IPLEY, GEORGE]. Review of Redburn. New York Daily Tribune ·
      (1 December).
          Redburn is not entirely free from the affectations of
      Mardi; nor does it have the freshness, gaiety, and natural
      frolicsomeness of Typee. It "has something about it which
      savours more of the bookmaker by profession, and shows
      that it is not the product of any innate necessity." But
      it is a decided improvement on Mardi. Melville's pictures
      of ocean life are drawn from nature; despite occasional
      exaggeration, his descriptions have all the fidelity of a
      Dutch painting. The Liverpool scenes are depicted "with a
      minute fidelity of touch that is hardly surpassed by the
      dark and lurid coloring of Crabbe." Melville is an artist
      of unparalleled merit in his own right; he should trust
      more to the natural play of his own fine imagination, "with-
      out goading it on to a monstrous activity." Reprinted in
      Branch, pp. 210-211.

148   ANON. Review of Redburn. New York Gazette of the Union,
      Golden Rule and Odd-Fellows' Family Companion, 11
      (1 December), 347.
          Brief introduction to extract, chapter 14, an example
      of Melville's graphic drawing of Redburn's experiences.
      Typee and Omoo have placed Melville "in the front rank of
      American or indeed living authors."

149   ANON. "Books of the Week." New York Literary World, No. 148
      (1 December), p. 469.
          Notes that "Blackwood has a paper on Melville's Redburn
      [see 1849.B110], sufficiently complimentary, but the writer's
      evident pains-taking and love of his subject are somewhat
      obscured by an occasional snobbish patronizing tone of
      expression of the London cockney school."

150   ANON. Review of Redburn. Newark Daily Advertiser (3 December).
          Redburn is an interesting book for juvenile readers and
      others who are much interested in the impulses of boyhood
      or the minute incidents of a seafaring life; but the reader

1849

who expects to find another romance like Typee will be
disappointed. It has commendable simplicity of style and
some entertaining and instructive incidents, "drawn out,
however, with rather tedious minuteness."

*151   ANON. Nantucket Enquirer (11 December).
          Comment on Blackwood's review of Redburn [see 1847.B110].
       Cited in Hetherington (1961), p. 150n.

152   ANON. Review of Redburn. Boston Littell's Living Age, 23
          (29 December), 580-583.
          Reprint of 1847.B104.

1850 A BOOKS - NONE

1850 B SHORTER WRITINGS

1   CHEEVER, HENRY T. The Island World of the Pacific. New York:
        Harper & Brothers, p. 37.
        Mention: "Cape Horn weather here [off the Falkland
     islands] begins, and the ship and her company put on their
     Cape Horn suit; which, so far as some of our men are con-
     cerned, is quite as unique and nondescript as the notable
     'White Jacket.'"

2   GREENWOOD, GRACE [LIPPINCOTT, SARA JANE]. "Letter from the
        Author of 'Typee.'" Greenwood Leaves: A Collection of
        Sketches and Letters. Boston: Ticknor, Reed, and Fields,
        pp. 294-296.
        Reprint of 1847.B93.

3   [MITCHELL, DONALD GRANT]. The Lorgnette: or, Studies of the
        Town. By an Opera Goer. Second Edition. New York:
        Stringer and Townsend, pp. 71, 277, 279.
        Reprint of 1850.B30 and 1850.B82.

4   MARVEL, IK [MITCHELL, DONALD GRANT]. Reveries of a Bachelor:
        or A Book of the Heart. New York: Baker & Scribner, p. 21.
        Asks if any family purse can be better filled "than the
     exceeding plump one, you dream of, after reading such pleas-
     ant books as Munchausen, or Typee."

5   WARTER, JOHN WOOD, ed. Southey's Common-Place Book. Third
        Series. London: Longman, Brown, Green, and Longmans, p. 585.
        Editor's footnote. A reference to volcanoes in Hawaii is
     quite "corroborated in those objectionable, but very graphic
     publications, Typee and Omoo, of the authenticity of which,
     I suppose, there can be no reasonable doubt."

6   ANON. Review of Redburn. New York Holden's Dollar Magazine, 5
     (January), 55-56.
          Redburn is not a romance, nor a satire, nor a narrative
     of actual events, "but a hodge podge of all three." The
     few palpable inventions, such as the story of the London
     Hell, do not give a very exalted idea of Melville's imag-
     inative capacities. The sober descriptions are the most
     valuable and interesting parts of the work. A few rhapso-
     dies are distracting. If Melville had confined himself to
     a simple record of facts, Redburn would have been more
     profitable; but it is exceedingly interesting, even with
     all its faults. Melville's fresh and poetic style lends
     charm to the commonplace incidents. There is hardly an
     English writer Melville so little resembles as Defoe, whose
     charm is in his simplicity of style and artistic accuracy
     of description. Melville is at times ambitiously gorgeous
     in style, and, at others, coarse and abrupt in his simplic-
     ity. His chief defect is "an ambitious desire to appear
     fine and learned which causes him to drag in by the head
     and shoulders remote images that ought not to be within a
     thousand miles of the reader's thoughts." Extract from
     chapter 59. Reprinted in Branch, pp. 213-215.

7   ANON. Review of Los Gringos by Lieut. Henry A. Wise.
     Philadelphia Godey's Magazine and Lady's Book, 40 (January),
     78.
          Wise's book ought to be as popular as Typee or Mardi.

8   ANON. Review of Redburn. Philadelphia Graham's Magazine, 36
     (January), 94-95.
          Melville has Defoe's power of realizing the details of a
     scene to his own imagination and of impressing them on the
     imaginations of others; but he also has "a bit of deviltry"
     in him that is not in Defoe. Redburn is less adventurous
     in style than Mardi and more interesting, though it hardly
     has the same intellectual merit. It will be invaluable to
     a large class of youthful sailors. The style sparkles with
     wit and fancy, but the book's great merit is rapidity of
     movement. Reprinted in Branch, p. 212.

*9   ANON. Review of The Whale and his Captors by H. T. Cheever.
     New York National Anti-Slavery Standard (3 January).
          Comparison with Typee. Cited in Mailloux and Parker,
     p. 13.

10   ANON. Review of Wandering Sketches of People and Things in
     South America, Polynesia, California, and Other Places by
     Wm. Maxwell Wood. New York Literary World, No. 153
     (5 January), p. 7.

1850

Reference to "Nukuheva and the Marquesas, the classic ground of Melville."

11   ANON. "Light Touchings. International Copyright." New York
      Home Journal (12 January), p. 2.
          Cites Melville as "one of the first and most signal
      realizers of the effect of the recent English repudiation
      of copyright," following which "an American author can no
      more sell a book in England than Dickens can sell one here."
      Prints extract of a letter from Melville in London, pro-
      fessing unconcern over his lack of money [Letters, p. 97].
      Reprinted in part in Log, p. 361.

12   ANON. Review of United States' Exploring Expedition, during
      the Years 1835-42 by James D. Dana. New York Literary
      World, No. 155 (19 January), p. 55.
          Mention: the Society Islands are "the group which all
      the accounts, from the early narratives of Cook and Kotzebue,
      down to the more apocryphal pages of Omoo the wanderer,
      have familiarized to our fancies as the paradise of the
      Pacific."

13   'An Importer of Foreign Books.' Letter to the Editor. London
      Times (22 January), p. 8.
          Claims that American authors have no copyright in Eng-
      land, just as English authors have no copyright in America.
      Cites the example of Melville, "who recently made a voyage
      to this country on purpose to sell the 'right' of his un-
      published White Jacket" and "wearily hawked this book from
      Piccadilly to Whitechapel, calling upon every publisher in
      his way, and could find no one rash enough to buy his
      'protected right.'" [See 1850.B14 for reply; see also
      1850.B35.] Reprinted in 1850.B33; reprinted in part in
      Log, pp. 361-362.

14   BENTLEY, RICHARD. Letter to the Editor. London Times
      (25 January), p. 4.
          Bentley replies to 1850.B13: White-Jacket "was in the
      first instance offered to me by the author himself, and I
      have become the purchaser of what I firmly believe to be
      the copyright, for a considerable sum--quite sufficient to
      make me in earnest to defend that right, should the 'Im-
      porter,' or any of his friends, attempt to invade it."
      Reprinted in 1850.B35; reprinted in part in Log, p. 362.

15   ANON. Review of White-Jacket. London Sun (28 January).
          Admires the interesting variety of characters in White-
      Jacket and agrees with the remarks on flogging. The

"natural delineation of a master-hand" is visible in all of Melville's varied pictures.

16   ANON. Review of St. Leger; or, the Threads of Life. New York Holden's Dollar Magazine, 5 (February), 123.
Notes that the "two most popular writers among us, just now, are Melville and Headley; and much of their success is undoubtedly owing to the perfect fearlessness with which they thrust themselves bodily before their countrymen." Reprinted in 1850.B27.

17   ANON. Review of Redburn. New York Merchants' Magazine and Commercial Review, 22 (February), 252.
Reviewer has scarcely found time to read a dozen pages but predicts success for Redburn. The freshness, vigor, and grotesqueness of Melville's style must fascinate all.

18   ANON. Review of Redburn. Philadelphia Godey's Magazine and Lady's Book, 40 (February), 149.
"A sensible book, and one that will do more for the author's reputation than ten thousand such as 'Mardi.' Without becoming Munchausenish, it tells some wonderful stories, and the interest is admirably sustained to the last page." [Complete review.]

19   ANON. Review of Redburn. Philadelphia Peterson's Magazine, 17 (February), 115.
Considers Redburn far more interesting than Mardi and equal to Typee and Omoo, though there is a little affectation of simplicity in the style, a little affectation of rusticity in the author.

20   ANON. Review of Redburn. Philadelphia Sartain's Union Magazine, 6 (February), 174.
There is a wild, fascinating spirit of adventure about Melville, not only in what he relates, but in his manner of relating it. He imitates nobody. Reprinted in part in Log, p. 367.

21   ANON. Review of White-Jacket. London Athenaeum, No. 1162 (2 February), pp. 123-125.
Melville is unique among sea writers, such as Hall, Cooper, Marryat, and their imitators, in his manner of giving "the poetry of the Ship"; his sea creatures, calms, and storms belong to the dreamy tone of "The Ancient Mariner." Melville has more vivacity, fancy, color, and energy than 99 out of 100 sea writers. Extracts from chapters 1, 9, 26, 56, and 57. Reprinted in part in Log, p. 365, and Branch, pp. 217-218.

1850

22   ANON. Review of <u>White-Jacket</u>. London <u>John Bull</u> (2 February),
      pp. 74-75.
         Melville is a vastly improved writer, no longer the
      wanton boy indulging in refined licentiousness of descrip-
      tion and the smart daredevil style of remark; the rattling
      youngster has grown into the thoughtful man without any
      abatement of his sparkling wit. In the minutely graphic
      <u>White-Jacket</u>, a caustic critique of the American navy
      assumes the form, and possesses all the attraction, of a
      first-rate sea novel, while embodying Melville's philosophy
      of life. The characters are admirable life pictures, ex-
      hibiting each man in the complete individuality of his per-
      son and office. Regrettably, Melville's religious views
      are little calculated to edify his readers; in <u>White-Jacket</u>
      there is far too great a freedom in touching upon sacred
      subjects and a philosophy which ill accords with the truth
      of revelation. Extracts from chapters 12, 34, 52, 38, 65,
      and "The End." Reprinted in Branch, pp. 220-221.

23   ANON. Review of <u>White-Jacket</u>. London <u>Spectator</u> (Supplement),
      23 (2 February), 3-4.
         In form it is the narrative of a voyage, but "as general
      rather than particular incidents, characters, and nautical
      manners, are professed to be delineated," <u>White-Jacket</u> has
      "some of the properties of fiction." There is nothing like
      a continuous story; and the incidents are not always as
      striking as they might have been made, nor always as fresh.
      But the book conveys a good idea of the economy and charac-
      ter of the U.S. navy. Melville's tone is more sober and
      his views are more sensible than the tone and views of
      platform sophists. There is not always a ready answer to
      his religious, legal, or constitutional logic. But in his
      quiet ridicule of many ceremonies and customs of the service
      he seems to forget the necessity of forming habits of
      obedience, readiness, activity, and vigilance. Extracts
      from chapters 38 and 14. Reprinted in Branch, pp. 222-224.

24   ANON. Review of <u>White-Jacket</u>. London <u>Atlas</u> (9 February).
         Hall, Marryatt, Chamier, Cooper, and others have written
      of sea life from the quarter-deck; Melville has the same
      subject, "but with the forecastle for his point of sight."
      We are admitted behind the scenes and see the seamy side of
      the canvas. The whole narrative in <u>White-Jacket</u> is marked
      by all the sobriety of truth, though enlivened by Melville's
      sparkling and racy style. The prevailing tone of the book
      is one of discontent. Melville "seems conscious of no in-
      fluence in the thought of duties gallantly and silently
      performed." Extracts from chapters 30, 31, and 25. Re-
      printed in part in Branch, pp. 224-226.

25   ANON. Review of <u>White-Jacket</u>. London <u>Literary Gazette</u>,
        No. 1725 (9 February), pp. 102-105.
            <u>White-Jacket</u> is a very clever story, a stirring compound,
        interesting, even for English readers, to the very end.
        Extracts from chapters 3, 11, 24, 32, and 33.

26   ANON. "Facts and Opinions." New York <u>Literary World</u>, No. 158
        (9 February), p. 134.
            Notes Melville's return from Europe and the forthcoming
        publication of <u>White-Jacket</u>; anticipates an interesting
        story and "some light" on "the important Naval Reform ques-
        tions of the day."

27   ANON. "Holden's Dollar Magazine." New York <u>Literary World</u>,
        No. 158 (9 February), p. 130.
            Reprint of 1850.B16.

28   ANON. Review of <u>White-Jacket</u> and <u>The Petrel</u>. London <u>Daily
        News</u> (11 February).
            <u>The Petrel</u> is "a sea-life viewed through the telescope
        of a superior officer," paternal, romantic, gentlemanly,
        and sentimental; whereas <u>White-Jacket</u> is "a sailor's produc-
        tion, full of his raciness, his oddities, his sufferings,
        his endurance."

29   ANON. Review of <u>White-Jacket</u>. London <u>Morning Post</u>
        (12 February).
            "Fresh, bold, original, acquainted with the more striking
        passages of history, and animated with the spirit of the
        most brilliant poets," Melville brings out the stories of
        his reading and imagination in sudden bursts, without wait-
        ing to consider whether the allusion he makes is far-fetched
        or the sentiment he breathes misplaced. In <u>White-Jacket</u> the
        "mind of young America, keen, sensitive, but unmatured, lies
        before us." Melville lacks taste, delicacy, and good judg-
        ment, as when he introduces the subject of Christ's nature
        into a sea novel and disposes of it in an unthinking sum-
        mary way. But <u>White-Jacket</u> is a work of distinguished
        merit, the genuine outpouring of a vigorous mind. It con-
        sists of the most familiar incidents of real life, given in
        new, striking, and forcible colors. Melville's language is
        poetical and noble; his thoughts are in no way inferior to
        his graceful and unaffected power of expressing them. Ex-
        tracts from chapter 50 and "The End."

30   [MITCHELL, DONALD GRANT]. "Ways of Getting into Society."
        New York <u>Lorgnette</u> (14 February).

1850

"Taste, upon the whole, appears to be rather a dangerous
element in the character of an aspirant.... On some topics,
indeed, a little latitude is allowable, such as Forti's
singing, or Melville's last book, or Mrs. Butler's horse-
back riding...." Reprinted in 1850.B3.

*31   ANON. Nantucket Enquirer (15 February).
        Reprint of 1850.B26. Cited in Hetherington (1961),
        p. 165.

 32   ANON. Review of White-Jacket. London Britannia (23 February).
        The sketches in White-Jacket are worked up with skill
        and power, but the lack of continuity of interest is pain-
        fully felt; the book exhibits something of the monotony of
        the long voyage. The faces of the crew weary us; we see
        too much of them and long for land and change of company.
        The work "labours under the defect of want of motive"; the
        elaborate descriptions lead to no end. Melville and the
        great majority of his countrymen who aspire to literary
        eminence aim to astonish and horrify rather than to elevate
        and please; they revel in exaggeration of all kinds.
        Melville has strength but is not skillful in the use of
        it; his genius requires the direction of taste. But White-
        Jacket deserves some attention for its incidental notices
        of the state and discipline of the American navy. One won-
        ders how the abuses and tyranny could have arisen under the
        jealous eye of republican rule. Extracts from chapters 88,
        34, and 53. Reprinted in part in Branch, pp. 218-219
        [dated 2 February].

 33   ANON. "International Copyright." New York Literary World,
        No. 160 (23 February), p. 179.
        Reprints 1850.B13.

 34   ANON. Review of White-Jacket. London Bentley's Miscellany,
        27 (March), 309-310.
        The great charm of the marine stories of such writers as
        Cooper, Marryat, and Hall is literal truthfulness. But
        Melville "bathes the scene in the hues of a fanciful and
        reflective spirit, which gives it the interest of a creation
        of genius. He is everywhere original, suggestive, and indi-
        vidual." White-Jacket is remarkable for its concentration
        of rare qualities--brilliancy and profundity, shrewdness,
        vivacity, and energy. In such a book there must be great
        faults--the faults of a superabundant fancy and a prodigal
        genius. White-Jacket takes first place among Melville's
        works.

35   ANON. "Mr. Melville and Copyright in England." New York
      Literary World, No. 161 (2 March), p. 205.
          Reprints Richard Bentley's letter to the London Times
      [1850.B14] and prints a letter from "K." of New York City
      in reply to 1850.B33. "K." claims that Melville "had not
      the slightest difficulty in making an arrangement for the
      publication of White-Jacket with Mr. Bentley, the publisher
      of Mr. Melville's previous work, and what is more, such
      arrangement was concluded promptly, without impediment or
      finesse. Mr. Melville is not the man to 'hawk' his wares
      in any market, and Mr. Bentley not the publisher to allow
      so capital a book to escape him."

36   ANON. Review of White-Jacket. London Globe and Traveller
      (4 March).
          The keenness of Melville's powers of observation enable
      him, within so narrow a sphere and without any extraordinary
      incident, to maintain the interest of White-Jacket through-
      out. But "the picture is provokingly marred, at times, by
      conceits such as the reader would look for only if he knew
      the narrative was purely fanciful." In some of the best
      passages Melville seems to have been straining for an un-
      necessary air of smartness. These blemishes are the result
      of the need to produce "much and fast." Extracts from chap-
      ters 38, 25, 7, 39, and 34.

*37   ANON. Review of White-Jacket. London Morning Herald (4 March).
      Cited in Hetherington (1961), p. 163.

*38   HAWKINS, H. R., JR. Letter. Lansingburgh Gazette (14 March).
          Melville's account of the missionaries in Typee and Omoo
      is truthful. Cited in Log, p. 368.

39   ANON. "Mr. Melville's White Jacket." New York Literary World,
      No. 163 (16 March), pp. 271-272.
          The union of culture and experience, thought and observa-
      tion, distinguishes Melville's narratives from other works
      of the same class. The sailor as a man, seen with a genial
      philosophy and seen from the forecastle, has been reserved
      for him; the effect is startling and novel. In White-Jacket
      there is no sentimentality, no effort to elevate the "people"
      or degrade the commodores; all the characters are interest-
      ing "as genuine Shakespearean, that is human personages."
      The book is thoroughly American and democratic. A quaint,
      satirical, yet genial humor is Melville's grand destructive
      weapon. Extracts from chapters 8, 11, 61, 68, 4, and 50.
      Reprinted in part in Recognition, pp. 23-27, and Branch,
      pp. 226-229.

1850

*40   ANON. Review of <u>White-Jacket</u>. Troy <u>Daily Budget</u> (21 March).
        Cited in Hetherington (1961), p. 166.

41   ANON. Notice of <u>White-Jacket</u>. Boston <u>Daily Evening Transcript</u>
        (23 March).
        The author of <u>Typee</u> is himself again in this volume.

42   ANON. "Mr. Melville's White Jacket." New York <u>Literary World</u>,
        No. 164 (23 March), pp. 297-299.
        Devoted to the hardships and the abuses of power in the
        navy, with extracts from chapters 70, 33, and "The End."
        In Melville's narrative you find "no shirking of duty or
        unmanly mawkish solicitudes" White Jacket is not a blubber-
        ing sentimentalist, but he is a man of commonsense and
        common feeling.

43   ANON. Review of <u>White-Jacket</u>. Boston <u>Daily Evening Transcript</u>
        (25 March).
        Praises Melville for returning to the best vein of <u>Typee</u>
        and <u>Omoo</u> and for exposing the flogging and grogging system
        in the navy. As long as Melville sticks to the ship, there
        is truth enough in his fictions to give them vitality. Ex-
        tract from chapter 4.

44   ANON. Review of <u>White-Jacket</u>. New York <u>Sun</u> (26 March).
        If anything, <u>White-Jacket</u> is more interesting than any
        of Melville's other works.

45   ANON. Review of <u>White-Jacket</u>. Boston <u>Daily Evening Traveller</u>
        (27 March), p. 1.
        The sketches of <u>White-Jacket</u> are spirited, full of inter-
        est and instruction. The man-of-war seen by the common
        sailor is entirely different from that seen from the quarter-
        deck, "whence most of our glimpses of sea life have been
        obtained."

46   ANON. Review of <u>White-Jacket</u>. New York <u>Evangelist</u> (28 March).
        If it were not a little too ambitious, <u>White-Jacket</u>
        would be pronounced one of the most able and beautiful
        pictures of sea life ever drawn; it displays the highest
        order of descriptive talent, keen wit, shrewd good sense,
        and (its chief merit) sympathy for the poor sailor, and
        opens the secrets of the man-of-war.

47   ANON. New York <u>Evening Post</u> (28 March).
        Mention of favorable English reception of <u>White-Jacket</u>.

48   ANON. Review of White-Jacket. Philadelphia Public Ledger and
      Daily Transcript (28 March).
        The man-of-war is depicted graphically and amusingly.

49   ANON. Review of White-Jacket. New York Commercial Advertiser
      (29 March).
        Suspects that a full knowledge of White-Jacket's graphic
      power can only be obtained by reading it consecutively.

*50   ANON. Review of White-Jacket. New York Commercial Advertiser
      (29 March).
        Partial reprint of 1850.B39. Cited in Hetherington
      (1961), p. 166.

51   ANON. Review of White-Jacket. New York Evening Mirror
      (29 March).
        Considers sea stories superior to novels of fashionable
      life since they teach "lessons of humanity." White-Jacket,
      however, is not a sea novel but a picture of actual man-of-
      war life, veritable, honest, and drawn with a steady hand,
      for a serious and generous purpose. It valuably does for
      the navy what Dana's Two Years Before the Mast did for the
      merchant service.

*52   ANON. Review of White-Jacket. Buffalo Courier (30 March).
        Cited in Hetherington (1961), p. 169.

53   ANON. Review of White-Jacket. New York Albion, NS 9
      (30 March), 153.
        Admires the touches of humor, pathos, wit, and practical
      philosophy seasoning the lighter parts of White-Jacket; the
      nautical sketches are unsurpassed. In its serious parts,
      White-Jacket must draw the attention of serious men. Its
      revelations of the inner life of a frigate have more truth
      than poetry to recommend them; Melville takes away much of
      the romance of the sea. In order to illustrate the oppres-
      sive rigor of naval laws, he has not peopled his quarter-
      deck with demons and his forecastle with angels.
      White-Jacket is a work of rare merit. Extracts from chap-
      ters 72, 34, 7, 8, 11, 12, 16, 20, 21, 50, 63, and 76.
      Reprinted in part in Log, pp. 370-71, and Recognition,
      pp. 27-30.

54   ANON. Review of White-Jacket. New York's Saroni's Musical
      Times, 1 (30 March), 317-318.
        Accounts of man-of-war's men have previously been written
      in the melodramatic style, with heroic sailors, epic quarter-
      deck characters, romantic incidents, and stirring sea

1850

scenes. Melville remorselessly and truthfully tears the
veil that has been cast over the man-of-war world, though
not in a cynical spirit. No thread of fiction binds his
recollections of the sea; the identity of White Jacket himself furnishes the sole unity of interest. White Jacket
speaks eloquently "on the popular side" on the subject of
flogging; carried away by his very natural sympathy, he has
substituted rhetoric for logic and viewed the question from
one side only. The reviewer has also "done long and griev-
ous penance in a man-of-war." Extracts from chapters 7,
20, and 21. Reprinted in part in Branch, pp. 229-231.

55 ANON. Review of White-Jacket. New York Spirit of the Times,
     20 (30 March), 72.
        White-Jacket is one of Melville's best works. Reprinted
     in Flanagan, p. 60.

*56 ANON. Review of White-Jacket. Philadelphia American Courier
      (30 March).
         Cited in Hetherington (1961), p. 163.

57 ANON. Review of White-Jacket. Springfield (Mass.) Republican
     (30 March), p. 1.
        Unlike the broad and coarse narratives of Marryat and the
     pretending and high-wrought romances of Cooper, Melville's
     tales bring out the beauties of humble natures and deal in
     pure and simple pictures. In White-Jacket Melville has
     devoted himself to the important office of illustrating the
     baneful effect of the "cat" and the spirit ration.

58 ANON. Review of Redburn. Charleston (S.C.) Southern Quarterly
     Review, NS 1 (April), 259-260.
        Rather cold and prosaic, Redburn is in direct contrast
     with the wild, warm, and richly fanciful Mardi, but is much
     more within the range of popular sympathies. It is fash-
     ioned somewhat after the school of Defoe and Marryat, em-
     ploying their simplicity and numerous details. But Redburn
     as a character is not consistent and all the "foreign graf-
     fing" is not proper to such a story, though Melville's im-
     agination naturally becomes restive in the monotonous details
     of a career such as Redburn's. Wild, improbable, and fan-
     tastic as it was, Mardi showed more proof of real powers in
     reserve. Reprinted in Branch, pp. 215-216.

59 ANON. Notice of White-Jacket. New York American Whig Review,
     11 [NS 5] (April), 442.
        The chapters the reviewer has read have decidedly whetted
     his appetite for more.

60   ANON. Review of White-Jacket. New York United States Magazine
     and Democratic Review, 26 (April), 384.
          The manners and customs of the man-of-war are most agree-
     ably sketched, but White-Jacket is manufactured for the Eng-
     lish market: all the seamen heroes are Britons and all the
     English admirals are oracles. London pays Melville better
     for his copyright than New York. Reprinted in Branch,
     p. 231.

61   ANON. Review of White-Jacket. Richmond Southern Literary
     Messenger, 16 (April), 250-252.
          Practical forecastle experience, uniting with a love of
     elegant learning and an educated taste, distinguishes
     Melville from all other writers of his class. Redburn and
     White-Jacket differ from his previous works in being written
     with a definite purpose: Redburn to reform the discipline
     of the merchant service; White-Jacket to draw attention to
     flogging in the navy. White-Jacket abounds with Melville's
     peculiar beauties and is full of fine thoughts nobly ex-
     pressed. But the reviewer cannot admire the levity
     Melville exhibits in introducing sacred things to his narra-
     tive. Extracts from chapter 50 and "The End."

62   ANON. "Marine Intelligence." Honolulu Friend (1 April), p. 28.
          Reports that natives of the Marquesas Islands recently
     robbed whaleship deserters of their boat and clothing,
     leaving them destitute on the beach; adds that the
     Marquesans "have doubtless, laid aside the mildness and
     innocence of their natures" since Melville visited the
     Typees.

63   ANON. "Twilight Musings." Honolulu Friend (1 April), p. 29.
          Sarcastic reference to Melville in item on the need for
     Protestant missionaries to the Marquesas Islands. Recom-
     mends that "the dashing Melville" take a trip with his
     young bride to scenes of earlier days; perhaps "the gentle
     Fayaway would stand upon the beach to extend a cordial
     welcome."

64   ANON. Review of White-Jacket. Worcester (Mass.) Palladium
     (3 April), p. 3.
          Melville gives his descriptions of sea life all the
     force of reality. Extract from chapter 1.

65   ANON. Review of White-Jacket. Albany Daily State Register
     (4 April).
          Readers' knowledge of the strange economy of a man-of-war
     has hitherto been derived from those who wrote from the

cabin; White-Jacket is a voice from before the mast, speaking the feelings of those who seldom find a means of utterance.

66 ANON. Review of White-Jacket. New Bedford Mercury (4 April), p. 2.

White-Jacket, a most entertaining volume, is more substantial than any of Melville's other works, with "a matter-of-fact minuteness of detail that makes the narrative as everyday-ish as the life of a hotel." White-Jacket "is to the navy what Dana's book is to the merchant service." But Melville has an unaccountable penchant for fine writing and relapses continually into "lavender phrases and fantastic comparisons"; he is also bent on airing his literature. Jack Chase's address to the captain and commodore at Rio is hardly credible in any human being with a rational purpose in his brain.

67 ANON. Review of White-Jacket. New York Daily Tribune (5 April), p. 1.

Melville works up his ample materials into a narrative of great power and interest. He always tells a story well and plenty of stories are related in White-Jacket. He has performed an excellent service in revealing the secrets of his prison house and calling public attention to the indescribable abominations of naval life. His remarks on naval discipline coincide with the prevailing tendences of the public mind. White-Jacket would have been a more valuable book if confined to what Melville had heard and seen: the moral and metaphysical reflections he sets forth in bad Carlylese are only incumbrances to the narrative and often become intolerable. Reprinted in 1850.B91; reprinted in part in Branch, p. 232.

68 ANON. Review of White-Jacket. New York Evening Post [Supplement] (6 April), p. 1.

The book is "full of piquant and clever sketches." Extracts from chapters 8, 11, 68, 61, 38, and 26.

69 ANON. "Literary Items." New York Home Journal (6 April), p. 2.

"The first edition of Melville's new work, the 'White Jacket,' was sold as soon as published." [Complete item.]

70 ANON. Review of White-Jacket. New York Literary American, 4 (6 April), 277.

Melville's narrative is perfectly easy and natural, his descriptions are graphic, his plots and episodes enchanting. White-Jacket is more matter-of-fact than Typee or Omoo and less polished but its free and easy style will make it popular.

71   ANON. "Mr. Colton's Cruise." New York Literary World, No. 166
      (6 April), p. 347.
           Review of Rev. Walter Colton's Deck and Port. Two brief
      mentions of Melville's views on chaplains and flogging and
      grogging in White-Jacket.

72   ANON. Review of White-Jacket. New York Spirit of the Times,
      20 (6 April), 79.
           White-Jacket "is no French soup made from a potato and
      an onion, a mere dilution ingeniously flavored, but one
      which contains solid nutritive substance, while the cookery
      adds a zest worthy of any Careme." While the ingenious
      narrative and abundant incident will attract general readers,
      curiosity will excite the navy corps, and the important and
      clearly stated facts will appeal to legislators. Melville
      excels particularly in life-like portraiture, not mere
      caricatures. Extract from chapter 26. Reprinted in part
      in Flanagan, p. 61.

73   ANON. Review of White-Jacket. Boston Post (10 April).
           In White-Jacket Melville goes in for "abstractions and
      perfections," without recognizing the practical considera-
      tions and compromises always necessary to "the administra-
      tion of terrestrial affairs." In his extreme and bitter
      discussion of naval abuses, he is "liable to prejudice the
      intelligent reader against even the good" in him and has
      made himself and his good cause ridiculous by going so far
      into theoreticals. White-Jacket is inferior to anything
      Melville has previously written, with the exception of
      Mardi; though it has interesting and instructive passages,
      its best passages are not equal to the best passages of
      Typee or Redburn. Its few real characters are also inferior.
      The constant attempt to be smart, witty, and entertaining
      on no capital becomes very tedious before the end of the
      book. Reprinted in part in Branch, pp. 233-235.

74   ANON. Review of White-Jacket. New York Christian Intelligencer
      (11 April).
           White-Jacket is written in a very flowing and easy style
      and is well calculated by its incidents and narration to
      keep the reader's attention to the end.

75   ANON. Review of White-Jacket. New York Independent (11 April).
           Though his moralizing is awkward, Melville excels in
      description and storytelling. White-Jacket will enlighten

1850

thousands as to the abominations of grog and the "cat" and the necessity of abolishing both. On the subject of flogging, W. G. Haynes has published a fly sheet, "which gives a fearful array of statistics." Reprinted in Monteiro (Fourth Quarter 1974), p. 435.

76   ANON. Review of White-Jacket. New York Home Journal (13 April).
         Values White-Jacket for its "series of highly finished pictures," its vigorous and graphic descriptions, its fresh and abundant humor, and its intense relish for character; the great charm of Melville's books is their vividity and truthfulness. Melville is one of the most original of writers, a mixture of Chaucer, Crabbe, Defoe, Charles Lamb, and Dickens without being a copy of any one of them; in spite of his evident familiarity with books, his writings owe little or nothing to others. The passion to see for himself and to describe is so great that it "overpowers all inclination to repeat the impressions produced by other men's thoughts." His perceptions are "of that positive, vigorous and intense kind which amount to passion." Melville has clearness of eye and tongue, an honest and manly taste, and a love of humanity too broad and catholic to be imposed upon by conventionalism or pretension. His "elaboration of trifles, his redundancy and often incongruity of metaphor, his quaintness of expression" are parts of his suggestiveness, "the fulness, the fun and humor of his soul." A triumph of art in White-Jacket, the uncertainty whether all its incidents are actual occurrences, may weaken Melville's testimony as a reformer of naval abuses. Reviewer commends White-Jacket to legislators and advocates specific naval reforms. Extracts from chapters 8, 86, 33, and 87.

77   ANON. Review of Ned Allen; or, the Past Age, by David Hannay. New York Literary World, No. 167 (13 April), p. 373.
         Melville is listed among authors who "are delighting everybody around at the literary feast of the month."

78   ANON. Review of White-Jacket. Baltimore American and Commercial Daily Advertiser (17 April), p. 1.
         Brilliant and dashingly spirited descriptions abound in White-Jacket, which is written in Melville's best style and will add to his reputation.

79   ANON. Review of White-Jacket. Boston Puritan Recorder (18 April).
         White-Jacket seems to be rather less exceptionable than Melville's other lively, unprincipled books, some of which

are "of an irreligious character, and even of demoralizing
tendency." There are "no jack-a-nape flings at missionaries in this book."

80 ANON. Review of Deck and Port by Rev. Walter Colton. Albany
    Semi-Weekly State Register (19 April).
        Reviewer took up Colton's book with more interest from
    having just read White-Jacket; it gives "a much brighter
    view of naval life than that furnished from the fore
    castle."

81 ANON. "Literary Notices." New York Home Journal (20 April),
    p. 3.
        Item on the high standard of Harper and Brothers publica-
    tions. Notes that White-Jacket is "enjoying universal favor"
    and in both the United States and England "seems, by common
    consent, to have taken its place among standard works" in
    its department of literature. Reprinted in part in Log,
    p. 372.

82 [MITCHELL, DONALD GRANT]. "Authors and Authorlings." New York
    Lorgnette (24 April).
        Article on literary diseases. The Typee disorder was a
    novel one, which attacked with peculiar virulence adventur-
    ous schoolboys and romantic young ladies; after publication
    of Mardi the disorder assumed a threatening malignancy;
    latterly Peregrine Pickle and Robinson Crusoe are safe cures
    for Redburn and White-Jacket. A kind of African fever after
    publication of Kaloolah was not unlike the Typee "affection."
    Reprinted in 1850.B3.

83 ANON. Review of White-Jacket. Washington National Era
    (25 April).
        White-Jacket offers reality, not romance. There is
    plenty of incident, but it is made subservient to the very
    laudable purpose of exhibiting the condition of the navy,
    its discipline, treatment of sailors, and abuses. The book
    should be given to every member of Congress. Reprinted in
    1850.B102 and McElderry.

84 ANON. "Publishers' Circular." New York Literary World,
    No. 169 (27 April), p. 427.
        Note that Murray's American publications "have been
    further invaded by the cheap republication" of Typee and
    Omoo "at one shilling each."

85 ANON. Review of White-Jacket. Boston Christian Examiner and
    Religious Miscellany, 48 [4th Series 13] (May), 512.

1850

Though not the most brilliant, White-Jacket is by far the most instructive and valuable of Melville's writings and to a landsman seems fair and impartial in its moralizings.

86   ANON. Review of White-Jacket. New York Holden's Dollar Magazine, 5 (May), 314-315.
      The descriptions in White-Jacket "are the finest, most accurate and entertaining of any narrative of sea life that has ever been published; neither Cooper's nor Marryat's will compare with them for fidelity and spirit." The book is an eloquent, humorous, and faithful picture of man-of-war life and a thorough exposure of the enormities, defects, and evil tendencies of the whole naval system. Much good must result from it.

87   ANON. Review of White-Jacket. New York Knickerbocker, 35 (May), 448.
      After the failure of Mardi, Redburn was reassuring and in White-Jacket Melville is on the right ground again at last, exciting continuous interest. Without the aid of much imagination, but with a "daguerreotype-like naturalness of description," he has written a book which is continually reminiscent of Dana's Two Years Before the Mast "in its evident truthfulness and accuracy of personal and individual delineation." A "vein of sly humor percolates through the book" and "a sort of unctuous toying with verbal double-meanings" is occasionally found. White-Jacket is especially valuable for its descriptions of almost indiscriminate flogging, a matter of present public interest. Reprinted in Recognition, pp. 30-31, and Branch, pp. 235-236.

88   ANON. Review of White-Jacket. Philadelphia Peterson's Magazine, 17 (May), 231.
      Since the publication of Typee, Melville has published nothing equal to White-Jacket, which excels in animated pictures of sea life.

89   ANON. Review of White-Jacket. Syracuse Literary Union, 2 (May), 293-296.
      Melville is one of the very few novelists who writes with a design of correcting certain specific abuses or of inculcating an important moral. Navy regulations are little better known to the American public than the genealogy of the Feejean chiefs or the judicial system of Japan. Extracts from chapters 1 and 9. Reprinted in Pollin (October 1975), p. 8.

90   ANON. Review of White-Jacket. Philadelphia Pennsylvanian
      (3 May).
      White-Jacket is uncommonly well written, in a fresh and
      sparkling style, but is calculated to dishonor the United
      States. It was printed in England and seems to have been
      written for the British market. There is a studious injus-
      tice to the American navy that is infamous; many of
      Melville's allegations seem spitefully exaggerated or wholly
      untrue. The book is so defaced with calumny as to affect
      all its influence for good. Reprinted in Heflin, pp. 8-9
      [dated 2 May].

91   ANON. Review of White-Jacket. Boston Littell's Living Age,
      25 (4 May), 230-232.
      Reprint of 1850.B67.

92   ANON. "The Mexican War." New York Literary World, No. 172
      (18 May), p. 491.
      After the publication of a forthcoming volume on the
      Mexican war, future writers on the same subject will need
      "the vein of a Melville or Ik Marvel" to compete with it.

93   ANON. "Book Notices." New Orleans De Bow's Commercial Review
      of the South and West, 8 (June), 590.
      Quotes favorable judgments in 1850.B29 approvingly.

94   ANON. Review of White-Jacket. Philadelphia Godey's Magazine
      and Lady's Book, 40 (June), 418.
      The exceedingly pleasant White-Jacket is likely to become
      the most popular of Melville's works.

95   ANON. "Book Notices." Philadelphia Sartain's Union Magazine,
      6 (June), 434.
      Reviewer regrets he has not been able to read "this in-
      viting volume" and suspects that readers of White-Jacket are
      "destined to a rare entertainment." Summarizes the book's
      preliminary "Note."

96   ANON. Review of White-Jacket. Andover (Maine) Biblical
      Repository and Classical Review, Third Series 6 (July), 561.
      White-Jacket is brimful of Melville's characteristic
      faults: "a swaggering air, extravagant speech, and out-
      rageous sentiment, profane expressions, amounting at times
      almost to blasphemy, and a reckless, care-for-nothing manner
      of life." But as a sketch of the real world of a naval ship
      it is intensely exciting, has wonderful power, and is painted
      with consummate skill and intense energy of expression. Its
      keen wit, pointed irony, sarcastic humor, biting invective,

1850

and fearless exposure of wrong "do prodigious execution."
As an exposé, it is really withering and often heartrending.
White-Jacket is commended to all friends of seamen and the
naval authorities. Reprinted in part in Log, p. 381.

97   ANON. Review of White-Jacket. Charleston (S.C.) Southern
      Quarterly Review, NS 1 (July), 514-520.
         White-Jacket is a history and an argument, not a story.
      Melville aims at nothing fanciful and seeks none of the
      successes of the artist or romancer. His role is that of
      the reformer, and there is no reason to suspect him of
      coloring too highly his complaints of the evils in the navy;
      his discussion of abuses deserves the equal consideration of
      government and people. The interest of the book is derived
      from the regular details of life on the ship, which is neces-
      sarily a prison. The picturesque is introduced through oc-
      casional events that disturb the monotony of a ship's
      progress. The narrative is seldom sparkling or brilliant;
      but Melville shows himself everywhere a shrewd, sensible,
      well-informed, thoughtful, and practical man. Extracts from
      chapters 7, 16, 21, 22, 27, and 34.

98   ANON. "Red-Jacket." New York Holden's Dollar Magazine, 6
      (July), 431.
         Spoof review. Reprinted in Pollin (April 1975), p. 61.

99   ANON. Review of White-Jacket. New York Methodist Quarterly
      Review, 32 [Fourth Series 2] (July), 478-479.
         White-Jacket is not a mere novel; it is in fact no story
      at all but a most graphic picture of the real life of a man-
      of-war with what may be called a series of essays on the
      evils of the American Naval Service. It is for the American
      people to decide whether barbarities of this Algerine kind
      shall be continued in their name. Extract from chapter 87.

100   ANON. Review of The Vale of Cedars; or the Martyrs by Grace
      Aguilar. New York Literary World, No. 179 (6 July), p. 8.
         Imagines that numerous early readers thought Nathaniel
      Hawthorne and Herman Melville were noms de plume, "the
      harmony between the name and the spirit of the printed page,
      seeming too great to be the result of accident."

*101 ANON. "Personal" New York Morning Express (20 July).
         Report that Melville has gone on a cruise to Europe once
      more and that another of his amusing and peculiar books may
      be anticipated as a result. Cited in Log, p. 380.

102   ANON. Review of <u>White-Jacket</u>. Honolulu <u>Friend</u>, 8 (1 August), 59.
         Reprints 1850.B83. Adds paragraph stating that Melville was not altogether unqualified to speak of the man-of-war world, having taken French leave of several whalers in the Pacific and shipped on the <u>United States</u>.

103   [MATHEWS, CORNELIUS]. "Several Days in Berkshire. 'Introductory.'" New York <u>Literary World</u>, No. 186 (24 August), p. 145.
         First part of an account of a visit to Broad-Hall and surrounding countryside. [Melville a member of the party.] Continued in 1850.B104.

104   [MATHEWS, CORNELIUS]. "Several Days in Berkshire. Part II. The Mountain Festival." New York <u>Literary World</u>, No. 187 (31 August), p. 166.
         Continued from 1850.B103. Account of excursion to Monument Mountain; Melville and Hawthorne members of the party. Continued in 1850.B107.

*105   du MONDES, JACQUES. [BUTLER, WILLIAM ALLEN]. Washington <u>Weekly National Intelligencer</u> (31 August).
         Report that Melville is summering in an old mansion near Pittsfield, instead of being in England, "as the newspaper paragraphs have announced." Cited in <u>Log</u>, p. 390.

106   R., W. S. W. "Education in the Navy." Richmond <u>Southern Literary Messenger</u>, 16 (September), 524-526.
         Article reprints all but the last two paragraphs of chapter 27 in <u>White-Jacket</u>. As a whole, <u>White-Jacket</u> is a romantic caricature but has "strong pretensions to consideration." Statesmen and politicians are responsible for the excessive numbers of naval officers, and not the officers themselves.

107   [MATHEWS, CORNELIUS]. "Several Days in Berkshire. Part III. The Grand Fancy Dress-Ball." New York <u>Literary World</u>, No. 188 (7 September), pp. 185-186.
         Continued from 1850.B104.

108   ANON. "American Copyright in England." New York <u>Literary World</u>, No. 189 (14 September), pp. 213-214.
         Report that publisher Murray "has made applications in the Vice-Chancellor's Court to enjoin Bohn and Routledge, who have issued cheap editions of the works, from the publication of the books of Washington Irving and Herman Melville.... The defence, it is understood, will rest on

1850

the ground of the authors being aliens, and according to a recent decision unprotected by the English law."

*109   [BUTLER, WILLIAM ALLEN]. "Our Literary Lions." Philadelphia Pennsylvanian (30 September), p. 1.
         Reprint of 1850.B105. Cited in Heflin, p. 9.

110   ANON. "Mr. Melville and South-Sea Missions." London Eclectic Review, NS 28 (October), 425-436.
         Attempts to show that, in his statements about the Protestant mission in Tahiti, Melville is "guilty of deliberate and elaborate misrepresentation" and that he is "a prejudiced, incompetent, and truthless witness." Reprinted in 1850.B116 and 1850.B118; reprinted in part in Anderson (March 1939), pp. 25-26.

111   ANON. "Facts and Opinions." New York Literary World, No. 193 (12 October), p. 296.
         Item on American copyright in England (reprinted from London Athenaeum); quotes Richard Bentley, who claims to have given Prescott, Cooper, and Melville "between £15,000 and £16,000."

112   ANON. Pittsfield (Mass.) Sun (17 October).
         Report that the Morewoods have bought "the Melvill Farm" and that Melville has bought a farm from Dr. J. M. Brewster.

113   ANON. "English Literary Intelligence." New York Literary World, No. 195 (26 October), p. 338.
         Notes publication of 1850.B110, without comment.

114   ANON. New York International Miscellany of Literature, Art, and Science, 1 (1 November), 472.
         Hopes Melville has not abandoned literature with his purchase of a farm. He is at fault in his more recent works in coming too much before the reader in his own person.

115   ANON. New York International Miscellany of Literature, Art, and Science, 1 (1 November), 478.
         Notes the severity of the review of Omoo in 1850.B110 and thinks that Melville has been very unfortunate in his hostility to the missions. Remembers that earlier a writer in the New York Tribune "by very ample and satisfactory evidence proved him to be altogether wrong in facts and opinions."

116   ANON. "Mr. Melville and South-Sea Missions." Boston Littell's Living Age, 27 (16 November), 325-330.
         Reprint of 1850.B110.

1851

117   ANON. "Facts and Opinions." New York <u>Literary World</u>, No. 198
       (16 November), pp. 393-394.
           Reply to commentary on <u>Omoo</u> in 1850.B110. With the anti-
       popery mania in his head, <u>the Eclectic's</u> reviewer evidently
       considers Melville a Jesuit in disguise, bent on the destruc-
       tion of Protestantism in the Islands. The stupidity into
       which a leading idea sometimes betrays a man was never more
       ludicrously illustrated.

118   ANON. "Mr. Melville and the South Sea Missions." New York
       <u>Eclectic Magazine</u>, 21 (December), 553-559.
           Reprint of 1850.B110.

<u>1851 A BOOKS - NONE</u>

<u>1851 B SHORTER WRITINGS</u>

   1   CHASLES, PHILARÈTE. <u>Ètudes Sur la Littérature et les Moeurs</u>
        <u>des Anglo-Américains au XIXe Siècle</u>. Paris: Amyot,
        pp. 185-235.
            Incorporates 1846.B67, 1846.B68, and 1849.B59.

   2   [CURTIS, GEORGE WILLIAM]. <u>Nile Notes of a Howadji</u>. New York:
        Harper & Brothers, p. 201.
            Impressionistic account of the "dreamy depths" of <u>Mardi</u>.
        <u>Mardi</u> "is unrhymed poetry, but rhythmical and measured. Of
        a low, lapping cadence is the swell of those sentences, like
        the dip of the sun-stilled, Pacific waves. In more serious
        moods, they have the grave music of Bacon's Essays. Yet
        who but an American could have written them?"

   3   [LUCETT, EDWARD]. <u>Rovings in the Pacific</u>. Vol. 1. London:
        Longman, Brown, Green, and Longmans, pp. 293-296.
            By his own showing Melville "has been a most reckless
        loafer, caring not a pin what enterprises were ruined so
        long as he could indulge the gratification of his own pro-
        pensities." Regardless of "all truth, gratitude, or man-
        liness," he has "grossly scandalized by name some worthy
        men living at Tahiti," particularly Dr. Johnstone.
        Melville's sketches are amusing and skillfully drawn but
        bear little relation to truth. While temporarily imprisoned
        in the calliboose at Tahiti, Lucett was attacked by one of
        the mutineers from the <u>Lucy Ann</u>, who he thinks was Melville.

   4   WARREN, JOHN ESAIAS. <u>Para; or, Scenes and Adventures on the</u>
        <u>Banks of the Amazon</u>. New York: G. P. Putnam, p. 31.
            The same reference to Fayaway as in 1848.B3.

1851

5   ANON. "The Earl of Carlisle's View of America." New York
     Literary World, No. 207 (18 January), p. 41.
         The earl's view that America contains the fewest miser-
     able and the fewest happy people in the world is based on
     an insufficient definition of happiness as "the dolce far
     niente of the Southern races, the luxury of indolence,
     tropical fruits, out of door gratifications—the unthinking
     enjoyments of races troubled little with work and not at all
     with conscience, who sin pleasantly and grow jolly enor-
     mously—the merry races of Mr. Melville's Typee, among whom
     it is misery to introduce schools, garments, or the Christ-
     ian religion."

6   ANON. "Authors and Books." New York International Magazine
     of Literature, Art, and Science, 3 (1 July), 467.
         Notes that Melville "will soon be again before the pub-
     lic in a romance," believed to be "in press."

7   ANON. Review of Para by John Esaias Warren. New York Literary
     World, No. 231 (5 July), p. 5.
         Mention: there is "a faint attempt, repeated at inter-
     vals throughout the book, with rather indifferent success
     to get up a 'Fayaway,' after the style of the romantic
     nautical Herman Melville. All travellers in the tropics
     are bound henceforth, it would appear, to be voluptuous...."

*8   ANON. Pittsfield (Mass.) Sun (10 July).
         Brief report of visit by Chief Justice Shaw to Arrowhead.
     Cited in Log, p. 416.

9   ANON. Review of Godfrey Malvern by Thomas Miller. New York
     Literary World, No. 236 (9 August), p. 109.
         Notes the "present season of unexampled scarcity in the
     reading world...while Hawthorne is silent, and Melville's
     new romance, like a certain holiday, is coming, but has not
     come."

10   'HOWADJI' [CURTIS, GEORGE WILLIAM]. "Summer Notes of a
     Howadji." New York Daily Tribune (10 September), p. 3.
         Episode by Lake George; narrator sees a boat drive
     silently into a cove, "and a hushed tumult of low laughter
     trembled through the trees. For that moment I was a South-
     sea islander, a Typeean, a Herman Melville, and down the
     ruined steps I sprang to catch a moonlight glimpse of
     Fayaway, but saw only the rippling brilliance of the rapidly
     fading boat." Reprinted in 1852.B3.

11   D[UYCKINCK], E[VERT], A. "Notes of Excursions.--No. III.
      Glimpses of Berkshire Scenery." New York Literary World,
      No. 243 (27 September), pp. 241-242.
         Remembers a day's excursion in the Taconic range "with
      two pleasantly named and to be named authors, whose Scarlet
      Letters and White Jackets are gleaming here and there about
      the world in the light of quickening fancies...." In dis-
      cussion of the landscape's power of nourishing the heart and
      head: "Herman Melville, in the vistas of his wood and the
      long prospective glance from his meadows to the mountains,
      blends the past and the future on his fancy-sprinkled page."

12   ANON. Notice of The Whale. London Household Narrative of
      Current Events (28 September-28 October), p. 239.
         Melville "relates more of the ocean experiences of his
      Typees and Omoos in a motley book called The Whale." [In
      a discussion of "voyages and travels," which precedes a dis-
      cussion of recent novels.] Reprinted in Doubloon, pp. 12-13.

13   ANON. New York Literary World, No. 244 (4 October), p. 270.
         Notes that the October issue of Harper's Magazine con-
      tains "a spirited chapter, 'The Town-ho's Story,' from
      Melville's forthcoming book."

14   ANON. "Literary Intelligence." New York Literary World,
      No. 244 (4 October), p. 273.
         Melville's forthcoming book is announced by the Harpers.
      "Its title is simply 'The Whale.'"

15   ANON. Review of The Whale. London Morning Herald
      (20 October).
         Melville is on the right track now in The Whale, where
      we see a concentration of all his powers. For vigor, orig-
      inality, and interest it has never been surpassed. Re-
      printed in Doubloon, pp. 1-2.

16   ANON. Review of The Whale. London Morning Advertiser
      (24 October).
         The Whale is a book of various merits: "High philosophy,
      liberal feeling, abstruse metaphysics popularly phrased,
      soaring speculation, a style as many-coloured as the theme,
      yet always good, and often admirable; fertile fancy, ingen-
      ious construction, playful learning, and an unusual power
      of enchaining the interest, and rising to the verge of the
      sublime, without overpassing that narrow boundary which
      plunges the ambitious penman into the ridiculous." It shows
      an ability to express the ideas which in ordinary men refuse
      to shape themselves in words and a dramatic ability for

producing a prose-poem. "Now we have a Carlylism of phrase, then a quaintness reminding us of Sir Thomas Brown, and anon a heap of curious out-of-the-way learning" after the fashion of Burton. The Spouter Inn and its inmates "are pencilled with the mastery and minuteness of Washington Irving." The whaling adventures are "wild as dreams, and powerful in their cumulated horrors." Extracts from chapters 7, 5, and 24. Reprinted in Doubloon, pp. 2-7; reprinted in part in Branch, pp. 251-252.

17 ANON. Review of The Whale. London Athenaeum, No. 1252 (25 October), pp. 1112-1113.
    The Whale is a wild, absurd book, an ill-compounded mixture of romance and matter-of-fact, showing only occasionally the idea of a connected and collected story. The style in places is disfigured by mad (rather than bad) English; the catastrophe is hastily, weakly, and obscurely managed. The book might have been acceptable as an extravaganza if Melville had been consistent; there is a place for everything in imaginative literature—"for rant as well as for reserve; but the rant must be good, honest, shameless rant, without flaw or misgiving. The voice of 'the storm wind Euroclydon' must not be interrupted by the facts of Scoresby and the figures of Cocker." In The Whale, ravings and scraps of useful knowledge are flung together salad-wise. The "Extracts" suggest that a substantial work on the whale may have been originally contemplated; either Melville's purpose changed, or his power fell short. There is a wild humorous poetry in some of his terrors "which distinguishes him from the vulgar herd of fustian-weavers." Melville must be henceforth numbered with the incorrigibles "who occasionally tantalize us with indications of genius, while they constantly summon us to endure monstrosities, carelessnesses and other such harassing manifestations of bad taste." Extracts from chapters 2 and 3. Reprinted in part in Log, pp. 430-431; Rountree, pp. 22-23; Branch, pp. 253-254; reprinted in Doubloon, pp. 7-8.

18 ANON. Review of The Whale. London John Bull (25 October), p. 687.
    Of all Melville's extraordinary books, this is the most extraordinary. Few books professedly dealing in metaphysics or claiming the parentage of the muses contain as much true philosophy and as much genuine poetry as this. It is brimful of matters of deepest interest; Melville has succeeded in investing objects apparently the most unattractive with an absorbing fascination. The book has a power of thought and force of diction suited to the huge dimensions of its

subject. The flashes of truth, the profound reflections
uttered by the actors, and the graphic representations of
human nature in startling disguises combine to raise The
Whale far beyond the level of an ordinary work of fiction.
It unfolds not a mere tale of adventures, but a whole philosophy of life. It is all the greater pity that Melville
should have defaced his pages by occasional thrusts against
revealed religion which add nothing to the interest of his
story. Extracts from chapters 109, 68, and 70. Reprinted
in Doubloon, pp. 9-10, and Branch, pp. 255-256.

19 ANON. "Herman Melville's Whale." London Spectator, 24
    (25 October), 1026-1027.
       In The Whale, the usual sea matter of whaling is expanded
    by a variety of digressions on the nature of the sperm whale,
    the history of the fishery, and similar things, in which a
    little knowledge is made the excuse for a vast many words.
    The "marvellous" injures the book by disjointing the narra-
    tive, as well as by its inherent lack of interest, and pas-
    sages of rhapsody repel the reader. The soliloquies and
    dialogues of Ahab induce weariness or skipping. Perhaps
    the earliest chapters are the best; their topics are fresher
    to English readers than the whale chase, and they have more
    direct satire. The strongest point of the book is its char-
    acters, the harpooners, mates, and several of the seamen;
    Ishmael is little more than a mouthpiece. Melville violates
    rules of narrative by describing things impossible for him
    to know, since all the Pequod's crew perish; and by begin-
    ning in the autobiographical form and changing ad libitum
    into the narrative. Extracts from chapters 12 and 16.
    Reprinted in 1851.B76; Recognition, pp. 33-35; Doubloon,
    pp. 10-12; Branch, pp. 257-259; reprinted in part in
    Vincent, pp. 2-4.

20 ANON. "Literary Intelligence." New York Literary World,
    No. 247 (25 October), p. 233.
       Notes that Moby-Dick "is now very nearly ready."

21 ANON. Review of Peter the Whaler by William H. G. Kingston.
    New York Literary World, No. 247 (25 October), p. 328.
       The boy's "introduction to the service reminds us of
    Mr. Melville's Redburn, though with no pretensions to the
    humor and picturesqueness of that delightful book."

22 ANON. "Chronicle of Passing Events." New York North American
    Miscellany, NS 3 (November), 166.
       Notes that Melville's new work, The Whale, will also
    shortly be published in London.

1851

23   ANON. Review of The Whale. London Atlas (1 November),
        pp. 697-698.
            In some respects The Whale is Melville's greatest effort.
        None of his previous works contain finer or more highly
        soaring imaginative powers, so many profound and original
        veins of philosophic speculation, such wonderfully graphic
        descriptions of seafaring and whaling matters, or a more
        thorough command over the strength and beauties of the
        language. Extravagance is the bane of the book; Melville
        allows his fancy to run riot and abandons commonsense.
        There are fine poetic elements in the conception of Ahab,
        but its intensity is impaired by the constant rigmarole
        rhapsodies placed in his mouth. Most of the conversation
        of the seamen, too, is in a wild rhapsodic vein, destitute
        of sense or appropriateness. Melville's sketches of his
        shipmates are among the poorest things he has done. His
        reveries on whales and whaling are full of strange and
        novel beauties, strangely mixed with ingenious and daring
        speculation, and written in a tone of exaltation and poetic
        sentiment which ultimately makes the reader look upon the
        whale as a sort of awful and unsoluble mystery. The classi-
        fication of whales is ingenious; the descriptions of the
        sperm whale wonderfully minute. Extracts from chapters 99,
        36, and 45. Continued in 1851.B27. Reprinted in Doubloon,
        pp. 13-18.

24   R., A. B. Review of The Whale. Illustrated London News, 19
        (1 November), 539.
            One of the two "works of fancy" currently attracting the
        most attention is Melville's last and best and most wildly
        imaginative story. The controversial novel is remarkable
        for fairness, good temper, and good humor, "and the person-
        ages are so conceived as to be types of the principal dif-
        ferent parties and classes into which the late Aggression
        agitation split up the community." The book will worthily
        support Melville's "reputation for singularly vivid and
        reckless imaginative power--great aptitude for quaint and
        original philosophical speculation, degenerating, however,
        too often into rhapsody and purposeless extravagance--an
        almost unparalleled power over the capabilities of the
        language." Reprinted in Doubloon, pp. 18-19; reprinted in
        part in Branch, pp. 259-260.

25   ANON. "Authors and Books." New York International Magazine
        of Literature, Art, and Science, 4 (1 November), 559.
            Notes that The Whale will be published in a few days,
        simultaneously by the Harpers and by Bentley of London.

26 ANON. Review of <u>The Whale</u>. London <u>News of the World</u>
(2 November).
"There are people who delight in mulligatawny. They
love curry at its warmest point. Ginger cannot be too hot
in the mouth for them. Such people, we should think, con-
stitute the admirers of Herman Melville. He spices his
narrative with uncommon courage, and works up a story amaz-
ingly. If you love heroics and horrors he is your man...."
Extracts from chapters 2, 3, and 68. Reprinted in Parker
(March 1972), p. 183.

27 ANON. Review of <u>The Whale</u>. London <u>Atlas</u> (8 November),
pp. 714-715.
Continued from 1851.B23. Mainly summary, with extracts
from chapters 48, 61, and 135. Melville continually alter-
nates with the strangest coolness from the grandest to the
smallest themes, oscillating from rhapsodically expressed
tirades on the doctrine of metempsychosis to a closely
argued demonstration that the skin of a whale is its blubber. The ordinary whaling adventures are told with rare
and impassioned power. Closing <u>The Whale</u>, "we feel as if
waking from what was partly a gorgeous vision, partly a
night-mare dream, but both vision and dream intense, over-
mastering in their power[,] the spell of a magician who
works wildly, recklessly, but with a skill and a potency
which few...will be disposed either to deny or resist."
Reprinted in <u>Doubloon</u>, pp. 19-22.

28 ANON. Review of <u>The Whale</u>. London <u>Britannia</u> (8 November).
<u>The Whale</u> is a most extraordinary work, with so much
eccentricity in style and construction and in the original
conception and gradual development of the strange, improb-
able story that the reviewer is "at a loss to determine in
what category of works of amusement to place it." The plot
is meager beyond comparison. But Melville displays a rare
versatility of talent: he has a thorough acquaintance with
whaling; and in his descriptions of character and analysis
of the motives of actions he displays a considerable knowledge of the human heart. He makes his narrative intensely
interesting and has a fund of humor at command. Ahab is a
most eccentric conception, well contrasted with the commonplace mates. Queequeg is made a most interesting hero
among whale slayers. Except for a few Americanisms, the
language of the work is appropriate and impressive. The
cetological information will have little interest for the
general reader. Extracts from chapters 133 and 135. Reprinted in <u>Doubloon</u>, pp. 22-24; reprinted in part in Branch,
pp. 260-261.

1851

29   ANON. Review of The Whale. London Examiner (8 November),
      p. 709.
            If not carelessness, so much willfulness in The Whale
      results in small enjoyment even of what is remarkably clever
      in it. All the regular rules of narrative or story are
      spurned and set at defiance. Melville has kindly taken up
      the narrative which must otherwise have gone to the bottom
      with Ishmael. The sole survivor is Moby Dick, properly
      perhaps in a book which "presents not a particle of interest
      connected with humanity to compare with that which it yields
      in regard of cetology." Melville is a man of too real an
      imagination, and a writer with too singular a mastery over
      language and its resources, to have satisfied readers' ex-
      pectations by such an extravaganza as this. Reprinted in
      Doubloon, pp. 24-25.

30   ANON. Review of The Whale. London Leader, 2 (8 November),
      1067-1069.
            The Whale is a strange, wild, weird book, full of poetry
      and full of interest. The ghostly terrors Melville evokes
      have a strange fascination. "The book is not a romance,
      nor a treatise on Cetology. It is something of both: a
      strange, wild work with the tangled overgrowth and luxuriant
      vegetation of American forests, not the trim orderliness of
      an English park. Criticism may pick many holes in this
      work; but no criticism will thwart its fascination." Ex-
      tracts from chapters 28, 42, 58, 64, and 55. Reprinted in
      Doubloon, pp. 25-27; reprinted in part in Branch,
      pp. 262-263.

31   ANON. Notice of Moby-Dick. Albany Evening Journal
      (12 November).
            Looks forward with pleasure to reading Moby-Dick, which
      opens promisingly. Reprinted in Doubloon, p. 28.

32   ANON. Notice of Moby-Dick. Boston Daily Evening Transcript
      (12 November).
            Welcomes Melville back to the field where he has won so
      many laurels and predicts that he will be at home among the
      whalers. Reprinted in Doubloon, p. 28.

33   ANON. Review of Moby-Dick. Albany Argus (14 November).
            Moby-Dick is the work of a man of genius, abounding in
      bright, witty, attractive things; telling many things about
      the whale, both true and untrue; and, unhappily, pervaded
      by an air of irreverence in many parts. Reprinted in
      Doubloon, p. 28.

34   ANON. Editorial. London <u>Morning Chronicle</u> (14 November),
      p. 4.
           Mention: "...without the smallest desire to misconstrue
      the evidences of progress, and with something more than dis-
      dain for calumniators of the Melville school, typifying, as
      they generally do, the very men who have wrought the mis-
      chief, we are forced to avow our belief that the mission-
      aries have not effected all that might have been expected
      of them...." Reprinted in 1852.B19.

35   ANON. Review of <u>The Whale</u>. London <u>Morning Post</u> (14 November).
           <u>The Whale</u> is a book of extraordinary merit, a work of
      great power and beauty. Despite the occasionally improbable
      character of the incidents, there is a wild and wonderful
      fascination in the story; the spell of genius is upon us;
      Melville's radiant imagination enthralls us in a delicious
      bondage. His descriptive powers are so vivid and appealing
      that we share with him the perils he so graphically pic-
      tures and merge our own identity in his. The book is brim-
      ful of interest; the adventures are deliciously exciting.
      One of the cleverest, wittiest, and most amusing of modern
      books. Extracts from chapters 14, 24, 35, and 48. Reprinted
      in <u>Doubloon</u>, pp. 28-31.

36   ANON. Review of <u>Moby-Dick</u>. <u>Morning Courier and New-York</u>
      <u>Enquirer</u> (14 November).
           <u>Moby-Dick</u> is as attractive as Melville's previous books
      and has more of a "witching interest" since his fancy has
      taken a wilder play than ever before. Melville writes with
      racy humor and the gusto of true genius, setting off a vast
      variety of characters and subjects with an artistic effect
      that irresistibly captivates the attention. Reprinted in
      1852.B23; Potter, p. 65; <u>Doubloon</u>, pp. 31-32; reprinted
      in part in <u>Log</u>, pp. 433-434.

37   ANON. Review of <u>Moby-Dick</u>. Boston <u>Daily Evening Traveller</u>
      (15 November), p. 1.
           <u>Moby-Dick</u> seems a sort of hermaphrodite craft, half fact
      and half fiction, in which it is not easy to separate the
      two. Many of Melville's descriptions are extremely graphic,
      lifelike and entertaining, but frequent profaneness and
      occasional indelicacies materially detract from a book
      showing much tact, talent, and genius. Reprinted in
      <u>Doubloon</u>, p. 32.

38   ANON. Review of <u>Moby-Dick</u>. Hartford (Conn.) <u>Daily Courant</u>
      (15 November), p. 2.

1851

As Melville writes, he continues to improve in the minor
details of incident, management, and style. In all his
stories there is "the same want of unity of subject--of a
regular beginning and end--of the form and shape and outline
of a well built novel--which we find in real life." But
there is a little too much romance and adventure to be
anything but fiction. Moby-Dick is well worth reading as
a book of amusement. Reprinted in Doubloon, pp. 32-33,
and Branch, p. 263.

39   ANON. Notice of Moby-Dick. New Haven Daily Register
     (15 November).
        The book "will undoubtedly have a great run." Reprinted
     in Doubloon, p. 33.

40   ANON. Review of Moby-Dick. New York Literary World, No. 250
     (15 November), pp. 381-383.
        The "catastrophe" of Moby-Dick is the same as the destruc-
     tion of the Ann Alexander, even to very many of the details.
     Moby-Dick is "a natural-historical, philosophical, romantic
     account of the person, habits, manners, ideas of the great
     sperm whale" and of the not less remarkable individuals who
     hunt him. "Nothing like it has ever before been written of
     the whale; for no man who has at once seen so much of the
     actual conflict, and weighed so carefully all that has been
     recorded on the subject, with equal powers of perception
     and reflection, has attempted to write at all on it." The
     "Extracts" are in lieu of the old style chapter headings
     of Scott, Cooper, and others; they "may be taken as a kind
     of bitters, a whet and fillip to the imagination." Extracts
     from chapters 91 and 81. Continued in 1851.B63. Reprinted
     in 1851.B73, and Doubloon, pp. 33-36; reprinted in part in
     Recognition, pp. 37-39; Vincent, pp. 5-8; Branch, pp. 264-265.

41   ANON. Review of Moby-Dick. Philadelphia Dollar Newspaper
     (15 November).
        Moby-Dick contains 135 distinct sketches, presented in
     the easy and yet racy style so characteristic of the author.
     Paragraphs 1-3 of chapter 80 printed as representative
     extract. Reprinted in Pollin (April 1975), p. 58.

42   ANON. Notice of Moby-Dick. New York Atlas (16 November).
        Melville's name will ensure Moby-Dick an immense sale.
     Reprinted in Doubloon, p. 36.

43   ANON. Notice of Moby-Dick. Albany Daily State Register
     (17 November).

Recalls sinking of the Ann Alexander and reprints part
of 1851.B40. Extract from chapter 81 (written in Melville's
best style and "no ordinary every-day writing"). Reprinted
in 1851.B48.

44   ANON. Review of Moby-Dick. New Haven Daily Palladium
     (17 November).
     Moby-Dick has all the interest of the most exciting fic-
     tion and also conveys much valuable information about nat-
     ural history, commerce, and ship life. It has numerous
     thrilling sketches, but in some of the sailors' talk there
     is a little more irreverence and profane jesting than was
     necessary, however true to life. Reprinted in Doubloon,
     pp. 36-37.

45   ANON. Review of Moby-Dick. New York Morning Express
     (17 November), p. 1.
     Expects to find in Moby-Dick a great deal of amusement
     and instruction, combined with Melville's usual felicity.
     Reprints part of 1851.B36. Reprinted in Doubloon, p. 37.

46   ANON. Review of Moby-Dick. Springfield (Mass.) Republican
     (17 November).
     Around "this cumbrous bulk of romance," Melville has
     woven "a large and interesting web of narrative, informa-
     tion, and sketches of character and scenery, in a quaint
     though interesting style, and with an easy, rollicking
     freedom of language and structure, characteristic of him-
     self." All of Melville's books are greatly superior to
     the sea books of Marryat. Reprinted in Doubloon, pp. 37-38,
     and Branch, pp. 268-269.

47   ANON. Review of Moby-Dick. New Bedford Daily Mercury
     (18 November).
     "We have had before volume upon volume of narratives of
     whaling voyages, and adventures with the leviathans of the
     deep, but never before a work combining so much of natural
     history of Moby-Dick, nor in so attractive guise...."
     Reprinted in Doubloon, p. 38, and Branch, p. 269; reprinted
     in part in Log, p. 436.

48   ANON. Review of Moby-Dick. Boston Daily Bee (19 November),
     p. 4.
     Reprint of 1851.B43. [Extract from chapter 81 concluded
     20 November.] Reprinted in Doubloon, pp. 38-39.

49   ANON. Review of Moby-Dick. Utica (N.Y.) Daily Gazette
     (19 November).
     The subject of Moby-Dick affords the finest field for
     Melville's rich imaginative powers and seafaring experience.

1851

Few authors have got up stories of deeper interest in more attractive style. Reprinted in <u>Doubloon</u>, p. 39.

50   ANON. Review of <u>Moby-Dick</u>. Worcester (Mass.) <u>Palladium</u> (19 November).
There is life, elasticity, and freedom from restraint in Melville's manner as a writer and originality and freshness in his matter. <u>Moby-Dick</u> will be as popular as his previous works. Reprinted in <u>Doubloon</u>, p. 39.

51   ANON. Review of <u>Moby-Dick</u>. Boston <u>Daily Atlas</u> (20 November).
Does not admire Melville's works, but to those who do commends <u>Moby-Dick</u> as fully equal in interest to any of its predecessors. Reprinted in <u>Doubloon</u>, p. 39.

52   ANON. Review of <u>Moby-Dick</u>. Boston <u>Post</u> (20 November).
Agrees with, and quotes from, 1851.B17. <u>Moby-Dick</u> is "a crazy sort of affair, stuffed with conceits and oddities of all kinds, put in artificially, deliberately and affectedly, by the side of strong, terse and brilliant passages of incident and description." It is not worth the money asked for it [$1.50], either as a literary work or a mass of printed paper. Reprinted in <u>Doubloon</u>, p. 40.

53   ANON. Review of <u>Moby-Dick</u>. New Bedford <u>Daily Mercury</u> (20 November), p. 1.
In Melville's lively description, even the implements of whaling gear acquire a degree of interest which is almost fascinating. Extracts from chapters 60 and 61. Reprinted in <u>Doubloon</u>, pp. 40-41.

54   ANON. Review of <u>Moby-Dick</u>. New York <u>Christian Intelligencer</u> (20 November).
<u>Moby-Dick</u> shows that no one can excel Melville in his delineations of the sea and its wonders. Marryat is not capable of making "such a correct use of English undefiled" or even of painting so beautifully. Reprinted in <u>Doubloon</u>, p. 41.

55   ANON. Review of <u>Moby-Dick</u>. New York <u>Evangelist</u> (20 November), p. 4.
Admires the extraordinary descriptive powers, the graphic and terrible portraitures of hairbreadth escapes, the exquisitely humorous, sharp delineation of character, and the passages of great eloquence. Melville grows wilder and more untameable with every adventure and has reached the very limbo of eccentricity in <u>Moby-Dick</u>. The book will add to his repute as a writer. Reprinted in <u>Doubloon</u>, p. 41, and Branch, p. 270.

56   H.   Review of Moby-Dick. New York Independent (20 November).
         The realities and fabrications of whaling life are dashed
     into with a bold hand; and mixed with a great deal of myth
     and mystery, there are exciting descriptions, curious in-
     formation, and strange adventures. Melville shows powers
     "that make us ashamed of him that he does not write some-
     thing better and freer from blemishes." But it is doubtful
     that he could, "for there is a primitive formation of pro-
     fanity and indecency that is ever and anon shooting up
     through all the strata of his writings," making it impos-
     sible for a religious journal heartily to commend any of
     his works. Reprinted in Parker (March 1972), p. 184, and
     Monteiro (Fourth Quarter 1974), p. 436.

57   ANON. Review of Moby-Dick. New York Observer (20 November),
         p. 374.
         Moby-Dick is a complete exhibition of the art and mystery
     of whaleology; its graphic pictures of the whaler's life are
     presented with Melville's peculiar tact. Reprinted in
     Doubloon, p. 42.

58   ANON. Review of Moby-Dick. New York Sun (20 November).
         Moby-Dick abounds with thrilling narratives of dangers
     and hairbreadth escapes, is written in a singularly attrac-
     tive style, and conveys much interesting knowledge of whales
     and whaling. Reprinted in Parker (March 1972), pp. 184-185.

59   ANON. Review of Moby-Dick. Toronto Globe. (20 November).
         Moby-Dick is equal to any of Melville's former works.
     There is a close resemblance in his subjects but a differ-
     ence in their handling gives constant variety. Melville
     has few equals as a describer of the manners of seamen, and
     in Moby-Dick there is a store of information on all sorts
     of subjects which surprises and delights in a work of fic-
     tion. Reprinted in Parker (March 1972), p. 185.

60   ANON. "Killing a Whale." New Haven Journal and Courier
         (22 November).
         Extract from chapter 61--the most absorbingly interest-
     ing and vivid of many accounts of the chase and capture of
     the sperm whale. Reprinted in 1851.B67; 1851.B75; Doubloon,
     p. 42.

61   ANON. Review of Moby-Dick. New York Albion, NS 10
         (22 November), 561.
         Moby-Dick is not lacking much of being a great work. In
     the conception of Ahab lies the most original thought of the
     whole book, stamping it decidedly as the production of a man

of genius. The book contains thrilling adventures and an
immense amount of reliable information. The characters are
all vivid sketches done in Melville's best style, with wondrous elaborateness of detail. It is only when Melville
puts words in their mouths that his cunning fails him: not
one of them talks pure seaman's lingo. Ahab spouts stuff
and nonsense. His rarely-imagined character is ruined "by
a vile overdaubing with a coat of book-learning and mysticism"; the chief feature of the book is a perfect failure
and the work itself inartistic. But there is abundant
choice reading for those who can skip a page now and then,
judiciously. The Pequod's fate is the same as the Ann
Alexander's. Extracts from chapters 36, 44, 45, 99, 135,
108, 49, and 82. Reprinted in part in Log, pp. 437-438,
and Branch, pp. 271-272; reprinted in Doubloon, pp. 42-47.

62   ANON. Review of Moby-Dick. New York Daily Tribune
      (22 November), p. 6.
      Moby-Dick is a wildly imaginative and truly thrilling
story, the best production yet of Melville's seething brain,
in spite of its lawless flights which put all regular criticism at defiance. The book is a "Whaliad" or Epic of the
old leviathan of Nantucket and New Bedford tradition, with
a great mass of instruction about whales and the strategems
of their pursuers. The interest of the work pivots on Ahab.
The narrative is constructed in Melville's best manner, combining the chief attractions of his style and commendably
free from his previous faults. The intensity of the plot
is happily relieved by minute descriptions of the most
homely processes of the fishery. Occasional touches of
subtle mysticism are safely mixed up with tangible and
odorous realities. Extracts from chapters 10, 60, 61, and
133. Reprinted in Recognition, pp. 35-37; Vincent,
pp. 11-13; Doubloon, pp. 47-49; reprinted in part in Branch,
pp. 273-274.

63   ANON. Review of Moby-Dick. New York Literary World, No. 251
      (22 November), pp. 403-404.
      Continued from 1851.B40. In their resistance to dis-
tinct classification as fact, fiction, or essay, Melville's
books resemble "Jean Paul's German Tales, with an admixture
of Southey's Doctor." Combining "personal observation,
actual fidelity to local truthfulness in description, a
taste for reading and sentiment, a fondness for fanciful
analogies, near and remote, a rash daring in speculation,
reckless at times of taste and propriety, again refined and
eloquent," Moby-Dick "may be pronounced a most remarkable
sea-dish--an intellectual chowder of romance, philosophy,

natural history, fine writing, good feeling, bad sayings."
It is two if not three books rolled into one: Book 1, a
thorough, exhaustive account of the sperm whale, the information minute and brilliantly illustrated; Book 2, the
romance of Ahab and his crew, striking characters of the
romantic spiritual cast of the German drama; Book 3, perhaps a fourth of the book, "a vein of moralizing, half
essay, half rhapsody, in which much refinement and subtlety,
and no little poetical feeling, are mingled with quaint conceit and extravagant daring speculation." Ahab is a striking conception, but too long drawn out. If Melville
intended to exhibit in Ishmael the painful contradictions
of the self-dependent, self-torturing agency of a vacillat-
ing mind, the result was successful but not admirable.
Regrettably, Melville runs down creeds and opinions and
violates and defaces the most sacred associations of life.
Reprinted in 1851.B73; Norton <u>Moby-Dick</u>, pp. 613-616;
<u>Recognition</u>, pp. 39-43; Vincent, pp. 8-10; <u>Doubloon</u>,
pp. 49-52; Branch, pp. 265-268; reprinted in part in <u>Log</u>,
p. 437.

64   ANON. Notice of <u>Moby-Dick</u>. New York <u>Spirit of the Times</u>, 21
      (22 November), 475.
          Announces publication of "this excellent work," which
      will be given an extended notice in the next issue. [See
      1851.B80.]

65   ANON. Review of <u>Moby-Dick</u>. Philadelphia <u>American Saturday
      Courier</u> (22 November).
          Melville is "one of the most spirited, vigorous, good-
      natured writers in existence; as sparkling and racy as old
      wine and sweet as nuts, with a constant flow of animating
      description and thrilling incident...." For real, easy,
      pleasant, social enjoyment, <u>Moby-Dick</u> is decidedly the
      richest book out. Readers will be better prepared to credit
      all its wonders after reading of the whale shipwreck in
      last week's <u>Courier</u>. Reprinted in <u>Doubloon</u>, pp. 52-53.

66   ANON. Review of <u>Moby-Dick</u>. New York <u>Commercial Advertiser</u>
      (28 November).
          There are few readers who will not be at first repulsed
      by the eccentricity of <u>Moby-Dick</u>. "Such a salmagundi of
      fact, fiction and philosophy, composed in a style which
      combines the peculiarities of Carlyle, Marryatt and Lamb,
      was never seen before." The science of cetology is pleas-
      antly interwoven with the legend of Ahab and Moby Dick, but,
      regrettably, Melville is guilty of sneering at the truths
      of revealed religion. Reprinted in <u>Doubloon</u>, p. 53.

1851

67   ANON. "Killing a Whale." Hartford <u>Daily Courant</u>
        (29 November).
            Reprint of 1851.B60.

68   ANON. Review of <u>The Whale</u>. London <u>Weekly News and Chronicle</u>
        (29 November).
            <u>The Whale</u> is a wild weird book, full of strange power
        and irresistible fascination. Its blemish is occasional
        extravagance and exaggeration; one result is that Ahab
        becomes a melodramatic caricature of what, with a little
        more simplicity, might have been a striking and original
        picture. The fate of the <u>Pequod</u> is that of the <u>Essex</u> and
        the <u>Ann Alexander</u>. The excitement felt about Moby Dick is
        singularly increased by every kind of dramatic artifice;
        the eagerness of expectation becomes at last most pleasur-
        ably painful. "Cetology" contains admirable analysis of
        the different varieties of whales, and the various processes
        of whaling are described with the minute and graphic vivid-
        ness of an attentive and gifted eye-witness. <u>The Whale</u>
        is by far the most powerful and original contribution
        Melville has yet made to the Romance of Travel. Extracts
        from chapters 3, 35, and 41. Reprinted in Parker (January
        1970), pp. 586-588, and <u>Doubloon</u>, pp. 53-56.

69   ANON. "Whale Killing." New York <u>Evening Post</u> (29 November).
            In <u>Moby-Dick</u> Melville probably lets us into the realities
        of actual whaling as minutely and faithfully as any sea
        author has ever done. Extract from chapter 61. Reprinted
        in <u>Doubloon</u>, p. 56.

70   ANON. Review of <u>Moby-Dick</u>. New York <u>Home Journal</u> (29 November).
            Melville has treated of the whale under three points of
        view--as the nucleus of maritime adventure, as a subject of
        scientific curiosity, and as a kind of hero of romance. The
        result is a very racy, spirited, curious, and entertaining
        book which affords quite an amount of information. Melville
        has apparently decided to combine all his popular character-
        istics in <u>Moby-Dick</u>. Reprinted in part in <u>Log</u>, p. 438;
        reprinted in <u>Doubloon</u>, p. 56.

71   ANON. Review of <u>Moby-Dick</u>. New York <u>Eclectic Magazine</u>, 24
        (December), 572.
            Despite its faults and its severe handling in 1851.B17,
        <u>Moby-Dick</u> bears the marks of such unquestionable genius
        that it cannot fail to add to Melville's reputation. Re-
        printed in <u>Log</u>, p. 439, and <u>Doubloon</u>, p. 57.

72   ANON. Review of <u>Moby-Dick</u>. New York <u>Harper's New Monthly</u>
     <u>Magazine</u>, 4 (December), 137.
          In richness and variety of incident, originality of
     conception, and splendor of description, <u>Moby-Dick</u> surpas-
     ses all of Melville's other works. On its slight framework
     of a story, Melville has constructed a romance, a tragedy,
     and a natural history, "not without numerous gratuitous
     suggestions on psychology, ethics, and theology." Beneath
     the whole story, the subtle imaginative reader may perhaps
     find a pregnant allegory, intended to illustrate the mys-
     tery of human life. Frequent rapid, pointed hints penetrate
     deep into the heart of things, showing that Melville's
     genius for moral analysis is scarcely surpassed by his
     wizard power of description. Frequent graphic and instruc-
     tive sketches of the fishery and of the manners and customs
     of strange nations are interspersed with excellent artistic
     effect among the thrilling scenes of the story. These sud-
     den and decided transitions are wrought with consummate
     skill and constantly pique the attention of the reader,
     keeping curiosity alive and presenting the charm of sur-
     prise and alternation. The introductory chapters are per-
     vaded by a fine vein of comic humor. Ahab exercises a wild,
     bewildering fascination; all members of the ship's crew are
     strongly individualized and present a unique picture gallery.
     Moby Dick may be the same monster whose destruction of an-
     other ship is just announced from Panama. Reprinted in
     Norton <u>Moby-Dick</u>, pp. 616-617; <u>Recognition</u>, pp. 43-45;
     Rountree, pp. 24-25; <u>Doubloon</u>, pp. 57-58; Vincent, pp. 14-
     16; Branch, pp. 274-276.

73   ANON. Review of <u>Moby-Dick</u>. New York <u>Holden's Dollar Magazine</u>,
     8 (December), 267-272.
          Reprint of 1851.B40 and 1851.B63.

74   ANON. New York <u>North American Miscellany</u>, 3 (December), 222.
          Notes, and quotes from, the unfavorable <u>Athenaeum</u> review
     [1851.B17]. Reprinted in Doubloon, p. 59.

75   ANON. "Killing a Whale." New Bedford <u>Daily Evening Standard</u>,
     (1 December), p. 1.
          Reprint of 1851.B60.

76   ANON. "Herman Melville's Whale." New York <u>International</u>
     <u>Magazine of Literature, Art, and Science</u>, 4 (1 December),
     602-604.
          The subject of <u>Moby-Dick</u> is the monster first written
     about by J. N. Reynolds 10 or 15 years ago in "Mocha Dick,"
     a paper for <u>Knickerbocker</u>. Reprints 1851.B19. Reprinted
     in <u>Doubloon</u>, p. 59.

1851

77 ANON. Review of <u>Moby-Dick</u>. Newark <u>Daily Advertiser</u>
    (5 December), p. 2.
        Melville's evident object is to portray plainly the
    daily adventures and dangers of whaling men. It is doubt-
    ful that the whale has ever been so scientifically described,
    and Melville's account is worthy to be included in all fu-
    ture natural histories. A semi-marvelous narrative connects
    the various chapters and retains the interest of the reader
    till the last page. For all his numerous works on similar
    subjects, Melville repeats himself very little, whereas
    even Cooper continued many of his characters in successive
    tales. With each succeeding book there is an improvement
    in the work's artistic character, but the metaphysical dis-
    cussions of <u>Moby-Dick</u> might well be omitted. Reprinted in
    <u>Doubloon</u>, pp. 59-60.

78 ANON. Review of <u>The Whale</u>. London <u>Literary Gazette</u>, No. 1820
    (6 December), pp. 841-842.
        An odd book, professing to be a novel; wantonly eccen-
    tric; outrageously bombastic; in places charmingly and
    vividly descriptive. There are sketches of sea scenes,
    whaling adventures, storms, and ship life equal to any.
    But the cetological learning makes bad stuffing; the story
    scarcely deserves the name. Melville's original intention
    in spinning his preposterous yarn is impossible to guess
    and was evidently never carried out. How Ishmael, who
    appears to have drowned with the rest, communicated his
    notes for publication is not explained. Melville should
    not waste his strength on such purposeless and unequal
    doings. Extract from chapter 48. Reprinted in <u>Doubloon</u>,
    pp. 60-62, and Branch, pp. 276-278.

79 ANON. Review of <u>Moby-Dick</u>. New York <u>Churchman</u> (6 December).
        <u>Moby-Dick</u> is a strange compound of rare ability, stirring
    adventures, brilliant descriptions, apparently accurate
    knowledge of the whale, much wild rhapsody and bad philoso-
    phy, and many violations of good taste and delicacy. The
    character of Ahab is a novelty and powerfully drawn, but
    it is pitiable to see so much talent perverted to sneers
    at revealed religion and the burlesquing of sacred passages
    of Holy Writ. Reprinted in Parker (March 1972), p. 185.

80 ANON. Review of <u>Moby-Dick</u>. New York <u>Spirit of the Times</u>,
    21 (6 December), 494.
        <u>Typee</u>, <u>Omoo</u>, <u>Redburn</u>, <u>Mardi</u>, and <u>White-Jacket</u> are equal
    to anything in the language and have quickened the humani-
    ties of the world. As matters of art, they are among the
    largest and freshest contributions of original thought and

observation in many years. Moby-Dick is a many-sided book;
mingled with much curious information about whales and
whaling are a fine vein of sermonizing, a good deal of
keen satire, much humor of the finest order, and a story
of peculiar interest. But it is in the personal adventures
of the whalers that our highest interest is excited. This
mingling of human adventure with new, startling objects
and pursuits constitutes one of the chief charms of
Melville's books. Moby-Dick is a drama of intense interest.
The usual staple of novelists is entirely missing. Extracts
from chapter 91. Reprinted in Recognition, pp. 45-48, and
Doubloon, pp. 62-64; reprinted in part in Flanagan, pp. 61-
62; Vincent, pp. 17-20; Branch, pp. 278-280.

81   ANON. Review of Moby-Dick. St. John (New Brunswick) News
      (10 December).
          The whole story is full of interest and will give a vast
      amount of entertainment to the man who loves adventure. It
      is a fair sample of the "Romance of real life." Its ten-
      dency is useful and instructive, and it is free from "those
      pernicious and deceptive ingredients, with which many of
      the tales of the present age are impregnated."

82   ANON. "Hear the 'Blubber!'" New Bedford Daily Evening
      Standard (11 December).
          Quotes the "very handsome compliment" to New Bedford
      girls at the end of chapter 6 in Moby-Dick, which is pre-
      sumably just but, regrettably, "may make the dear creatures
      proud." Reprinted in Log, p. 440, and Doubloon, pp. 64-65.

83   ANON. Notice of Moby-Dick. Boston Christian Freeman and
      Family Visiter (12 December), p. 131.
          Notes the book's "wide and diversified scope" in treat-
      ing whaling and other seafaring business. Reprinted in
      Doubloon, p. 65.

84   ANON. North Adams (Mass.) Greylock Sentinel (13 December).
          Reprint of 1851.B67.

85   ANON. Review of Moby-Dick. Washington National Intelligencer
      (16 December).
          Opens with a long essay on the critic's role as devil's
      advocate. Does not propose to play devil's advocate with
      Melville; but objects to his "querulous and cavilling
      innuendoes...against objects that should be shielded from
      his irreverent wit." Neither good taste nor good morals
      can approve the "forecastle scene" in chapter 40 of Moby-
      Dick. But no one can deny Moby-Dick to be the production

of a man of genius. A prose epic on whaling, it presents
a most striking and truthful portraiture of the whale and
his capture. Melville's descriptive powers are unrivalled.
Language in the hands of this master becomes like a magician's wand, evoking at will "thick-coming fancies."
Melville has a strange power to reach the sinuosities of
a thought. His delineation of character is actually
Shakespearean--more so in Moby-Dick than in any of his
previous works. Melville's humor is like the subdued but
unquenchable humor of Sterne. Irresistibly comic passages
are scattered through Moby-Dick, and occasionally there are
traces of the "wild imagining" which throws such a weird-
like charm over Coleridge's "The Ancient Mariner," which
undoubtedly suggested many of the scenes and objects of
Moby-Dick. But the reviewer is far from considering
Melville a greater artist than Defoe in the general design
of his romantic pictures. Reprinted in part in Norton Moby-
Dick, pp. 618-619; Doubloon, pp. 65-69; Branch, pp. 281-284.

86   ANON. "Herman Melville's Whale." London Morning Chronicle
      (20 December), pp. 2-3.
         In his early books, Melville was thoroughly original.
      There never was an author "more instinct with the flush of
      power and the pride of mental wealth." A perception of the
      picturesque and beautiful, an imagination of singular force,
      and a genuine, hearty, and genial earnestness marked Melville
      not for a man of talent but for a genius. His style was
      just as characteristic in its strength and vitality. But
      even the best parts of the best books were marked by his
      tendency to rhapsody, a constant leaning toward wild and
      aimless extravagance, which has since drowned the human
      interest in so great a part of his works. The storm of
      extravagance burst forth in Mardi; and even amidst the
      Dutch painting of White-Jacket comes an occasional dash of
      raving. In The Whale Melville is in all his pristine pow-
      ers, with all his mental energy, with strange, wild and
      original themes as ever, with his store of quaint informa-
      tion and his "old mingled opulence and happiness of phrase."
      With his old extravagance, too; Melville raves and rhapso-
      dizes in chapter after chapter, unchecked, it seems, by the
      slightest remembrance of judgment or commonsense. Every-
      thing about Ahab is enveloped in a jumble of mysticism and
      rhapsody; the author's shipmates are even more phantomlike,
      unhuman, and vaguely uninteresting. But apart from the
      rhapsody, the entire book reads like a ghost story done
      with rare imaginative power and noble might of expression.
      The many chapters devoted to the natural history of the
      whale contain some of the most delightful pages in the book;

the whales are described in wonderful detail, with vivid
picturesqueness and freshness of language; there are masses
of vivid detail about whale fishing. Extracts from chapters
36, 40, 61, 87, 60, and 135. Reprinted in <u>Doubloon</u>, pp. 69-
78; reprinted in part in Branch, pp. 284-288.

87   ANON. Review of <u>The Imperial Guard of Napoleon</u> by J. T.
      Headley. New York <u>Literary World</u>, No. 255 (20 December),
      p. 482.
         Brief allusion to the "lukewarm priests in the Sandwich
      islands of whom Mr. Melville writes."

1852 A BOOKS - NONE

1852 B SHORTER WRITINGS

1   ANON. <u>The Men of the Time or Sketches of Living Notables</u>.
     New York: Redfield, pp. 350-351.
        Lengthy biographical paragraph, mainly on Melville's
     "sailor-life." Lists Melville's books to 1851 without
     critical comment. Reprinted in 1852.B49; 1853.B1; Sealts
     (1974), pp. 89-90.

2   CHASLES, PHILARÈTE. <u>Anglo-American Literature and Manners</u>.
     New York: Charles Scribner, pp. 118-146.
        Translation of 1851.B1, with omission of long summary
     of <u>Typee</u>.

3   CURTIS, GEORGE WILLIAM. <u>Lotus-Eating: A Summer Book</u>. New
     York: Harper & Brothers, p. 132.
        Reprint of 1851.B10, slightly revised.

4   GREYLOCK, GODFREY [SMITH, J. E. A.]. <u>Taghconic; or Letters
     and Legends about our Summer Home</u>. Boston: Redding and Co.,
     pp. 13, 16, 41-43, 211.
        Claims that the lightning-scarred Pittsfield Old Elm
     suggested Ahab's scar; mentions Melville's estate as adjoin-
     ing Dr. Holmes's; gives account of the "Memnon" stone and
     its naming; and names Melville as one of Hawthorne's friends.
     Melville passages reprinted in Sealts (1974), pp. 194-195.

5   HAWTHORNE, NATHANIEL. <u>A Wonder-Book for Girls and Boys</u>.
     Boston: Ticknor, Reed, and Fields, pp. 252-253.
        "On the hither side of Pittsfield sits Herman Melville,
     shaping out the gigantic conception of his 'White Whale,'
     while the gigantic shape of Graylock looms upon him from
     his study-window." (Complete reference.)

1852

6   PARKER, E. M. WILLS.   The Sandwich Islands As They Are, Not
    As They Should Be.   San Francisco: Burgess, Gilbert &
    Still, p. 7.
        "We are apt to associate something of romance with the
    inhabitants of the Pacific isles, especially after reading
    Melville's happy delineations; but I have looked in vain
    for his noble warriors, or graceful Fayaway, in the wide-
    mouthed, flat-nosed creatures around me, whose only beauty
    is grossness, and only expression, sensuality." (Complete
    reference.)

7   ROORBACH, O. A.   Bibliotheca Americana. New York: Orville A.
    Roorbach, p. 361.
        Lists Mardi, Moby-Dick, Omoo (1848), Pierre, Redburn,
    Typee (1849) and White-Jacket. Reprinted in 1855, 1858,
    and 1861.

8   ANON.   Review of The Whale.   London New Quarterly Review, 1
    (First Quarter), 66-67.
        Mainly summary and extracts (from chapters 36 and 135).
    Remembers the recent destruction (20 August 1851) of the
    Ann Alexander by a sperm whale, adding "and yet already
    has Mr. Bentley, with the assistance of that prolific writer
    Mr. Herman Melville, presented the public with a three-
    volume novel, of which the above incident forms the entire
    plot!" No tale of love is interwoven with the "strange ana"
    of which The Whale is compounded and so the term "novel" is
    perhaps inappropriate. As there was no survivor of the
    catastrophe, how did Melville or Bentley become "possessed
    of all these minute and painful details?" Reprinted in
    Doubloon, pp. 78-79.

9   ANON.   Review of Moby-Dick.   Charleston (S.C.) Southern
    Quarterly Review, NS 5 (January), 262.
        All the parts of Moby-Dick about whales or whaling will
    keep the reader's interest alive and his attention fully
    rewarded. In all other respects the book is sad stuff,
    dull and dreary, or ridiculous. Melville's Quakers are the
    wretchedest dolts and drivellers and his mad captain a
    monstrous bore. His ravings and the ravings of other
    characters and Melville himself, "meant for eloquent decla-
    mation, are such as would justify a writ de lunatico against
    all the parties." Reprinted in Norton Moby-Dick, p. 619;
    Doubloon, p. 80; Branch, p. 289.

10 ANON.   Review of The Whale.   London Bentley's Miscellany, 31
    (January), 104-105.

The Whale is certainly one of the most remarkable books
that has appeared for many years. The extraordinary character of Ahab, the forceful descriptions, the many passages
of vigorous thought and glowing fancy settle what has been
debated since the beginning of Melville's literary career--
that he is a man of the truest and most original genius.
Reprinted in Doubloon, pp. 80-81, and Rountree, p. 26.

11   ANON. Review of Moby-Dick. New Haven Church Review and
      Ecclesiastical Register, 4 (January), 627.
         People who believe in laughing, the side-splitting ex-
      plosion of genuine mirth, are referred to Moby-Dick. It is
      unquestionable that Melville (whose whole soul is rapt in
      his subject) has genius, wit, mirth, a vigorous, imaginative
      style, great command of the language, and uncommon power of
      description; he is also at times shockingly irreverent,
      without any great proof of wit, thereby repelling many he
      might otherwise amuse. Moby Dick, the presiding genius of
      the story, years ago used to be called Mocha Dick. Reprinted
      in Pollin (May 1975), pp. 3-4.

12   ANON. Review of Moby-Dick. New York Democratic Review, 30
      (January), 93.
         After his first passable works Melville's books have
      become increasingly exaggerated and increasingly dull.
      Redburn was a stupid failure, Mardi hopelessly dull, White-
      Jacket worse than either, Moby-Dick worse yet. In bombast,
      caricature, rhetorical artifice (generally as clumsy as
      ineffectual) and low attempts at humor each one of his vol-
      umes has been an advance on its predecessors. Melville
      never writes naturally; his sentiment, wit, and enthusiasm
      are all forced. He has survived his reputation; his vanity
      (his desire to be first among the book-making tribe) has
      destroyed all his chances of immortality or even of a good
      name with his own generation. Moby-Dick is recommended to
      all readers who wish to find examples of bad rhetoric, in-
      volved syntax, stilted sentiment, and incoherent English.
      Reprinted in Doubloon, pp. 83-84, and Branch, pp. 290-291.

13   ANON. Review of Moby-Dick. New York Harper's New Monthly
      Magazine, 4 (January), 277.
         Notes that the book has excited a general interest among
      the critical journals of London and quotes from the London
      Atlas review [1851.B23] as one of the most discriminating.
      Reprinted in Doubloon, pp. 81-82.

14   ANON. Review of Moby-Dick. New York Hunt's Merchants' Maga-
      zine, 26 (January), 140.

1852

> An agreeable and entertaining volume, though in some
> parts it may be rather diffuse. Reprinted in Doubloon,
> p. 82.

15   ANON. Review of Moby-Dick. New York Knickerbocker, 39
>   (January), 109.
>   In Moby-Dick Melville has taken up Mocha Dick (whose
> story appeared some years ago in the Knickerbocker) and
> made him the subject of one of his characteristic and
> striking romances. His ocean pictures are exceedingly
> graphic, his descriptions of taking the whale a succession
> of moving pictures. Reprinted in Doubloon, p. 82.

16   ANON. Review of Moby-Dick. New York Methodist Quarterly
>   Review, 34 [Fourth Series 4] (January), 154.
>   Moby-Dick is a wonderful mixture of fact and fancy, of
> information about the whale and of the wildest whimsies of
> a seething brain, displaying the same power of vivid picture-
> painting which characterizes all of Melville's other works.
> But the book contains flings at religion and even vulgar
> immoralities that render it unfit for general circulation.
> Reprinted in Doubloon, pp. 82-83.

17   ANON. Review of Moby-Dick. Philadelphia Peterson's Magazine,
>   21 (January), 84.
>   Moby-Dick is like a compound of Typee and Mardi, both a
> skillfully told narrative of sea adventures and a philosoph-
> ical romance. If it had been compressed one-half and all
> the transcendental chapters omitted, it would have been the
> best sea novel in the English language. It is nonetheless
> a very superior work, and the last three chapters are really
> beyond rivalry (the catastrophe recalling the recent news
> of a ship run down by a whale). Nowhere can so authentic
> an account of the whale be found. Reprinted in Doubloon,
> p. 84.

18   ANON. "Retrospective Survey of American Literature." London
>   Westminster Review, NS 1 (1 January), 304.
>   "The new writers who have been heard of in England are,
> Hawthorne, first and greatest;...Melville, a man of unques-
> tionable genius, who struck out for himself a new path in
> Typee, Omoo, and his last book, 'The Whale.'"

19   ANON. "Tahiti." Boston Littell's Living Age, 32 (3 January),
>   36-37.
>   Reprint of 1851.B34.

20 ANON. Review of The Book of Ballads edited by Bon Gualtier.
    New York Literary World, No. 257 (3 January), p. 7.
         Ends review, after lengthy quotation from ballads, with:
    "Shades of Typee, is not this most 'admirable fooling?'"

21 ANON. "Marks and Remarks." New York Literary World, No. 257
    (3 January), p. 9.
         In a passage on "literary celebrities" notes that
    Hawthorne has moved from Lenox to Newton, "while Herman
    Melville, close-reefed in his library at Pittsfield, is
    doubling old Saddleback and winter, with a thermometer
    below zero, it is rumored on a new literary tack for the
    public when he next emerges in Cliff street."

22 ANON. Review of Moby-Dick. To-day: A Boston Literary Journal,
    1 (10 January), 20-21.
         Reviewer has been disappointed by all of Melville's books
    after Typee; Moby-Dick is a new disappointment. Over its
    curious mixture of fact and fancy "is thrown a veil of a
    sort of dreamy philosophy and indistinct speculation just
    sufficient to obscure the value of the facts stated" with-
    out improving the quality of the tale. The parts of the
    book dealing with whales and whaling "would be of much value
    if their connexion with other parts of so totally different
    a character did not cast a shade of uncertainty over their
    accuracy." Melville also has a regrettable "loose way of
    stating matters as facts." Some of the adventures of
    Ishmael and Queequeg are narrated inimitably and are almost
    sufficient to excuse any faults in other parts of the book.
    Yet the humor of those parts where sacred things are made
    light of is revolting to good taste and may be dangerous to
    many of those most likely to read the book. Reprinted in
    Doubloon, pp. 84-86.

23 ANON. Review of Moby-Dick. Boston Littell's Living Age, 32
    (17 January), 130.
         Reprint of 1851.B36.

24 ANON. "Editorial Splinters." Boston Museum (31 January).
         Reports that Melville was once driven out of his country
    town school "by two naughty boys."

25 FRANCIS, JOHN WAKEFIELD. "Personal and Historical Reminiscences.
    From an Address before the Typographical Society." New
    York Literary World, No. 261 (31 January), pp. 91-93.
         Short passage celebrates American authors: extends "the
    cordial hand" to Melville for Typee. Reprinted in 1852.B28.

1852

26   ANON. "A Budget of Novels." <u>Dublin University Magazine</u>, 39
        (February), 220-223.
            Review of <u>The Whale</u>. The work is as strange as its
        title. "All the rules which have been hitherto understood
        to regulate the composition of works of fiction are despised
        and set at naught. Of narrative, properly so called, there
        is little or none; of love, or sentiment, or tenderness of
        any sort, there is not a particle whatever; and yet, with
        all these glaring defects, it would be in vain to deny that
        the work has interest." It "contains some scenes of stir-
        ring interest; and scattered through its motley pages the
        reader will find more curious and varied information about
        the whale...than in any other treatise, probably, extant."
        Since everyone drowns at the conclusion, how is the author
        alive to tell the story? Summary; extracts from chapters
        3 and 133. Reprinted in <u>Doubloon</u>, pp. 86-88.

27   ANON. Review of <u>Moby-Dick</u>. New Orleans <u>De Bow's Southern and
        Western Review</u>, 12 [NS 2] (February), 223.
            <u>Moby-Dick</u> is another of the attractive series of sea
        stories by Melville which English critics have extravagantly
        praised. Reprinted in <u>Doubloon</u>, pp. 88-89.

28   FRANCIS, JOHN W. "Reminiscences of Printers, Authors, and
        Booksellers in New York." New York <u>International Magazine</u>,
        5 (February), 265. Reprint of 1852.B25.

29   ANON. Review of <u>Moby-Dick</u>. Philadelphia <u>Godey's Magazine and
        Lady's Book</u>, 44 (February), 166.
            The book is a perfect literary whale, worthy of Melville's
        pen. Reprinted in <u>Doubloon</u>, p. 89.

30   ANON. Review of <u>Moby-Dick</u>. Philadelphia <u>Graham's Magazine</u>,
        40 (February), 219.
            <u>Moby-Dick</u> sparkles with the raciest qualities of
        Melville's voluble and brilliant mind, with passages of
        description and narration equal to his best, his rhetoric
        reveling and rioting in scenes of nautical adventure with
        more than usual glee and gusto. The style is dashing, head-
        long, strewn with queer and quaint ingenuities moistened
        with humor, a capital specimen of deliberate and felicitous
        recklessness in which a seeming helter-skelter movement is
        guided by real judgment; even the tasteless passages bear
        the impress of conscious and unwearied power. Melville's
        late books convey the impression of a new originality. Re-
        printed in <u>Doubloon</u>, p. 89.

31   ANON. "The American Drama." New York <u>American Review</u>, 9
        (March), 234-235.

Characterizes the present as the Age of Respectability;
Tennyson, Browning, Horne, Marsten, Carlyle, Irving,
Melville, Mathews, and Boker "are all what the world calls
respectable men." Although generally loving the gay rather
than the grave, "our men of genius" have become "the prom-
inent exponents of the leading spirit of the age." Concludes that "a literature which boasts Cooper, Hawthorne,
and Mayo, among its novelists; Poe as a critic; Halleck,
Dana, Bryant, Stoddard, Wallace, and Longfellow, as poets;
Willis, Irving, Melville, and Emerson as essayists...has
more to show for her last thirty years than any other nation whose first century is not yet accomplished." Reprinted
in Yannella (1976), p. 14.

32   ANON. "Literary Notices." New York Harper's New Monthly
     Magazine, 4 (April), 711.
          Reprints first paragraph of 1851.B30. Reprinted in
     Doubloon, pp. 89-90.

33   ANON. Review of Recollections of a Journey through Tartary
     by E. R. Huc. New York Literary World, No. 271 (10 April),
     p. 261.
          Huc understands telling a story and his yarn, "though
     from the most opposite point of view of a Roman Catholic
     Missionary, and from the antipodes of the globe, reminds
     us not a little of the mode of telling of Mr. Melville's
     Typee."

34   ANON. "Chronicle of Passing Events." New York North American
     Miscellany and Dollar Magazine, 4 (June), 213.
          "Our authors have been for the last two or three years
     building themselves substantial edifices at a very encour-
     aging rate.... Melville has bought a farm at Stockbridge.
     Irving and Paulding have splendid seats on the Hudson."
     Gives details of contemporary authors' book profits, but
     not Melville's.

35   ANON. "Nathaniel Hawthorne." London Eliza Cook's Journal,
     7 (19 June), 121-124.
          Notes the great popularity of American books in England;
     asks "in Fiction, can we produce any sea novels equal to
     those of Cooper and Herman Melville?"

36   ANON. "The Literary World." New York Herald (29 July), p. 7.
          Gossip item, reporting that in Pierre Melville is said to
     have dressed up and exhibited in Berkshire some of the an-
     cient and most repulsive inventions of the George Walker
     and Ann Radcliffe sort.

1852

37 ANON. Review of Pierre. Albany Evening Journal (31 July),
    p. 2.
        Pierre is an attractive character everyone will wish to
    know and his history is full of stirring incidents.

38 ANON. Notice of Pierre. Boston Daily Evening Transcript
    (2 August).
        Has not yet had leisure to discover how successfully
    Melville has ventured on a regular story of life and love
    and tragic personal adventure on shore.

39 ANON. Review of Pierre. Lansingburgh (N.Y.) Gazette
    (3 August).
        Pierre is a fine character, well conceived and admirably
    sustained. The book is full of sterling incidents and fine
    passages. Frailty and vice are delineated with energy and
    acuteness and the most glowing language. Pierre places
    Melville indisputably in the highest list of eloquent
    writers.

40 ANON. Review of Pierre. Boston Post (4 August), p. 1.
        Melville might be a vivid and brilliant author if he
    chose to criticize himself and "lop off the puerility, con-
    ceit, affectation and insanity" which he exhibited in Mardi
    and Moby-Dick. But Pierre is perhaps the craziest fiction
    extant. It has scenes and descriptions of unmistakable
    power, vivid characters, however false to nature, and many
    of the thoughts reveal an intense and cultivated intellect.
    "But the amount of utter trash in the volume is almost
    infinite--trash of conception, execution, dialogue and
    sentiment." The plot is a tissue of unnatural horrors.
    Even considered as a prose poem the book "might be supposed
    to emanate from a lunatic hospital." Melville "has produced
    more and sadder trash than any other man of undoubted abil-
    ity among us." Reprinted in 1852.B48; 1852.B62; Recognition,
    pp. 48-50; Branch, pp. 294-296.

41 ANON. Notice of Pierre. Hartford Daily Courant (4 August).
        After slight examination Pierre appears to be very
    exciting. The style is strange, "not at all natural and
    too much in the mystic, transcendental vein of affectation
    that characterizes some of our best writers."

42 ANON. Notice of Pierre. Baltimore American & Commercial Daily
    Advertiser (6 August).
        Melville has produced "a regular romance of love and its
    dangers and difficulties, and of bold and successful daring."
    Without having read the book "entirely through," the

reviewer has no doubt that it will be found quite as entertaining as Melville's previous popular works.

43   ANON. Review of Pierre. Boston Daily Advertiser (7 August),
      p. 2.
          Melville has taken his hero from the country's very
      highest aristocracy, so high one hardly knows where to look
      for it, and the scene is entirely on land.

44   ANON. Review of Pierre. New York Journal of Commerce
      (7 August).
          The mechanical execution of Pierre is very fair, and
      the style of writing vivacious and attractive. Reprinted
      in Parker (October 1972), p. 4.

*45   ANON. Review of Pierre. New York Atlas (8 August).
          Cited in Hetherington (1961), p. 230.

*46   ANON. Review of Pierre. Albany Argus (10 August).
          Cited in Hetherington (1961), p. 230.

47   ANON. Review of Pierre. New York Commercial Advertiser
      (11 August).
          The highest literary reputation would be demolished by
      the publication of a few volumes of such trash as Pierre,
      "the plot of which is monstrous, the characters unnatural,
      and the style a kind of prose run mad." Reprinted in Parker
      (October 1972), p. 4.

48   ANON. Review of Pierre. Philadelphia Public Ledger
      (11 August).
          Reprints most of 1852.B40.

49   ANON. Review of The Men of the Time. New York Literary World,
      No. 289 (14 August), pp. 99-101.
          Reprints Melville entry of 1852.B1. Notes that its
      "matter-of-fact account" will show that Melville's various
      romances "rest on a more substantial basis than has been
      sometimes supposed."

50   ANON. Notice of Pierre. New York Sun (16 August).
          Recommends Pierre to readers without having read it,
      supposing it to be "a love story to the full," though not
      one of "the every day sickening sort" but "daintily told
      and in merry cheerful language." Reprinted in Parker
      (October 1972), p. 4.

1852

51   ANON. Review of Pierre. Springfield (Mass.) Republican
     (16 August).
          "Genteel hifalutin, painful, though ingenious involutions
     of language, and high-flown incidental detail" characterize
     Pierre "to the uprooting of our affection for the graceful
     and simple writer" of Typee and Omoo. The new Melville dis-
     plays more subtleness of thought, more elaborateness of man-
     ner (or mannerism), and a higher range of imagination, but
     at a sad sacrifice of simplicity and popular appreciation.
     Reprinted in Branch, p. 296.

52   ANON. Review of Pierre. Boston Daily Evening Traveller
     (17 August), p. 1.
          Pierre is even more unnatural and improbable than
     Melville's previous productions, the interest extremely
     disagreeable and tragical in character. But throughout,
     the book bears the marks of Melville's unquestionable genius.
     The plot is complex and involved, but on the whole skill-
     fully managed; the characters, though exceedingly unnatural,
     are held with a firm grasp.

53   ANON. Review of Pierre. Washington National Era (19 August),
     p. 134.
          Pierre is a mass of incongruities, ambiguities, hetero-
     geneities, absurdities, and absolute impossibilities, the
     largest part a slough of metaphysical speculation; the
     characters are absurdly paradoxical and greatly overdrawn,
     and the incidents impossible in real life. It contains a
     vast deal of power but amounts to nothing. Melville is
     more at home in the intricacies of a ship's rigging than
     amid the subtleties of psychological phenomena. Reprinted
     in Branch, p. 297.

54   ANON. Review of Pierre. New York Albion, NS 11 (21 August),
     405.
          Pierre is a dead failure, an objectionable tale clumsily
     told. Melville works up his situations cleverly enough to
     the point where Pierre has to choose between Lucy and Isabel,
     but he might have hit upon "a less Frenchified mode" of
     carrying us through the conflict and bringing about the
     catastrophe. He heaps up horrors and trash to the last.
     In several places "the ambiguities are still further thick-
     ened by hints at that fearfullest of all human crimes, which
     one shrinks from naming." Lucy does not differ much "from
     some scores of Lucies in your book acquaintance, if it be
     extensive"; it is hard to decide if Isabel is "more ridicu-
     lously sublime or sublimely ridiculous." There is scarcely
     a page of dialogue that is not absurd to the last degree.

Melville should wash out the remembrance of Pierre by
writing a fresh romance of the ocean without a line of
dialogue in it. Lengthy summary. Reprinted in part in
Branch, pp. 298-299.

55   ANON. Review of Pierre. New York Literary World, 11
      (21 August), 118-120.
         Melville's purpose, vaguely hinted, "seems to be to
      illustrate the possible antagonism of a sense of duty,
      conceived in the heat and impetuosity of youth, to all the
      recognised laws of social morality; and to exhibit a con-
      flict between the virtues." The work violates truth and
      nature, "the germinal principles of all true art."
      Melville's aim, perhaps, has been "not to delineate life
      and character as they are or may possibly be, but as they
      are not and cannot be." The "most immoral moral of the
      story, if it has any moral at all, seems to be the imprac-
      ticability of virtue"; the "Chronometricals and
      Horologicals" chapter, "if it has any meaning at all,
      simply means that virtue and religion are only for the
      gods and not to be attempted by man." But "ordinary novel
      readers will never unkennel this loathsome suggestion." In
      the sacrilegious supersensuousness with which the holy rela-
      tions of the family are described, an incestuous relation
      between Pierre and Isabel seems to be vaguely hinted at.
      Cites "incoherencies of thought" and "infelicities of ex-
      pression"; only fragmentary elements of beauty. Lengthy
      summary; extracts from Book 6, chapter 3, and Book 2,
      chapter 4. Reprinted in part in 1852.B58; Willett, pp. 2-3;
      Branch, pp. 300-302; reprinted in Recognition, pp. 51-56.

56   ANON. Review of Pierre. Morning Courier and New-York
      Enquirer (21 August).
         There are passages in Pierre that absolutely glitter
      with genius, scenes and portraitures that nothing but the
      most extraordinary skill could execute. Yet it abounds
      with defects and even positive deformities. It would be
      difficult to match its extravagant ideas and absurd forms
      of expression. Reprinted in Parker (October 1972), p. 5.

57   ANON. Review of Pierre. Philadelphia Church's Bizarre for
      Fireside and Wayside, NS Part 10 (21 August), p. 307.
         Pierre is an original book, with depth, passion, even
      genius; but it is "wild, wayward, overstrained in thought
      and sentiment, and most unhealthy in spirit." In style it
      is "barbarously outré, unnatural and clumsy beyond measure."
      No true, fluent inspiration produced these 500 pages.

1852

58 ANON. Review of <u>Pierre</u>. New York <u>Evening Mirror</u> (27 August).
      Quotes summary of <u>Pierre</u> from 1852.B55. The book evokes
    alternate feelings of pleasure and disgust. It is marked
    by great intellectual ability, and some of the descriptive
    parts are transcendantly beautiful. But the metaphysics
    are abominable; the whole tone of the work is morbid and
    unhealthy; the action and plot are monstrously unnatural;
    and there is no natural sequence in the accumulated misery
    that overwhelms every character.

59 ANON. Review of <u>Pierre</u>. New York <u>Spirit of the Times</u>, 22
      (28 August), 336.
      <u>Pierre</u> outstrips all Melville's former works and is
    quite equal to <u>Moby-Dick</u>. It is certainly one of the most
    exciting and interesting books ever published. Reprinted in
    Flanagan, p. 68.

60 ANON. Review of <u>Pierre</u>. Richmond <u>Southern Literary Messenger</u>,
      18 (September), 574-575.
      Lengthy summary. Points out inconsistencies in Pierre
    and concludes that Melville's "theory is wrong. It should
    be the object of fiction to delineate life and character
    either as it is around us, or as it ought to be.... Pierre
    never did exist, and it is very certain that he never ought
    to exist." Consequently Melville has deviated from the
    legitimate line of the novelist. Bad as a work of art,
    <u>Pierre</u> is infinitely worse in its moral tendency: Melville
    seeks to enlist our sympathies with Pierre for the reason
    that throughout all his follies and crimes his sense of
    duty struggles with and overcomes every law of religion and
    morality. <u>Pierre</u> must be left unbought "if one does not
    desire to look at virtue and religion with the eye of
    Mephistopheles, or, at least, through a haze of <u>ambiguous</u>
    meaning, in which they may readily be taken for their oppo-
    sites." Melville seems to have been writing under an un-
    lucky star since <u>Typee</u> and has written himself out. Re-
    printed in <u>Recognition</u>, pp. 56-59, and Branch, pp. 304-307.

61 ANON. "The Editor's Shanty." Toronto <u>Ango-American Magazine</u>,
      1 (September), 273.
      Unfavorable review in the form of a humorous dialogue.
    <u>Pierre</u> is a gigantic blunder, with hardly one redeeming
    feature. Reprinted in Branch, pp. 303-304.

62 ANON. Review of <u>Pierre</u>. Boston <u>Littell's Living Age</u>, 34
      (4 September), 480.
      Reprint of 1852.B40.

63   ANON. Review of Pierre. New York Home Journal (4 September).
     Melville's original power "is manifest in the very
     eccentricity of his invention. The story is not artistically
     contrived, but it is psychologically suggestive. It is sub-
     tle, metaphysical, often profound, and has passages of be-
     wildering intensity." Reprinted in Parker (October 1972),
     p. 5.

64   ANON. "Herman Melville Crazy." New York Day Book
     (7 September).
     Quotes judgment of a "critical friend" that Pierre
     "appeared to be composed of the ravings and reveries of a
     madman," and reports having learned that Melville "was
     really supposed to be deranged" and that "his friends were
     taking measures to place him under treatment." Concludes:
     "We hope one of the earliest precautions will be to keep
     him stringently secluded from pen and ink."

65   'TACONIC.' "Literary Correspondence. Homes of Literary Men
     in Berkshire, Mass." New York Norton's Literary Gazette
     and Publishers' Circular, 2 (15 September), 167-168.
     Brief comments on several Berkshire literary figures.
     Notes that the author of Typee and Omoo lives within sight
     of Dr. Holmes's house.

66   ANON. Review of Pierre. New York Herald (18 September).
     Pierre is one "long brain-muddling, soul-bewildering
     ambiguity" without beginning or end, "a labyrinth without
     a clue," the "dream of a distempered stomach, disordered by
     a hasty supper on half-cooked pork chops." It is uncertain
     whether Pierre's actions are those of a lunatic or are
     "mere forms of eccentricity, outward symptoms of the genius
     latent within." The murder and suicides in the book are
     appalling to contemplate. Melville will rue his desertion
     of the forecastle for the drawing room: mere "analytical
     description of sentiment, mere wordy anatomy of the heart"
     are not enough for the modern novel, which requires deeds
     and room for the reader to exercise his own judgment. No
     book "was ever such a compendium of Carlyle's faults, with
     so few of his redeeming qualities" as Pierre: it has "the
     same German English--the same transcendental flights of
     fancy--the same abrupt starts--the same incoherent ravings,
     and unearthly visions." Melville has violated nature in
     his departures from the style of ordinary dialogue--a fault
     attributable perhaps to Martin Farquhar Tupper. He should
     study the classic writers of English and the plain, honest
     Saxon style. Reprinted in Branch, pp. 308-312.

1852

67 ANON. Review of <u>Pierre</u>. Charleston (S.C.) <u>Southern Quarterly</u>
   <u>Review</u>, 22 [NS 6] (October), 532.
    Fears that Melville has gone "clean daft" and recommends
   he be put in ward. <u>Pierre</u> is a very mad book in which the
   <u>dramatis personae</u> are all as mad as March hatters.

68 ANON. "National Humor: A Fragment." New York <u>American Whig</u>
   <u>Review</u>, 16 (October), 311.
    Melville named in list (which includes Irving, Lowell,
   Whittier, Hawthorne, Donald Grant Mitchell) of Americans
   who have "originated a new style of humor." Reprinted in
   Yannella (1976), pp. 14-15.

69 ANON. Review of <u>Pierre</u>. New York <u>Hunt's Merchants' Magazine</u>,
   27 (October), 526.
    <u>Pierre</u> is more imaginative than Melville's previous
   works but perhaps not as interesting as some of them. It
   aims to present the workings of an over-sensitive spirit.
   The story is well told as usual. Reprinted in Pollin
   (April 1975), p. 60.

70 ANON. Review of <u>Pierre</u>. Philadelphia <u>Godey's Magazine and</u>
   <u>Lady's Book</u>, 45 (October), 390.
    Suggests Melville may have been satirizing the ridiculous
   pretensions of some modern literati in <u>Pierre</u> and parodies
   its style, finding in "the insignificant significances of
   that deftly-stealing and wonderfully-serpentining melodious-
   ness" an "infinite, unbounded, inexpressible mysteriousness
   of nothingness." Melville has strangely mistaken his powers in leaving his native element, the ocean. Reprinted in
   Falk (Grove), p. 86; Falk (Twayne), p. 98; Branch,
   pp. 312-313.

71 ANON. Review of <u>Pierre</u>. Philadelphia <u>Graham's Magazine</u>, 41
   (October), 445.
    None of Melville's works equals <u>Pierre</u> in force, subtlety
   of thinking and unity of purpose. Many of the scenes are
   wrought with great vigor and Melville describes with mas--
   terly distinctness "some of the most evanescent phenomena
   of morbid emotions." The book's merit is in clearly presenting the psychology of Pierre's madness. But the spirit
   pervading the whole book is intolerably unhealthy. In
   attempting to combine the peculiarities of Poe and Hawthorne,
   Melville has produced only "a powerfully unpleasant caricature of morbid thought and passion." A provoking perversion
   of talent and waste of power. Reprinted in Branch, p. 313.

72 ANON. "Fatal Occurrence." New York <u>Lantern</u>, 2 (2 October),
    127.
        Humorous item: report of an intelligent young man who
    was seen to "deliberately purchase" a copy of <u>Pierre</u> and
    who "has, of course, not since been heard of."

73 ANON. Review of <u>Pierre</u>. New York <u>Lantern</u>, 2 (16 October),
    153.
        Melville should either resign his pen altogether or
    choose different subjects; he "must not dance on the tight
    rope between morality and indecency longer--dullness is
    better than meretriciousness."

74 ANON. Review of <u>Pierre</u>. New York <u>American Whig Review</u>, 16
    [NS 10] (November), 446-454.
        Long, sardonic, at times outraged, summary and analysis.
    <u>Pierre</u> is a bad book, affected in dialogue, unnatural in
    conception, repulsive in plot, inartistic in construction,
    its style "disfigured by every paltry affectation of the
    worst German school," its ideas "perfectly unparalleled
    for earnest absurdity." Melville "dares to outrage every
    principle of virtue" and "strikes with an impious, though,
    happily weak hand, at the very foundations of society."
    <u>Pierre</u>'s feelings toward Isabel "can never be any thing
    but repulsive to a well constituted mind." Melville should
    have known that certain ideas are so repulsive to "the gen-
    eral mind" that they are kept out of sight, while every-
    thing "that might be supposed to even collaterally suggest
    them is carefully shrouded in a decorous darkness."
    Melville's style is probably the most extraordinary thing
    an American press ever beheld, particularly in its "boldness"
    with metaphors and tendency to add "est" and "ness" to
    "every word to which they have no earthly right to belong."
    <u>Pierre</u> proves that Melville is wholly unfitted for the task
    of writing wholesome fictions. The uncouth and mysterious
    syllables in the titles of his earlier works probably had
    much to do with their success. Extract from Book 2, chapter
    3. Reprinted in part in Branch, pp. 314-321, and Rountree,
    pp. 27-30.

75 ANON. Review of <u>Anglo-American Literature and Manners</u> by
    Philarète Chasles. New York <u>Harper's New Monthly Magazine</u>
    5 (November), 857.
        Chasles's strictures on Melville and other American
    authors are often acute--more acute than profound or con-
    vincing--and not unfriendly to American genius.
    [<u>See</u> 1852.B2.]

1852

76   ANON. Notice of <u>Pierre</u>. New York <u>National Magazine</u>, 1
      (November), 476.
          Notes the severity of the reviews of <u>Pierre</u> and quotes
      briefly from a "Boston paper" which pronounces it "abomin-
      able trash--an emanation from a lunatic rather than the
      writing of a sober man."

77   ANON. Review of <u>Pierre</u>. London <u>Athenaeum</u>, No. 1308
      (20 November), pp. 1265-1266.
          <u>Pierre</u> is second-hand Germanism, with nothing American
      or original in its pages, a diffuse dose of transcendental-
      ism. Its plot is one of its inexplicable ambiguities, the
      style is a prolonged series of spasms, and the characters
      are a marrowless tribe of phantoms. "We take up novels to
      be amused--not bewildered,--in search of pleasure for the
      mind--not in pursuit of cloudy metaphysics...." Reprinted
      in <u>Recognition</u>, pp. 60-62, and Branch, p. 322.

78   ANON. "Whales and Whale Fishing." London <u>Eliza Cook's Journal</u>,
      8 (11 December), 106-109.
          Article ends by recommending readers "to peruse the great
      Whale Epic of Herman Melville--certainly one of the most
      curious, instructive, imaginative, and graphic books of
      the present day." Reprinted in 1853.B10.

<u>1853 A BOOKS - NONE</u>

<u>1853 B SHORTER WRITINGS</u>

1   ANON. <u>Men of the Time or Sketches of Living Notables</u>. London:
      David Bogue, pp. 310-311.
          Reprints 1852.B1 and adds that <u>Pierre</u> is an unhealthy
      mystic romance, which met with a decided non-success. Re-
      printed, with slight alteration, in 1856, 1857 [<u>see</u> 1857.B1],
      and 1859.

2   GERSTAECKER, F. <u>Narrative of a Journey Round the World</u>.
      Vol. 2. London: Hurst and Blackett, p. 209.
          Visits what he believes is "the same valley that Hermann
      Melville has described so well in his 'Adventures in the
      South Seas'" and hears of a couple of white men who lived in
      the neighborhood (at Emao) and "raised potatoes."

3   HANNAY, JAMES. "The Life and Genius of Edgar Allan Poe," in
      <u>The Poetical Works of Edgar Allan Poe</u>. Ed. James Hannay.
      London: Addey and Co., p. xii.
          Notes that English readers are beginning to get acquainted
      with American writers like Emerson and Hawthorne "who are

really national." Adds "from whom but an American could we
have expected such a book as we had the other day in the
'Whale' of Herman Melville,--such a fresh, daring book--
wild, and yet true,--with its quaint, spiritual portraits
looking ancient and also fresh,--Puritanism, I may say,
kept fresh in the salt water over there and looking out
living upon us once more! These writers one sees, at all
events, have our old English virtue of Pluck. They think
what they please and say what they think."

4   HUNT, T. DWIGHT. The Past and Present of the Sandwich Islands.
    San Francisco: Whitton, Towne & Co., pp. 28-29.
        The picture in books like Typee and Omoo of the luxuries
    and liberties, nobility and dignity of barbarous tribes is
    as false as it is fair.

5   [STEVENS, ABEL]. "The Editor's Table." New York National
    Magazine, 2 (January), 87-88.
        Essay on Hawthorne. Melville's "late miserable abortion,"
    Pierre, included in list of examples of the "morbid propen-
    sity for morbid characters--bizarre anomalies of human na-
    ture," which seems to be developing in American literature.

6   [GODWIN, PARKE]. "The Homes of American Authors." New York
    Putnam's Monthly, 1 (January), 23-30.
        Melville named with other writers who have "reaped large
    rewards from their publications," and with others who are
    no mere imitators of European writers. He is also part of
    "a new and vigorous tendency" in narratives of travel.

7   ANON. "Literature, Books of the Week, Etc." New York
    Literary World, No. 310 (8 January), p. 24.
        "Captain Mayne Reid has written a new work for youth,
    'The Boy Hunters, or Adventures in search of a White Buf-
    falo'--as Captain Ahab went in search of a white whale."
    (Complete Melville reference.)

8   [O'BRIEN, FITZ-JAMES]. "Our Young Authors." New York Putnam's
    Monthly, 1 (February), 155-164.
        Impressionistic survey. After sea novels had been run
    into the ground by Marryat, Chamier, and Cooper, Melville
    produced a brilliant new amalgam of fresh land scenery and
    clever ship life, the contrast of sea and shore episodes
    making one of his greatest charms. Melville "is essentially
    exoterical in feeling. Matter is his god. His dreams are
    material. His philosophy is sensual." His language is
    rich and heavy; he has a barbaric love of ornament, and
    his sensual pleasure in words frequently leads him to write

at random. Melville can deal capably with events of matter-
of-fact life, but his sensual power holds the secret of his
first successes. All of his works have their merits, except for the wild, inflated, repulsive Pierre. For all its
defects in taste and style, there is something very charming about Mardi, with its deliberate plagiarisms of
Sir Thomas Browne; the philosophical parts are the worst:
when Melville condescends to be intelligible, he is stale
and trite. White-Jacket, a pure sea book, but very clever,
has less of Melville's faults than almost any of his works
and is distinguished for clear, wholesome satire, and a
manly style. His later books are a decided falling-off,
Pierre being a mad mosaic of all his many affectations of
style, with a bad moral. His hard-earned fame in jeopardy,
Melville needs to diet himself on Addison for a year or two
and avoid Sir Thomas Browne. Reprinted in part in Recognition, pp. 62-68; Willett, p. 3; Branch, pp. 323-329.

9   FORGUES, E.-D. "Moby Dick." Paris Revue des Deux Mondes, 1
       (1 February), 491-515.
          Long summary. Admires Melville's talent, wit, invention,
       and picturesque style, but warns him to be on his guard in
       the use of eccentricities, purely external to his subject,
       and which consist in a huge prodigality of bizarre titles,
       unlooked for digressions, out of place bibliography, and
       superfluous erudition. Melville is imbued, perhaps more
       than necessary, with the philosophy of which Emerson is the
       apostle. Reprinted in part in Doubloon, pp. 93-94.

10   ANON. "Whales and Whale Fishing." Cincinnati Pen and Pencil,
       1 (26 February), 267-270.
          Reprint of 1852.B78.

11   ANON. "Literature, Books of the Week, Etc." New York
       Literary World, No. 320 (19 March), p. 228.
          Notes French translation of Moby-Dick in New York
       Courier des Etats-Unis [unlocated] and quotes from commen-
       tary of translator, E.-D. Forgues.

12   ANON. "A Missionary wanted for Marquesas." Honolulu Friend
       (1 April), p. 28.
          Hopes a missionary will visit the Marquesas islands, in
       spite of Melville's picture of the people as living in a
       happy, natural society and certain to be corrupted if mis-
       sionaries go there. Relates anecdote of a joker who ordered
       50 copies of Typee for circulation in Honolulu, "but to com-
       plete the joke, his agent sent out the '2d' instead of the
       '1st' edition, which was expurgated of nearly every

paragraph that breathed an anti-missionary spirit. The
books lay for a long time unsold on the shelves of the
auctioneer's store!"

13 ANON. "Literature, Books of the Week, Etc." New York
     Literary World, No. 322 (2 April), p. 268.
         Notes the "abstract" of Moby-Dick in 1853.B9.

14 ANON. Review of The Captive in Patagonia by Benjamin Franklin
     Bourne. New York Literary World, No. 323 (9 April), p. 286.
         Notes that Patagonia "is not exactly a Typee. There are
     no damsels delicately arrayed in flowers there, and philo-
     sophic Melvillean savages don't lounge about there with the
     gentlemanly ease of Broadway club-men."

15 ANON. Cincinnati Pen and Pencil, 1 (16 April), 500.
         Claims that "the present system of literary piracy" dis-
     courages authors in the United States from writing books on
     which a lasting reputation could be founded. "Hawthorne and
     Melville are our only writers of elaborate fiction...."

16 ANON. Review of The Captive in Patagonia by Benjamin Franklin
     Bourne. Cincinnati Pen and Pencil, 1 (23 April), 539.
         "On the whole, the 'Captive' is a sort of dismal Typee
     or Omoo, though the subject is very unattractive compared
     to those in which Herman Melville revelled of old.... It
     seems to us that 'the natives' are very much alike in all
     books of travels, that is to say they are savages in appear-
     ance, and in other respects incomprehensible. However, we
     would rather meet the swimming girls of Typee than the greasy
     thieves of Patagonia, even between the covers of a volume."

17 ANON. "Literature, Books of the Week, Etc." New York
     Literary World, No. 326 (30 April), p. 356.
         Notes story in London Household Words, No. 159, of
     Daniel Dash, a whaler shipwrecked in the Marquesas, taken
     prisoner, and tattooed by the "savages"; he "encounters
     pretty much the same observations of life and manners re-
     corded by Herman Melville."

18 ANON. "Where is our Literature?" Cincinnati Pen and Pencil,
     1 (21 May), 662.
         Article on the dearth of original literature. "Where are
     the new novelists? We cannot live on one romance by
     Hawthorne, and half a one by Melville per annum."

19 'SIR NATHANIEL.' "American Authorship. No. IV--Herman
     Melville." London New Monthly Magazine, 98 (July), 300-308.

1853

Survey. Values <u>Typee</u> for its "strange visions of out-
landish things," its incidents and portrait gallery of
natives, <u>Omoo</u> for its lively sketches of ship and ship's
company; but <u>Mardi</u> bores. <u>Redburn</u> was an improvement, with
good sketches, but is "prosy, bald, and eventless," as
deficient in romance and adventure as <u>Mardi</u> was overfraught
with them. The adventures of <u>White-Jacket</u> are detailed
with the eager vivacity and sometimes unlicensed extravagance that are characteristic of Melville. <u>The Whale</u> contains much vigorous description, much wild power, many
striking details, but the effect is marred throughout by
an extravagant treatment of the subject; the style is maniacal. There is no lack of rude power and character in Ahab's
"presentment," but it is spoiled "by the Cambyses' vein in
which he dissipates his vigour," raving "by the hour in a
lingo borrowed from Rabelais, Carlyle, Emerson, newspapers
transcendental and transatlantic, and the magnificent
proems of our Christmas pantomimes." Melville is two men
rolled into one--"the one sensible, sagacious, observant,
graphic, and producing admirable matter--the other maunder-
ing, drivelling, subject to paroxysms, cramps, and total
collapse, and penning exceeding many pages of unnacountable
'bosh.'" <u>Pierre</u> is his worst production. Reprinted in
1853.B21; 1853.B23; 1853.B24; reprinted in part in Norton
<u>Moby-Dick</u>, pp. 619-621; <u>Recognition</u>, pp. 69-71; <u>Doubloon</u>,
pp. 94-96; Branch, pp. 330-336.

20   'ANTHONY AUTOGRAPH, ESQ.' "A Stroll through New Amsterdam."
      New York <u>Literary World</u>, No. 341 (13 August), p. 40.
         Loose paraphrase of short passage in <u>Moby-Dick</u>, chapter
      1.

21   'SIR NATHANIEL.' "American Authorship--Herman Melville."
      Boston <u>Littell's Living Age</u>, 38 (20 August), 481-486.
         Reprint of 1853.B19.

*22   ANON. "Pittsfield Portraits." Pittsfield (Mass.) <u>Berkshire</u>
      <u>County Eagle</u> (26 August).
         Short paragraph noting that author Melville is a resident
      of Pittsfield, to be seen driving an old brown lumber wagon
      with an old horse; he is unassuming, but very popular.
      Cited in <u>Log</u>, p. 479.

23   'SIR NATHANIEL.' "Herman Melville." New York <u>Eclectic Maga-</u>
      <u>zine</u>, 30 (September), 46-52.
         Reprint of 1853.B19.

24   'SIR NATHANIEL.' "American Authorship. No. IV.--Herman
     Melville." Augusta (Ga.) Southern Eclectic Magazine, 1
     (November), 181-186.
          Reprint of 1853.B19.

25   ANON. "Literature, Books of the Week, Etc." New York
     Literary World, No. 356 (26 November), p. 278.
          "Cock-A-Doodle-Doo!" (in the December issue of Harper's
     New Monthly Magazine) "is an imaginative, descriptive, sen-
     timental paper, dramatically moralizing in a northern New
     England landscape, the sound of the farmyard trumpeter--in
     a strain for humor and poetry which would make merry the
     heart of old Dan Chaucer. It is not at all difficult to
     recognise, in this paper, the best qualities of one of the
     foremost of American writers. Herman Melville never was in
     better trim than in this resonant 'article.'"

26   ANON. "The Missions of Polynesia." London Quarterly Review,
     94 (December), 80-122.
          Passage on the Marquesas (p. 107) notes that Melville
     has made many better acquainted with the islanders than
     more authentic narratives might have done, for whatever
     amount of romance there may be in Typee and Omoo he
     describes scenes and life with which he is evidently famil-
     iar. Remembers Fayaway's pair of tattooed epaulettes.

27   ANON. "Literature, Books of the Week, Etc." New York
     Literary World, No. 357 (3 December), p. 295.
          Notes that "Mr. Melville's 'Bartleby, the Scrivener,' a
     Poeish tale, with an infusion of more natural sentiment,
     is concluded," in the December issue of Putnam's Monthly.

1854 A BOOKS - NONE

1854 B SHORTER WRITINGS

1   ELWES, ROBERT. A Sketcher's Tour Round the World. 2nd ed.
     London: Hurst and Blackett, pp. 222-223.
          Elwes was a passenger on the same vessel sailing from
     Honolulu to Papeete as "Dr. Johnston," who was "excessively
     angry" at Melville's description of him in Omoo and "always
     threatened an action against Mr. Murray for publishing it."

2   PERKINS, EDWARD T. Na Motu: or, Reef-Rovings in the South
     Seas. New York: Pudney & Russell, pp. 321-323.
          Perkins meets the carpenter in Omoo (Ch. 76), now married
     to his native girl and somewhat displeased by Melville's
     portrayal of him.

1854

3   ANON. Notice of "The Encantadas." New York <u>Evening Post</u>
     (14 February).
        Looks forward to "another of those Pacific elysiums,"
     which "the oriental imagination" of the author of <u>Typee</u>
     can so richly reproduce, with the forthcoming publication
     of "The Encantadas" in the next issue of <u>Putnam's Monthly</u>.
     Melville "has awakened from that uneasy sleep, during which
     his genius was disturbed by such distempered dreams" as
     <u>Mardi</u> and "frightful nightmares" like <u>Pierre</u>. Reprinted
     in 1854.B4.

4   ANON. Pittsfield (Mass.) <u>Berkshire County Eagle</u> (24 February).
     Reprint of 1854.B3.

*5   ANON. Review of "The Encantadas." Pittsfield (Mass.) <u>Berkshire
     County Eagle</u> (10 March).
        Cited in <u>Log</u>, p. 485.

*6   ANON. Notice of "The Encantadas." Pittsfield (Mass.)
     <u>Berkshire County Eagle</u> (7 April).
        Cited in <u>Log</u>, p. 486.

7   ANON. "Life in An American Man-O'-War." London <u>National
     Miscellany</u>, 3 (May), 100–109.
        Mainly a "brief digest" of information given in <u>White-
     Jacket</u>, which is "a perfectly reliable and conscientiously
     written picture of the life of an American man-o'-war's
     crew," though Melville occasionally indulges in eccentrici-
     ties of imagination; "so far as graphic and appropriate
     language is concerned, there is no living author who can
     treat such subjects in a style at all approachable to
     Melville."

8   ANON. Notice of "The Encantadas." New York <u>American
     Phrenological Journal</u>, 19 (May), 120.
        The continuation of this work, "believed to be from the
     pen of Herman Melville," is among the more notable articles
     in the excellent April issue of <u>Putnam's Monthly</u>.

*9   ANON. "Notice of "The Encantadas." Pittsfield (Mass.)
     <u>Berkshire County Eagle</u> (4 May).
        Cited in <u>Log</u>, p. 487.

*10 LOWELL, JAMES RUSSELL. Letter to Charles F. Briggs. New York
     <u>Putnam's Monthly Magazine</u> (12 May).
        Cited in Ricks and Adams, p. 201.

11   ANON. Notice of "Poor Man's Pudding and Rich Man's Crumbs."
New York <u>Citizen</u> (10 June).
    Comments that the story, in the June issue of <u>Harper's
Monthly</u>, is "a somewhat foolish, but no doubt highly in-
structive tale."

*12 ANON. Notice of <u>Israel Potter</u> serial. New York <u>Commercial
Advertiser</u> (3 July).
    Cited in Mailloux and Parker, p. 61.

*13 ANON. Notice of <u>Israel Potter</u> serial. New York <u>Evangelist</u>
(6 July).
    Cited in Mailloux and Parker, p. 61.

*14 ANON. Notice of <u>Israel Potter</u> serial. Pittsfield (Mass.)
<u>Berkshire County Eagle</u> (7 July).
    Cited in <u>Log</u>, p. 490.

*15 ANON. Pittsfield (Mass.) <u>Berkshire County Eagle</u> (21 July).
    Reprints item from Honolulu <u>Friend</u>, 6 May 1854, on the
capture of the whale which sank the <u>Ann Alexander</u> and comments that Moby Dick is "tuk." Cited in <u>Log</u>, p. 490.

*16 ANON. Notice of <u>Israel Potter</u> serial. <u>Morning Courier and
New-York Enquirer</u> (after July 31).
    Cited in <u>Log</u>, pp. 490-491.

17   ANON. "New Publications." New York <u>Evangelist</u> (3 August).
    Notes the continuation of Melville's "fine tale of
Israel Potter" in the August issue of <u>Putnam's Monthly</u>.

*18 ANON. Notice of <u>Israel Potter</u> serial. Pittsfield (Mass.)
<u>Berkshire County Eagle</u> (25 August).
    Cited in <u>Log</u>, p. 491.

19   ANON. Notice of <u>Israel Potter</u> serial. <u>Morning Courier and
New-York Enquirer</u> (29 August).
    The continuation of the serial in the September issue of
<u>Putnam's Monthly</u> "preserves the direct simplicity of style
which has thus far marked it." Reprinted in <u>Log</u>, p. 491.

20   ANON. "Serials for September." New York <u>Citizen</u>
(2 September), p. 555.
    Melville "is reaping fresh honors" in his <u>Israel Potter</u>.

21   ANON. Notice of <u>Israel Potter</u> serial. <u>Morning Courier and
New-York Enquirer</u> (30 September).
    The serial "is continued with unflagging interest" in
the October issue of <u>Putnam's Monthly</u>.

1854

*22 ANON. Notice of <u>Israel Potter</u> serial. New York <u>Citizen</u>
    (4 November).
        Cited in Mailloux and Parker, p. 61.

23 ANON. Review of <u>Na Motu: or, Reef-Rovings in the Pacific</u> by
    Edward T. Perkins. London <u>Athenaeum</u>, No. 1411 (11 November),
    pp. 1360-1361.
        Byron's "Island" and Melville's <u>Typee</u> and <u>Omoo</u> "are the
    distinguished literary fruits of the Polynesian Archipelago";
    they have done for those islands what <u>Paul and Virginia</u> did
    for the Mauritius, or <u>Tom Cringle's Log</u> for the West Indies,
    or Fenimore Cooper for the Prairies. The traces of the
    author of <u>Omoo</u> in <u>Na Motu</u> will interest admirers of a
    writer who is a little too fond of surrounding himself with
    a haze of mystery. [<u>See</u> 1854.B2.]

24 ANON. "A Visit to the Scene of the Typee." New Bedford
    <u>Whalemen's Shipping List</u>, 12 (5 December), 306.
        An "extract from a letter by an officer of the British
    Pacific squadron, published in the London journals," noting
    that <u>Typee</u> "gives a most interesting account of these
    [Marquesas] Islands, although rather romanced."

*25 GREENE, RICHARD T. Sandusky (Ohio) <u>Mirror</u> (7 December).
        Passage in Greene's column referring to his time with
    Melville in the Marquesas. Cited by Gohdes (1944), p. 54.

26 ANON. Notice of <u>Israel Potter</u> serial. New York <u>Citizen</u>
    (30 December), p. 827.
        Israel Potter "is a stirring narrative, and admirably
    written; so that if you begin you must finish it."

*27 ANON. Notice of <u>Israel Potter</u> serial. New York <u>Ledger</u>
    (30 December).
        Cited in Mailloux and Parker, p. 61.

<u>1855 A BOOKS - NONE</u>

<u>1855 B SHORTER WRITINGS</u>

1 ANON. <u>Hand-Book of American Literature, Historical, Biograph-</u>
    <u>ical, and Critical</u>. Philadelphia: J. B. Lippincott & Co.
    [1855?], p. 189.
        Notes the increasing popularity of tales of adventure,
    by land and sea, as practical life becomes tame and monot-
    onous. The romances of Mayo and Melville "must be received
    as reports of the fluent, careless, and often brilliant

talk of imaginative travellers, or dreamers of travel, who
have written without any care for rules of art, or fear of
critics." The wildness of Melville's stories--Typee, Omoo,
Mardi, and others--seems to be infectious. Reprinted in
Doubloon, p. 97.

2   DUYCKINCK, EVERT A. and GEORGE L. "Herman Melville," in
Cyclopaedia of American Literature. Vol. 2. New York:
Charles Scribner, pp. 672-676.
     The fullest biographical account to date, with details
of several of Melville's ancestors. Brief critical comments on the novels. For pleasant, easy narrative, Omoo
is the most natural and agreeable of Melville's books. In
Moby-Dick he opposed the metaphysical energy of despair to
the physical sublime of the ocean. "Cock-A-Doodle Doo!"
is one of his most lively and animated productions. Prints
chapter 14 of Redburn. Reprinted in part in Branch, pp.
345-348; reprinted in Sealts (1974), pp. 91-95.

3   HOWE, HENRY, ed. Life and Death on the Ocean: A Collection
of Extraordinary Adventures in the Form of Personal Narratives. Cincinnati: Henry Howe, p. 261.
     Footnote to abridgment of White-Jacket refers to
Melville as a writer of great ability in his peculiar line.
White-Jacket "gives the most faithful sketches of any work
of the kind extant."

4   'JET' [TUEL, J. E.]. Putnam Portraits. New York: Crayon &
Co., pp. 22-23.
     Verses on Melville. Reprinted in Birss (December 1933),
p. 402.

*5   ANON. Morning Courier and New-York Enquirer (28 February).
     Mention of Israel Potter. Cited in Mailloux and Parker,
p. 62.

*6   ANON. Notice of Israel Potter serial. New York Commercial
Advertiser (2 March).
     Cited in Mailloux and Parker, p. 62.

*7   ANON. Notice of Israel Potter serial. Boston Daily Advertiser
(7 March).
     Cited in Log, p. 499.

8   ANON. Review of Israel Potter. New Bedford Mercury
(12 March).
     Melville's works are unequal but never dull; he is
especially at home on his native soil, with a keen sense

1855

of the picturesqueness of its scenery and the peculiarities
of the Yankee character at the revolutionary period. Israel
Potter is a mixture of fun, gravity, romance, and reality,
and equal to the best of its predecessors. Reprinted in
Branch, p. 337.

*9 ANON. Review of Israel Potter. Reading (Pa.) Gazette
(before 15 March).
Quoted in advertisement in New York Commercial Advertiser,
15 March 1855.

10 ANON. Review of Israel Potter. Boston Post (15 March), p. 4.
Melville "has made a most interesting book from the
facts at his command--a book, not great, not remarkable
for any particular in it, but of a curt, manly, independent
tone, dealing with truth honestly, and telling it feelingly."
Paul Jones and Benjamin Franklin are not without a spice of
his former "humors," but on the whole the book's style,
sentiment and construction are far above those of Pierre
and some of its predecessors. Reprinted in Branch, p. 338.

11 ANON. Review of Israel Potter. New York Evangelist
(15 March), p. 44.
In some respects Israel Potter is the best thing
Melville has ever done; it abounds in sharp delineations
of character, stirring incident, and rich historic
allusions.

12 ANON. Review of Israel Potter. New York Norton's Literary
Gazette and Publishers' Circular, NS 2 (15 March), 121.
Israel Potter offers rich and novel entertainment, not
excelled by any of Melville's previous works. It is something of a disappointment, after following the hero's adventures for five years to lose his track for more than 40
years in London; but taken as a whole, read through at one
sitting, the interest of the story is intense, each scene
appearing real. Melville's powerful imagination is probably
more responsible for this eager interest, however, than
Israel's autobiography.

13 W., J. G. "Putnam's Monthly." Washington National Era
(15 March), p. 43.
Praises Putnam's magazine. "Tennyson, Carlyle, and
De Quincey, occasionally write for English Magazines, but
neither [sic] of them can be regarded as a regular contrib-
utor. Setting these aside, what names have Blackwood, or
Tait's, or Dublin University Magazines to offer, which will
compare with those of Bryant, Longfellow, Curtis, Mellville
[sic], Russell Lowell, and Bayard Taylor?"

14   ANON. Review of Israel Potter. New York Albion, NS 14
         (17 March), 129.
         The masculine vigor and fantastical ruggedness of
      Israel Potter give it a distinctness and raciness of flavor.
      Franklin and Paul Jones are admirable sketches of character,
      but the sea is Melville's special element. The fight be-
      tween the Serapis and the Bon Homme Richard is a masterpiece
      of writing, the imagery helping the description wonderfully.
      Melville can also be effectively plain spoken. Reprinted
      in Branch, pp. 339-340.

15   ANON. Review of Israel Potter. New York Evening Post
         (17 March).
         Brief summary. The story is delightfully told by
      Melville, one of the most popular American writers in his
      peculiar department.

16   ANON. Review of Israel Potter. Morning Courier and New-York
         Enquirer (17 March), p. 4.
         A very simple yet graphic recital of interesting adven-
      ture, Israel Potter is equal to any of Melville's works,
      though in quite a different vein. Its style is remarkably
      manly and direct and in this respect a pleasant contrast to
      his last book. It "is occasionally somewhat coarse for the
      refinement of our day; but so are Robinson Crusoe and The
      Pilgrim's Progress."

17   ANON. Review of Israel Potter. New York Commercial Advertiser
         (21 March).
         Israel Potter is an original and extremely graphic story
      of the revolutionary era and is thoroughly saturated with
      American sentiment. It is quite equal in a literary way to
      Melville's previous works and much superior to them in other
      respects.

18   ANON. Review of Israel Potter. Boston Puritan Recorder
         (22 March), p. 45.
         Brief summary. The material Israel Potter is made of is
      deeply interesting; but it is molded with so much skill
      that it has all the effect of a most thrilling romance.
      The account of Israel's return to the spot where he was
      born is exquisitely beautiful.

19   ANON. Review of Israel Potter. New York Quarterly, 4
         (April), 153-154.
         The detail of Israel Potter's narrative is "not too in-
      teresting, and for purposes of romantic interest not too
      well chosen," New England and its customs being too familiar

1855

to most readers "to be considered novel without the aid of
brilliant or startling appendages." In the main, Melville
fails to sustain the flights of fancy and rhetoric in the
dedication and first chapter. Reprinted in Pollin
(October 1975), p. 7.

20   ANON. Review of Westward Ho! The Voyages and Adventures of
      Sir Amyas Leigh by Charles Kingsley. Boston Post (5 April),
      p. 4.
          Compares Westward Ho! and Israel Potter, each "an oddity
      in itself." Both are modern imitations of bygone styles of
      writing and talking, both are the supposed biographies of
      real personages, and are based more or less on undoubted
      fact. Israel Potter is more truthlike, pithy, vigorous,
      and readable; but Westward Ho! is far superior in scope,
      brilliancy, tone, and character. Reprinted in part in Log,
      p. 500.

21   ANON. Review of Israel Potter. Newark Daily Advertiser
      (5 April), p. 2.
          A most charming tale, Israel Potter is one of the most
      genuine of Melville's numerous books and will be most
      popular for its patriotic interest.

22   ANON. Review of Israel Potter. New York Citizen (7 April).
          Israel Potter is a racy volume, abounding with lively
      sketches of character and graphic scenes on land and sea.

23   ANON. Notice of "The Paradise of Bachelors and the Tartarus
      of Maids." New York Home Journal (7 April).
          Ascribes the sketches (in the April issue of Harper's
      Monthly Magazine) to Melville on the basis of internal
      evidence; they are written in his best vein.

24   ANON. Review of Israel Potter. Boston Christian Examiner and
      Religious Miscellany, 58 (May), 470–471.
          Israel Potter scarcely sustains the reputation Melville
      won by his early works where he entered a comparatively
      uncultivated field and gained popularity by the freshness
      of his manner and the romantic interest of his narrative.
      The style of Israel Potter is generally flowing and grace-
      ful, its tone genial and healthy; it has some fine passages
      and skillful descriptions. But in his hero Melville gives
      only a feeble delineation of a very commonplace person, who
      lacks those elements which arrest the reader's attention.
      The other characters are no more skillfully portrayed. A
      battle as sanguinary and brutal as that between the Bon
      Homme Richard and the Serapis cannot form an attractive

1855

episode in a work of high art. Reprinted in Branch,
pp. 340–341.

25   ANON. Review of Israel Potter. New York National Magazine,
      6 (May), 477–478.
          Israel Potter is written in a half-comic, half-patriotic
      vein, yet is exceedingly attractive and not a little instruc-
      tive. The Yankee character is well sustained in Israel's
      adventures. A tinge of obscure sarcasm pervades the book.

26   ANON. "Editorial Notes--Literature." New York Putnam's
      Monthly, 5 (May), 548.
          Quotes from title page of Israel Potter's Life and Adven-
      tures and claims that the book is not as rare as Melville
      suggests in his dedication to Israel Potter. Notes that
      Melville departs considerably from his original in his
      narrative.

27   ANON. Review of Israel Potter. New York Christian
      Intelligencer (3 May).
          Brief summary, praising Melville's "smooth and nimble
      pen." Melville has done better as a romancer than as the
      vilifier and traducer of missionaries and of Christianity.
      Next to Irving he is the best living American writer of
      prose.

28   ANON. Review of Israel Potter. London Leader, 6 (5 May), 428.
          In its first 14 chapters Israel Potter is incomparably
      Melville's best work; the subject is treated with vigor,
      freshness, and artist-like skill, the characters are con-
      ceived with genuine dramatic feeling; the incidents are all
      striking; and the style, except for an occasional American-
      ism, is hearty and graphic. After chapter 14 the book
      grows duller and duller, apart from one or two scenes,
      mainly because the least successful character, Paul Jones,
      is the one most fully developed in the second half and be-
      cause Melville generalizes about Israel's fortunes instead
      of following them with his earlier minuteness. Israel
      Potter is the work of an original thinker and vigorous
      writer, damaged by lack of constructive ability. Extract
      from chapter 5. Reprinted in Branch, pp. 341–343.

29   ANON. "American Travelers." New York Putnam's Monthly, 5
      (June), 566.
          Notes that many younger American authors have made their
      literary debut by books of travel; Melville included in list
      of examples.

1855

30 ANON. Review of <u>Israel Potter</u>. London <u>Athenaeum</u>, No. 1440
   (2 June), p. 643.
     Unable to decide whether Israel is a fictional character
   or was an actual American. Melville tries for power and
   commands rhetoric but becomes wilder and more turgid with
   each book. The portraits of Franklin and Paul Jones are
   additional weaknesses in <u>Israel Potter</u>. But the book is
   not a bad shilling's worth for a railway reader. Reprinted
   in <u>Recognition</u>, pp. 72-73, and Branch, pp. 343-344.

31 ANON. Review of <u>Israel Potter</u>. London <u>Weekly Chronicle</u>
   (2 June).
     The book seems to have been carefully and purposely ren-
   dered commonplace. It suggests that Melville is capable of
   something much better, "but for a freak is resolved to curb
   his fancy and adhere to the dustiest routine." It is written throughout in an abrupt, condensed style. Brief summary;
   extract from chapter 5. Reprinted in Parker (January 1970),
   pp. 588-589.

32 MONTÉGUT, ÉM. "Israël Potter: Légende Démocratique
   Américaine." Paris <u>Revue des Deux Mondes</u>, 25 (1 July),
   5-56.
     <u>Israel Potter</u> attempts to show essential qualities of
   the American spirit. Melville creates a legendary figure
   in Israel, making him the symbol of all the virtues of the
   revolutionary generation and the symbol of democracy in an
   aristocratic land. Israel represents the American character at the moment it was still being formed; he is also the
   representative of the anonymous self-sacrificing masses to
   whom America owes its independence. He is the free man,
   who fears nothing and is always ready for anything. Long
   summary.

*33 ANON. Review of <u>Putnam's Monthly</u>. New York <u>Citizen</u>
   (5 August).
     Refers to "The Lightning-Rod Man" (in the August issue
   of <u>Putnam's</u>) as "a sketchy trifle." Cited in Mailloux and
   Parker, p. 66.

34 ANON. "Our Berkshire Pleasures." Pittsfield (Mass.)
   <u>Berkshire County Eagle</u> (14 September).
     Description of a fancy-dress picnic the previous week on
   the Morewood estate at Melville Lake. The Herman Melvilles
   attended.

35 ANON. Review of <u>Putnam's Monthly</u>. New York <u>Citizen</u>
   (6 October).

Notes that "Benito Cereno," an "animated tale," is commenced in the October issue of Putnam's.

36   ANON. Notice of "Benito Cereno." New York Dispatch
      (25 November).
            Notes conclusion of the story in the December issue of
      Putnam's Monthly and ascribes it to Melville. Predicts
      that thousands will read with pleasure the closing up of
      the mystery.

1856 A BOOKS - NONE

1856 B SHORTER WRITINGS

1   ANON. "A Trio of American Sailor-Authors." Dublin University
     Magazine, 47 (January), 47-54.
           [The trio are Cooper, Dana, and Melville.] Survey, but
     no mention of Pierre. Redburn contains some clever chap-
     ters, but much of it is outrageously improbable and cannot
     be read with pleasure or profit. In his next work [sic],
     Mardi, after the first half of volume one, all Melville's
     powers are wasted on a theme nobody can understand; the
     book is "one of the saddest, most melancholy, most deplor-
     able, and humiliating perversions of genius of a high order
     in the English language" and will repulse most readers with
     its total want of human interest and sympathy. White-Jacket
     is Melville's very best work, the best ever picture of life-
     before-the-mast in a ship of war, though Melville has bor-
     rowed expressions and incidents from nautical books without
     acknowledgment and at times seems deficient in practical
     knowledge of seamanship. The Whale is as eccentric and
     monstrously extravagant as Mardi in many of its incidents,
     but is a very valuable book because of its unparalleled mass
     of information on whaling. Melville is a man of genius: no
     living author rivals him in his poetical and original powers
     of describing scenes at sea and sea life; he never scruples
     to make use of information from his prodigious reading but
     is undoubtedly an original thinker with amazing powers of
     expression; he is also often mystical and unintelligible.
     If he does not eventually rank as one of America's greatest
     literary giants it will be owing solely to his own incorrig-
     ible perversion of his rare and lofty gifts. Reprinted in
     1856.B3; reprinted in part in 1856.B40; Anderson (March 1939),
     pp. 35-36; Recognition, pp. 73-81; Doubloon, pp. 98-99;
     Branch, pp. 349-353.

1856

*2   ANON. Editorial. New York <u>Life Illustrated</u> (9 February).
        On "benevolent societies"; <u>Typee</u> mentioned. Cited in
       <u>Log</u>, p. 512.

3   ANON. "A Trio of American Sailor-Authors." Boston <u>Littell's
       Living Age</u>, 48 (1 March), 560-566.
        Reprint of 1856.B1.

4   ANON. New York <u>Dispatch</u> (4 May).
        Finds "The Apple-Tree Table" (in the May issue of
       <u>Putnam's Monthly</u>) "an amusingly written chapter on Spiri-
       tual Manifestations."

5   X., GRS. "Dottings About Island Coasts." New York <u>Spirit of
       the Times</u>, 26 (24 May), 170-171.
        Author visited Nukuheva in 1855. All that Melville
       writes of Polynesian scenery and life may be relied upon;
       but he is a poet and therefore condemned by the inductive
       and scientific men of the day. Melville's fault was in
       painting exclusively bright pictures of Typee life. Whaling
       captains who visit the Pacific islands can tell truer tales
       of Marquesan women than are found in <u>Typee</u>. Fayaway died
       early, perhaps of a broken heart; one of her friends told
       the author she never "got over" Melville's desertion.

6   ANON. Review of <u>The Piazza Tales</u>. New York <u>Atlas</u> (25 May).
        Volume contains stories of more than ordinary interest,
       which will captivate the reader's attention. "The Encan-
       tadas" is more in the style of Melville's first works, and
       contains an exceptionally vivid picture of the Galapagos.
       The simple announcement of a new work from Melville will
       probably create an instant demand for it.

7   ANON. Review of <u>The Piazza Tales</u>. New York <u>Daily News</u>
       (26 May), p. 1.
        Can find nowhere in Melville's writings "the slightest
       rational symptom of deterioration"; their different styles
       only prove the versatility of his pen. "The Piazza" is one
       of the most charming sketches in the language; each of the
       tales is a gem. The wild humor and melodramatic effects
       of "The Lightning-Rod Man" and "The Bell-Tower" recall Poe
       in his strangest mood. "The Encantadas" can be read again
       and again like a gorgeous poem. Melville's prose, particu-
       larly in his descriptions of "scenery, sea and cloud-land,"
       resembles Tennysonian verse. Marianna of "The Piazza" has
       "a distinct and yet not traceable relationship to 'Marianna
       in the Moated Grange.'"

8   ANON. Review of The Piazza Tales. Pittsfield (Mass.)
     Berkshire County Eagle (30 May).
          The Piazza Tales is decidedly Melville's most readable
     work since Typee and Omoo. Without so many striking pas-
     sages as Moby-Dick and some others, the book is more uni-
     formly excellent and freer from blemishes than any of his
     later works. "The Piazza" will be especially interesting
     to Pittsfield readers for its description of familiar
     scenery. "Bartleby" is one of Melville's best ever "bits
     of writing." Reprinted in Log, p. 515.

9   ANON. Review of The Piazza Tales. New York American Pub-
     lishers' Circular and Literary Gazette, 2 (31 May), 318.
     Evincing the excellent characteristics of their popular
     author, the tales were instrumental, in no small degree, in
     making Putnam's the best of all American monthlies.

10   ANON. Review of The Piazza Tales. New York Criterion, 2
     (31 May), 74.
          Capital stories, or sketches, though "The Lightning-Rod
     Man" shows that Melville can write a very indifferent paper
     if he chooses. "Bartleby" is based on living characters.

11   ANON. Review of The Piazza Tales. Richmond Southern Literary
     Messenger, 22 (June), 480.
          Melville writes with much of his former freshness and
     vivacity in The Piazza Tales. The best paper is "The
     Encantadas." "The Lightning-Rod Man" is a very flat recital.
     Reprinted in Recognition, p. 81, and Branch, p. 354.

12   ANON. Review of The Piazza Tales. Boston Daily Evening
     Traveller (3 June), p. 4.
          Five of the tales are gorgeous in their way, but deeply
     affected by Melville's peculiarity of travelling into the
     mystic regions of fairyland where he can seldom be under-
     stood. For originality of invention and grotesqueness of
     humor, "Bartleby," the sixth tale, is equal to anything by
     Dickens, "whose writings it closely resembles, both as to
     the character of the sketch and the peculiarity of the
     style."

13   ANON. Review of The Piazza Tales. Boston Post (4 June), p. 1.
          All of the tales are readable and forcibly written.
     Reprinted in Recognition, p. 82.

14   ANON. Review of The Piazza Tales. New Bedford Daily Mercury
     (4 June), p. 2.

Admires the strong and picturesque sentences in The
Piazza Tales and the thoughtful truths of a writer who
leaves some space for the reader to try his own ingenuity
upon. In copiousness of fancy and gentility of imagination
Melville more nearly resembles Charles Brockden Brown "than
either of our other American story-tellers." Hawthorne is
more dry, prosaic, and detailed; Irving more elegant, careful, and popular. Melville is a kind of wizard, writing
strange, mysterious things that belong to other worlds.
Reprinted in Branch, p. 355.

15   ANON. Review of The Piazza Tales. Boston Puritan Recorder
      (5 June).
          All of the tales are characterized by a singularly
      graphic power. Not for the first time, Melville shows
      himself equally at home in every kind of description.

16   ANON. Review of The Piazza Tales. Milwaukee Daily Wisconsin
      (5 June), p. 3.
          The interesting sketches are prefaced by "The Piazza," a
      "most happy reflection upon that fault-finding ideality
      which considers imaginary fancyings the true heaven of
      delights.... It is given in abrupt sentences, which shows
      [sic] a particular nervousness in the writer that makes it
      a rich literary treat, being so different from the old mule-
      team of authorship, that one feels new life in its perusal."
      Its influence "will profit." Reprinted in 1856.B24.

17   ANON. Review of The Piazza Tales. New York Churchman
      (5 June).
          Perhaps above any of "our home writers," Melville is
      remarkable for "a certain taking variety of style." In
      The Piazza Tales he has achieved the "just mean" between
      the two extreme styles of Typee and Moby-Dick. Melville
      is "a close observer and reverent student of Nature under
      her wilder as well as her sunnier aspects" and is not less
      at home in the portrayal of human character and passion.
      Extracts from "The Piazza" and "The Bell-Tower."

18   ANON. Review of The Piazza Tales. New York Evening Post
      (5 June).
          The tales are well characterized by Melville's vivid
      imagination and wonderful faculty of description, "in which
      latter respect they will remind the reader agreeably of his
      earliest and best works."

19   ANON. Review of The Piazza Tales. Boston Evening Transcript
      (6 June), p. 1.

Each tale is "peculiar in its way," and Melville's great powers of description appear to admirable advantage. The book will have a wide circulation in cultivated circles. Reprinted in Branch, p. 356.

20   ANON. Review of The Piazza Tales. Morning Courier and New-York Enquirer (6 June).
Three of the tales are fine specimens of Melville's widely recognized power as a storyteller. The first part of "Bartleby" has a singular fascination, which it was impossible in the nature of things to keep up; "The Encantadas" is "more in the vein of the wondrous traveller's tales"; and "The Bell-Tower" is "a happy emulation, though not an imitation, of the style of Poe."

21   ANON. Review of The Piazza Tales. Philadelphia North American and United States Gazette (7 June), p. 1.
A pleasant volume with Melville's "characteristics, mannerisms and all" and "as desirable an afternoon book as one may meet."

22   ANON. Review of The Piazza Tales. New York Dispatch (8 June).
"Benito Cereno" and "The Encantadas" are the two best tales in the collection. "Benito Cereno" sustains its Poe-like mysticism to the end. "The Encantadas" is a romance, a sort of mixture of Mardi and Robinson Crusoe, though far more interesting than Mardi. Not the least merit of the tales is their simplicity and purity of style. Melville's name is a passport to public favor, and the book will command a large sale.

23   ANON. Review of The Piazza Tales. New York Sun (9 June), p. 1.
These "dreamy, wild, sketchy narrations, and far-away, hazy scenes" make a "delightful companion for an afternoon lounge." Melville has a vivid fancy and the art of conveying deep expression by simple touches, each suggestive of a picture. His style is felicitously adapted to the subject.

24   ANON. Review of The Piazza Tales. Milwaukee Weekly Wisconsin (11 June), p. 4.
Reprint of 1856.B16.

25   ANON. Review of The Piazza Tales. Amherst (Mass.) Hampshire and Franklin Express (13 June).
The book is full of graphic description, the various characters are life-like, and the portraiture is natural

1856

and beautiful. Melville is an entertaining and cultivated
writer whose works all have a peculiar charm.

26   ANON. Review of The Piazza Tales. Boston Christian Freeman
      and Family Visiter (13 June), p. 26.
         Melville is justly regarded among the first writers of
      fiction of the present day, possessing in an eminent degree
      two indispensable requisites for a successful romance
      writer--vivid imagination and remarkable descriptive powers.
      "Benito Cereno" is unsurpassed in the descriptive and keeps
      the reader's imagination constantly exercised. "The Encan-
      tadas" could not have been written by a man of ordinary
      imagination.

27   ANON. Review of The Piazza Tales. Newark Daily Advertiser
      (18 June).
         The tales are in the real Omoo and Typee vein. "One
      reads them with delight and with rejoicing that the author
      has laid his rhapsodizing aside, which savored too much of
      Swift, Rabelais and other such works...." Reprinted in
      Branch, p. 356.

28   ANON. Notice of The Piazza Tales. New York Christian Advocate
      and Journal (19 June).
         Notes that Melville "is well known as one of the most
      popular writers of the day" and lists the titles of the
      tales.

29   ANON. Review of The Piazza Tales. New York Daily Tribune
      (23 June), p. 3.
         The peculiar traits of Melville's genius are present in
      the tales, though in a less decided form than in most of
      his previous works. They show "something of the boldness
      of invention, brilliancy of imagination, and quaintness of
      expression which usually mark his writings, with not a lit-
      tle of apparent perversity and self-will, which serve as a
      foil to their various excellences." "Bartleby" is the
      book's most original story and has unquestionable merit as
      a curious study of human nature. "Benito Cereno" and "The
      Encantadas" are not improvements on Melville's previous
      popular sea romances. Reprinted in Branch, p. 357.

30   ANON. Review of The Piazza Tales. Salem Gazette (24 June).
         Claims that everything from Melville's pen "is eagerly
      sought by his numerous admirers" and reprints the first
      three sentences of 1856.B20.

31 ANON. Review of The Piazza Tales. Salem Register (26 June).
     "The characteristics of Melville's style, and the pecul-
     iar turn of his mind are known to a multitude of readers,
     who will recognize in these tales their true paternity."

32 ANON. Review of The Piazza Tales. New York Daily Times
     (27 June), p. 5.
     Taken as a whole the tales will not augment Melville's
     high reputation. "Benito Cereno" is melodramatic, not
     effective. "The Encantadas" is the best piece; "The Piazza"
     is full of freshness and beauty. The author of Typee
     "should do something higher and better than Magazine arti-
     cles." Reprinted in Branch, p. 357.

33 ANON. Review of The Piazza Tales. Boston Christian Examiner
     and Religious Miscellany, 61 (July), 152.
     Melville's tales will accomplish all they aim at--the
     amusement of his readers.

34 ANON. Review of The Piazza Tales. New York Mrs. Stephen's
     Illustrated New Monthly, 1 (July), 54.
     The tales are fine reading.

35 ANON. "Christian Missions: Their Principle and Practice."
     London Westminster and Foreign Quarterly Review, NS 10
     (1 July), 8-10, 20-22, 25.
     Quotes from Typee and Omoo on the evils accompanying
     missionary activity in the Sandwich islands, accepting
     Melville's testimony.

36 ANON. Review of The Piazza Tales. New York Albion, NS 15
     (5 July), 321.
     Imperfect as they are, even these tales show that the
     brilliant author of Typee, Omoo, "and other South Sea
     phantasies" is brimful of talent. The "Bell-Tower" is a
     fine conception, rather bunglingly worked out.

37 ANON. Review of The Piazza Tales. Springfield (Mass.)
     Republican (9 July), p. 1.
     Marked by "a delicate fancy, a bright and most fruitful
     imagination, a pure and translucent style, and a certain
     weirdness of conceit," the tales are not unlike, and seem
     not inferior to, the "best things" of Hawthorne. "The
     Piazza," one of the most graceful specimens of American
     writing, is essentially a poem, lacking only rhythm and
     form. Reprinted in Branch, p. 358.

1856

38   ANON. Review of The Piazza Tales. London Athenaeum, No. 1500
     (26 July), p. 929.
          Melville might deserve to be added to the list of Amer-
     icans who excel in short tales, a list including Irving,
     Poe, and Hawthorne; but in The Piazza Tales he gives merely
     indications, not fulfillment. Under the idea of being ro-
     mantic and pictorial in style, he is sometimes barely intel-
     ligible. The legends have a certain wild and ghostly power,
     but the exaggeration of their teller's manner appears to be
     on the increase. Extract from "The Bell-Tower." Reprinted
     in Recognition, pp. 82-83, and Branch, pp. 358-359.

39   ANON. "The Islands of the Pacific." New York Putnam's
     Monthly, 8 (August), 142-156.
          Melville mentioned at end of article. The reader will
     dwell with delight on the stories of the Encantadas in The
     Piazza Tales.

40   ANON. "Herman Melville." Pittsfield (Mass.) Berkshire County
     Eagle (8 August), p. 1.
          Reprints 1856.B1 in part and adds postscript on The
     Piazza Tales, by far the most popular of Melville's works
     since Omoo and Typee. "The Bell-Tower" is "a picturesque
     and arabesque tale well fitted to inspire an artist, as it
     did one in New York who has made four striking sketches
     from it...." Reprinted in part in Log, p. 519.

41   ANON. Review of The Piazza Tales. New York Knickerbocker,
     48 (September), 330.
          Though "partaking of the marvellous," the tales are
     written with Melville's usual felicity of expression and
     minuteness of detail. "Benito Cereno" is most painfully
     interesting. Reprinted in Branch, p. 359.

42   ANON. Review of The Piazza Tales. New York United States
     Democratic Review, 38 [NS 7] (September), 172.
          Melville seems to have lavished even more than his usual
     care on the tales; all of them exhibit the peculiar richness
     of language, descriptive vitality, and splendidly sombre
     imagination which are his characteristics. Admirers of Poe
     will perhaps see an imitation of his concentrated gloom in
     "Bartleby"; and the broad tinge of German mysticism in "The
     Bell-Tower" also has some resemblance to Poe. Reprinted in
     Recognition, pp. 83-84, and Branch, p. 360.

43   ANON. Review of The Piazza Tales. Philadelphia Godey's Lady's
     Book and Magazine, 53 (September), 277.

Cannot read Melville's works with much satisfaction.
His style has an affectation of quaintness, which renders
it very confused and wearisome.

44   ANON. Pittsfield (Mass.) <u>Berkshire County Eagle</u> (5 September).
Reports "Annual Fancy Pic-nic" the previous Wednesday at
the Morewoods. Mrs. Melville was there as the "Genius of
Greylock."

45   ANON. "Herman Mellvill." Pittsfield (Mass.) <u>Berkshire County
Eagle</u> (10 October).
Notes Melville's forthcoming trip to Europe. Melville
"much needs this relaxation from his severe literary labors
of several years past, and we doubt not that he will return
with renovated health and a new store of those observations
of travel which he works so charmingly."

<u>1857 A BOOKS - NONE</u>

<u>1857 B SHORTER WRITINGS</u>

1   ANON. <u>Men of the Time or Sketches of Living Notables</u>
(London: Kent & Co.), pp. 310-311.
Reprint of 1853.B1, with slight alteration. Reprinted
in 1859.

2   ANON. London <u>Mr. Murray's General List of Works</u> (February),
p. 24.
Lists <u>Typee</u> and <u>Omoo</u>.

3   [O'BRIEN, FITZ-JAMES]. "Our Authors and Authorship. Melville
and Curtis." New York <u>Putnam's Monthly</u>, 9 (April), 384-393.
In style and form, <u>Typee</u> exhibited a rare degree of
ripeness and perfection, though it was deformed with un-
graceful locutions and the simple flow of narrative was
sometimes broken. Since then, Melville has been going
wrong. <u>Typee</u> showed a constant tendency to vague and whim-
sical speculation; Melville had all the metaphysical tendencies belonging so eminently to the American mind. But in
<u>Mardi</u> and <u>Moby-Dick</u> he becomes incomprehensible. Melville
is a man born to see who insists on speculating; he has
indulged himself in a trick of metaphysical and morbid
meditations until he has almost perverted his fine mind
from its healthy productive tendencies"; he has vitiated
his thought and style into an appearance of the wildest
affectation and untruth. <u>Redburn</u> is an almost unique mixture of sense and nonsense, accuracy and extravagance, exact

portraiture and incredible caricature. The Confidence-Man
belongs to "the metaphysical and Rabelaistical class" of
Melville's works, but is more reasonable, and more respect-
ful of probabilities and possibilities, though very few
will understand it. Melville should give up metaphysics
"and take to nature and the study of mankind." Reprinted
in part in Recognition, pp. 84-93; Doubloon, pp. 101-102;
Branch, pp. 361-368.

4   ANON. Review of The Confidence-Man. Albany Evening Journal
    (2 April), p. 2.
        The Confidence-Man, regrettably, is like Melville's
    other recent works--"a story in which the incidents and
    characters are chosen with a view to convey a theoretic
    moral, not a vivid, graphic delineation based upon real
    life" like Typee and Omoo. But his reputation would ensure
    the sale of the book even if its merits were much less than
    they are. Reprinted in 1857.B8 and Norton The Confidence-
    Man, p. 269.

5   ANON. Review of The Confidence-Man. Boston Evening Transcript
    (3 April), p. 1.
        Commends the book as "a unique affair." Any work from
    Melville is sure to find a host of readers.

6   ANON. Review of The Confidence-Man. Philadelphia North Amer-
    ican and United States Gazette (4 April).
        A sketchy affair, like other tales by Melville. "Sly
    humor peeps out occasionally, though buried under quite too
    many words, and you read on and on, expecting something more
    than you ever find, to be choked off at the end of the book
    like the audience of a Turkish story teller, without getting
    the end of the story." Reprinted in Norton The Confidence-
    Man, p. 269.

7   ANON. Review of The Confidence-Man. New York Dispatch
    (5 April).
        Melville cannot write badly, but he "appears to have
    adopted a quaint, unnatural style, of late, which has little
    of the sparkling vigor and freshness of his early works."
    The Confidence-Man has all the faults of style peculiar to
    Mardi without the romance of that strange book. Reviewer
    closed it, "finding nothing concluded, and wondering what on
    earth the author has been driving at." Melville should read
    the article in the latest issue of Putnam's [1857.B3] and
    try to profit by it. It is trespassing too much on the
    patience and forbearance of the public when a writer of
    Melville's talent publishes such puerilities as The

Confidence-Man. Reprinted in Norton The Confidence-Man,
pp. 269-270, and Branch, pp. 369-370.

8   ANON. Review of The Confidence-Man. Salem Register (6 April),
p. 2.
The theme of the book is "confidence or the lack of it
in ordinary life." Melville has a dashing, off-hand way of
telling a story, but his later works do not have the charm
of Omoo and Typee. Reprints most of 1857.B4.

9   ANON. Review of The Confidence-Man. Boston Daily Advertiser
(8 April), p. 2.
The "Confidence Man" succeeds in drawing passenger's
money with rather more facility than is quite natural. The
"grand morale" of the book appears to be that the world
is full of knaves and fools, and that a man who believes
what is told him, is necessarily a fool.

10   ANON. Review of The Confidence-Man. New York Sun (8 April).
Melville never suffers his readers to get the blues or
go to sleep. The Confidence-Man is his last but by no
means the worst of his efforts.

*11   ANON. Pittsfield (Mass.) Sun (9 April).
Reports that Melville is expected to return soon from
his European tour in greatly improved health. Cited in
Log, p. 569.

12   '-KNICK.' Review of The Confidence-Man. Boston Evening
Transcript (10 April), p. 2.
Melville has added to the number of original subjects
with his "Confidence Man"--one of "the indigenous characters
who has figured long in our journals, courts, and cities."
Melville is an author who deals equally well "in the mate-
rial description and the metaphysical insight of human life."
Reprinted in Norton The Confidence-Man, pp. 270-271, and
Branch, p. 370.

13   ANON. Review of The Confidence-Man. London Athenaeum, No. 1537
(11 April), 462-463.
The Confidence-Man "is a morality enacted by masqued
players." Some of Melville's readers, "possibly, may wait
for a promised sequel to the book before deciding as to the
lucidity or opaqueness of the author's final meaning."
There is a stage, with a set of elaborate scenery, but there
is strictly no drama, the incidents being those of a masquerade. Melville "is lavish in aphorism, epigram, and
metaphor. When he is not didactic, he is luxuriously

1857

picturesque; and, although his style is one, from its peculiarities, difficult to manage, he has now obtained a mastery over it...." The table of contents is like a reflection
of "The Ancient Mariner," interspersed with some touches
vaguely derived from the dialecticians of the eighteenth
century. Full of thought, conceit, fancy, affectation, and
originality, The Confidence-Man is not unexceptionably meri-
torious, but is invariably graphic, fresh, and entertaining.
Extracts from chapters 2 and 45. Reprinted in part in Log,
p. 570, and Branch, pp. 371-372; reprinted in Recognition,
pp. 94-97.

14   ANON. Review of The Confidence-Man. London Leader, No. 308
(11 April), p. 356.
In The Confidence-Man festoons of exuberant fancy decor-
ate the discussion of abstract problems, the narrative is
almost rhythmic, the talk is cordial, and bright American
touches are scattered over the perspective. The charm of
the book "is owing to its originality and to its constant
flow of descriptions, character-stretching [sic], and
dialogue, deeply toned and skilfully contrasted." Melville
has added satire to his repertory "and, as he uses it scru-
pulously, he uses it well." His fault "is a disposition to
discourse upon too large a scale, and to keep his typical
characters too long in one attitude upon the stage." Reprinted in part in Log, pp. 570-571; reprinted in Norton
The Confidence-Man, p. 271, and Branch, pp. 372-373.

15   ANON. Review of The Confidence-Man. London Literary Gazette,
No. 2099 (11 April), pp. 348-349.
The Confidence-Man professes to inculcate philosophical
truths through the medium of nonsensical people talking
nonsense. It is not a novel, "unless a novel means forty-
five conversations held on board a steamer, conducted by
personages who might pass for the errata of creation, and
so far resembling the Dialogues of Plato as to be undoubted
Greek to ordinary men." Melville has violated certain ill-
defined but sufficiently understood rules of probability.
In Mardi and Moby-Dick the language was extraordinary, but
the speakers were extraordinary, too; in The Confidence-Man
Melville has put extravaganzas in the mouths of Yankee cabin
passengers. This "tangled web of obscurity is shot with
many a gleam of shrewd and subtle thought"; there are often
"bright, brief bubbles of fancy and wit"; but Melville has
ruined this book as he did Pierre by a strained effort after
excessive originality. Extracts from chapters 33, 29 and 1.
Reprinted in part in Log, p. 571; reprinted in Norton The
Confidence-Man, pp. 271-275, and Branch, pp. 373-376.

16   ANON. Review of The Confidence-Man. London Spectator, 30
      (11 April), 398-399.
          Melville's design in The Confidence-Man is not very
      clear. "Satire on many American smartnesses, and on the
      gullibility of mankind which enables those smartnesses to
      succeed, is indeed an evident object of the author. He
      stops short of any continuous pungent effect; because his
      plan is not distinctly felt, and the framework is very in-
      artistical; also because the execution is upon the whole
      flat, at least to an English reader, who does not appre-
      ciate what appear to be local allusions." There seems "too
      great a success on the part of the rogues, from the great
      gullibility of the gulls." One cannot implicitly rely on
      the fiction as a genuine sketch of American society; the
      spirit of the satire seems drawn from seventeenth and eight-
      eenth century European writers with some of Melville's own
      Old World observations superadded. Extract from chapter 19.
      Reprinted in Recognition, pp. 97-98, and Branch, pp. 376-77.

17   ANON. "Books of the Week." New York Daily Times [Supplement]
      (11 April), p. 1.
          The Confidence-Man is almost as ambiguous an apparition
      as Pierre. But in The Confidence-Man "there is no attempt
      at a novel, or a romance, for Melville has not the slightest
      qualifications for a novelist, and therefore he appears to
      much better advantage here than in his attempts at story
      books." Though full of book learning, the work "is as
      essentially Western and Indianesque as one of Cooper's
      Leather-Stocking Tales"; it is "a Rabelaisian piece of
      patch-work without any of the Rabelaisian indecency." Some
      of the local descriptions are "as striking and picturesque
      as the best things in Typee, and the oddities of thought,
      felicities of expression, the wit, humor, and rollicking
      inspirations are as abundant and original" as in any of
      Melville's works. Reprinted in part in Log, p. 570; re-
      printed in Branch, p. 378.

18   ANON. Review of The Confidence-Man. Morning Courier and New-
      York Enquirer (11 April).
          The Confidence-Man differs in character from Melville's
      previous works and is much inferior.

19   ANON. Review of The Confidence-Man. London Critic, 16
      (15 April), 174-175.
          There is a vividness and an intensity about Melville's
      style which is almost painful for the constant strain upon
      the attention. Of all his works, readers will find The
      Confidence-Man the hardest nut to crack. There is a dry

1857

vein of sarcastic humor running throughout which suggests
another meaning hidden in the depths of the subject other
than that which lies near the surface. The book's apostle
of geniality may be "an arch-imposter of the deepest dye."
Extracts from chapters 16, 22, and 30. Reprinted in part
in Log, pp. 572-573.

20   ANON. Review of The Confidence-Man. Boston Puritan Recorder
     (16 April), p. 61.
         "This book was got up for amusement, and in that view, it
     is no failure. Its reading may be very useful to dyspeptics."
     (Complete review.)

21   ANON. Review of The Confidence-Man. New York Day Book
     (17 April).
         Melville has not greatly improved since Typee and has a
     rather queer way of telling a story, but The Confidence-Man
     is a clever delineation of Western characteristics. Without
     being a really great or philosophical novelist, Melville
     gives pleasant delineations of nature and a considerable
     insight into the springs of human nature. Reprinted in
     Norton The Confidence-Man, p. 275.

22   ANON. Review of The Confidence-Man. London Examiner
     (18 April), p. 245.
         The book consists "not so much of a single narrative as
     of a connected series of dialogues, quaintly playing upon
     the character of that confidence of man in man which is or
     ought to be the basis of all dealing. It is not altogether
     what it ought to be," Melville hints in his satire.

23   ANON. Review of The Confidence-Man. New York Atlas
     (19 April).
         There are passages here and there in The Confidence-Man
     worthy of Melville but in general it seems a remarkably
     lazy book. It looks too much like a job of bookmaking,
     instead of a work of love stimulated by the best faculties
     of the intellect. Melville has expended much labor to lit-
     tle purpose.

24   ANON. Review of The Confidence-Man. Worcester (Mass.)
     Palladium (22 April), p. 2.
         There are bright flashes in The Confidence-Man, scintil-
     lations of poetic light, and much common sense well expressed,
     but the book as a whole is somewhat heavy and written in a
     careless and rambling style. But since it pictures nine-
     teenth century notions it will command attention. We see
     "The Confidence Man" every day. Reprinted in Branch, p. 379.

25   ANON. Review of The Confidence-Man. Boston Christian Freeman
      and Family Visiter (24 April), p. 206.
          The Confidence Man is a wonderful genius, at least in
      Melville's hands; the many characters he "personates" are
      described in Melville's peculiar, inimitable style.

26   ANON. Review of The Confidence-Man. Burlington (Vt.) Daily
      Free Press (25 April).
          "The story of the chap who managed to diddle many out of
      their property lamenting their want of confidence in him
      till they were willing to prove its reality by trusting
      him with a watch, a gold pencil case or a five dollar bill,
      never to be seen again by their owners, has furnished the
      hint on which the volume is made up." The book will not
      add to Melville's reputation. The world is not made up of
      cheats and their victims. Reprinted in Orth, p. 48, and
      Norton The Confidence-Man, p. 275.

27   ANON. Review of The Confidence-Man. London Illustrated Times,
      4 (25 April), 266.
          Reviewer is uncertain whether The Confidence-Man is a
      novel, comedy, collection of dialogues, or repertory of
      anecdotes, but "the work is a fiction, at all events."
      There are scenes of admirable dramatic power and pages of
      the most vivid description. Some of the stories are inter-
      esting enough, and all are well told; the anecdotes are
      highly amusing. But there is almost no beginning to the
      central story and altogether no end to it. The characters
      seem intended not for actual living beings but for philo-
      sophical abstractions. The book is a sad jumble, though the
      jumble of a very clever man. It contains "a mass of anec-
      dotes, stories, scenes, and sketches undigested, and...
      indigestible." Reprinted in Norton The Confidence-Man,
      pp. 275-278; reprinted in part in Branch, pp. 379-381.

28   ANON. Notice of The Confidence-Man. New York Porter's Spirit
      of the Times, 2 (25 April), 120.
          Reviewer has not read the book, but Melville's name is a
      guarantee of its interest and literary merit. Reprinted in
      Flanagan, p. 63.

29   ANON. Review of The Confidence-Man. New York Churchman
      (30 April).
          The Confidence-Man is marked by the characteristic and
      defect of Melville's later works--"a disposition to meta-
      physical speculation, for which the subject affords him a
      wide scope."

1857

30   ANON. Review of The Confidence-Man. London John Bull and
     Britannia (9 May).
          No thread of a story ties together these sketches of
     American life. But a vein of philosophy runs through the
     book, and the conflict between trust and distrust, which
     is in every human breast, has not often been so forcibly
     and amusingly illustrated as in the incoherent ramblings
     of The Confidence-Man. Reprinted in part in Log, p. 578.

31   ANON. Review of The Confidence-Man. New York Independent
     (14 May), p. 8.
          A worse book than Typee, in its moral tone and tendency,
     has rarely been published. Melville presented himself,
     autobiographically, as one of the vilest of those runaway
     sailors who escape from work and civilization and give
     themselves to the indulgences of a brutish life in the
     Pacific islands. A partial reading of The Confidence-Man
     shows that Melville may have learned some decency since
     then but that there is no prospect of any good to be got
     by reading farther. Reprinted in Monteiro (Fourth Quarter
     1974), p. 437.

32   ANON. "The Sandwich Islands. Their History." Chicago Maga-
     zine, 1 (15 May), pp. 226-227.
          The "unanimous testimony of intelligent natives" de-
     scribes "a state of things very different from the Paradis-
     iacal innocence and happiness ascribed to the aborigines by
     Hermann Melville & Co."

33   ANON. Review of The Confidence-Man. Springfield (Mass.)
     Republican (16 May), p. 1.
          The Confidence-Man is the oddest, most unique, and the
     most ingenious thing Melville has yet done. The book is
     very interesting and very well written, but it seems like
     the work of one not in love or sympathy with his kind;
     human nature gets badly "cut up."

34   ANON. Review of The Confidence-Man. London National Era
     (17 May).
          "A strange book, the object of which is difficult to
     detect, unless it be to prove this wicked world still more
     full of wickedness than even the most gloomy philosophers
     have supposed." The Confidence Man is "the villain who,
     with the Scripture in his mouth, has mammon in his heart,
     and a fiendish principle of deceiving all men influencing
     his every word." Does Melville mean that "no one lives
     who acts up to Christian principle? that to profess to act
     from good feeling is a sign that we are acting solely with

the base view of our own interest?" The reverse of this
is not so uncommon as The Confidence-Man might lead us to
suppose. The book is thoroughly original in plot and
written in the brilliant and masterly style Melville exhibited in Typee and Omoo. The pictures, if dark in satire,
are full of wit and cleverness.

35 ANON. Review of The Confidence-Man. London Saturday Review,
      3 (23 May), 484.
      Melville's view that the world consists of those who
cheat and those who are cheated should be condemned if it
were gravely intended. But he has no such intention. He
has fully attained his aim in The Confidence-Man of minis-
tering to "the implied wish of the more indulgent lovers of
entertainment, before whom harlequin can never appear in a
coat too parti-coloured, or cut capers too fantastic." He
also vividly portrays the "money-getting spirit which appears
to pervade every class of men in the States, almost like a
monomania"; as a satirist he is attacking "the most dangerous and the most debasing tendency of the age." The practical commentary on the mystic philosopher's philosophy
attacks "severely, and with considerable power, the pre-
tended philanthropical, but really hard and selfish optimist
school, whose opinions seemed not long ago likely to gain
many disciples." Occasional irreverent use of Scriptural
phrases, doubtless inadvertent, mars Melville's wit and
blunts the edge of his satire. The characters in The
Confidence-Man are all wonderfully well sustained and linked
together. Reprinted in part in Log, p. 579; reprinted in
Branch, pp. 381-383.

36 ANON. Review of The Confidence-Man. Newark Daily Advertiser
      (23 May), p. 2.
      A man of great talent, Melville manages to write the most
unreadable of books; but those who read police reports will
relish the record of trickery and deceit in The Confidence-
Man. It seems as if Melville is afraid to write as well as
he can.

37 ANON. Pittsfield (Mass.) Sun (28 May).
      Notes Melville's return from abroad and the London pub-
lication of The Confidence-Man, which "is critically noticed
at large in most of the London literary papers."

38 ANON. "Domestic Intelligence." New York Harper's Weekly,
      1 (30 May), 342.
      Reports Melville's return on May 20 "in the steamer City
of Manchester, from Liverpool, after a seven months' absence
abroad."

1857

39 ANON. "Literary Gossip from Abroad." New York <u>Weekly Times</u>
    (30 May).
        Reports favorable reception of <u>The Confidence-Man</u> in
    England.

40 ANON. Review of <u>The Confidence-Man</u>. New York <u>Mrs. Stephens'</u>
    <u>Illustrated New Monthly Magazine</u>, 2 (June), 288.
        <u>The Confidence-Man</u> is the most singular of Melville's
    many singular books. Melville seems bent upon obliterating
    his early successes. His style has become "more individual-
    ized--more striking, original, sinewy, compact; more reflec-
    tive and philosophical." Yet his recent books are
    "confessedly inferior" to his earlier ones. The Confidence
    Man assumes innumerable disguises with no clear object;
    there is no apparent object in the masquerade. Reprinted
    in part in <u>Log</u>, p. 580; reprinted in Branch, p. 384.

41 ANON. "The Confidence Man." Pittsfield (Mass.) <u>Berkshire</u>
    <u>County Eagle</u> (19 June), p. 2.
        Notes that <u>The Confidence-Man</u> "is much praised in the
    English papers" and quotes from 1857.B35, adding: "We need
    not say to those who have read the book that as a picture of
    American society, it is <u>slightly</u> distorted." Reprinted in
    Norton <u>The Confidence-Man</u>, p. 278.

42 ANON. Review of <u>The Confidence-Man</u>. London <u>Westminster and</u>
    <u>Foreign Quarterly Review</u>, NS 12 (July), 310-311.
        <u>The Confidence-Man</u> shows Melville in the new character
    of satirist. "It required close knowledge of the world, and
    of the Yankee world, to write such a book and make the sat-
    ire acute and telling, and the scenes not too improbable
    for the faith given to fiction. Perhaps the moral is the
    gullibility of the great Republic, when taken on its own
    tack. At all events, it is a wide enough moral to have
    numerous applications, and sends minor shafts to right and
    left." Several capital anecdotes are well told; "but we
    are conscious of a certain hardness in the book, from the
    absence of humour, where so much humanity is shuffled into
    close neighbourhood. And with the absence of humour, too,
    there is an absence of kindliness. The view of human
    nature is severe and sombre.... It wants relief, and is
    written too much in the spirit of Timon." Few Americans
    write so powerfully as Melville or in better English.
    <u>The Confidence-Man</u> will add to his reputation. Reprinted
    in part in <u>Log</u>, p. 581; reprinted in <u>Recognition</u>, pp. 98-99,
    and Branch, pp. 385-386.

43   [GREENE, RICHARD TOBIAS]. Letter to the Editor. New York
      Putnam's Monthly, 10 (July), 140.
            Replying to the April number of Putnam's [see 1857.B3],
      "Toby" claims that he is often spoken of as Melville's valet
      or "man Friday" or as a myth; in fact he "stood on the same
      footing with Melville." Reprinted in Log, p. 581.

44   ANON. Review of The Confidence-Man. New York Hunt's
      Merchants' Magazine and Commercial Review, 37 (August), 270.
            Admirers of The Piazza Tales, Omoo, and Typee "will not
      forego the gratification of a story though somewhat differ-
      ent from the others, equal, if not surpassing in interest,
      either of his previous performances." Reprinted in Pollin
      (April 1975), p. 60.

*45   ANON. Concord (N.H.) Patriot (18 November).
            Announcement of the 24 November lecture at Concord on
      Roman statuary. Cited in Sealts (1957), p. 22.

46   ANON. "Melville's Lecture." Lawrence (Mass.) Courier
      (25 November), p. 2.
            Review of the 23 November lecture at Lawrence on "Roman
      Statuary." The subject might be called "The men of ancient
      Rome, studied in their busts and statues." The studies were
      "marked throughout by keen insight, honest independence,
      bold originality, and great justness of vision." Melville's
      nervous, vigorous style was perhaps too highly wrought and
      he spoke so low that many could not hear the lecture. Re-
      printed in Lloyd, pp. 392-393; reprinted in part in Log,
      p. 584.

47   ANON. "Institute Lectures." New York Journal and Courier
      (25 November).
            Advertisement for the Young Men's Institute's winter
      lecture series. Melville "was first made known to the
      reading public by his wonderfully graphic and Robinson
      Crusoe-like record of the vagabond life he led, while a
      runaway sailor...." Reprinted in Cameron, p. 92.

48   ANON. "Mercantile Library Association. Lecture by Herman
      Melville." Boston Daily Courier (3 December), p. 2.
            Summary of the 2 December lecture at Boston on "Statuary
      in Rome." Reprinted in 1858.B7; reprinted in part in Log,
      p. 585.

49   ANON. "Lecture on the Statuary of Rome." Boston Daily Evening
      Bee (3 December), p. 2.
            Summary of the 2 December lecture. Refers to Melville as
      "a gentleman of decided position in American literature, and

1857

the author of several unquestionably original and eccentric
works." His appearance in Boston was regarded "as an 'event'
ranging up to a 'sensation' point," and "a large and distinguished character-dotted audience" was present. The
lecture, "though quite able, and delivered with considerable
enthusiasm, excited but little applause," but was listened
to with complimentary attention.

50   ANON. "Mercantile Library Lectures." Boston Daily Evening
     Transcript (3 December).
         Review of the 2 December lecture at Boston on Roman
     statuary. A large audience listened with evident satisfac-
     tion. Melville showed himself as much at home in the lec-
     ture room "as in prosecuting his peculiar vocation, i.e.,
     the weaving of sparkling fancies into a web of incident
     and fact--the result of extended observation and travel."
     The lecture contained many trenchant passages, reminiscent
     of his writings. One defect: the subject was too vast for
     one hour. Reprinted in part in Log, p. 586.

51   ANON. "Mercantile Library Lectures." Boston Evening Traveller
     (3 December), p. 1.
         Summary of the 2 December lecture at Boston on "Statuary
     in Rome." Melville spoke in a clear and distinct voice,
     and on the whole it was a most interesting lecture, "though
     too long by one-fifth, covering an hour and a quarter."
     The audience was not as large as on the two previous eve-
     nings. Reprinted in part in Log, p. 586.

52   ANON. "Mercantile Library Lectures--Herman Melville on the
     Statuary of Rome." Boston Journal (3 December).
         Summary of the 2 December lecture at Boston. "The lec-
     ture was quite interesting to those of artistic tastes, but
     we fancy the larger part of the audience would have pre-
     ferred something more modern and personal." Reprinted in
     part in Log, pp. 585-586.

53   ANON. "Mercantile Library Association." Boston Post
     (3 December).
         Summary of the 2 December lecture on "Statuary in Rome"
     at Boston, "before a large audience."

*54 ANON. Montreal Commercial Advertiser (10 December).
         Advance notice of the lecture in Montreal on Roman
     statuary. Reprinted in Sealts (1957), p. 25.

55   ANON. "Mercantile Library Association." Montreal Gazette
     (14 December), p. 2.

Review of the 11 December lecture at Montreal on "'Sight
seeing in Rome,' or rather 'Statuary in Rome.'" Some passages of the lecture were very fine, but on the whole it was
somewhat disappointing. The subject was too large to be
condensed into a single lecture.

56 ANON. "Lecture on Sight-Seeing in Rome." Montreal <u>Daily
Transcript and Commercial Advertiser</u> (16 December), p. 1.
Summary of the 11 December lecture at Montreal. The
audience was "numerous and respectable."

57 ANON. "Lectures." Montreal <u>Witness</u> (19 December).
Reference to the 11 December lecture at Montreal. It
"was an insult to a Christian audience to invite to lecture
before it, a man who has libelled Christian Missionaries,
and shown himself to be an enemy to Christian Missions."
The ideas of some of the lecturers in this series "make
their lectures undesirable, not to say dangerous, for young
men." Reprinted in 1857.B59 and Sealts (1957), p. 25.

58 ANON. Saratoga Springs (N.Y.) <u>Daily Saratogian</u> (24 December),
p. 3.
Review of the 21 December lecture at Saratoga Springs on
"Statues in Rome." The subject was handled in a style at
once graceful and instructive. With only a day's notice,
the audience was quite small "but decidedly select in its
literary appreciation." Reprinted in Sealts (1957), p. 26.

59 ANON. "The Mercantile Library Association and the 'Montreal
Witness.'" Montreal <u>True Witness and Catholic Chronicle</u>
(25 December).
Reprints 1857.B57. The meaning of this tirade is that
Melville did not provide the anticipated "anecdotes illustrative of the '<u>Corruptions of Romanism</u>'" and had previously
told a few unpleasant facts about the Methodist missions to
the Pacific islands, which had never been refuted. In
"Sight Seeing in Rome" he furnished a rich intellectual
treat. Reprinted in Kennedy, pp. 134-136.

*60 ANON. "Mr. Melville's Lecture." New Haven <u>Daily Palladium</u>
(30 December), p. 2.
Announcement of the 30 December lecture at New Haven on
Roman statuary. Reprinted in Cameron, p. 96.

61 S. "Mr. Herman Melville and his Lecture." New Haven <u>Journal
and Courier</u> (30 December), p. 2.
Advance notice of the 30 December lecture at New Haven
on "Roman Statuary." Gives biographical details and notes
that without "the best advantages of culture in his early

1857

youth," Melville "has advanced over difficulties of considerable magnitude, to a position of peculiar elevation as an
American literary man." Expects a large audience. Reprinted in A.S.P., pp. 111-112; reprinted in part in Log,
p. 588.

1858 A BOOKS - NONE

1858 B SHORTER WRITINGS

1   FRANCIS, JOHN W. Old New York; or, Reminiscences of the Past
     Sixty Years. New York: Charles Roe, pp. 363-364.
        In a passage noting "the worldlike reputation" secured
     by prominent American writers: "the romances of Hawthorne
     and of Melville...have met with a reception flattering to
     the most aspiring author...."

*2   ANON. Auburn (N.Y.) Daily Advertiser (2 January).
        Advance notice of the 5 January lecture at Auburn on
     Roman statuary. Cited in Sealts (1957), p. 28.

*3   ANON. Ithaca (N.Y.) Journal and Advertiser (5 January).
        Announcement of the 6 January lecture at Ithaca on
     Roman statuary. Cited in Duffy, p. 58.

4   ANON. Review of Lecture. Auburn (N.Y.) Daily Advertiser
     (6 January), p. 5.
        Review of the 5 January lecture at Auburn on "the Statues
     in Rome." The lecture was "by far the most chaste and clas-
     sic of the season," exhibiting the elevating conceptions
     and masterly description of a finely cultivated and appre-
     ciative mind. But it was completely spoiled by Melville's
     feeble and "inexcusable blundering, sing song, monotonous
     delivery." As a result, the lecture probably did not please
     twenty in the large audience. Reprinted in part in Sealts
     (1957), pp. 29-30.

5   ANON. Review of Lecture. Auburn (N.Y.) Daily American
     (6 January), p. 3.
        Melville's 5 January lecture at Auburn on Roman statuary
     was worthy of his talents and reputation but was not a very
     popular one.

6   ANON. Notice of Lecture. Cincinnati Evening Herald
     (11 January).
        Predicts that Melville's readers will want to see the
     genius who created the singular productions Typee, Omoo,
     Mardi, and Moby-Dick, and that the lecture hall will be
     crowded.

7 ANON. Notice of Lecture. Cincinnati <u>Morning Leader</u>
   (11 January).
       Expects something fine from the "talented and distin-
   guished author of <u>Omoo</u>, <u>Typee</u>, <u>Mardi</u>, and <u>Maybe Dick</u>" (on
   the subject of Roman statuary). Reprints summary of lec-
   ture from 1857.B48.

*8 ANON. Review of Lecture. Cincinnati <u>Morning Herald</u>
   (12 January).
       Review of the 11 January lecture in Cleveland on Roman
   statuary. Cited in <u>Log</u>, p. 589, and in Sealts (1957), p. 31.

9 ANON. "Melville's Lecture." Cleveland <u>Morning Leader</u>
   (12 January), p. 3.
       Review of the 11 January lecture at Cleveland on "Roman
   Statuary"--one of the most interesting of the season. The
   "prevailing <u>practicality</u> of pioneer society" and lack of "that
   cultivation of nature and taste necessary to a fine and general appreciation of Art" explain why the hall was not full.
   Melville's mind is "untrammeled by the mannerisms of the
   schools, yet keenly alive to the beautiful in Nature, and in-
   timately familiarized therewith by eager, loving, and extended
   observation." His lecture was distinguished by remarkable
   "word-<u>chiseling</u>." Review ends with description of Melville
   and notes a slight indistinctness in his articulation. Reprinted in part in <u>Log</u>, p. 589, and Sealts (1957), pp. 31-32.

10 ANON. "Melodeon." Cleveland <u>Plain Dealer</u> (12 January).
       Notes that the audience for the 11 January lecture at
   Cleveland on "Roman Statuary" was not large but appeared
   to be "very well satisfied" with the lecture.

11 ANON. Review of Lecture. Ithaca (N.Y.) <u>Journal and Advertiser</u>
   (13 January), p. 3.
       Review of the 7 January lecture at Ithaca Town Hall on
   "Ancient Statuary." In comparing the statues with the people they represented, Melville evinced a fine, quick, per-
   ceptive imagination and a rare appreciation of the beauties
   of statuary. But his subject must necessarily be an unat-
   tractive one to the masses. Reprinted in Duffy, p. 58.

12 ANON. "Mr. Melville's Lecture." Detroit <u>Daily Free Press</u>
   (14 January), p. 1.
       Detailed summary of the 12 January lecture at Detroit on
   "Roman Statuary." Notes that Melville is well known to the
   literary world as the author of <u>Omoo</u>, <u>Typee</u>, and <u>Moby-Dick</u>.

13 ANON. "Herman Melville." Cleveland <u>Ohio Farmer</u> (23 January),
   p. 28.

1858

Review of the 11 January lecture at Cleveland on "Roman
Statuary." In style the lecture was superior to nine-tenths
of the lectures usually given. There is a dreamy beauty
about Melville's utterances, a "boozy elocution." His
respect for heathenism is profound and sincere. An undercurrent of regret, or sorrow, or malice at the introduction
of Christianity seemed to pervade the whole lecture, marring
enjoyment of the fine observation, beautiful sentiments, ex-
quisite choice of terms, and fine portraiture of character.
Melville is already well known to readers of light literature as the author of Typee, Omoo, and Moby-Dick. Reprinted
in part in Sealts (1957), p. 34.

*14   ANON. Montreal Witness (23 January).
News item, reprinted from the American Presbyterian, on
the cannibals of the "celebrated valley of Typee" and sarcastic reference to "those paradisical innocents with whom
the author of Typee and Omoo passed his time so agreeably."
Cited in Kennedy, p. 136.

15   ANON. Review of Lecture. Clarksville (Tenn.) Jeffersonian
(27 January), p. 2.
Melville's 22 January lecture at Clarksville on "The
Statues of Rome" was "one of the events of the season,"
attracting a large and fashionable audience. The subject
was not one calculated to excite general interest or much
enthusiasm, but all admired Melville's mastery of it and
his finished and scholarly composition.

16   ANON. "Herman Melville." Clarksville (Tenn.) Chronicle
(29 January), p. 3.
Review of the 22 January lecture at Clarksville on
"Statues in Rome." The subject was faultless in conception
and execution. With "that true instinct of genius, which
turns aside from lofty and high sounding themes," Melville
"selected one of unpretending title, from which to educe
noble and inexhaustible thought, and quiet, but none the
less striking philosophy." The "expression of doubt, and
dark groping of human speculation, in the ideal statuary of
that age, when the old mythology was passing away, and men's
minds had not yet reposed in the new faith, was finely
portrayed." The superiority of art over science was never
so triumphantly and eloquently sustained as in the closing
remarks. Some of the audience objected to Melville's subdued delivery. Reprinted in part in Sealts (1957), p. 39.

*17   ANON. Notice of Lecture. Cincinnati Daily Commercial
(1 February).
Announcement of the 2 February lecture at Cincinnati on
Roman Statuary, identifying Melville as "one of the most

popular writers in the United States" and giving a brief
biographical sketch. Cited in Sealts (1957), pp. 42-43.

*18   ANON. Announcement of Lecture. Chillicothe (Ohio) Scioto
       Gazette (2 February).
            Notes that wherever Melville has lectured, "he has re-
       ceived the general commendation of the press and the people.
       His fame as a writer is world-wide, and his fine descriptive
       powers, as exhibited in 'Omoo' and 'Typee' cannot fail to
       make his lecture a rich intellectual treat to his audience."
       Cited in Sealts (1957), p. 45.

19   ANON. Notice of Lecture. Cincinnati Daily Commercial
       (2 February).
            Announcement of the lecture at Cincinnati the same day
       on Roman Statuary. Notes that Melville's lectures are said
       to be admirably written and that the public is "extremely
       desirous" to see and hear him, anticipating a rich literary
       repast. Advises Melville to avoid'the usual objection
       against lectures by speaking distinctly and with animation.
       Reprinted in part in Log, p. 590.

20   ANON. "Third Lecture Before the Y.M.M.L.A. by Herman
       Melville, Esq." Cincinnati Daily Commercial (3 February).
            Detailed summary of the 2 February lecture at Cincinnati
       on "Statues in Rome." As a literary production the lecture
       was very superior, abounding with happy gems of thought and
       beautiful word painting, a department of literature Melville
       greatly excels in. Review ends with a description of
       Melville ("rather an attractive person, though not what any-
       body would describe [as] good looking") and his delivery
       ("not sufficiently animated for a Western audience," enun-
       ciates "with only tolerable distinctness"). Reprinted in
       1858.B25; reprinted in part in Kummer, pp. 34-35; Mead,
       p. 76; Log, p. 591.

21   ANON. "'The Statues of Rome'--Lecture by Herman Melville, Esq.,
       last Evening." Cincinnati Daily Gazette (3 February).
            In appearance Melville is "about such a man as one might
       see from reading his works; an adventurous, determined
       traveler, free in the expression of opinions, and yet a
       close observer of matters passing around him." The lecture
       was rather interesting throughout, but the high interest of
       the opening passages was not maintained to the end. Sum-
       mary of lecture. Reprinted in Pilkington and Alsterlund,
       pp. 68-70; reprinted in part in Log, p. 591.

22   ANON. "Y.M.M.L. Lectures--Herman Melville on 'Statues in
       Rome.'" Cincinnati Enquirer (3 February).

1858

> Brief summary of Melville's literary career before sum-
> mary of the 2 December lecture at Cincinnati. Typee is the
> best of his works, The Confidence-Man decidedly the worst,
> "one of the dullest and most dismally monotonous books we
> remember to have read." Fayaway is the most attractive and
> best known of Melville's characters. Pierre, an example of
> his later works "more akin to the modern novel," is highly
> extravagant and unnatural, but original and interesting in
> its construction and characters. The lecture lasted nearly
> two hours and was "exceedingly interesting and eloquent,
> abounding in admirable specimens of such word-painting as
> his best works contain." The delivery "was monotonous and
> often indistinct, but not devoid of impressiveness, which
> sometimes approached the ministerially solemn." Reprinted
> in part in Log, pp. 590–591, and Sealts (1957), p. 44;
> reprinted in Norton The Confidence-Man, p. 279.

*23   ANON. Clarksville (Tenn.) Daily Enquirer (3 February).
>   Review of the 22 January lecture at Clarksville on Roman
> statuary. Cited in Log, p. 590.

24   ANON. Review of Lecture. Chillicothe (Ohio) Advertiser
>   (5 February), p. 3.
>   Review of the 3 February lecture at Chillicothe on "Stat-
> ues in Rome." "Altogether, to those familiar through writers
> of the day with Rome and its attractions, the lecture was a
> string of indifferent Pearls, genuine indeed, but sadly
> wanting in that polish which gives even to trite common
> places a passing interest and endows the germ of original-
> ity with the power of life and beauty." Nevertheless, the
> audience in general was highly appreciative; and the lecture
> was by no means void of interest or instruction. Melville's
> delivery was impaired by quite a severe cold. Reprinted in
> Kummer, p. 35; reprinted in part in Log, p. 591, and Sealts
> (1957), p. 46.

25   ANON. "Herman Melville's Lecture." Chillicothe (Ohio)
>   Advertiser (5 February), p. 2.
>   Reprints the summary of "Statues in Rome" and description
> of Melville's appearance and delivery from 1858.B20, lest
> it be imagined the strictures of 1858.B24 do Melville an
> injustice.

26   ANON. "The Lecture." Chillicothe (Ohio) Scioto Gazette
>   (9 February), p. 3.
>   Review of the 3 February lecture at Chillicothe on
> "Statues in Rome." The audience's expectations of a rare
> intellectual treat were not disappointed. Melville makes
> no attempt at eloquence but showed that his brilliant imag-
> ination and charming descriptive powers can hold hearers as

well as readers entranced. The lecture was replete with
rich imagery. Melville's voice was rich and mellow despite
a severe cold; he speaks with earnestness and enunciates
distinctly. Reprinted in Sealts (1957), p. 45.

27   ANON. "Mishawum Lectures." Charlestown (Mass.) <u>Advertiser</u>
     (10 February).
          Review of the 9 February lecture at Charlestown on
     "Statuary." An interesting and instructive lecture, its
     style neither dry nor verbose but elegant and mostly free
     from artificialities. Brief summary. Reprinted in Birss,
     (1943), pp. 11-12.

28   ANON. "Mishawum Lectures, No. XI." Charlestown and Boston
     (Mass.) <u>Bunker-Hill Aurora and Boston Mirror</u> (13 February),
     p. 2.
          Review of the 9 February lecture at Charlestown on
     "Statuary in Italy." A well written but particularly dull
     lecture, a monotonous description of such "dead heads" as
     Demosthenes, Julius Caesar, Seneca, Plato, Tiberius and
     Apollo. No man could reasonably hope to interest a common
     audience on such a subject. Common people care precious
     little about Italy or its statues. Melville's "draughts
     upon the classical Dictionary were frequent and heavy, too
     heavy for the comfort and edification of his auditors."
     Reprinted in part in <u>Log</u>, p. 592.

29   ANON. Announcement of Lecture. Rochester <u>Democrat and
     American</u> (18 February).
          Announcement of the 18 February lecture at Rochester on
     Roman statuary, anticipating "one of the most interesting
     lectures of the season." <u>Typee</u>, <u>Omoo</u>, "etc." are found in
     every well-selected home library. Melville "has abstained
     from producing books latterly, and entered the lecture
     field, where his success has been entirely commensurate
     with his exalted literary reputation previously attained."

30   ANON. Notice of Lecture. Rochester <u>Union and Advertiser</u>
     (18 February).
          Advance notice of the 18 February lecture at Rochester
     on Roman statuary. Melville's reputation should entitle
     him to a full house; the vast number interested in his sub-
     ject will be present.

31   ANON. "Mr. Melville's Lecture." Rochester <u>Democrat
     and American</u> (20 February), p. 3.
          Review of the 18 February lecture at Rochester on "the
     Statues of Rome." The lecture was well written, knowledge-
     able, and critically appreciative, but not particularly
     interesting to the miscellaneous audience. Melville erred

in his choice of theme. The mass of people are not deeply versed in ancient literature and are not very interested in ancient statues. Reprinted in Pilkington and Alsterlund, p. 68; reprinted in part in Log, p. 593, and Sealts (1957), p. 48.

32　ANON. "The Lyceum--Thirteenth Lecture. By Herman Melville." New Bedford Daily Evening Standard (24 February), p. 2.
　　Summary of the 23 February lecture at New Bedford on "The Remains of Ancient Art in Rome." The lecture was a well written and scholarly essay which would be read with much pleasure, but was not calculated to interest as a lecture.

33　ANON. "Lyceum Lectures." New Bedford Daily Mercury (24 February), p. 2.
　　Summary of the 23 February lecture at New Bedford on "the Sculptures of Rome." An interesting and instructive lecture, with many suggestive and thoughtful criticisms on art interspersed. Reprinted in part in Log, p. 593.

34　ANON. The Seven Travelers. New York Emerson's Magazine and Putnam's Monthly, 7 (November), 462.
　　A character misquotes from Pierre, Book III, chapter 2. ("From without no wonderful effect is wrought within ourselves, unless some interior, corresponding wonder welcome it.")

35　ANON. "Local Intelligence." Pittsfield (Mass.) Sun (11 November).
　　Reports that Melville is ready to receive applications to lecture.

36　ANON. "Local Items. Lectures." Pittsfield (Mass.) Berkshire County Eagle (19 November).
　　Announcement of the 14 December lecture at Pittsfield on the South Seas.

37　'Herr Honeytown.' Letter to the Editor. Yonkers (N.Y.) Examiner (8 December).
　　Sarcastic reaction to the 6 December lecture at Yonkers on the South Seas. "We must be in our second childhood, for up to Monday evening last we were ignorant of the fact that the Pacific Ocean extended from Tierra del Fuego to Kamschatka, and that the said pool was...'infested with islands, densely peopled with sharks, and some natives.'" Reprinted in Sealts (1957), pp. 73-74.

*38 ANON. Pittsfield (Mass.) <u>Sun</u> (9 December).
     Announcement of the 14 December lecture at Pittsfield
     on the South Seas. Cited in Sealts (1957), p. 76.

39   ANON. "Melville's Lecture." Yonkers (N.Y.) <u>Examiner</u>
     (9 December), p. 2.
     Review of the 6 December lecture at Yonkers on the South
     Seas. Melville's success as a humorist, "if it be newly
     tried," should encourage him, for his large audience was
     very sympathetic and in continuous merriment. He could not
     "forbear making a splenetic allusion to the missionaries,
     concerning whom his feelings are well-known, and are too
     bitter to be impersonal." Melville's "excessively florid
     style" was seen before in <u>Typee</u>: each noun has its adjec-
     tive, each sentence its parenthesis, "till we are aghast
     at the profuseness." His delivery is anything but pleasant.
     Reprinted in Birss (February 1934), pp. 51-52; reprinted
     in part in <u>Log</u>, pp. 596-597, and Sealts (1957), pp. 72-74.

40   ANON. Announcement of Lecture. Pittsfield (Mass.) <u>Berkshire
     County Eagle</u> (10 December).
     Announcement of the 14 December lecture at Pittsfield
     on "the South Seas." Nothing need be said to induce
     Pittsfield people to hear such a man on such a subject.
     Melville is a familiar speaker, "abounding in quaint and
     original thoughts, which adorn and enliven a story told
     with extraordinary powers of narrative and description."
     Reprinted in <u>Log</u>, p. 597.

41   ANON. "The Lecture Course." Pittsfield (Mass.) <u>Berkshire
     County Eagle</u> (17 December), p. 2.
     Review of the 14 December lecture at Pittsfield, on the
     "South Seas." The lecture was pleasant and instructive,
     written in the style of Melville's best books, quaint,
     simple, polished, and sparkling with original thoughts.
     The hall was full, though the night was the most stormy
     and uncomfortable of the winter. Reprinted in part in <u>Log</u>,
     p. 597.

<u>1859 A BOOKS - NONE</u>

<u>1859 B SHORTER WRITINGS</u>

1   ANON. <u>The Tricks and Traps of Chicago. Part 1</u>. New York:
     Dinsmore & Co., p. 51.
     Mention: "Whoever has read Hermann Melville's 'Confidence
     Man' will have formed a very clear and accurate idea of this

1859

species of the genus homo, as exhibited in many of his
chamelion-like phases."

2   ANON. "Lecture by Herman Melville--South Sea Adventures."
    Boston Atlas and Daily Bee (1 February), p. 2.
        Summary of the 31 January lecture at Boston. Melville's
    reputation called out a somewhat larger audience than
    usual, "though not so numerous as should have been the
    case." The lecture was quite interesting and frequently
    elicited applause.

3   ANON. "Mechanic Apprentices' Lectures." Boston Daily
    Advertiser (1 February), p. 4.
        Summary of the 31 January lecture at Boston, on "The
    South Sea." Melville's description of the natives and
    their customs was graphic and humorous. The lecture was
    a fine production and received the close attention of the
    large audience. Reprinted in part in Log, p. 599.

4   ANON. "Herman Melville at the Tremont Temple." Boston
    Daily Courier (1 February), p. 1.
        Summary of the 31 January lecture at Boston on "South
    Sea Adventures." Reprinted in part in Log, pp. 598-599.

5   ANON. "Mechanic Apprentices' Lectures." Boston Daily Evening
    Traveller (1 February), p. 4.
        Summary of the 31 January lecture at Boston on "The
    South Seas." The lecture abounded with numerous anecdotes
    and facts of great interest. The hall was not more than
    half full.

6   ANON. "Mechanic Apprentices' Lectures." Boston Evening
    Transcript (1 February), p. 2.
        The 31 January lecture at Boston on the "South Sea" con-
    tained much fine writing, and vividly described the manners
    and customs of the natives of some of the South Sea islands.

7   ANON. "Mechanic Apprentices' Lecture." Boston Herald
    (1 February), p. 2.
        Brief mention of Melville's "interesting lecture" on
    "South Sea Adventures," 31 January at Boston.

8   ANON. "Lecture on the South Seas, by Herman Melville, Esq."
    Boston Journal (1 February), p. 4.
        Summary of the 31 January lecture at Boston. The lecture
    gave the most ample satisfaction and was frequently applauded.
    The audience was not large but about equal to the usual
    attendance for the course of lectures.

9   ANON. "Herman Melville before the Mechanic Apprentices'
     Association." Boston <u>Post</u> (1 February), p. 4.
          Summary of the 31 January lecture at Boston on "The
     South Sea." Notes that the audience was not large.

*10   ANON. New York <u>Daily Tribune</u> (5 February).
          Advance notice of the 7 February lecture in New York on
     the South Seas. Cited in Sealts (1957), p. 78.

11   ANON. Announcement of Lecture. Baltimore <u>Sun</u> (8 February).
          Announcement of the 8 February lecture at Baltimore on
     the South Seas. Melville's "charming books of Life and
     Adventure" in the South Seas "first truly presented to the
     world men and manners in this enchanting region." Reprinted
     in Gifford, p. 245.

12   ANON. "South Sea Islands." New York <u>Daily Tribune</u>
     (8 February), p. 7.
          Brief summary of the 7 February lecture at New York.
     Melville related many interesting incidents of the islands'
     inhabitants and was listened to with great attention by a
     fair audience.

13   ANON. "N.Y. Historical Society Lecture." New York <u>Evening
     Express</u> (8 February), p. 3.
          Summary of the 7 February lecture on the "South Seas,"
     which was ably treated, full of rich, valuable information,
     and delivered with ease and grace. The hall "was nearly
     filled by an audience highly respectable, and comprising
     some of our most eminent <u>literati</u>."

14   ANON. Review of Lecture. New York <u>Evening Post</u> (8 February),
     p. 3.
          Brief summary of the 7 February lecture at New York on
     "The South Sea." Melville's descriptions of the phenomena
     observed in this region were replete with interest.

15   ANON. "'The South Seas'--A Lecture By Herman Melville,
     Delivered Before The Mercantile Library Association."
     Baltimore <u>American and Commercial Advertiser</u> (9 February),
     p. 1.
          Long, detailed summary of the 8 February lecture at
     Baltimore, which "drew a fine audience." Melville had
     delighted them from time to time through several years past
     with his graphic and graceful books suggested by the same
     romantic subject. Reprinted in part in <u>Log</u>, p. 601.

1859

16 ANON. "Mercantile Library Lectures." Baltimore <u>Sun</u>
(9 February), p. 1.
Summary of the 8 February lecture at Baltimore on "The
South Seas." The lecture abounded in interesting personal
narratives and held the interest of the audience to the
close. Reprinted in 1859.B17 and Gifford, pp. 245-246.

17 ANON. "Mercantile Library Lectures." Baltimore <u>Weekly Sun</u>
(12 February).
Reprint of 1859.B16.

18 ANON. "Herman Melville--'South Seas.'" New York <u>Century</u>
(12 February), p. 6.
Summary of the 7 February lecture at New York. A very
interesting lecture, none the less so for its modest and
unpretending composition and delivery. Reprinted in part
in Sealts (1957), pp. 79-80.

19 ANON. "Herman Melville's Lecture." Chicago <u>Daily Journal</u>
(25 February).
Review of the 24 February lecture, "to a large and
fashionable audience" at Metropolitan Hall, Chicago, on
the "South Seas." Out of charity forbears criticism, but
notes Melville's limited vocal powers and the intrinsic
defects in the lecture; compares Melville's performance
unfavorably to "the matchless word-painting and clear-
ringing cadences of the handsome Bayard [Taylor]," a previous lecturer. Refers to the many admirers of the really
charming books <u>Typee</u>, <u>Omoo</u>, "etc."

20 ANON. "The South Seas--Mr. Melville's Lecture." Chicago
<u>Daily Press and Tribune</u> (25 February), p. 1.
Summary of the 24 February lecture at Chicago. Melville's
discourse, "in the warm coloring, the voluptuous odors and
romantic drapery with which he invested it," was fully up
to public expectation. But those at some distance from
the stage lost a large share of the admirable entertainment.
Reprinted in part in 1859.B25 and <u>Log</u>, p. 602.

*21 ANON. Milwaukee <u>Daily Wisconsin</u> (25 February).
Advance notice of the 25 February lecture in Milwaukee
on the South Seas. Cited in Sealts (1957), p. 84.

22 ANON. "Herman Melville's Lecture." Milwaukee <u>Daily Free
Democrat</u> (26 February), p. 3.
Review of the 25 February lecture at Milwaukee on the
"South Sea Islands." Perhaps most of Melville's large audi-
ence were disappointed in the lecturer and his lecture,

which was a literary effort below mediocrity and too bookish
to please. His remarks were so general they failed to create much interest; he merely told what the primary geogra-
phies tell. The few illustrations in the lecture were bare
and colored more by Melville's attempts at word painting
than by any inherent or thrilling interest in them. He
received limited applause at the end. Reprinted in part in
Sealts (1957), p. 85.

23   ANON. "An Antartic Hour. Lecture of Herman Melville before
     the Young Men's Association Last Night." Milwaukee Daily
     Sentinel (26 February).
        Summary of the 25 February lecture at Milwaukee on the
     South Seas. As a lecturer Melville sustains the idea
     formed of him in Typee--"a soft, voluptuous ease is the
     predominant characteristic. Romance is breathed into the
     sterile topography of his subject, and the same drowsy en-
     chantment that makes his writings so fascinating radiates
     from the speaker...." Reprinted in part in Log, pp.
     pp. 602-603.

24   ANON. "Herman Melville's Lecture Last Night." Milwaukee
     Daily Wisconsin (26 February), p. 1.
        Long, detailed summary of the 25 February lecture at
     Milwaukee on the "South Seas," which was "a pleasant,
     richly colored story" rather than a stilted lecture. There
     was no labored effort at profound syllogisms nor soaring
     rhetorical flights. It was such a feast as one would like
     to sit down to in a club room; both entertaining and in-
     structive. A large and appreciative audience. Reprinted
     in Davis (1941), pp. 48-51; reprinted in part in Log,
     p. 603, and Sealts (1957), p. 86.

25   ANON. "The South Seas. Herman Melville's Lecture." Rockford
     (Ill.) Daily News (1 March), p. 2.
        Review of the 28 February lecture at Rockford. A large
     and appreciative audience "listened with great pleasure to
     the discussion of a subject invested with all the gorgeous
     coloring, and glowing romance of Mr. Melville's peculiar
     genius." Reprints summary of lecture from 1859.B20.

26   ANON. "Young Men's Association Lecture Course." Rockford
     (Ill.) Republican (3 March), p. 2.
        Review of the 28 February lecture at Rockford on "The
     South Seas." The lecture was an uncommonly "painful in-
     fliction" on the audience. Instead of drawing on his per-
     sonal experience, Melville gave "a simple presentation of
     historical facts, few in number, very common placed, and

to be found in books on the shelves of almost any library."
Melville lacks depth, earnestness, consecutiveness, and
finish, the necessary qualities of a permanently successful
lecturer. There was not one really good point in the entire lecture. Brief sarcastic summary. Reprinted in Davis
(1941), pp. 52-54; Log, p. 603; Sealts (1957), pp. 88-89.

27   ANON. "Association Lectures." Rockford (Ill.) Register
      (5 March), p. 2.
          Review of the 28 February lecture at Rockford on "The
      South Seas." The lecture was a disappointment: instead
      of relating his personal experiences "in one of the most
      delightful portions of the world," as expected, Melville
      recorded a few general historical facts which could be
      found in almost any well selected library. He cannot take
      his eyes from his manuscript for one minute. Bayard
      Taylor's lecture the following evening was far more inter-
      esting. Reprinted in part in Davis (1941), p. 53; Log,
      p. 604; Sealts (1957), pp. 89-90.

*28   ANON. Lynn (Mass.) Weekly Reporter (12 March).
          Announcement of the 16 March lecture at Lynn on the
      South Seas. Refers to Melville as "the celebrated adven-
      turer." Cited in Log, p. 604.

29   'NOGGS.' Review of Lecture. Lynn (Mass.) Weekly Reporter
      (19 March).
          Review of the 16 March lecture at Lynn on the South Seas.
      The lecture "didn't touch the innermost, as did those of
      Emerson and Lowell" but "was good, though, of its kind, and
      went off very well." Reprinted in Log, p. 604.

1860 A BOOKS - NONE

1860 B SHORTER WRITINGS

1   BOTTA, ANNE C. LYNCH. Handbook of Universal Literature.
      Boston: Ticknor and Fields, p. 538.
          Notes that in "adventurous description" Melville's Omoo
      and Typee and Mayo's Kaloolah and Berber have gained an
      extensive popularity.

2   ANON. "Dowse Institute. Fourteenth Lecture.--By Herman
      Melville. Travel." Cambridge (Mass.) Chronicle
      (25 February).
          Summary of the 21 February lecture at Cambridgeport,
      Mass., on traveling. Reprinted in Birss (December 1934),
      pp. 725-727, and Sealts (1957), pp. 181-185.

3 ANON. "Herman Melville." Pittsfield (Mass.) <u>Berkshire County Eagle</u> (31 May).

Reports that Melville "left home last week for a voyage round the world, in pursuit of relaxation, renewed vigor, and, we hope, material for another charming volume on sea-life, which he will now see in a new phase."

4 ANON. "A Noted Author Coming to San Francisco." San Francisco <u>Daily Evening Bulletin</u> (12 October).

Item notes Melville's imminent arrival on the <u>Meteor</u> and that he is traveling in pursuit of health and "new experiences to turn to account in a literary way." Suggests Melville might be available for lectures. Reprinted in <u>Log</u>, p. 627, and Fracchia, p. 2.

5 ANON. "Hermann Melville." San Francisco <u>Daily Alta Californian</u> (18 October).

Notes that the "well known author" intends to return to New York by the next steamer; that, like Dana, he is on "a tour of observation," and has made the trip to benefit his health; hopes for a lecture or two from him before his departure. Reprinted in <u>Log</u>, p. 628, and Fracchia, p. 3.

6 ANON. San Francisco <u>Daily Evening Bulletin</u> (20 October).

Reports Melville's departure on the <u>Cortes</u>, a steamer bound for Panama. Reprinted in <u>Log</u>, p. 628 and Fracchia, p. 3.

7 ANON. "Herman Melville." Pittsfield (Mass.) <u>Berkshire County Eagle</u> (8 November), p. 2.

Announces arrival of the <u>Meteor</u>, captained by Melville's brother, at San Francisco. Notes that Melville has not fully recovered on the voyage out and hopes that he will return home in his former "full vigor of health." Reprinted in part in <u>Log</u>, p. 630.

1861 A BOOKS - NONE

1861 B SHORTER WRITINGS

1 ANON. "Melville, Herman." <u>A Dictionary of Contemporary Biography: A Handbook of the Peerage of Rank, Worth and Intellect</u>. London and Glasgow: Richard Griffin and Co., p. 272.

Three sentences. <u>Typee</u>, a great success, was followed by <u>Omoo</u>, <u>Mardi</u>, "and a number of others."

1861

2   ANON. "Melville, Herman." The New American Cyclopaedia: A
     Popular Dictionary of General Knowledge. Eds. George Ripley
     and Charles A. Dana. Vol. 11. New York and London:
     D. Appleton and Co., pp. 370-371.
         Mainly details of Melville's career as a sailor and
     adventurer. Lists his books (Typee is told in a spirited
     and graceful style) and states that in 1860 he sailed again
     on a voyage round the world in a whaling vessel. Reprinted
     in 1866 and 1872.

3   ANON. Pittsfield (Mass.) Berkshire County Eagle (12 December),
     p. 2.
         Reports that Melville has left town for the winter, which
     he is to spend in New York and Boston. Reprinted in Log,
     p. 643.

1862 A BOOKS - NONE

1862 B SHORTER WRITINGS

1   ANON. Men of the Time: A Biographical Dictionary of Eminent
     Living Characters, (Including Women). London: Routledge,
     Warne, & Routledge, pp. 543-544.
         New shorter entry [see 1853.B1]; brief biographical
     details to 1847. After list of works (excluding The Piazza
     Tales) adds that Melville is the author of "several arti-
     cles in magazines and periodicals." Reprinted in 1865.B1,
     with slight alterations.

2   ANON. "Accident to Herman Melvill." Pittsfield (Mass.)
     Berkshire County Eagle (13 November), p. 2.
         Reports injuries to Melville and J. E. A. Smith after
     being thrown from wagon. Reprinted in Log, p. 655.

1863 A BOOKS - NONE

1863 B SHORTER WRITINGS

*1   ANON. Celebration of the Semi-Centennial Anniversary of the
     Albany Academy. Albany (N.Y.).
         Notes that Melville's reputation as an author has honored
     the Academy worldwide. Cited in Log, p. 660.

2   HAWTHORNE, NATHANIEL. Our Old Time: A Series of English
     Sketches. Boston: Ticknor and Fields, p. 17.

An American who had been wandering about England for more than a quarter of a century, all the while wishing to get home again, reminds Hawthorne of Melville's "excellent novel or biography" of Israel Potter, with its "somewhat similar" idea.

3   ANON. "Local News." Pittsfield (Mass.) <u>Berkshire County Eagle</u> (21 May), p. 2.
Reports that Allen [sic] Melville has bought Arrowhead from Herman for a summer residence. Reprinted in <u>Log</u>, p. 659.

4   T[UCKERMAN], H.T. "Authors at Home: Authors in Berkshire." Philadelphia <u>American Literary Gazette</u>, 2 (16 November), 40.
Melville included with Hawthorne, Holmes, and others. <u>Typee</u>, <u>Omoo</u>, <u>Moby-Dick</u> and Melville's other adventurous writings "have more of the genuine Robinson Crusoe spell about them than any American writings." <u>Moby-Dick</u>, "for curious and eloquent descriptions and details about the whale and whale fishing, rivals Michelet's brilliant and copious brochures on the sea, woman, and other generic themes; but Melville is more scientific as to his facts, and more inventive as to his fiction." <u>Moby-Dick</u> "has the rare fault of redundant power; the story is wild and wonderful enough without being interwoven with such a thorough, scientific, and economical treatise on the whale; it is a fine contribution to natural history and to political economy, united to an original and powerful romance of the sea." Among Melville's "more casual things, indicative of great versatility" are <u>Israel Potter</u> and "his remarkable sketch of a Wall Street scrivener in 'Putnam's Monthly.'" Reprinted in 1863.B5; <u>Log</u>, p. 664; <u>Doubloon</u>, p. 103; Branch, pp. 386-387.

5   [TUCKERMAN, H. T.] "Authors in Berkshire." Pittsfield (Mass.) <u>Berkshire County Eagle</u> (10 December), p. 1.
Reprint of 1863.B4.

6   ANON. Pittsfield (Mass.) <u>Berkshire County Eagle</u> (10 December), p. 2.
Corrects inaccuracies in 1863.B5. "Mr. Melville did not come to Berkshire to secure health but to enjoy it. He has now removed to New York to secure its restoration."

<u>1864 A BOOKS - NONE</u>

1864

1864 B SHORTER WRITINGS

1   NICHOLS, THOMAS L.   Forty Years of American Life.   Vol. 2.
    London: John Maxwell and Co., pp. 344-346.
        While Nichols was in Gansevoort Melville's law office,
    Allan Melville gave him the manuscript of Typee to read.
    Nichols advised Gansevoort to have it issued in London
    simultaneously with its New York publication, feeling "sure
    that the reviews of the English press would make its Amer-
    ican success" and "not at all sure that the process could
    be reversed." Nichols subsequently met Melville: "He was
    a simple-hearted, enthusiastic, gentlemanly sailor, or
    sailorlike gentleman. His subsequent works have been marked
    by certain eccentricities, but have, on the whole, sustained
    the promise of his maiden production." Melville wrote a
    book every year till 1860 when "he started off again on a
    whaling voyage round the world." Reprinted, with some
    alteration, in 1874.B2.

1865 A BOOKS - NONE

1865 B SHORTER WRITINGS

1   ANON. Men of the Time: A Biographical Dictionary of Eminent
    Living Characters of Both Sexes. London: George Routledge
    and Sons, p. 586.
        Reprint of 1862.B1, with slight alterations; includes
    "Piazza Tales" in list of works. Reprinted in 1868.B1,
    with slight alterations.

2   ANON. Review of The Refugee. Philadelphia Godey's Lady's
    Book and Magazine, 70 (May), 465.
        Review of the T. B. Peterson and Brothers' pirated edi-
    tion of Israel Potter (Philadelphia, 1865). A well-written
    story of Revolutionary times.

3   THOMSON, JAMES. "Mr. Kingsley's Convertites." London National
    Reformer, NS 6 (24 September), 606.
        The chapter of Kingsley's Hypatia in which Raphael Ben
    Ezra's Pyrrhonism "disported itself 'on the floor of the
    bottomless,' seems to have been, in great measure, borrowed
    from the talk of one Babbalanja in Herman Melville's Mardi;
    perhaps, however, both were borrowed direct from Jean Paul's
    gigantic grotesque, Titan." Reprinted in 1884.B6.

1866 A BOOKS - NONE

1866 B SHORTER WRITINGS

1 ANON. New York Herald (12 August), p. 5.
   Announcement of publication of Battle-Pieces, with
   parenthetical comment "for ten years the public has won-
   dered what had become of Melville."

2 ANON. Review of Battle-Pieces. New York Times (27 August),
   p. 2.
   Mainly summary of the "Supplement." The poems "all dis-
   play marked poetic ability, although the unusual metres now
   and then selected give a stiffness to the movement which
   might have been avoided." They "make all the more pleasant
   a contribution to the literature of the war, because they
   are not marked by those extravagances in which nearly all
   our bellicose poets have so freely indulged." Reprinted in
   Scholnick, pp. 423-424.

3 ANON. Review of Battle-Pieces. Springfield (Mass.) Republican
   (29 August), p. 1.
   Melville has tried his hand at verse with moderate success. None of the poems are absolutely bad, but many of
   them cannot be called good. The general tone of the pieces
   is conservative rather than radical, and there is hardly a
   broad enough grasp of the causes, purposes, and results of
   the Civil War. Among the best pieces are "America" and "The
   Scout toward Aldie." Reprinted in Kaplan (1972), p. xxix.

4 ANON. Review of Battle-Pieces. New York National Quarterly
   Review, 26 (September), 390-393.
   There is much more truth than poetry in Battle-Pieces.
   Melville is a sensible man with respectable literary talents
   but not a poet; he would have awakened a deeper interest by
   plain prose. The supplement contains more poetry than his
   most elaborate verses. Melville has great faith in difference of type, sometimes printing whole pages in italics, as
   if he thought that would render them more poetical. Brief
   discussion of "Lyon," "Donelson," "The Swamp Angel," "Lee
   in the Capitol," and "The Victor of Antietam."

5 ANON. Review of Battle-Pieces. New Bedford Daily Mercury
   (1 September), p. 2.
   The prose supplement "might have been omitted without
   detriment, to say the least." There are some pieces of
   rare merit, but on the whole the volume will not add to the
   reputation Melville has won by his rich poetic prose.

1866

6   ANON. Review of <u>Battle-Pieces</u>. Philadelphia <u>American Literary</u>
     <u>Gazette and Publishers' Circular</u>, 7 (1 September), 190.
          Melville has abundant force and fire, "and his words
     will kindle afresh the patriotic flame. But he has written
     too rapidly to avoid great crudities. His poetry runs into
     the epileptic. His rhymes are fearful." Reprinted in part
     in <u>Log</u>, p. 682; reprinted in Kaplan (1972), p. xxx.

7   ANON. Review of <u>Battle-Pieces</u>. New York <u>Herald</u> (3 September),
     p. 5.
          Many of the lines "are not inappropriately rugged enough."
     So far from spoiling the symmetry of the book, the supple-
     ment completes it, and "converts it into what is better than
     a good book--into a good and patriotic action." The supple-
     ment is welcome not only as the deliberate, impartial tes-
     timony of a highly cultivated individual mind, but as a
     hopeful sign of a change in public opinion and sentiment.
     Extract from supplement. Reprinted in part in <u>Log</u>,
     pp. 682-683; reprinted in Kaplan (1972), pp. xxx-xxxv, and
     Branch, pp. 388-389.

8   ANON. "More Poetry of the War." New York <u>Nation</u>, 3
     (6 September), 187-188.
          Nature did not make Melville a poet. <u>Battle-Pieces</u> con-
     tains at best little more than the rough ore of poetry. In
     some of the poems it is difficult to discover rhythm, mea-
     sure, or consonance of rhyme. The thought is often in-
     volved and obscure. The sentiment is weakened by
     incongruous imagery (as in "The Portent"). There are
     occasional gleams of imaginative power; very few pieces
     are as direct in expression and as natural in thought as
     "Ball's Bluff," but there are single lines, couplets, or
     quatrains in which genuine power is shown as well as genu-
     ine feeling. The Civil War has inspired only one truly
     great and lasting poem--Lowell's "Commemoration Ode."
     Reprinted in part in <u>Log</u>, p. 683; reprinted in Kaplan (1972),
     pp. xxxvi-xxxix, and Branch, pp. 389-392.

9   ANON. Review of <u>Battle-Pieces</u>. New York <u>Albion</u>, 44
     (15 September), 441.
          No one but Melville could have written this volume, and
     few besides him would have cared to write it. Its merit is
     blended with much that is worthless. At no time a literary
     artist, Melville is less an artist now than ever. His con-
     ceptions are frequently obscure; his style is uncouth and
     harsh. Of verse as verse he knows little, seldom writing a
     stanza that is melodious throughout. Some of his discords
     are fine, but music has other and higher qualities than

mere discords. Melville lacks Whitman's power of placing
us en rapport with the events he writes about. His most
sustained poem is "Donelson"; "Malvern Hill" and "The
Victor of Antietam" are both good, though the diction of
the latter is rather turgid; best of all is "Sheridan at
Cedar Creek." Reprinted in Monteiro (September 1977), p. 12.

10 ANON. Review of Battle-Pieces. New York Round Table, 4
    (15 September), 108-109.
        Like everything Melville has written, Battle-Pieces
    bears the stamp of his peculiar idiosyncracy and is nothing
    if not original. But there is "something wayward" in
    Melville's mind "which drives him to commit many sins in
    authorship." From the start he appears not to have compre-
    hended the laws which govern prose--the radical difference
    and irreconcilable antagonism between prose and poetry--
    and, consequently, his prose is not so much prose proper
    as poetry in a prosaic form--the "dreariest reading."
    Melville has some of the elements of a poet in his nature
    but is not a poet: he disregards the laws of verse, has
    little sense of melody and almost no sense of proportion.
    He has imagination, but it lacks clearness and purpose; he
    has wealth of language, but he squanders it. In Battle-
    Pieces he is often obscure; in not more than half of his
    poems does he appear to have understood what he wished to
    accomplish. Some of his rhymes are positively barbarous.
    But there are occasionally nervous phrases and energetic
    passages and fine bits of description. The "best thing"
    in the volume is "Sheridan at Cedar Creek." Brief discus-
    sion of "Shiloh." Reprinted in Scholnick, pp. 425-428.

11 ANON. Review of Battle-Pieces. New York Evening Post
    (10 October).
        Melville's war lyrics are full of martial fire and some-
    times are really artistic in form; but often the thought is
    too vaguely expressed. His style in verse is as unfettered
    by ordinary precedents as in such of his prose works as
    Pierre. Reprinted in part in Log, p. 683; reprinted in
    Kaplan (1972), pp. xxxix-xl [dated 12 October].

12 ANON. Review of Battle-Pieces. New York World (19 October),
    p. 6.
        Battle-Pieces exemplifies the fact that the poetic
    nature and the technical faculty of poetry are not identical.
    Whole pages of Melville's prose are in the highest sense
    poetic and nearly all the poems in Battle-Pieces would be
    much more poetic "if they were thrown into the external
    prose form." Melville's habit of mind is not lyric but

1866

historical, "and the genre of historic poetry in which he
most congenially expatiates finds rhythm not a help but a
hindrance. The exigencies of rhyme hamper him still more,
and against both of these trammels his vigorous thought
habitually recalcitrates...." Multitudes of strong and
beautiful images show that the nature of his thought is
not at fault. Without one poem "of entire artistic
ensemble," Battle-Pieces has numerous passages of beauty
and power. Brief discussion of "The March into Virginia"
and "Lyon." Reprinted in Sealts (1971), pp. 360-362, and
Branch, pp. 393-395.

13   ANON. Review of Battle-Pieces. Cincinnati Ladies' Repository,
      26 (November), 699.
         "Another book of poems, war-inspired, not exhibiting a
      very high order of poetry, but interesting as detailing
      in measured form many of the stirring incidents and events
      of our country's great strife."

14   ANON. Notice of Battle-Pieces. Philadelphia Godey's Lady's
      Book and Magazine, 73 (December), 540.
         The volume will, doubtless, find many admirers. Re-
      printed in Kaplan (1972), p. xl, and Branch, p. 392.

1867 A BOOKS - NONE

1867 B SHORTER WRITINGS

1   ANON. Review of Battle-Pieces. New York Harper's New Monthly
      Magazine, 34 (January), 265.
         Among these poems are some which will stand as among the
      most stirring lyrics of the war. Reprinted in part in Log,
      p. 685; reprinted in Kaplan (1972), p. xli, and Branch,
      p. 395.

2   ANON. Review of Battle-Pieces. New York Independent
      (10 January).
         In Battle-Pieces Melville seems a humble medium alter-
      nately influenced by the overmastering personalities of
      Whitman, Dante, Emerson, Brownell, and Mother Goose. Some-
      times fanciful, often grotesque, rarely imaginative, he has
      remarkable ease of versification, much vividness and pictur-
      esqueness. He coins words and phrases with the prodigality
      of Elizabeth Browning without her fine fitness. He wholly
      disdains rhythm and "discourteously entreats" rhyme. Yet
      real power underlies Melville's vagaries, carelessness, and
      crudities. There are lines strong as Robert Browning,

pictures vivid as life, phrases clearcut as Emerson. The
ideas in the supplement are unconvincing and dangerous.
Brief discussion of "The Victor of Antietam," "The Cumber-
land," "Sheridan at Cedar Creek," and "A Canticle." Reprinted in Monteiro (Fourth Quarter 1974), pp. 437-439.

3   ANON. Review of Battle-Pieces. Boston Atlantic Monthly, 19
     (February), 252-253.
          Melville's work "possesses the negative virtues of orig-
     inality in such degree that it not only reminds you of no
     poetry you have read, but of no life you have known." His
     skill is "so great that we fear he has not often felt the
     things of which he writes, since with all his skill he fails
     to move us." In some respects the poems are admirable.
     Melville treats events as realistically as one can to whom
     they seem to have presented themselves as dreams. His
     faculty is well fitted to deal with certain moods or ab-
     stractions of the common mind during the war: "the unrest,
     the strangeness and solitude, to which the first sense of
     the great danger reduced all souls, are reflected in his
     verse, and whatever purely mystic aspect occurrences had
     seems to have been felt by this poet, so little capable of
     giving their positive likeness." A tender and subtle music
     is felt in many of the verses, and the eccentric metres are
     gracefully managed. Brief discussion of "The Portent,"
     "Lyon," and "The Scout toward Aldie." Reprinted in part in
     Log, p. 685; reprinted in Recognition, pp. 100-102; Kaplan,
     pp. xli-xliv; Branch, pp. 396-398.

4   ANON. Review of Wild Life Among the Pacific Islanders by
     E. H. Lamont. London Athenaeum, No. 2061 (27 April),
     p. 542.
          Review begins, "Mr. Melville's 'Typee,' the authenticity
     of which, it may be recollected, was in some quarters ques-
     tioned, was not fuller of wonders than this book."

5   COAN, TITUS. "The First Missionary Trip of the New 'Morning
     Star.'" Honolulu Supplement to The Friend, NS 18 (1 July),
     58.
          Coan visited the Typee and Happar Valleys and saw places
     on the island Melville passed through before reaching Typee.
     Gives distances between various points on the island. Re-
     vised version in 1882.B1.

6   ANON. "Miscellaneous Despatches." Boston Daily Advertiser
     (13 September), p. 1.
          "The inquest today on the body of Malcolm Melville, a
     native of Massachusetts, who committed suicide yesterday

by shooting himself with a pistol, brought in a verdict of suicide while temporarily insane."

7   ANON. "News of the Day. Local." New York *Times* (13 September), p. 4.
        "Malcolm Melville, a youth 18 years of age, son of a well-known literary gentleman, committed suicide yesterday by shooting himself with a pistol."

8   ANON. New York *Evening Post* (16 September).
        Statement by jurors at the inquest on Malcolm Melville, designed "to correct any erroneous impressions" drawn from their verdict of "suicide."--"We believe that his death was caused by his own hand, but not that the act was by premeditation or consciously done, no motive for it having appeared during the inquest or after it...whether the act was committed in a state of aberration incident to disturbed or somnambulistic sleep, or whether the death arose from an accident in carelessly pulling out the weapon from under his head, it is impossible now to determine." Followed by letter dated 16 September 1867 from the Rev. Dr. Samuel Osgood, stating that "there is sufficient reason to think that he [Malcolm] came to his end by the accidental discharge of a pistol which he kept under his pillow, and was known by his companions to handle sometimes too freely, and with something of the boyish recklessness of a newly-made soldier." Reprinted in 1867.B9; reprinted in part in *Log*, p. 690.

    H[OADLEY], J. C. "Malcolm Melville." Boston *Daily Advertiser* [Supplement] (28 September), p. 2.
        Vindication of Malcolm and details of his death. "Those who knew this pure, genial, healthful young man, know that he could be neither insane nor a self-murderer." His fellow clerks "had remonstrated with him for his carelessness in handling his pistol." Malcolm was out "until three o'clock in the morning of the night before his death; but he had never been seen in the slightest degree under the influence of liquor; and his manner as he kissed his mother, who was sitting up for him, sat down by her side, put his arm round her neck, begged her pardon for keeping her up so long, promised not to do so again, and told her all about the manner in which he had spent his evening, must have proved to her his innocence, his purity, and his truth, and must give assurance to her wounded heart that her darling boy never harbored a single thought prompting to self-destruction." Quotes recent letter from Melville [see *Letters*, p. 228]. Reprints 1867.B8. Reprinted in part in *Log*, p. 687.

1868 A BOOKS - NONE

1868 B SHORTER WRITINGS

1   ANON. <u>Men of the Time: A Dictionary of Contemporaries, Con-</u>
<u>taining Biographical Notices of Eminent Characters of Both</u>
<u>Sexes</u>. London: George Routledge and Sons, p. 575.
    Reprint of 1865.B1, with slight alterations. Reprinted
in 1872.B1.

2   HAWTHORNE, NATHANIEL. <u>Passages from the American Note-Books</u>
<u>of Nathaniel Hawthorne</u>. Vol. 2. Boston: Ticknor and
Fields, pp. 172-173.
    Entries for August 5 and 7, 1850: brief mentions of
Melville, in company with others.

3   BRIGGS, CHARLES F. "The Old and the New. A Retrospect and a
Prospect." New York <u>Putnam's Magazine</u>, NS 1 (January), 3.
    Wonders what has happened to Melville, "that copious and
imaginative author, who contributed so many brilliant articles to the <u>Monthly</u>." Melville reference reprinted in <u>Log</u>,
p. 694.

4   S., R. "Marquesas Islands.--Melville's 'Typee.'" London
<u>Athenaeum</u>, No. 2113 (25 April), pp. 595-596.
    Recounts recent visit to the Marquesas and corroborates
details of the topography and people described in <u>Typee</u>.
R. S. and party were told "that Fa-a-wa and a daughter of
Melville's were still living, the former an old woman."
Reprinted in Gohdes (1937), pp. 527-531.

5   ANON. "Books, Authors and Art." Springfield (Mass.)
<u>Republican</u> (24 June), p. 2.
    Melville included in list of literary men working as
clerks in the New York custom house. Such positions might
not leave them entirely free to write independent political
articles or criticisms on American life.

6   ANON. "Literary Invalids." Richmond <u>Southern Opinion</u>
(4 July).
    Report that the Customs House in New York "appears to be
a kind of hospital for literary invalids" and that Melville,
"who delighted the publick with his 'Typee' and 'Omoo,' and
ended with such trash as 'Pierre' and the 'Confidence Man'"
is "thoroughly written out, and so very unpractical that he
needs some such position to live." Reprinted in Hubbell,
pp. 58-59.

1869

1869 A BOOKS - NONE

1869 B SHORTER WRITINGS

1   ANON. "Melville, Herman." <u>Beeton's Dictionary of Universal</u>
    <u>Biography</u>. London: Ward, Lock and Co., p. 708.
        One paragraph; brief biographical details to 1847; in-
    cludes <u>Peter</u> in list of Melville's works (but not <u>Moby-Dick</u>,
    <u>The Piazza Tales</u>, <u>The Confidence-Man</u>, or <u>Battle-Pieces</u>).
    Melville's style became by degrees eccentric and unequal.

2   ANON. Springfield (Mass.) <u>Republican</u> (20 September).
        Melville listed among "the notabilities" summering at
    Curtis's hotel in Lenox.

1870 A BOOKS - NONE

1870 B SHORTER WRITINGS

1   DILLINGHAM, JOHN H. "Herman Melville," in Supplement to <u>The</u>
    <u>Prose Writers of America</u> by Rufus Wilmot Griswold.
    Philadelphia: Porter and Coates, pp. 665-666.
        Headnote to extracts from <u>Typee</u>, chapter 18, and <u>Omoo</u>,
    chapter 24. Brief biographical details, mainly to 1847.
    For pleasant, easy narrative, <u>Omoo</u> is the most natural and
    agreeable of Melville's books [cf. 1855.B2]. <u>Mardi</u> will
    pay nobody to wade through, despite its many delicate
    traits and fine bursts of fancy. In <u>Moby-Dick</u> the details
    of the fishery and the natural history of the whale are well
    told, but the metaphysical portions of the narrative destroy
    its interest. Concluding assessment of Melville (an orig-
    inal thinker with amazing powers of expression but often
    mystical and unintelligible) taken from 1856.B1. Reprinted
    in part in <u>Doubloon</u>, pp. 103-104.

2   GODWIN, PARKE. "American Authorship," in <u>Out of the Past</u>.
    New York: G. P. Putnam & Sons, pp. 176-195.
        Reprint of 1853.B6.

3   HAWTHORNE, NATHANIEL. <u>Passages from the English Note-Books of</u>
    <u>Nathaniel Hawthorne</u>. Boston: Fields, Osgood, & Co.
    Vol. 1, p. 140; Vol. 2, pp. 155-160.
        Entry for 25 December 1854: Commodore Perry asked
    Hawthorne to recommend someone suitable to prepare his
    notes and material for publication of an account of his
    voyage to Japan; Hawthorne "spoke of Herman Melville, and
    one or two others...." Entry for 30 November 1856:

Melville's visit to Hawthorne at Liverpool and their visit together to Chester (with passages deleted).

4   MARTIN, FREDERICK. "Melville, Herman," in Handbook of Contemporary Biography. London: MacMillan and Co., p. 183.
        Three-line entry. Melville the author of Typee, Omoo, White-Jacket, Israel Potter, The Piazza Tales, "and other works."

5   THOMAS, JOSEPH. "Melville, Herman," in Universal Pronouncing Dictionary of Biography and Mythology. Vol. 2. Philadelphia: J. B. Lippincott and Co., p. 1565.
        Among Melville's principal works are Typee, Omoo, White-Jacket, and The Piazza Tales. Frequent reprintings.

1871 A BOOKS - NONE

1871 B SHORTER WRITINGS

1   ALLIBONE, S. AUSTIN. "Melville, Herman," in A Critical Dictionary of English Literature and British and American Authors. Vol. 2. Philadelphia: J. B. Lippincott & Co., pp. 1264-1265.
        Brief biographical sketch to 1847. Several "descriptive volumes" give ample evidence that Melville "was no unobservant spectator of the peculiar phases of society which he encountered during his travels." List of works to 1857, each followed by quotations from contemporary British reviews. Concluding extract from 1856.B1.

2   PHILLIPS, LAWRENCE B. The Dictionary of Biographical Reference Containing One Hundred Thousand Names. New York: Scribner, Welford, & Co., p. 643.
        Melville included as American author. [Cf. 1881.B1.]

1872 A BOOKS - NONE

1872 B SHORTER WRITINGS

1   ANON. Men of the Time: A Dictionary of Contemporaries, Containing Biographical Notices of Eminent Characters of Both Sexes. Ed. Thompson Cooper. London: George Routledge and Sons, p. 674.
        Reprint of 1868.B1. Adds The Confidence-Man to list of works and notes that Melville "has contributed largely to reviews and periodicals"; also adds that in 1860 "he made another voyage round the world in a whaling vessel."

1872

2   ANON. "Melville, Herman," in The New American Cyclopaedia:
       A Popular Dictionary of General Knowledge. Eds. George
       Ripley and Charles A. Dana. Vol. 11. New York:
       D. Appleton and Co., pp. 370-371.
          Reprint of 1861.B2.

3   DRAKE, FRANCIS S. "Melville, Herman," in Dictionary of Amer-
       ican Biography, Including Men of the Time. Boston:
       James R. Osgood and Co., p. 615.
          Brief biographical sketch (including a whaling voyage
       round the world in 1860). List of works (Israel Potter and
       Battle-Pieces omitted), without critical comment.

4   FIELDS, JAMES T. Yesterdays with Authors. Boston:
       James R. Osgood and Co., pp. 52-53.
          Account of excursion to Monument Mountain with party
       including Melville, Hawthorne, Holmes, and Duyckinck.
       Frequent reprintings.

5   UNDERWOOD, FRANCIS H. "Herman Melville," in A Hand-Book of
       English Literature. Intended for the Use of High Schools.
       Boston: Lee and Shepard, p. 458.
          Headnote, mainly biographical, to extract from Typee,
       chapter 29. Typee and Omoo are among the most delightful
       travel books in the language; the style is charmingly easy,
       the descriptions are novel and picturesque, and the inci-
       dents related with an air of verisimilitude. Moby-Dick, an
       imaginative story, is not altogether probable; The Piazza
       Tales contain some powerfully drawn pictures. Reprinted in
       1893.B9 and Recognition, pp. 103-104.

6   STODDARD, CHARLES WARREN. "A Prodigal in Tahiti." Boston
       Atlantic Monthly, 30 (November), 620.
          Stoddard saw the "calabooses" where Melville "got some
       chapters" of Omoo and many times "tracked the ground of
       that delicious story." Reprinted in 1873.B3.

1873 A BOOKS - NONE

1873 B SHORTER WRITINGS

1   ANON. "Melville, Herman," in The Best Reading. New York
       G. P. Putnam's Sons, p. 98.
          Lists Typee, Mardi, Moby-Dick, Pierre, Omoo, Redburn,
       White-Jacket, Israel Potter, with prices.

2   HART, JOHN S. <u>A Manual of American Literature: A Textbook for Schools and Colleges</u>. Philadelphia: Eldredge and Brother, p. 486.

        List of Melville's principal works omits <u>Moby-Dick</u> and <u>Pierre</u>; his two best works are perhaps <u>Typee</u> and <u>Redburn</u>. Melville is a writer of forcible and graceful English, although in some of his works he lapses into mysticism. Reprinted in <u>Recognition</u>, p. 103.

3   STODDARD, CHARLES WARREN. <u>South-Sea Idyls</u>. Boston: James R. Osgood and Co., pp. 314, 353-354.

        Account of sailing past Nouka Hiva: "A moist cloud, far up the mountain, hung above a serene and sacred haunt, and under its shelter was hidden a deep valley, whose secret has been carried to the ends of the earth; for Herman Melville has plucked out the heart of its mystery, and beautiful and barbarous Typee lies naked and forsaken." Reprints 1872.B6. [<u>See</u> 1874.B3.]

4   THAXTER, CELIA. <u>Among the Isles of Shoals</u>. Boston: James R. Osgood and Co., p. 1.

        The Isles of Shoals are enchanted in a better sense of the word than "the great Gallipagos of which Mr. Melville discourses so delightfully" in "The Encantadas."

5   ANON. Review of <u>Kaloolah</u> by W. S. Mayo. San Francisco <u>Overland Monthly</u>, 10 (January), 103-104.

        The success of <u>Kaloolah</u> on its first appearance in 1849 "might have been aided by the desire for graphic and picturesque literature awakened by the advent of Herman Melville's fascinating story of <u>Typee</u>." <u>Kaloolah</u> is second only to Melville's "unrivaled Polynesian romances."

6   [BAGGER, LOUIS]. "The Sailors' Snug Harbor." New York <u>Harper's New Monthly Magazine</u>, 46 (January), 188-197.

        Recounts meeting with Melville's brother Thomas, governor of the Sailors' Snug Harbor rest home, Staten Island. No mention of Herman. [<u>See</u> discussion in Parker (1965), pp. 24-25.]

7   ANON. "A Curiosity relating to a Literary Author." Honolulu <u>Friend</u>, NS 22 (1 August), 71.

        Prints contract between Melville and Isaac Montgomery, signed at Honolulu, 1 June 1843, indenturing Melville as clerk to Montgomery. Melville's literary fame "imparts an interest to the document."

1873

8   GORDON, CLARENCE. "Mr. DeForest's Novels." Boston <u>Atlantic
     Monthly</u>, 32 (November), 611-621.
         <u>Typee</u> included in list of the dozen American "tales"
     next in merit after the works of "our pre-eminent literary
     artist, Hawthorne."

9   ANON. Review of <u>South-Sea Idyls</u> by Charles Warren Stoddard.
     New York <u>Independent</u> (18 December), p. 1577.
         Stoddard "has written from a strong imagination, already
     prepossessed with the exquisite South Sea pictures of
     Herman Melville...."

1874 A BOOKS - NONE

1874 B SHORTER WRITINGS

1   FIELD, MAUNSELL B. <u>Memories of Many Men and of Some Women.</u>
     New York: Harper & Brothers, pp. 198, 202.
         Account of visit to Melville at Arrowhead and visit with
     Melville to Holmes: "Somehow, the conversation drifted to
     East India religions and mythologies, and soon there arose
     a discussion between Holmes and Melville, which was con-
     ducted with the most amazing skill and brilliancy on both
     sides. It lasted for hours...." Reprinted in <u>Log</u>, p. 506.

2   NICHOLS, T. L. <u>Forty Years of American Life</u>. London:
     Longmans, Green, & Co., pp. 227-228.
         Reprint of 1864.B1, with some alteration. Refers to
     Melville as "a simple-hearted, enthusiastic man of genius,
     who wrote with the consciousness of an impelling force, and
     with great power and beauty." Omits reference to the
     "eccentricities" of Melville's works after <u>Typee</u>. Reprinted
     as <u>Forty Years of American Life, 1821-1861</u> by Thomas Low
     Nichols. New York: Stackpole Sons, 1937, pp. 212-213.

3   STODDARD, CHARLES WARREN. <u>Summer Cruising in the South Seas.</u>
     London: Chatto and Windus, pp. 279, 312.
         English edition of 1873.B3.

4   'B.V.' [THOMSON, JAMES]. "Walt Whitman." London <u>National
     Reformer</u>, NS 24 (30 August), 135.
         "I know but one other living American writer who
     approaches him [Whitman] in his sympathy with all ordinary
     life and vulgar occupations, in his feeling of brotherhood
     for all rough workers, and at the same time in his sense of
     beauty and grandeur, and his power of thought; I mean
     Herman Melville, the author of 'Typee,' 'Omoo,' 'Mardi,'

'The Whale,' etc.; but Melville is sometimes strangely unequal to his better self, and has lavished much strength
in desultory doings; while Whitman has concentrated himself
from the beginning on one great strenuous endeavour, with
energies reinforced and multiplied by the zeal and enthusiasm of the consciousness of a mission." Reprinted in
1910.B4; reprinted in part in Log, p. 740.

5   ANON. Review of Nimrod of the Sea; or, The American Whaleman
by William M. Davis. New York Nation, 19 (29 October), 290.
A readable book, but in interest and fullness of information inferior to Moby-Dick, "which describes the sperm-
whale fishery at a later time than that of Mr. Davis's
journal, and with an accuracy not less remarkable than the
poetic and imaginative faculty which has made the work a
classic among sea-tales."

1875 A BOOKS - NONE

1875 B SHORTER WRITINGS

1   ANON. "Melville, Herman," in Chambers's Encyclopaedia: A
Dictionary of Universal Knowledge for the People. Vol. 6.
Philadelphia: J. B. Lippincott Co., p. 397.
One paragraph; brief biographical details to 1847 and
list of works. Comment only on Typee ("a spirited account"
of Melville's residence in the Marquesas) and Mardi ("a
strange philosophical romance"). Reprinted, with slight
alteration, in 1886.B1.

2   ANON. Men of the Time: A Dictionary of Contemporaries, Con-
taining Biographical Notices of Eminent Characters of Both
Sexes. Ed. Thompson Cooper. London: George Routledge and
Sons, pp. 718-719.
New entry (see 1872.B1). Adds brief details of
Melville's life after 1847 (including "a new voyage round
the world" in 1860). After list of works notes that
Melville wrote "several notable magazine papers," before
his literary activity ended in 1857, including "The Town-
Ho's Story" and "Cock-A-Doodle-Doo!"

3   DUYCKINCK, EVERT A. and GEORGE L. "Herman Melville," in
Cyclopaedia of American Literature. Edited to date by
M. Laird Simons. Vol. 2. Philadelphia: Wm. Rutter & Co.,
pp. 636-639.
Reprint of 1855.B2.

1875

4   GANSEVOORT, HENRY SANFORD. <u>Memorial of Henry Sanford</u>
     <u>Gansevoort</u>. Ed. J. C. Hoadley. Boston: Franklin Press,
     Rand, Avery, & Co., p. 214.
          "'With undulating, long-drawn flow,
            As rolled Brazilian billows go
            Voluminously o'er the line.' ["America"]
          This is Herman Melville's description of the wavy folds
     of the star spangled banner. It is good...." [Letter of
     19 April 1867.]

5   JOHNSON, ROSSITER. <u>Little Classics</u>. <u>Authors</u>. Boston:
     James R. Osgood and Co., pp. 172-173.
          Brief biographical sketch and list of works. [<u>Tragedy</u>,
     volume 3 of <u>Little Classics</u> (1874) printed "The Bell-Tower."]

<u>1876 A BOOKS - NONE</u>

<u>1876 B SHORTER WRITINGS</u>

1   LATHROP, GEORGE PARSONS. <u>A Study of Hawthorne</u>. Boston:
     James R. Osgood and Co., pp. 226, 230-231.
          Brief reference to Hawthorne's friendship with Melville;
     prints extract from Melville's letter to Hawthorne, 16?
     April? 1851 [<u>Letters</u>, pp. 123-125]. Melville's analysis
     of <u>The House of Seven Gables</u> is "really profound." Re-
     printed in 1886.B2.

2   SMITH, J. E. A. <u>The History of Pittsfield, (Berkshire County,)</u>
     <u>Massachusetts, From the Year 1800 to the Year 1876</u>.
     Springfield: C. W. Bryan & Co., pp. 7-8.
          At Arrowhead Melville wrote <u>Moby-Dick</u>, "and other ro-
     mances of the sea," <u>The Piazza Tales</u>, "My Chimney and I"
     [sic] ("a quaintly humorous essay"), and "October Mountain"
     ("a sketch of mingled philosophy and word-painted land-
     scape," inspired by "a prominent and thickly-wooded spur
     of the Hoosac mountains" as seen from the south-eastern
     windows of Arrowhead). [<u>See</u> discussion in Sealts (1950),
     pp. 178-182.] Reprinted in 1879.B2.

3   ANON. "Literary Notes." New York <u>Daily Tribune</u> (12 January).
          Notes that a narrative and descriptive poem on the Holy
     Land by Melville is "in press" by Putnams.

4   ANON. Review of <u>Clarel</u>. New York <u>Daily Tribune</u> (16 June).
          <u>Clarel</u> has no plot and the theological doubts, questions,
     and disputations indulged in by the characters have no log-
     ical course and lead to no distinct conclusions. "The

reader soon becomes hopelessly bewildered, and fatigues
himself vainly in the effort to give personality to speakers
who constantly evade it, and connection to scenes which per-
versely hold themselves separate from each other. The
verse, frequently flowing for a few lines with a smooth,
agreeable current, seems to foam and chafe against unman-
ageable words like a brook in a stony glen: there are
fragments of fresh, musical lyrics, suggestive both of
Hafiz and of William Blake; there are passages so rough,
distorted, and commonplace withal, that the reader impa-
tiently shuts the book." Clarel is "a mixture of skill and
awkwardness, thought and aimless fancy, plan shattered by
whim and melody broken by discords." There are many admirable lines and couplets and many passages whose sense "is
only reached with difficulty, and then proves to be hardly
worth the trouble of seeking." Reprinted in part in Log,
p. 750; reprinted in Recognition, pp. 104-107, and Branch,
pp. 399-402.

5 ANON. "Herman Melville's Clarel." New York World (26 June),
   p. 2.
        There is no plot in Clarel to sustain the interest of
   the reader, who is "harassed by constant doubt whether the
   fact that he hasn't apprehended its motive and moral is due
   to his own obtuseness, or...to the entire absence of either."
   The poem contains much "jog-trot versifying" and an occasional "passage of striking original thought, or possessing
   the true lyrical ring"; its best passages, as a rule, are
   the descriptive ones. Its philosophizing is its least agreeable part, and its analysis of character cannot receive
   much higher praise. Clarel is not a work of art in any
   sense or measure. Reprinted in part in Log, pp. 750-751;
   reprinted in Recognition, pp. 107-109; Sealts (1971),
   pp. 363-364; Branch, pp. 402-403.

6 ANON. Review of Clarel. New York Independent (6 July), p. 9.
        Clarel "is a vast work, extending through a couple of
   16mo volumes" and "destitute of interest or metrical skill."

7 ANON. Review of Clarel. New York Times (10 July), p. 3.
        Clarel is not without signs of the power one expects
   from Melville and has occasionally delicate and vigorous
   pieces of description. But the poem as a whole should have
   been written in prose; Melville does not write with facility
   in verse. The reader will have some difficulty in decipher-
   ing the thread of the story in Clarel; and if Melville "has
   any special tenets of religion to advance he has chosen a
   vehicle somewhat at variance with intelligibility."

1876

Reprinted in part in Log, p. 751, and Branch, pp. 404-406;
reprinted in Recognition, pp. 109-112.

8   ANON. Review of Clarel. Springfield (Mass.) Republican
     (18 July).
         Melville's "literary reputation will remain, what it has
     fairly become, a thing of the past,--for all that his new
     book will do for it." Clarel is laboriously finished,
     sometimes elegant, but "the masculinity, the rich imagina-
     tion, the singular picturesqueness" of Omoo, Typee, and
     Moby-Dick are lacking. Reprinted in Log, p. 953, and
     Leyda (1954), p. 247.

9   ANON. Review of Clarel. New York Galaxy, 22 (August), 282.
         Reviewer cannot praise Melville's "poem or pilgrimage,
     or poem-pilgrimage"; it is sadly uninteresting. Reprinted
     in Log, pp. 753-754 and Branch, p. 406.

10   ANON. Review of Clarel. New York Library Table, 1 (August),
     108.
         The poem is a long one and might judiciously be somewhat
     curtailed but will doubtless "meet with some readers who
     will not object to linger with the author by the way and
     who will think it none too long." The verse is flowing
     and musical. Reprinted in part in Log, p. 753; reprinted
     in Recognition, pp. 112-114, and Branch, pp. 407-408.

11   ANON. Review of Clarel. London Academy, 10 (19 August), 185.
         "The scenes of the pilgrimage, the varying thoughts and
     emotions called up by them, are carefully described, and
     the result is a book of very great interest, and poetry of
     no mean order. The form is subordinate to the matter, and
     a rugged inattention to niceties of rhyme and metre here
     and there seems rather deliberate than careless. In this,
     in the musical verse where the writer chooses to be musical,
     in the subtle blending of old and new thought, in the unex-
     pected turns of argument, and in the hidden connexion be-
     tween things outwardly separate, Mr. Melville reminds us
     of A. H. Clough. He probably represents one phase of Amer-
     ican thought as truly as Clough did one side of the Oxford
     of his day." Reprinted in part in Log, pp. 953-954; re-
     printed in Recognition, pp. 112-114, and Branch, pp. 407-408.

12   ANON. Review of Clarel. London Saturday Review, 42
     (26 August), 276.
         An unusual phenomenon of a poem in two volumes, Clarel
     is not remarkable either for elevation of sentiment or for
     poetic excellence.

13   ANON. Review of <u>Clarel</u>. Philadelphia <u>Lippincott's Magazine</u>,
      18 (September), 391–392.
           In <u>Clarel</u> Melville takes some pains at characterization,
      but they are thrown away, as there is no story, no plot.
      No new light is thrown upon the topics of religious doubt
      and disbelief which occupy his characters. Melville has
      facility in rhyming but trouble with versification. There
      are a few striking descriptions and some good images and
      metaphors, "but generally there is a want of point and
      distinctness, whether it be in the figures of speech, word-
      painting or dialogue: it produces a confusion of ideas and
      clumsiness of outline, arising not from obscurity of thought,
      but of expression, and that arises originally from...
      Melville's imperfect command of metre and rhythm." He dis-
      plays wide but superficial information, presenting a great
      quantity of things one has heard before rather than any-
      thing new. The poem is almost unreadable because of its
      length "and the dead average commonplace level along which
      it stretches." There is nothing in it which could not have
      been said as well or better in prose. Reprinted in part
      in <u>Log</u>, pp. 755–756.

14   ANON. Review of <u>Clarel</u>. Springfield (Mass.) <u>Republican</u>
      (8 September).
           Reports that <u>Clarel</u> "receives kindlier countenance" in
      England than in America and quotes from 1876.B11. Reprinted
      in Leyda (1954), pp. 247–248.

15   ANON. Review of <u>Clarel</u>. London <u>Westminster Review</u>, 105
      (October), 577–578.
           Reviewer describes <u>Clarel</u> as a long poem of about
      27,000 lines, of which he does not understand a single
      word. Talleyrand, who "used to say that he always found
      nonsense singularly refreshing," would have valued <u>Clarel</u>
      highly.

16   ANON. "Books and Poems." Washington <u>Centennial Post</u>
      (31 December).
           Cited in <u>Extracts</u>, No. 32, p. 10. Actually a fake review,
      written for a guide to a bicentennial exposition at the
      Smithsonian. [<u>See</u> <u>Extracts</u>, No. 33, p. 22.]

<u>1877 A BOOKS – NONE</u>

<u>1877 B SHORTER WRITINGS</u>

 1   ANON. Review of <u>Clarel</u>. New York <u>International Review</u>, 4
      (January), 107–108.

1878

The poem might properly be called <u>Clarel, or the Ambi-
guities</u>. It is one of those works which the writer writes
for himself and not for the reader, "wherein he simply fol-
lows the bent of his own interests and fancies, and relies
either upon his personal value or assumed height of achievement for his popular success"--an experiment Browning has
lately tried. Reviewer doubts that many readers are familiar enough with Melville's literary individuality to "venture upon the perusal of such a work, solely for the more
complete appreciation of its author." The poem is a chaos
of description, incident, conversation, and conflict of
ideas and beliefs, in which there is no single governing
and harmonizing conception. Reviewer is unable to say if
Melville has meant to give any coherent spiritual development
to his chief character: any modifications of belief "seem
to spring from the intimate personal intercourse of the
parties rather than from the arguments they use." Throughout the work we trace, "under many masks, the wanderings of
a questioning and unsatisfied soul: yet at the close we do
not feel clearly that peace has been attained, or, if it
has been, upon what basis." The literary character of the
poem, like the intellectual, is astonishingly unequal.
"Reading the best parts, we can not understand why the
whole poem is not greatly better: reading the worst, we
are surprised to find it so good."

1878 A BOOKS - NONE

1878 B SHORTER WRITINGS

1   COLANGE, L. "Melville, Herman," in <u>Zell's Popular Encyclopedia</u>.
        Vol. 2. Philadelphia: T. Ellwood Zell, Davis & Co., p. 1621.
        Brief biographical sketch to 1844 and partial list of
     works.

2   RICHARDSON, CHARLES F. <u>A Primer of American Literature</u>.
        Boston: Houghton, Osgood and Co., p. 79.
            Melville "has written lively sea tales." (Complete
     reference.) Reprinted in 1884.B4.

1879 A BOOKS - NONE

1879 B SHORTER WRITINGS

1   BACKUS, TRUMAN J. <u>Shaw's New History of English Literature</u>.
        New York: Sheldon & Co., pp. 378n, 383.

Melville included in list of travel writers whose works "may be justly commended, either for graces of style, effective description, or interesting narrative,--and, in some instances, for all these qualities combined." In a discussion of romantic fiction, focusing on Brown, Cooper, and Hawthorne, Melville is classed with Mayo as a writer of "adventurous and descriptive narration."

2   GREYLOCK, GODFREY [SMITH, J. E. A.]. Taghconic; The Romance and Beauty of the Hills. Boston: Lee and Shepard, pp. 35, 83-84, 198-200, 317-318.
    Revised and expanded version of 1852.B4, with slightly revised account of Melville's writings at Arrowhead in 1876.B2. Adds account of the beginning of Melville's friendship with Hawthorne, sheltering from a thundershower on Monument Mountain; reports story that Hawthorne knew Melville was the author of the Literary World review of The Scarlet Letter. [See discussion in Thorp (1942), pp. 302-305.] Melville passages reprinted in Sealts (1974), pp. 196-198.

3   SABIN, JOSEPH. A Dictionary of Books Relating to America. Vol. 11. New York: J. Sabin's Son, p. 72.
    Lists Battle-Pieces, Israel Potter, White-Jacket, The Confidence-Man, and Redburn.

1880 A BOOKS - NONE

1880 B SHORTER WRITINGS

1   CATHCART, GEORGE R. "A Dictionary of Some of the Most Familiar of British and American Authors," in The Literary Reader: Typical Selections from Some of the Best British and American Authors, from Shakespeare to the Present Time. New York and Chicago: Ivison, Blakeman, Taylor, and Co., p. 421.
    Melville listed as a fiction and travel writer.

2   ANON. "One Reward of Literary Labor." Boston Atlantic Monthly, 45 (June), 858.
    Author remembers that "Bartleby the Scrivener" and "other articles" were read on their publication by three boys in the backwoods "with that interest, curiosity, and wonder which they are calculated to inspire in youthful minds. The men who could write such articles were regarded with a degree of respect which belongs properly to beings who are above our common humanity.... The history of the various writers and their peculiarities were inquired into by

1881

> the boys. It came to be the prevailing ambition to excel in literature."

1881 A BOOKS - NONE

1881 B SHORTER WRITINGS

1   PHILLIPS, LAWRENCE B. The Great Index of Biographical Reference Containing Over One Hundred Thousand Names. Philadelphia: Gebbie & Co., p. 643.
      Melville included as American author. [Cf. 1871.B2.]

1882 A BOOKS - NONE

1882 B SHORTER WRITINGS

1   COAN, TITUS. Life in Hawaii: An Autobiographic Sketch of Mission Life and Labors (1835-1881). New York: Anson D. F. Randolph & Co., pp. 190, 199-200.
      Revised version of 1867.B5. Reprinted in part in Log, pp. 781-782.

2   NICHOL, JOHN. American Literature: An Historical Sketch, 1620-1880. Edinburgh: Adam and Charles Black, pp. 179-180.
      Typee and Omoo listed among "minor works worthy of note."

3   TUCKERMAN, BAYARD. A History of English Prose Fiction From Sir Thomas Malory to George Eliot. New York: G. P. Putnam's Sons, p. 312n.
      Melville included in list of "Other American writers of fiction."

1883 A BOOKS - NONE

1883 B SHORTER WRITINGS

1   LEE, HENRY. Sea Fables Explained. London: William Clowes and Sons, pp. 73-74.
      Quotes from Melville's "remarkable book," The Whale, on the subject of the "whale-spout."

2   RUSSELL, W. CLARK. "Going Aloft," in Round the Galley Fire. London: J. M. Dent & Sons; New York: E. P. Dutton & Co., pp. 15-16.

Summary and quotation from chapter 50 of Redburn, "one of Herman Merivale's [sic] delightful sea tales." The incident (Harry Bolton's being forced to climb aloft) is told with wonderful power and no exaggeration.

1884 A BOOKS - NONE

1884 B SHORTER WRITINGS

1   ADAMS, OSCAR FAY. "Melville, Herman," in A Brief Handbook of American Authors. Boston: Houghton, Mifflin and Co., p. 113.
     Melville the author of several tales of adventure, of which Typee, Omoo, Redburn and White-Jacket are the chief. "Style breezy and forcible."

2   ANON. "Melville, Herman," in The Illustrated Globe Encyclopaedia of Universal Information. Ed. John M. Ross. Vol. 7. London: Thomas C. Jack, p. 241.
     Partial list of works includes Toby Dick.

3   HAWTHORNE, JULIAN. Nathaniel Hawthorne and His Wife: A Biography. Boston: James R. Osgood and Co. Vol. 1, pp. 89, 362, 377-407 passim, 415, 417, 419, 422, 474-475; Vol. 2, pp. 134-136.
     Melville's friendship with Hawthorne. Prints parts of Melville's letters to Hawthorne 16? April? 1851; 29 June 1851; 1? June 1851; late November 1852 [Letters, pp. 123-125; 132-133; 126-131; 162-163]; and extracts from Hawthorne's journals mentioning Melville. [See 1885.B1.]

4   RICHARDSON, CHARLES F. A Primer of American Literature. Rev. ed. Boston: Houghton, Mifflin and Co., p. 78.
     Reprint of 1878.B2.

5   TAYLOR, BAYARD. Letters to Mary Agnew. Life and Letters of Bayard Taylor. Eds. Marie Hansen-Taylor and Horace E. Scudder. Vol. 1. Boston and New York: Houghton, Mifflin and Co., pp. 119-120, 188.
     In letter of 13 February 1848 Taylor writes: "Herman Melville will be there to-morrow night, and I am obliged to write a valentine for him"; in letter of 23 February 1848 Taylor writes that he became acquainted with Melville's sister at "the grand valentine party" at which nearly all "the author-tribe" were gathered; and in letter of 27 September 1850 he writes that he has been invited to dine with Melville.

1884

6   THOMSON, JAMES (B. V.). "Mr. Kingley's Convertites," in
    Satires and Profanities. London: Progressive Publishing
    Co., pp. 146-156.
       Reprint of 1865.B3.

7   [SCUDDER, HORACE E.]. "Books of the Month." Boston Atlantic
    Monthly, 53 (June), 865.
       Mention in review of Camping among Cannibals by Alfred
    St. Johnston--who "has not the art and glow of Melville."
    Reprinted in Monteiro (September 1973), p. 9.

8   HAWTHORNE, JULIAN. "The American Element in Fiction." New
    York North American Review, 139 (August), 175.
       Melville cannot be cited as treating the difficulties
    dealt with by Hawthorne, "for his only novel or romance,
    whichever it be, was also the most impossible of all his
    books, and really a terrible example of the enormities
    which a man of genius may perpetrate when working in a
    direction unsuited to him. I refer, of course, to 'Pierre,
    or the Ambiguities.'" Reprinted in Monteiro (September
    1973), p. 9.

9   RUSSELL, W. CLARK. "Sea Stories." London Contemporary
    Review, 46 (September), 343-363.
       Ranks Melville first among "the poets of the deep."
    Whoever has read Melville must feel disposed to consider
    Moby-Dick as his finest work. It is not a sea story, but
    "a medley of noble impassioned thoughts born of the deep,
    pervaded by a grotesque human interest, owing to the con-
    trast it suggests between the rough realities of the cabin
    and the forecastle, and the phantasms of men conversing in
    rich poetry, and strangely moving and acting...." "Midnight,
    Forecastle" (chapter 40) might have come down to us from
    some giant mind of the Shakespearean era. We do not need
    to be told that seamen do not talk as these men do; proba-
    bilities are not thought of in this story, which "is of the
    'Ancient Mariner' pattern, madly fantastic in places, full
    of extraordinary thoughts, yet gloriously coherent."
    Melville's account of the emigrants' sufferings in Redburn
    is unimpeachably accurate. There is remarkable character-
    drawing in Omoo. Reprinted in part in Log, pp. 785-786;
    Recognition, pp. 117-120; Doubloon, pp. 104-105; Branch,
    pp. 409-411.

1885 A BOOKS - NONE

1885 B SHORTER WRITINGS

1 HAWTHORNE, JULIAN. <u>Nathaniel Hawthorne and His Wife: A
   Biography</u>. London: Chatto and Windus. Vol. 1, pp. 89,
   362, 377-407 passim, 415, 417, 419, 422, 474-475; Vol. 2,
   pp. 134-136.
       First English edition. [<u>See</u> 1884.B3.]

2 STEDMAN, EDMUND CLARENCE. <u>Poets of America</u>. Boston:
   Houghton, Mifflin and Co., p. 49.
       Melville mentioned with others who have "native fire"
   in their lyrics.

3 ANON. London <u>Daily Telegraph</u> (16 January).
       Article on the South Sea islands. People's association
   of these islands with beauty and peace is owing "particularly to that delightful and original American sailor-
   writer, Herman Melville."

4 ANON. Review of <u>Nathaniel Hawthorne and His Wife</u> by Julian
   Hawthorne. Boston <u>Atlantic Monthly</u>, 55 (February), 263.
       Hawthorne's few American correspondents "betray habit-
   ually the tone of secondary minds, not of men meeting him
   on high ground." The book includes "nine consecutive pages
   of not very interesting epistles from Herman Melville."
   Hawthorne is "made to present to us, beyond all other intellectual men on record, the spectacle of avoidance of his
   proper compeers." Reprinted in part in <u>Log</u>, p. 789.

5 RUSSELL, W. CLARK. "Poets of the Deep." Philadelphia <u>Times</u>
   (21 June), p. 6.
       Reprints paragraph from 1884.B9, ranking Melville first
   among "the poets of the deep."

6 BUCHANAN, ROBERT. "Socrates in Camden, With a Look Round."
   London <u>Academy</u>, 28 (15 August), 102-103.
       Verses, partly in celebration of Melville, "sea-compelling
   man." Footnote adds: "Hermann Melville, author of <u>Typee</u>,
   <u>The White Whale, &c</u>. I sought everywhere for this Triton,
   who is still living somewhere in New York. No one seemed
   to know anything of the one great imaginative writer fit to
   stand shoulder to shoulder with Whitman on that continent."
   Reprinted in 1891.B2; 1921.A1, pp. 349-350; <u>Log</u>, p. 792;
   <u>Recognition</u>, p. 121.

*7 ANON. "The South Sea." Brooklyn <u>Eagle</u> (14 September).
       Reprint of 1885.B3. Cited in <u>Log</u>, p. 793.

1885

8   'STYLUS.' "Our New York Letter." Boston Literary World, 16
        (28 November), p. 448.
              Reports meeting Melville in bookstore. "Had he possessed
        as much literary skill as wild imagination his works might
        have secured for him a permanent place in American litera-
        ture." Melville reference reprinted in Log, p. 794.

1886 A BOOKS - NONE

1886 B SHORTER WRITINGS

1   ANON. "Melville, Herman," in Chambers's Encyclopaedia.
        Vol. 5. New York: Collier, p. 321.
              Reprint of 1875.B1 with minor revision and correction;
        adds that in 1860 Melville "embarked in a whaling-vessel
        for a new tour round the world." Reprinted in 1892.B2 and
        1892.B3.

2   LATHROP, GEORGE PARSONS. A Study of Hawthorne. Boston:
        Houghton, Mifflin and Co., pp. 226, 230-231.
              Reprint of 1876.B1.

3   LONGFELLOW, HENRY WADSWORTH. Life of Henry Wadsworth
        Longfellow. Ed. Samuel Longfellow. Vol. 2. Boston:
        Ticknor and Co.; London: Kegan Paul, Trench & Co., pp. 52,
        301.
              Journal entry for 29 July 1846: Longfellow finishes
        the first volume of Typee, "a curious and interesting book
        with glowing descriptions of life in the Marquesas." Entry
        for 1 July 1857: Longfellow receives from Baroness Elize
        von Hohenhausen a copy of her poem Die Marquesas-Insel,
        "founded on Melville's Typee."

*4   ANON. "Echoes of the Hour." New York Commercial Advertiser
        (14 January).
              Details of Melville's present life; he is "generally
        supposed to be dead." Cited in Log, p. 796.

5   ANON. "A 'Buried' Author." New York Commercial Advertiser
        (18 January).
              Prints verses on Melville by Professor J. W. Henry Canoll.
        Reprinted in Log, pp. 796-797.

*6   ANON. "Writers Who Lack College Training." St. Louis Globe
        Democrat (before 11 December).
              Melville included in discussion of writers without col-
        lege training. Once renowned as an author, he is "seldom

mentioned of late." His writings "show a thorough understanding of the force and delicacy of the English language,
which he seems to have learned instinctively." Only a
small proportion of American literary men who are
"conspicuous for clearness, vigor, purity and elegance of
style" have gone through academic courses. Reprinted in
1886.B7; reprinted in part in Log, p. 802.

7   ANON. "Writers Who Lack College Training." New York Critic,
      NS 6 (11 December), 296-297.
         Reprint of 1886.B6.

1887 A BOOKS - NONE

1887 B SHORTER WRITINGS

1   ANON. "A Literary Tone," in The Book of Berkshire. Great
      Barrington and Springfield (Mass.): Clark W. Bryan & Co.,
      p. 104.
         Details of Pittsfield literary life and personalities.
      Recalls that Melville resided for many years at Arrowhead.

2   BARROWS, CHARLES M. "Melville, Herman," in Acts and Anecdotes
      of Authors. Boston: New England Publishing Co., p. 382.
         Two-line entry. Among Melville's works are Typee, Omoo,
      White-Jacket, and Redburn.

3   MORRIS, CHARLES. "H. Melville," in Half-Hours with the Best
      American Authors. Philadelphia: J. B. Lippincott Co.,
      p. 230.
         Headnote to extract from Moby-Dick, chapter 61. As an
      accurate, detailed, and vivid description of the whale fish-
      ery, Moby-Dick could not well be surpassed. It also has
      much value as a novel, its characters being drawn with strik-
      ing force and originality. Chief among Melville's many
      other romances is Typee. Reprinted in Monteiro (Third
      Quarter 1975), pp. 406-407.

4   SONNENSCHEIN, WILLIAM SWAN. The Best Books: A Reader's
      Guide to the Choice of the Best Available Books. London:
      Swan Sonnenschein Lowrey & Co., p. 215.
         Lists Typee and Omoo in Geography of Australasia:
      Polynesia bibliography.

5   WHIPPLE, EDWIN PERCY. American Literature and Other Papers.
      Boston: Ticknor and Co., p. 125.
         "Herman Melville, after astonishing the public with a
      rapid succession of original novels, the scene of which was

1888

placed in the islands of the Pacific, suddenly dropped his
pen, as if in disgust of his vocation." (Complete reference.)

1888 A BOOKS - NONE

1888 B SHORTER WRITINGS

1   ANON. "Melville, Herman," in Appleton's Cyclopaedia of Amer-
     ican Biography. Eds. James Grant Wilson and John Fiske.
     Vol. 4. New York: D. Appleton and Co., pp. 293-294.
        Lengthy biographical paragraph, mainly on Melville's
     adventures in the Marquesas (with details and brief quota-
     tion from Typee). List of Melville's works, without com-
     ment except for Typee (in which the story of his "romantic
     captivity is told with remarkable vividness"). Reprinted
     in 1898.B1 and Sealts (1974), pp. 95-97.

2   ALEXANDER, JAMES M. Mission Life in Hawaii. Memoir of
     Rev. William P. Alexander. Oakland, Calif.: Pacific Press
     Publishing Co., pp. 72, 74, 80.
        Brief quotations from Typee in chapter on the Marquesas
     Islands, including the Typee Valley.

3   ANON. Review of The Voyage of the Fleetwing by C. M. Newell.
     New York Nation, 46 (19 April), 330.
        Newell's book is full of life but crude in style.
     Similar scenes are described with wonderful power and
     felicity in Moby-Dick, "the classic story of whaling adven-
     ture." Reprinted in part in Log, p. 807, and Doubloon,
     pp. 105-106.

4   HAWTHORNE, JULIAN. "Man-Books." Chicago America: A Journal
     of To-Day, 1 (27 September), 11-12.
        In Typee and Omoo, Moby-Dick, and White-Jacket, Melville
     "wrote books that were certainly not meant for women; but
     they were not exactly man-books, either, if we except 'Moby-
     Dick'; they were books of adventure--boys' books." Re-
     printed in part in Log, p. 810, and Doubloon, pp. 106-108.

5   ANON. Review of John Marr and Other Sailors. New York Mail
     and Express (20 November), p. 3.
        Forty years ago Melville was "the peer of Hawthorne in
     popular estimation" and by many considered his superior.
     His later writings did not equal his earlier, but with all
     his defects Melville is a man of unquestionable talent and
     considerable genius. His verse is marked by the same un-
     trained imagination which distinguishes his prose. The

poems in John Marr are "of varying degrees of merit, but
all with the briny flavor that should belong to songs of
the sea." Moby-Dick is probably Melville's greatest work.
Reprinted in part in Log, p. 811 [as from "an unidentified
newspaper"]; reprinted in Sealts (1971), p. 365, and Branch,
p. 412.

1889 A BOOKS - NONE

1889 B SHORTER WRITINGS

1 ANON. "Melville, Herman," in Alden's Cyclopedia of Universal
   Literature. New York: John B. Alden, p. 407.
      Headnote to extract from Redburn, chapter 14; brief
   biographical sketch and list of works.

2 ANON. "XX.--Whale-Fishing in the Indian Ocean," in Harper's
   Fifth Reader. New York: American Book Co., p. 474.
      Brief biographical note to extract from Moby-Dick,
   chapter 61.

3 CLAYDEN, P. W. Rogers and His Contemporaries. London:
   Smith, Elder & Co., pp. 342-343.
      Letter dated 3 September 1849 from Edward Everett in-
   troducing Melville to Samuel Rogers: "He is known to you
   and the entire reading world by his 'Typee' and 'Omoo'...
   while he is in London I want him to see a few of those
   choicest spirits, who even at the present day increase the
   pride which we feel in speaking the language of Shakespeare
   and Milton."

4 RICHARDSON, CHARLES F. "The Lesser Novelists," in American
   Literature, 1607-1885. Vol. 2. New York and London:
   G. P. Putnam's Sons, pp. 403-404.
      Melville seen as one of a number of writers searching
   for "novelty of theme, scene, and time." In his brisk and
   stirring tales of the sea or sketches of travel, "fact and
   fancy were mingled by the nervously impatient author, in
   the proportion desired by his immediate public." His brilliant power of delineation, which charmed the Hawthornes in
   conversation, was diminished by the exigencies of writing.
   Melville made attempts to combine "the improbably romantic
   and the obviously satirical" but failed completely for lack
   of a firm thought and a steady hand. His sprightly improvi-
   sations in literature are now forgotten. Reprinted in
   1902.B8; Melville references reprinted in Log, p. 812, and
   Doubloon, pp. 108-109.

1889

5   RUSSELL, W. CLARK. "The Honor of the Flag." Chicago America:
    A Journal of To-Day, 1 (24 January), 1-3.
        On several sea authors. The poetry, passion, and senti-
    ment interwoven in the fabric of Melville's narratives are
    lacking in Dana. No name in American letters deserves to
    stand higher than Melville's for beauty of imagination,
    accuracy of reproduction, originality of conception and
    for a quality of imagination that, as in Moby-Dick, "lifts
    some of his utterances to such a height of bold and swelling
    fancy as one must search the pages of the Elizabethan drama-
    tists to parallel." Reprinted in part in Log, p. 813.

6   BUCHANAN, ROBERT. "Imperial Cockneydom." London Universal
    Review, 4 (May), 78.
        Melville unknown to young men in America. When Buchanan
    went to America his first inquiry was about the author of
    Typee, Omoo, The Whale, and White-Jacket. E. C. Stedman
    seemed much astonished at his interest in the subject; said
    that Melville was living "somewhere in New York" and because
    of public neglect of his works had resolved never to write
    another line. Melville a Titan silenced, while the book-
    stalls are flooded with illustrated magazines. Reprinted
    in 1891.B3; reprinted in part in Log, p. 787.

7   SALT, HENRY S. "Herman Melville." London Scottish Art Review,
    2 (November), 186-190.
        Melville's books can be roughly divided into two classes:
    the predominantly practical and autobiographical (Typee,
    Omoo, Redburn, White-Jacket); and the predominantly fantas-
    tic (Mardi, Moby-Dick, and the later works). Melville was
    affected by the transcendental tendency of the age, and "his
    stories of what purported to be plain matter-of-fact life"
    are "gradually absorbed and swallowed up in the wildest,
    mystical speculations." The first volume of Mardi ranks
    with Melville's finest achievements; the rest had better
    have not been written. Moby-Dick is perhaps more success-
    ful as a whole than Mardi since its very extravagances "work
    in more harmoniously with the outline of the plot." Pierre
    is perhaps the ne plus ultra of metaphysical absurdity.
    Melville is at his best, as in Typee, when the mystic ele-
    ment is kept in check, and made subservient to the clear
    development of the story; or when, as in certain passages
    of Mardi and Moby-Dick, the two qualities are for the time
    harmoniously blended. Despite his early transcendental
    tendencies and final lapse into the "illimitable inane,"
    Melville possessed strong powers of observation, a solid
    grasp of facts, and a keen sense of humor. As a portrayer
    of character he is almost always successful. The tone of

his books is altogether frank and healthy. His best work
is <u>Typee</u>. Reprinted in part in <u>Log</u>, pp. 817-818; <u>Recogni-
tion</u>, pp. 122-130; <u>Doubloon</u>, pp. 109-110; Branch,
pp. 413-417.

8   ANON. "The Novelist of the Sea. An Interview with Mr. Clark
      Russell." London <u>Pall Mall Gazette</u> (20 December), pp. 1-2.
        Russell shows copy of <u>John Marr</u> to interviewer, who
      refers to Melville as "that magnificent American sea-
      novelist."

1890 A BOOKS - NONE

1890 B SHORTER WRITINGS

1   RUSSELL, W. CLARK. "To Herman Melville, Esq.," in <u>An Ocean
      Tragedy</u>. 3 vols. London: Chatto & Windus.
        Dedication in form of letter. "...My books have done
      more than ever I had dared dream, by winning for me the
      friendship and approval of the Author of 'Typee,' 'Omoo,'
      'Moby-Dick,' 'Redburn,' and other productions which top
      the list of sea literature in the English tongue...."
      Reprinted in <u>Log</u>, p. 820.

2   STEDMAN, ARTHUR. "Short Biographies of American Authors
      Represented in This Work," in <u>A Library of American Litera-
      ture from the Earliest Settlement to the Present Time</u>.
      Vol. 11. Eds. Edmund Clarence Stedman and Ellen MacKay
      Hutchinson. New York: Charles L. Webster & Co., p. 554.
        Brief biographical sketch and partial list of works.
      [Vol. 7 (1889), pp. 464-478, prints "The Bell-Tower," "The
      Stone Fleet," "Sheridan at Cedar Creek," and "In the Prison
      Pen."] Also published in 1890.B3. Reprinted in 1891.B20;
      1891.B28; Sealts (1974), p. 98.

3   STEDMAN, ARTHUR. "Melville, Herman," in <u>Short Biographies of
      American Authors Represented in "A Library of American
      Literature</u>." New York: Charles L. Webster & Co., p. 554.
        Same entry as in 1890.B2.

4   LUKENS, HENRY CLAY. "American Literary Comedians." New York
      <u>Harper's New Monthly Magazine</u>, 80 (April), 793.
        Melville is named in a long list of "native literary
      comedians of rare talent" in the period 1840-1860. No
      separate comment on Melville.

1890

5   BOK, EDWARD. "Notes on Authors." New York Publishers' Weekly,
    38 (15 November), 705.
        Most people believe him to be dead, but Melville is
    "still vigorous," though an old man now, and works for the
    Customs Revenue Service. His sea stories "have never been
    equalled perhaps in their special line." Reprinted in
    1890.B7; Log, p. 827; Branch, pp. 417-418.

6   ANON. "Here in Boston." Boston Post (19 November).
        Takes up report that Melville is alive but forgotten in
    New York [see 1890.B5]. Such "a state of things" would be
    impossible in Boston. Most readers probably associate
    Melville only with sailor adventures, but he wrote "such
    stories" as The Confidence-Man, "a volume of poems about
    the Civil War and two volumes on a pilgrimage to the Holy
    Land." Melville has satisfaction in knowing that his best
    work is "unsurpassed in its way in English literature."
    Reprinted in part in Log, p. 827.

7   ANON. Boston Literary World, 21 (6 December), 469.
        Reprint of 1890.B5.

8   ANON. New York Critic, NS 14 (13 December), 310.
        Claims that Melville's friends are annoyed by the pub-
    lished statement that practically no one knows of his ex-
    istence. Though Melville has gone out very little since
    the death of his son "some two years ago," in New York
    literary circles he is known to live in the city and to
    work for the Customs Revenue Service.

1891 A BOOKS - NONE

1891 B SHORTER WRITINGS

1   ANON. "Melville, Herman," in Chambers's Encyclopaedia.
        Vol. 7. London: William & Robert Chambers; Philadelphia:
        J. B. Lippincott Co., p. 129.
        New, shorter entry [see 1875.B1 and 1886.B1]. Notes
    that after Typee and Omoo Melville wrote a "number of tales
    and three volumes of poetry," but does not name them.

2   BUCHANAN, ROBERT. "Canto II. The First Haven. (Natura
        Naturans)," in The Outcast. London: Chatto & Windus,
        pp. 76-78.
        Buchanan dedicates his book to Hermann Melville, "Last
    of the grand Homeric race,/Great tale-teller of the marines."
    The canto ends with the verses on Melville in 1885.B6, with
    slight revisions and deletions, and without the footnote.

3 BUCHANAN, ROBERT. "Imperial Cockneydom," in The Coming Terror
   and Other Essays and Letters. London: William Heinemann,
   p. 239.
        Reprint of 1889.B6.

4 KIRK, JOHN FOSTER. "Melville, Herman," in A Supplement to
   Allibone's Critical Dictionary of English Literature and
   British and American Authors. Philadelphia: J. B.
   Lippincott Co., p. 1103.
        Lists Battle-Pieces and Clarel.

5 STEVENSON, ROBERT LOUIS. "The South Seas: A Record of Three
   Cruises." London Black and White, 1 (28 February), 114.
        "Or take the valley of Hapaa, known to readers of Herman
   Melville under the grotesque misspelling of Hapar. There
   are but two writers who have touched the South Seas with
   any genius, both Americans: Melville and Charles Warren
   Stoddard; and at the christening of the first and greatest,
   some influential fairy must have been neglected: 'He shall
   be able to see,' 'He shall be able to tell,' 'He shall be
   able to charm,' said the friendly godmothers, 'But he shall
   not be able to hear,' exclaimed the last." (Complete
   Melville reference.) Reprinted in 1896.B4 and 1900.B4.

6 ANON. "Recent Deaths." Boston Evening Transcript
   (29 September).
        Biographical details and list of works (including Plute
   Jacket and The Prazza Tales--cf. 1891.B12).

7 ANON. Obituary Notice. New York Daily Tribune (29 September).
        Typee was Melville's best work, "although he has since
   written a number of other stories, which were published more
   for private than public circulation." Reprinted in part in
   Log, p. 837.

8 ANON. "Death of a Once Popular Author." New York Press
   (29 September).
        Melville's books are now little known, probably because
   he stopped writing; probably even his own generation has
   long thought him dead. Reprinted in part in Log, p. 836.

9 ANON. "Obituary Notes." New York Times (29 September).
        Melville wrote Typee, Omoo, Mobie Dick [sic], "and other
   sea-faring tales, written in earlier years." Reprinted in
   Branch, p. 418.

*10 ANON. "Death of Herman Melville. Author of Several Volumes
    of Poems and Romances." New York World (29 September).
        Cited in Log, p. 837.

1891

*11   ANON. Obituary Notice. Boston Evening Transcript
      (30 September).
          Cited in Hetherington (1955), pp. 326-327.

12   ANON. Boston Morning Journal (30 September).
          Brief biographical sketch and list of works (including
      Plute Jacket and The Prazza Tales--cf. 1891.B6). Conclud-
      ing assessment (Melville "was undoubtedly an original
      thinker....yet he was often mystical and unintelligible")
      taken from 1856.B1.

*13   ANON. Obituary Notice. New York Sun (30 September).
          Cited in Hetherington (1955), p. 327.

14   ELLIS, A. B. "On Polyandry." New York Popular Science Monthly,
      39 (October), 801-809.
          On marriage among primitive peoples. Melville cited as
      an authority.

15   [STEDMAN, ARTHUR]. "Herman Melville's Funeral." New York
      Daily Tribune (1 October), p. 14.
          Brief biographical details, including Melville's recent
      life. Though much has been written, particularly in Eng-
      lish journals, about the neglect of Melville by contemporary
      authors in the United States, he was among the very first
      to be invited to join the Authors Club in 1882. His re-
      fusal of this invitation and social life generally is said
      to be due chiefly to "natural disposition" and partly to
      "the very adverse critical reception" of Pierre. His prac-
      tical abandonment of literary work some 25 years ago has
      allowed general interest in his books to die out. His best-
      known poem is "Sheridan at Cedar Creek." Prints "L'Envoi"
      from Timoleon. Reprinted in 1891.B31 and Sealts (1974),
      pp. 99-101; reprinted in part in 1891.B46 and Log, p. 837.

16   ANON. "Herman Melville." New York Town Topics (1 October),
      p. 3.
          Melville's career is a rare instance of literary fame
      won in youth with apparently no care about increasing or
      even maintaining a reputation in later life. Melville pro-
      duced three classic books: Typee, Omoo, and in a less
      degree Moby-Dick, are the very best books of their kind
      in the language. Reprinted in 1891.B49.

17   ANON. "Berkshire County." Springfield (Mass.) Daily
      Republican (1 October), p. 6.
          "Herman Melville, the author, who died at New York Monday,
      spent many years of his life in town at the Melville

homestead on the middle road to Lenox, opposite Col
Richard Lather's Abby lodge." (Complete item.)

18   ANON. "Here in Boston." Boston Post (2 October), p. 4.
           Some of Melville's books are out of print, but the copy
      of Moby-Dick, thumbed beyond repair, with broken back, is
      "testimony of the appreciation of frequenters of the Public
      Library." Brief comments on the other novels. Mardi was a
      compound of "transcendentalism, Rabelais, hashish and tar";
      White-Jacket "thoroughly delightful"; Pierre "a stupid book";
      The Confidence-Man baffling. Remembers the short stories
      with affection but found the poetry unreadable. Wishes
      Melville had explained before his death "the reasons of
      the fierce hatred" between the White Whale and Ahab.
      "L'Envoi" from Timoleon is printed separately in the pre-
      vious column. Reprinted in part in Doubloon, p. 111.

19   ANON. "Herman Melville." New York Times (2 October), p. 4.
           Contrasts Melville's earlier fame with his present
      obscurity. Melville died "an absolutely forgotten man,"
      so little known that only one newspaper contained an obit-
      uary of him. Years ago the books that made Melville's
      reputation had long been out of print and out of demand.
      Yet Melville was a "born romancer." His experience in the
      South Sea did not lead him to romance; "the irresistible
      attraction that romance had over him" led him to the South
      Sea. Few readers will forget Melville's "poetizing" of
      the trying-out of blubber in Moby-Dick; but the South
      Pacific is the field Melville mainly made his own "beyond
      rivalry." Stevenson has not bettered him there. Reprinted
      in part in 1891.B37; reprinted in Branch, pp. 418-420.

20   ANON. New York Critic, NS 16 (3 October), 175.
           Refers to Melville as "the once popular writer of ro-
      mances" and reprints 1890.B2.

*21   ANON. New York Daily Tribune (3 October).
           Response to 1891.B19. Cited in Hetherington (1955),
      p. 328.

22   ANON. Obituary Notice. Boston Sunday Herald (4 October),
      p. 14.
           Notes Melville's great popularity nearly half a century
      ago and long subsequent obscurity. He wrote graphically,
      eloquently, and originally about the South Sea Islands "on
      some such lines as those with which Robert Louis Stevenson
      has been lately favoring the readers of the Herald."

1891

23   ANON. "The Literary Wayside." Springfield (Mass.) <u>Sunday
      Republican</u> (4 October), p. 6.
          At his death Melville had long been forgotten, but prob-
      ably no American has written a work of imagination more
      powerful and poetic than <u>Moby-Dick</u>. In <u>Moby-Dick</u> he draws
      character with great power and gives an immense amount of
      knowledge about the whale; the book swells with a humor
      "often as grotesque as Jean Paul's, but not so genial as
      it is sardonic." Melville was also the first to describe
      "with imaginative grace based upon personal knowledge" the
      inhabitants of the South Sea islands. The dedication to
      Greylock in <u>Pierre</u> shows Melville's later tendency to ex-
      travagance of rhetoric, "which confused and diminished the
      effect of his real genius." <u>Battle-Pieces</u> shows vigor of
      verse and frequent flashes of prophetic fire; <u>Clarel</u> cannot
      be read except as a task. Quotes J. E. A. Smith as author-
      ity that Melville wrote <u>Moby-Dick</u>, <u>Pierre</u>, <u>The Piazza Tales</u>,
      "My Chimney and I" [sic], and "October Mountain" at Arrow-
      head [<u>see</u> 1876.B2 and 1879.B2]. Prints "The Portent,"
      stanzas from "Chattanooga," and "The College Colonel."
      Reprinted in part in Branch, pp. 420-423.

24   H[ILLARD], O. G. "The Late Hiram [sic] Melville. A Tribute
      to His Memory from One Who Knew Him." Letter to the Editor.
      New York <u>Times</u> (6 October), p. 9.
          One reason for Melville's obscurity--he "had shot his
      arrow and made his mark and was satisfied." Melville's
      proud and sensitive nature made him a recluse. If he had
      been offered the editorship of a magazine, he would probably
      have accepted the position and filled it well; but he was
      incapable of asking for that or any other position.
      Melville claimed he did not own a single copy of his books;
      eloquent in discussing general literature, he was dumb on
      the subject of his own writings. Reprinted in 1891.B37.

*25   SCHONBERG, JAMES. Obituary Notice. New York <u>Home Journal</u>
      (7 October).
          Cited in Hetherington (1955), p. 329.

26   STODDARD, RICHARD H. "Herman Melville." New York <u>Mail and</u>
      <u>Express</u> (8 October), p. 5.
          Melville's wealth of imagination was untrained. He saw,
      felt, and thought like a poet, but never attained any pro-
      ficiency in verse. His vocabulary was large, fluent, elo-
      quent, but excessive, inaccurate, and unliterary; he wrote
      too easily, at too great length. He never learned to con-
      trol the dark, mysterious elements in his nature, as
      Hawthorne did his from the beginning, and never turned

their possibilities into actualities. Not easy to determine why Melville's works after Moby-Dick added nothing to
his reputation since they were conceived in the same spirit
and informed with the same qualities as Typee and Omoo,
which are landmarks in American literature. Prints nearly
all of Melville's letter to Hawthorne, 1? June 1851. Reprinted in part in 1891.B48; Doubloon, pp. 111-112; Branch,
pp. 423-425.

27   ANON. "Old and New." St. Johnsbury (Vt.) Republican
      (8 October).
         Obituary notice; biographical sketch. In his day the
      most popular author in America, Melville died forgotten.
      Typee is a remarkable book and well deserves immortality.

28   ANON. Obituary Notice. Boston Literary World, 22 (10 October),
      366.
         Notes Melville's death and reprints 1890.B2.

*29   ANON. New York Critic (10 October).
         Reprint of 1891.B16. Cited in Hetherington (1955),
      p. 327.

30   ANON. "Herman Melville." New York Harper's Weekly Magazine,
      35 (10 October), 782.
         Mainly biographical. Melville was a man of brilliant
      genius who practically retired as a writer a quarter of a
      century ago in the prime of his powers, suddenly becoming
      "dumb and barren." After 1866 he withdrew from the world,
      his seclusion prompted perhaps by natural melancholy of
      temperament and perhaps by his anger at the critics' bitter
      attacks on Pierre.

31   [STEDMAN, ARTHUR]. "Herman Melville." New York Critic, NS 16
      (10 October), 190.
         Reprint of 1891.B15.

32   WINGATE, CHARLES E. L. "Boston Letter." New York Critic,
      NS 16 (10 October), 184-185.
         To Bostonians Melville's death should recall the fact
      that his grandfather [Major Thomas Melvill] was a prominent
      patriotic merchant in Boston during Revolutionary days and
      was one of the "Indians" in the famous tea-party; he is
      reported to have been the last man in the city to wear the
      old-fashioned cocked hat.

33   STEDMAN, ARTHUR. "Marquesan Melville. A South Sea Prospero
      who Lived and Died in New York." New York World
      (11 October), p. 26.

      Lengthy biographical account, including details of the publication of Melville's early books. Quotes from Melville's letter to Hawthorne, 29 June 1851. Quotes letter from Dr. Titus Munson Coan, recording his first impressions of Melville, and letter from W. Clark Russell to Melville, dated 21 July 1886, stating that Melville's reputation in England was "very great." Melville would have sold more of his books and kept his name before the public if he had joined in the literary movements of New York. Doubtful that he would have accepted a magazine editorship [see 1891.B24]; he could not bear business details or routine work. His important literary work was practically ended with the completion of Moby-Dick. Reprinted in part in 1891.B40; reprinted in Sealts (1974), pp. 101-110.

34   ANON. "Note and Comment." Springfield (Mass.) Daily Republican (12 October), p. 4.
      Melville's separation from his fellow-authors was voluntary and not due to their neglect. Melville was one of the first to be invited to join the Author's club in 1882 but declined. Few literary men and women in New York knew him; one of the few, naturally, was Edmund C. Stedman, "whose friendly acquaintance no recluse even would willingly forego."

35   ANON. "Literary Gossip." London Athenaeum, No. 3338 (17 October), p. 519.
      Brief biographical sketch to 1847. Melville published Typee, Omoo, "various novels which had admirable passages in them, and some volumes of poetry."

36   ANON. "Obituary." London Saturday Review, 72 (17 October), 434.
      The death of Melville, "the author, nearly half a century ago, of Typee and Omoo, recalls another of those curious, but by no means rare, instances where a man under some peculiar stimulus does absolutely capital work early, and then neither rests altogether, nor does bad work, but is simply ordinary."

37   ANON. "Herman Melville." New York Critic, NS 16 (17 October), 203.
      Partial reprint of 1891.B19 and reprint of 1891.B24. Editorial note draws attention to errors in the latter.

38   ANON. "Note and Comment." Springfield (Mass.) Daily Republican (19 October), p. 4.

Melville's grandfather, Major Thomas Melvill, is said to be the original of Holmes's poem "The Last Leaf."

39 ANON. Springfield (Mass.) Weekly Republican (23 October). Summaries of 1891.B15 and 1891.B33.

40 STEDMAN, ARTHUR. "Herman Melville." New York Critic, NS 16 (24 October), 222-223.
Partial reprint of 1891.B33.

41 SMITH, J. E. A. "Herman Melville: A Great Pittsfield Author-- Brief Biographical Sketch." Pittsfield (Mass.) Evening Journal (27 October), p. 4.
First installment of Melville biography. Gives account of Melville's grandfather, Major Thomas Melvill. Continued in 1891.B42, B50, B51, B53, B54; 1892.B8, B9, B10. All but 1891.B51 reprinted, with some alterations and deletions, in 1895.A1; all installments reprinted in Sealts (1974), pp. 119-149.

42 SMITH, J. E. A. "Herman Melville. A Great Pittsfield Author-- Brief Biographical Sketches." Pittsfield (Mass.) Evening Journal (29 October), p. 4.
Second installment of Melville biography begun in 1891.B41. Accounts of General Peter Gansevoort, Melville's education, and his uncle, Major Thomas Melvill. Reprinted in Sealts (1974), pp. 123-126.

43 WINGATE, CHARLES E. L. "Boston Letter." New York Critic, NS 16 (31 October), 235.
Two paragraphs on Melville's grandfather, Major Thomas Melvill. Quotes Oliver Wendell Holmes: "I remember Major Thomas Melville [sic] very well.... The figure of the sturdy old gentleman thumping round with his cane suggested my poem 'The Last Leaf.'"

44 ANON. London Bookman, 1 (November), 50.
The death of Melville, the author of Typee "and other works," recalls "the quantity of good literature" published by John Murray in his Home and Colonial Library, many volumes of which "are still worthy of reproduction." Reprinted in Recognition, p. 130.

45 ANON. London Bookman, 1 (November), 56.
Notes Melville's death and remembers "some pleasant pictures" of Melville in Julian Hawthorne's life of Hawthorne. His conversation was vivid; his letters were "lively, schoolboy like productions." Quotes Hawthorne: though Melville

learned his traveling habits by drifting about all over
the South Seas, "we seldom see men of less criticisable
manners than he."

46 STEDMAN, ARTHUR. New York <u>Current Literature</u>, 8 (November),
     339-340.
       Reprint of most of 1891.B15.

47 STEDMAN, ARTHUR. "Melville of Marquesas." New York <u>Review
     of Reviews</u>, 4 (November), 428-430.
       Biographical and critical. Probable that publication
     of Dana's <u>Two Years Before the Mast</u> in 1840 influenced
     Melville to follow the sea as a vocation and ship for
     Liverpool the following year [sic]. <u>Typee</u> and <u>White-Jacket</u>
     are Melville's two most consistent books; <u>Typee</u> contains
     Melville's most artistic work, though earlier critics agree
     with W. Clark Russell that <u>Moby-Dick</u> is his best book.
     Stedman agrees with earlier critics that Melville's power
     lay in describing his own experiences and scenes he had
     witnessed and investing them with romance; he failed as an
     inventor of characters and situations. Melville enjoyed
     to the full the enhanced reputation <u>Moby-Dick</u> brought him,
     but the great Harper fire destroyed the whole stock of his
     books and kept them out of print at a most important time.
     Details of Melville's financial arrangements with the Harpers.
     The best poems in <u>Battle-Pieces</u> are "The Stone Fleet," "In
     the Prison Pen," "The College Colonel," "The March to the
     Sea," "Running the Batteries," and "Sheridan at Cedar Creek."
     In <u>John Marr</u> and <u>Timoleon</u> the best of several fine lyrics
     is Melville's last poem, "The Return of the Sire de Nesle."
     <u>Clarel</u>, a long mystical poem, requires a dictionary, a
     cyclopaedia, and a copy of the Bible for its elucidation.
     Prints "The Return of the Sire de Nesle." Reprinted in
     Sealts (1974), pp. 110-115.

48 ANON. "Mr. Stoddard on Herman Melville." New York <u>Critic</u>,
     NS 16 (14 November), 272-273.
       Partial reprint of 1891.B26, with brief introduction.

49 ANON. "Herman Melville." Pittsfield (Mass.) <u>Evening Journal</u>
     (21 November), p. 8.
       Reprint of 1891.B16.

50 SMITH, J. E. A. "Herman Melville. A Great Pittsfield Author--
     Brief Biographical Sketch." Pittsfield (Mass.) <u>Evening
     Journal</u> (21 November), p. 4.
       Third installment of Melville biography begun in 1891.B41.
     Account of Melville's voyages in the South Seas, the

publication and success of Typee and Omoo, and a visit with
wife Elizabeth to Pittsfield. Reprinted in Sealts (1974),
pp. 126-129.

51 SMITH, J. E. A. "Herman Melville. A Great Pittsfield Author--
    Brief Biographical Sketches." Pittsfield (Mass.) Evening
    Journal (16 December), p. 2.
       Fourth installment of Melville biography begun in
    1891.B41. Account of life at Arrowhead; biographical de-
    tails of Hawthorne. Reprinted in Sealts (1974), pp. 129-132.

52 COAN, TITUS MUNSON. "Herman Melville." Boston Literary World,
    22 (19 December), 492-493.
       Mainly biographical. Typee and Omoo, mistaken by the
    public for fiction, were the most vivid truth. According
    to Coan's father, the Rev. Titus Coan, who "went over
    Melville's ground" in 1867, the descriptions in Typee were
    admirably true and the characterizations faultless in the
    main. Typee is a masterpiece, the outcome of an opportu-
    nity that will never be repeated. Melville was "the first
    and only man ever made captive in a valley full of Polyne-
    sian cannibals, who had the genius to describe the situa-
    tion, and who got away alive to write his book." The
    attacks on his books were not the cause of his withdrawal
    from society [see 1891.B15 and 1891.B30]. The cause was
    "intrinsic": his "extremely proud and sensitive nature and
    his studious habits." Quotes Melville: "My books will
    speak for themselves, and all the better if I avoid the
    rattling egotism by which so many win a certain vogue for
    a certain time." Reprinted in Sealts (1974), pp. 116-119.

53 SMITH, J. E. A. "Herman Melville. A Great Pittsfield Author--
    Brief Biographical Sketches." Pittsfield (Mass.) Evening
    Journal (19 December), p. 6.
       Fifth installment of Melville biography begun in 1891.B41.
    Accounts of Melville's friendship with Hawthorne, works
    written at Arrowhead (including "October Mountain" [see
    1876.B2 and 1879.B2]), Melville as lecturer, the removal
    from Pittsfield. Melville's philosophical talk with
    Hawthorne, "while it could well color Hawthorne's weird
    tales, where it had a place, had a very disastrous effect
    upon those of Melville where it had none." The "excessive
    intimacy" between Melville and Hawthorne was a misfortune
    to Melville "whose charm lay in the simplicity, vigor and
    naturalness with which he related his observations of men
    and nature and his expression of the common sense, but keen
    and often eloquent, thoughts which they had excited in him."
    Reprinted in Sealts (1974), pp. 132-135.

1891

54   SMITH, J. E. A. "Herman Melville. A Great Pittsfield Author--
      Brief Biographical Sketch." Pittsfield (Mass.) Evening
      Journal (24 December), p. 4.
          Sixth installment of Melville biography begun in 1891.B41.
      Gives reasons for the removal from Pittsfield and an account
      of Melville at the custom house. Reprinted in Sealts (1974),
      pp. 135-137.

1892 A BOOKS - NONE

1892 B SHORTER WRITINGS

1   ANON. "Melville, Herman," in Appleton's Annual Cyclopaedia
      and Register of Important Events of the Year 1891. NS 16.
      New York: D. Appleton and Co., pp. 503-505.
          Mainly biographical. Moby-Dick is perhaps the most
      graphic and truthful description of whaling life ever writ-
      ten, though it contains some of the objectionable character-
      istics of Mardi. Melville was led by his inclination for
      philosophical speculation to commit grave literary errors,
      which destroyed his popularity with the reading public.
      Reprinted in Sealts (1974), pp. 149-154.

2   ANON. "Melville, Herman," in The Columbian Cyclopedia.
      Vol. 19. New York: Garretson, Cox & Co., n.p.
          Reprint of 1886.B1, with slight alterations.

3   ANON. "Melville, Herman," in The International Cyclopaedia.
      Ed. H. T. Peck. Vol. 9. New York: Dodd, Mead & Co.,
      pp. 684-685.
          Reprint of 1886.B1, with slight alterations, adding
      date of Melville's death.

4   HAWTHORNE, JULIAN and LEONARD LEMMON. "Herman Melville, An
      Early Sea-Novelist," in American Literature: A Text-Book
      for The Use of Schools and Colleges. Boston: D. C. Heath,
      pp. 208-209.
          Melville's position in literature as a sea author is
      secure and solitary; he surpasses all writers of the sea,
      including Cooper. He possessed exhaustive technical knowl-
      edge of his chosen field and his talent for exploiting it
      amounted to genius. His books are founded on fact, with an
      artful flavoring of fiction. A fascination and mystery in
      the narrator's personality enhances the interest of the
      tale. But when Melville trusts to his imagination alone he
      becomes difficult and sometimes repulsive; now and then his

speculations and rhapsodies have a tinge almost of insanity.
Brief comments on Mardi, Redburn, and White-Jacket. Moby-
Dick is the most powerful of Melville's books and the last
of any literary importance. Pierre is a repulsive, insane,
and impossible romance. Reprinted in Recognition, pp. 131-
132, and Branch, pp. 426-427.

5   STEDMAN, ARTHUR. "Introduction to the Edition of 1892," in
    Typee. New York: United States Book Co., pp. xv-xxxvi.
       Mainly biographical, incorporating material from
    Stedman's previous articles [1891.B15, B33, B47] and ex-
    panding upon them. Typee, Omoo, and White-Jacket are
    directly autobiographical, Moby-Dick partially so; the less
    important Redburn is "between these two classes"; with some
    exceptions, Melville's other prose works were unsuccessful
    efforts at creative romance. Typee is a virile and artis-
    tic creation that will never lose its position as a classic
    of American literature. Melville's style in Typee and Omoo
    is rough in places but marvelously simple and direct. Mardi
    is burdened with an over-rich diction (the result of study
    of Sir Thomas Browne) which Melville never entirely outgrew.
    Moby-Dick represents, to a certain extent, the conflict be-
    tween his earlier and later methods of composition, but the
    gigantic conception of the White Whale permeates the whole
    work and lifts it bodily into the highest domain of romance.
    "Benito Cereno" and "The Bell-Tower" are equal to Melville's
    best previous work; the story of Israel Potter is well told,
    but the book is hardly worthy of the author of Typee; The
    Confidence-Man does not seem to require criticism. Next to
    Ahab, Dr. Long Ghost is Melville's most striking delinea-
    tion. Attributes "October Mountain" to Melville. [The
    1892 United States Book Company Melville edition comprised
    Typee, Omoo, White-Jacket, and Moby-Dick; for reviews of
    books in this edition, see 1892.B18, B19, B20, B21, B22,
    B23, B24; 1893.B10, B11, B15.] Reprinted in part in Doubloon,
    p. 114; reprinted in Sealts (1974), pp. 155-166.

6   TRENT, WILLIAM P. William Gilmore Simms. Boston: Houghton,
    Mifflin and Co., pp. 329-330.
       In quantity as well as quality of work, Simms is superior
    to romancers like Bird, Kennedy, Paulding, Sedgwick, Mayo,
    and Melville. Simms is their superior in imaginative vigor,
    power of description, and ability to give movement to his
    stories, and is their equal in style at his best.

7   ANON. "Obituary." New York Harper's New Monthly Magazine,
    84 (January), 321.
       Two-line entry; records Melville's death at age 73 in
    New York City on 27 September.

1892

8   SMITH, J. E. A. "Herman Melville. A Great Pittsfield Author--
     Brief Biographical Sketch." Pittsfield (Mass.) Evening
     Journal (12 January), p. 6.
         Seventh installment of Melville biography begun in
     1891.B41. Gives reasons for Melville's seclusion from
     society in New York; attempts to modify the impression of
     Melville as a "recluse and almost misanthrope," given by
     some New York newspapers. Reprinted in Sealts (1974),
     pp. 137-140.

9   SMITH, J. E. A. "Herman Melville. A Great Pittsfield Author--
     Brief Biographical Sketch." Pittsfield (Mass.) Evening
     Journal (16 January), p. 4.
         Eighth installment of Melville biography begun in 1891.B41.
     Records Melville's retirement from book-making some two
     years after he left Pittsfield. Neither the poems nor
     prose comments in Battle-Pieces show the least trace of the
     irrelevant philosophy or the mysticism which marred most of
     Melville's later works. The book did not meet with the
     favorable reception it deserved; others of Melville's later
     works also had merit, which would have been recognized but
     for "the shadow" of the justly condemned Pierre (which con-
     tains, however, keen and just thoughts and a score of pages
     of local interest). Melville's sensitiveness to the general
     criticism of his later works may have had much to do with
     his retirement from writing, though other circumstances
     contributed to it. Prints "The Portent," "The College
     Colonel," and the dedication to Greylock in Pierre. Re-
     printed in Sealts (1974), pp. 140-145.

10   SMITH, J. E. A. "Herman Melville. A Great Pittsfield Author--
     Brief Biographical Sketch." Pittsfield (Mass.) Evening
     Journal (25 January), p. 4.
         Ninth installment of Melville biography begun in 1891.B41.
     Extract from Pierre, Book VII, chapter 4; gives the "true
     story" of the naming of the Memnon Stone. Quotes from
     1891.B47 on Melville's poems. Prints "L'Envoi" from
     Timoleon. Reprinted in Sealts (1974), pp. 145-149.

11   ANON. "Herman Melville and Pittsfield." Pittsfield (Mass.)
     Evening Journal (25 January), p. 4.
         Notes the completion of the series of articles on
     Melville [see 1892.B10], "well nigh his complete biography."
     Melville's worldwide fame is a part of the town's.
     Melville made himself intensely a Berkshire man. Reprinted
     in Sealts (1974), p. 149.

12   RUSSELL, W. CLARK. "A Claim for American Literature." New
      York North American Review, 154 (February), 138-149.
          Dana and Melville were the first to show the world what
      happens in a ship's forecastle. By doing so, they expanded
      American literature immeasurably further than English lit-
      erature was expanded by the works of two-thirds of the poets
      in Johnson's Lives, or by the whole series of Waverley
      novels, or by half the fiction with much of the philosophy,
      theology, poetry, and history published since the death of
      Dickens. Melville is inferior to Dana in style (Dana's is
      as plain and sturdy as Defoe's), but his pictures of fore-
      castle life are marvelously and delightfully true.
      Melville was neglected at his death, but his name and works
      will not die. Reprinted in part in 1892.B15; Recognition,
      pp. 132-134; Rountree, p. 31; Branch, pp. 428-430.

13   ANON. "Notes." New York Public Opinion, 12 (20 February),
      517.
          Announcement of the United States Book Company edition,
      edited by Arthur Stedman [see 1892.B5]; Typee to appear
      shortly.

14   SALT, HENRY S. "'Marquesan Melville.'" London Gentleman's
      Magazine, 272 (March), 248-257.
          Biographical and critical. Melville was a sort of
      nautical George Borrow. Among his works, Typee is the
      most sure of lasting popularity, the masterpiece of his
      earlier period when his artistic sense was still predomi-
      nant over his later transcendental tendencies; Typee is
      unsurpassed in its kind in English literature. In Moby-Dick,
      less shapely and artistic than Typee, Melville casts off all
      conventional restrictions and riots in the prodigality of
      his imaginative vigor. Despite the turgid mannerisms of
      his transcendental mood, Moby-Dick is the supreme production
      of a master mind; no one should presume to pass judgment on
      American literature unless he has read and re-read it.
      Melville's habit of gorgeous and fantastic word painting
      is brilliantly effective at best, but degenerates at worst
      into mere bombast and rhetoric--a process discernible in
      the last parts of Mardi and reaching its fatal climax in
      Pierre. Of The Confidence-Man it is unnecessary to speak;
      in Israel Potter and The Piazza Tales Melville partly re-
      covered his old firmness of touch and delicacy of workman-
      ship. Despite his later obscurities and mannerisms,
      naturalness is his prime characteristic, in tone and style.
      His narratives are as racy and vigorous as Defoe's or
      Smollett's or Marryat's; his character sketches show keen
      observation, a keen sense of humor. Quotes from Melville's

1892

letters to Hawthorne, 1? June 1851, and to James Billson,
10 October 1884 and 22 January 1885 [Letters, pp. 126-131,
275-276, 277]. Reprinted in 1892.B16; reprinted in part in
1893.B6; 1893.B7; Doubloon, pp. 112-114; Branch, pp. 430-433.

15 RUSSELL, W. CLARK. "Clark Russell on Dana and Melville."
New York Critic, NS 17 (26 March), 189-190.
Partial reprint of 1892.B12.

16 SALT, HENRY S. "Marquesan Melville." New York Eclectic
Magazine, NS 55 (April), 517-523.
Reprint of 1892.B14.

17 STEDMAN, ARTHUR, ed. "Poems by Herman Melville." New York
Century Magazine, 44 [NS 22] (May), 104-105.
One paragraph headnote to "Art," "Monody," "The Night-
March," "The Weaver," and "Lamia's Song." Typee, Omoo, and
Moby-Dick soon became classics of American literature and
are likely to remain such; they have been continuously in
print in England, and new American editions are in course
of publication.

18 ANON. "Travels, Far and Near." New York Book Buyer, 9
(October), 386.
Review of the United States Book Company edition of
Typee. [See 1892.B5.] There is evidence besides Melville's
word, that the story is autobiographical, but he has invested the picture with a great deal of romantic color, and
some will probably think the story mainly fiction. "The
book has been edited as a classic rather than as one to be
placed unreservedly in the hands of the traditional 'young
person.'" Reprinted in Monteiro (May 1977), p. 13.

19 ANON. "The Romances of Herman Melville." Boston Literary
World, 23 (8 October), 352-353.
Review of the United States Book Company edition of Typee
and Omoo. [See 1892.B5.] Mainly summary. Melville's
novels answer the public's need for a good story; they have
the truthfulness and open air clearness of stories of actual
experience.

20 PAYNE, WILLIAM MORTON. "Pictures from the Pacific." Chicago
Dial, 13 (16 October), 244-246.
Review of the United States Book Company edition of Typee
and Omoo. [See 1892.B5.] Typee, Omoo, White-Jacket, and
Moby-Dick are classics of their kind and Melville's only
books likely to live; their vitality is due to the fact that
they were written in the flush of youth and mainly relate
Melville's own stirring experiences.

21   ANON. "Novels and Short Stories." New York <u>Book Buyer</u>, 9
(November), 439.
       Review of the United States Book Company edition of <u>Omoo</u>.
[<u>See</u> 1892.B5.] Mainly summary. The daily life of the
<u>Julia</u> is minutely and interestingly pictured, the sketch
of the first mate being particularly lifelike. The description of the natives, their manner of life and customs, is
very vivid and picturesque. Reprinted in Monteiro (May
1977), p. 12.

22   ANON. "A New Edition of Herman Melville." New York <u>Literary
News</u>, 13 (November), 338.
       Review of the United States Book Company edition. [<u>See</u>
1892.B5.] Melville's death has made known to the world
again the charms of his authorship. He did little in the
way of authorship after his last notable book, <u>Moby-Dick</u>.
In his introduction to <u>Typee</u>, Stedman has shown wide familiarity with his subject, excellent literary judgment, and
regard for Melville's memory.

23   ANON. "Survey of Current Literature." New York <u>Literary News</u>,
13 (November), 344.
       Review of the United States Book Company edition of
<u>Typee</u> and <u>Omoo</u>. [<u>See</u> 1892.B5.] Aside from the adventures
and charming descriptions of scenery, <u>Typee</u> and <u>Omoo</u> are
rich in rare information which has given them a permanent
place in all libraries.

24   ANON. "Herman Melville's Romances." New York <u>Critic</u>, NS 18
(3 December), 308-309.
       Review of the United States Book Company edition of
<u>Typee</u>. [<u>See</u> 1892.B5.] <u>Typee</u>, <u>Omoo</u>, <u>Moby-Dick</u>, and <u>White-
Jacket</u>, Melville's romances of real life, have never been
excelled for vividness, verisimilitude, recondite information, and miniature-like finish of detail. <u>Typee's Robinson
Crusoe</u>-like minuteness and realism carry the stamp of truth;
the book will remain a classic in spite of its well-directed
attacks on the pseudo-missionaries. Stedman's biographical
and critical introduction is welcome. Reprinted in Branch,
pp. 434-435.

<u>1893 A BOOKS - NONE</u>

1893

1893 B SHORTER WRITINGS

1   ANON. "Melville, Herman," in The National Cyclopaedia of
    American Biography. Vol. 4. New York: James T. White &
    Co., p. 59.
        One paragraph biography; no comment on works.

2   BLACKBURN, CHARLES F. "Herman Melville," in Rambles in Books.
    London: Sampson Low Marston & Co., p. 82.
        Brief comments on Typee, Omoo, Moby-Dick and White-
    Jacket. Melville gives an Englishman the best substitute
    for brighter skies and a climate less rude. Moby-Dick com-
    pletely takes one out of the monotony of home life and
    amounts to a monograph on the sperm whale.

3   BRIDGE, HORATIO. Personal Recollections of Nathaniel Hawthorne.
    New York: Harper & Brothers, p. 123.
        Quotes letter of 7 August 1850 from Hawthorne, at Lenox,
    to Bridge: "...Duyckink, of the Literary World, and Herman
    Melville are in Berkshire, and I expect them to call here
    this morning. I met Melville the other day, and liked him
    so much that I have asked him to spend a few days with me
    before leaving these parts."

4   GODWIN, PARKE. George William Curtis: A Commemorative Address
    Delivered Before the Century Association, New York,
    December 17, 1892. New York: Harper & Brothers, p. 17n.
        Melville, "of 'Typee' and 'Omoo' fame," is listed among
    the "promised contributors" to Putnam's Monthly at its in-
    ception. Reprinted in 1895.B1.

5   HUDSON, W. H. Idle Days in Patagonia. London: Chapman &
    Hall, pp. 112-119, 122, 233-234.
        Discusses Melville's "long dissertation" on the effects
    of whiteness in Moby-Dick--perhaps the finest thing in the
    book; Melville is mistaken in some of his assumptions and
    explanations. Quotes from next-to-last paragraph of chap-
    ter 26 in Moby-Dick--one of the most eloquent passages of
    Melville's finest work.

6   SALT, HENRY S. "Memoir of Herman Melville," in Omoo. London:
    John Murray, pp. xi-xxi.
        Reprint of 1892.B14, with some omissions, reorganization
    of material, and biographical additions.

7   SALT, HENRY S. "Memoir of Herman Melville," in Typee. London:
    John Murray, pp. xi-xxi.
        The same introduction as in 1893.B6.

8 STONE, HERBERT STUART. <u>First Editions of American Authors</u>.
   Cambridge, Mass.: Stone & Kimball, pp. 137-138.
   Checklist of first editions of Melville's books.

9 UNDERWOOD, FRANCIS H. <u>The Builders of American Literature</u>.
   First Series. Boston: Lee and Shepard, pp. 233-234.
   Reprints 1872.B5 (minus the extract from <u>Typee</u>), with
   slight alterations and additions. The 1892 edition of
   <u>Typee</u> and <u>Omoo</u> [<u>see</u> 1892.B5] is striking proof of the
   enduring interest in Melville's works.

10 ANON. "Omoo." New York <u>Critic</u>, NS 19 (11 February), 76.
    Review of the United States Book Company edition. [<u>See</u>
    1892.B5.] Mainly summary. <u>Omoo</u> is singularly graphic in
    its portrayals of Polynesian life and customs. Its repub-
    lication is most welcome.

11 ANON. "Moby-Dick; or, The White Whale." New York <u>Critic</u>,
    NS 19 (15 April), 232.
    Review of the United States Book Company edition. [<u>See</u>
    1892.B5.] Victor Hugo may have plagiarized <u>Moby-Dick</u> in
    <u>Les Travailleurs de la Mer</u>; the two books have an essential
    kinship. No romance of Hawthorne's surpasses <u>Moby-Dick</u> in
    witching power, grasp on the pulse, strength of description,
    and ability to quicken the blood. Melville is as fantasti-
    cally poetical as Coleridge in "The Ancient Mariner"; but
    the characters and events seem true to life because of their
    fresh treatment. Even the recondite information about
    whales and sea fisheries does not interfere seriously with
    the intended effect. Melville's extraordinary vocabulary
    is comparable only to Chapman's translations of Homer; his
    depiction of the sea is Whitmanesque in its intensity and
    realism. Reprinted in Norton <u>Moby-Dick</u>, pp. 622-623; re-
    printed in part in <u>Recognition</u>, p. 135.

12 [STRACHEY, J. ST. L.]. "Herman Melville." London <u>Spectator</u>,
    70 (24 June), 858-859.
    Review of Putnam edition of <u>Typee</u>, <u>Omoo</u>, <u>White-Jacket</u>,
    and <u>Moby-Dick</u>. Melville lacks the literary power of
    Stevenson, but <u>Typee</u> has a greater charm than <u>The Wrecker</u>,
    <u>Island Nights</u>, and Stevenson's studies of the Marquesas
    published in <u>Black and White</u>: it is the document <u>par excel-
    lence</u> of savage life, by one who knew how to write as well
    as look. If Melville's judgment had equalled his feeling
    for form, he might have ranked high in English literature
    on the ground of style alone; but he tended to let the last
    great master of style he had read run away with him. Yet
    Melville is a great artist and <u>Moby-Dick</u>, an epic of whaling,

1893

one of the best and most thrilling sea stories ever written,
a genuine piece of literature, in spite of the influence of
Sir Thomas Browne. Carlylisms mixed with dregs of Religio
Medici occasionally annoy the reader in White-Jacket, but
the book is still excellent reading. Melville's books
throughout show a pleasant strong feeling of brotherhood
with the English. Reprinted in Recognition, pp. 136-137.

13 RUSSELL, W. CLARK. "The Life of the Merchant Sailor." New
York Scribner's Magazine, 14 (July), 4-5.
The works of writers like Cooper, Dana, and Melville
give as clear an idea of what is happening now in merchant
ships as a voyage round the world in a new ship out of
Boston or the Thames. A merchant sailor reads Two Years
Before the Mast or Homeward Bound or Redburn and finds the
old life almost identical with the present.

14 CUTLER, JAMES TUCKER. "The Literary Associations of Berkshire."
Boston New England Magazine, NS 9 (September), 8-9.
Notes Melville's visits to Hawthorne at Lenox; it would
be difficult to find two men more unlike in character.
Typee and Omoo are "both somewhat Robinson Crusoe like in
construction." The Piazza Tales and "October Mountain"
[see discussion in Sealts (1950), pp. 178-182] exhibit more
distinctly the Berkshirean spirit.

15 ANON. "White Jacket." New York Critic, NS 20 (30 September),
206.
Review of the United States Book Company edition of
White-Jacket. [See 1892.B5.] Melville, like Dana and
Marryat, was a practical sailor; the realism of his romances
and their intense verisimilitude emanated from personal
experience. In White-Jacket he leaves fiction for truth,
romance for reality. There has been no keener examination
of a war vessel. Melville is good-natured, observant,
kindly yet caustic.

1894 A BOOKS - NONE

1894 B SHORTER WRITINGS

1 ANON. "Melville, Herman," in The Century Cyclopaedia of Names.
Ed. Benjamin E. Smith. New York: The Century Co., p. 674.
Short biographical paragraph; no comment on works. Re-
printed in 1911.

2   BEERS, H. A. "Melville, Herman," in <u>Johnson's Universal</u>
       <u>Cyclopaedia</u>. Vol. 5. New York: A. J. Johnson Co., p. 662.
          Short biographical paragraph; no comment on works.
       Reprinted in 1900.B1.

3   CARY, EDWARD. <u>George William Curtis</u>. Boston: Houghton,
       Mifflin and Co., p. 55.
          Notes that Melville, Dana, Donald G. Mitchell, and
       Bayard Taylor were the same age as Curtis, or nearly so,
       and that some of them were in his circle.

4   LOWELL, JAMES RUSSELL. <u>Letters of James Russell Lowell</u>.
       Ed. Charles Eliot Norton. Vol. 1. New York: Harper &
       Brothers, p. 141.
          Letter to Sydney H. Gay, September 1848: "This having
       to do with printers is dreadful business. There was a
       Mr. Melville who, I believe, enjoyed it, but, for my part,
       I am heartily sick of <u>Typee</u>."

5   WATKINS, MILDRED CABELL. <u>American Literature</u>. New York:
       American Book Co., pp. 47-48.
          <u>Typee</u>, <u>Omoo</u>, <u>White-Jacket</u>, and <u>Moby-Dick</u> are four wildly
       exciting tales of adventure, just the kind to please boys.

6   WHITCOMB, SELDEN L. "Melville, Herman, 1819-1891," in
       <u>Chronological Outlines of American Literature</u>. New York:
       Macmillan and Co., p. 265.
          A checklist of Melville's books, excluding <u>John Marr</u> and
       <u>Timoleon</u>.

7   LATHROP, ROSE HAWTHORNE. "The Hawthornes in Lenox. Told in
       Letters by Nathaniel and Mrs. Hawthorne." New York <u>Century</u>
       <u>Magazine</u>, 49 (November), 89-91, 93.
          Prints Melville's letters to Hawthorne, 22 July 1851
       and 17? November 1851; Sophia Hawthorne's letter to her
       mother, 4 September 1850, describing Melville; Hawthorne's
       letter to Sophia, 9 August 1851, mentioning a ride with
       Melville; and Sophia's letter to her mother, 19 August 1851,
       mentioning Melville's visits to Hawthorne during her absence.

<u>1895 A BOOKS - NONE</u>

<u>1895 B SHORTER WRITINGS</u>

1   GODWIN, PARKE. <u>Commemorative Addresses by Parke Godwin</u>. New
       York: Harper & Brothers, pp. 18-19.
          Reprint of 1893.B4.

1895

2   SMITH, J. E. A. The Poet Among the Hills. Oliver Wendell
    Holmes in Berkshire. Pittsfield, Mass.: George Blatchford,
    pp. 28-33.
        An account of Melville in Pittsfield, his habits and
    manners, and the beginning of his friendship with Hawthorne.
    Melville drew pictures for his tales from many of the re-
    sorts in Berkshire, including Balance Rock, Potter Mountain,
    and the rounded summit he named October Mountain. The
    Piazza Tales is the most locally interesting of his works.
    Melville passage reprinted in Sealts (1974), pp. 199-201.

3   SONNENSCHEIN, WILLIAM SWAN. A Reader's Guide to Contemporary
    Literature, Being the First Supplement to the Best Books.
    London: Swan Sonnenschein & Co., pp. 293, 583.
        Lists Typee and Omoo in Polynesian bibliography [cf.
    1887.B4], with brief annotation: they are thoroughly inter-
    esting, realistic, and curious, but with a strong admixture
    of fiction. In bibliography of "Minor American Topical
    Novels" lists Moby-Dick, Omoo, Typee, and White-Jacket.

4   WOLFE, THEODORE F. Literary Shrines: The Haunts of Some Famous
    American Authors. Philadelphia: J. B. Lippincott Co.,
    pp. 176-177, 185, 188, 190-192.
        Details of Melville's friendship with Hawthorne and of
    Arrowhead, including its window view of October Mountain,
    "whose autumn glories inspired that superb word-picture and
    metaphysical sketch." [See discussion in Sealts (1950),
    pp. 178-182.]

5   SEDGWICK, HENRY DWIGHT. "Reminiscences of Literary Berkshire."
    New York Century Magazine, 50 (August), 562-563.
        Sedgwick's recollection of a party of authors, including
    Melville and Hawthorne, on Monument Mountain in August 1850.

1896 A BOOKS - NONE

1896 B SHORTER WRITINGS

1   IRISH, FRANK V., ed. "Mellville, Herman," in American and
    British Authors: A Textbook on Literature. Columbus, Ohio:
    Frank V. Irish, p. 211.
        No selection from Melville's work. Melville listed in
    section "Additional American Authors" as the author of Typee,
    Omoo, Mardi, The Piazza Tales, The Confidence-Man, "etc."

2   MATTHEWS, BRANDER. "Other Writers," in <u>An Introduction to the</u>
     <u>Study of American Literature</u>. New York: American Book Co.,
     pp. 225-226.
         Though not to be classed as fiction, <u>Typee</u> and <u>Two Years</u>
     <u>Before the Mast</u> have all the fascination of Cooper's sea
     stories.

3   PATTEE, FRED LEWIS. <u>A History of American Literature</u>.
     Boston: Silver, Burdett & Co., pp. 152-153.
         Short biographical sketch; no comment on works. Quotes
     from 1892.B12. Reprinted in 1903.

4   STEVENSON, ROBERT LOUIS. <u>In the South Seas</u>. New York:
     Charles Scribner's Sons, p. 26.
         Reprints 1891.B5.

5   ANON. Review of The American Publishers Corporation edition
     of <u>Typee</u>. Boston <u>National Magazine</u>, 4 (July), 304-305.
         <u>Typee</u> is as bewitching a book as <u>Robinson Crusoe</u>. The
     whole narrative is interesting, affecting, and most romantic.
     Reprinted in Monteiro (May 1977), p. 14.

6   ANON. "New Books and New Editions." New York <u>Book Buyer</u>, 13
     (September), 479.
         "...three of Mr. Herman Melville's famous stories of
     salt water--<u>The White Jacket</u>, <u>Moby Dick</u>, and <u>Omoo</u>--are
     reprinted in paper covers for summer reading" [in the
     American Publishers Corporation edition].

7   ANON. Review of The American Publishers Corporation edition
     of <u>Moby-Dick</u>. Boston <u>National Magazine</u>, 5 (October), 111.
         The literary merits of <u>Moby-Dick</u> are of the highest order.
     The history of the great white whale is told in an absorbing
     manner. One of the many interesting features of the book is
     the faithful representation of seafaring men of different
     nationalities. Reprinted in Monteiro (Fourth Quarter 1976),
     pp. 534-535.

8   ANON. Review of The American Publishers Corporation edition
     of <u>Omoo</u>. Boston <u>National Magazine</u>, 5 (October), 112.
         <u>Omoo</u>, like <u>Typee</u>, is as valuable ethnologically as it is
     interesting to the lover of the strange and thrilling.
     There are no better sea stories or narratives of adventure
     than <u>Typee</u>, <u>Omoo</u>, <u>White-Jacket</u>, and <u>Moby-Dick</u>. Reprinted in
     Monteiro (Fourth Quarter 1976), p. 535.

9   ANON. Review of The American Publishers Corporation edition of
     <u>White-Jacket</u>. Boston <u>National Magazine</u>, 5 (October), 111.

1896

Melville is a delightfully interesting author. "His pictures of life in the forecastle, and his description of what takes place in the various sections of a man-of-war are not only instructive, but are as captivating as they are true." Reprinted in Monteiro (Fourth Quarter 1976), p. 534.

10 ANON. Review of The American Publishers Corporation Melville Edition. New York Bookman, 4 (October), 171-172.
[An edition of Typee, Omoo, White-Jacket, and Moby-Dick.] "No more famous romancer of the southern seas ever spun a yarn; not even Louis Becke has done anything better than Typee and Omoo." The world is the richer for Melville's stories (marvelous adventures), classic in their field. Reprinted in Monteiro (May 1977), p. 13.

11 ANON. "Herman Melville." New York Literary News, 17 (October), 304-305.
Occasioned by The American Publishers Corporation edition of Typee, Omoo, White-Jacket, and Moby-Dick. Biographical sketch. Omoo contains a remarkably accurate description of the condition of Tahiti. The Confidence-Man is an entertaining story. "Captain Melville [sic] was a great reader, and sometimes in later years his own fund of knowledge led him to put into the conversation of his characters words that seem unnatural; but aside from this blemish from an artistic standpoint, his writing is full of life and color...." Quotes from an unlocated review of the new edition in the Springfield (Mass.) Republican. Reprinted in Monteiro (Fourth Quarter 1976), pp. 533-534.

12 ANON. Review of The American Publishers Corporation Melville Edition. New York Book Reviews, 4 (November), 208.
[An edition of Typee, Omoo, White-Jacket, and Moby-Dick.] Commentary only on White-Jacket--an unacknowledged quotation from 1896.B9. Reprinted in Monteiro (May 1977), p. 13.

13 ANON. Review of Typee. New York Book Reviews, 4 (November), 212-213.
Reprint of 1896.B14. Reprinted in Monteiro (Fourth Quarter 1976), p. 535.

14 ANON. Notice of The American Book Publishers Melville Edition. New York Current Literature, 20 (November), 472.
[An edition of Typee, Omoo, White-Jacket, and Moby-Dick.] Typee is Melville's best work, a spirited and charming story. Nowadays Clark Russell is read, not "the brilliant and really original works" of Michael Scott, Chamier, Marryat, and Melville. Reprinted in 1896.B13.

1897 A BOOKS

1 SMITH, J. E. A. <u>Biographical Sketch of Herman Melville, 1891</u>.
Pamphlet reprinting 1891.B41, B42, B50, B53, B54;
1892.B8, B9, B10, with small alterations and deletions.

1897 B SHORTER WRITINGS

1 ADAMS, OSCAR FAY. "Melville, Herman," in <u>A Dictionary of</u>
<u>American Authors</u>. Boston: Houghton, Mifflin and Co.,
p. 253.
Melville's earliest writings were very popular but "had
nearly passed out of remembrance" before his death.

2 ANON. "Melville, Herman," in <u>Chambers's Biographical Dictionary</u>.
Eds. David Patrick and Francis Hindes Groome. London:
W. & R. Chambers, p. 649.
Short biographical paragraph; lists <u>Typee</u> and <u>Omoo</u>, with-
out comment, and notes that Melville also wrote tales and
three volumes of poetry. Reprinted in 1907.B2.

3 ANON. "Herman Melville (1819-1891)," in <u>A Library of the</u>
<u>World's Best Literature, Ancient and Modern</u>. Ed. Charles
Dudley Warner. New York: The International Society.
Vol. 25, pp. 9867-9869; New York: R. S. Peale and J. A.
Hill. Vol. 17, pp. 9867-9869.
Introduction to extracts from chapters 11, 18, 27, and
30 of <u>Typee</u> (pp. 9870-9885). Biographical and critical.
Melville was a man of moods, but with a peculiarly winning
and interesting personality, deferring to the conventional
opinions of others while expressing the wildest and most
emancipated ideas of his own. In his South Sea romances
there is little character drawing, and his heroines are a
little too subsidiary to scenery; but Melville should not
be judged too harshly: his great advantage is in placing
his stories in a sort of poetic or fairy precinct. His
vocabulary is perhaps too large and fluent, but what he
lacks in conciseness is atoned for in spontaneity. His
romances have a healthy, manly ring, as far from sensuous-
ness as from austerity.

4 BATES, KATHARINE LEE. "National Era: Prose Fiction," in
<u>American Literature</u>. New York: The Macmillan Co.; London:
Macmillan & Co., p. 276.
"Cooper outgoes all American competitors in extravagant
fabrications of salt-water adventure. Herman Melville's
South Sea stories are more direct and convincing, his <u>Typee</u>,
especially, having the realistic shudder of an author who

1897

    barely escaped a dishing up for cannibals, but William
Starbuck Mayo makes too extreme a claim upon credulity."
Frequent reprintings.

5   BECKE, LOUIS. <u>Wild Life in Southern Seas</u>. London: T. F.
Unwin, p. 292.
    The "white trader, and his white or native wife on
Savage Island, do not lead the dreamy, careless, and lazily
happy sort of life which Herman Melville has written in
those charming books--'Typee' and 'Omoo.'" (Complete
reference.)

6   FOLEY, P. K. <u>American Authors, 1795-1895: A Bibliography of
First and Notable Editions Chronologically Arranged With
Notes</u>. Boston: Printed for Subscribers, pp. 195-196.
    A checklist of first editions of Melville's books.

7   LATHROP, ROSE HAWTHORNE. <u>Memories of Hawthorne</u>. Boston:
Houghton, Mifflin and Co., pp. 134-135, 143, 145, 155-161,
200.
    Prints Sophia Hawthorne's letter to her mother,
4 September 1850, describing Melville; Sophia's diary
record of visits by Melville, 22 January and 12 March 1851;
Melville's letters to Hawthorne, 22 July 1851 and 17?
November 1851; Hawthorne's letter to Sophia, 9 August 1851,
mentioning a fine ride with Melville and two other men; and
a letter from Sophia to her mother describing Melville
talking with Hawthorne.

8   BRIGHT, EDWARD. "Fly Leaves." New York <u>Illustrated Amer-
ican</u>, 22(14 August), 218.
    Requests publication of John LaFarge's South Sea
journal. "...the South Sea Islands remain, comparatively
speaking, virgin soil. Even Stevenson fails to tell us all
we of a romantic turn of mind wish to know of them. Loti,
and Herman Melville and Charles Warren Stoddard come nearest
to being satisfactory. But the trouble with them is that
they are too reticent. We want to know more...about the
doings in the island of Tahiti and in the Marquesas." Reprinted in Monteiro (June 1976), p. 13.

1898 A BOOKS - NONE

1898 B SHORTER WRITINGS

1   ANON. "Melville, Herman." <u>Appleton's Cyclopaedia of American
Biography</u>. Eds. James Grant Wilson and John Fiske. Vol. 4.
New York: D. Appleton & Co., p. 293.

Reprint of 1888.B1, adding <u>John Marr</u> and <u>Timoleon</u> to list of works.

2 FRANKLIN, S. R. <u>Memories of a Rear-Admiral</u>. New York and London: Harper & Brothers, pp. 33, 64-66.
Vaguely remembers a maintop-man in a white jacket on the <u>United States</u>; vividly remembers Jack Chase, about as fine a specimen of a seaman as Franklin ever saw. Claims that Melville subsequently became famous as a writer and admiralty lawyer and credits <u>White-Jacket</u> with the abolition of flogging in the navy. In <u>White-Jacket</u> Melville mentions a number of officers it is easy to recognize from their sobriquets.

3 KIPLING, RUDYARD. <u>A Fleet in Being</u>. London: Macmillan and Co., p. 52.
Kipling, writing of a captain's lonely life at sea: "Herman Melville has it all in <u>White Jacket</u>, but it is awesome to see with bodily eyes."

4 SALT, HENRY S. <u>The Life of James Thomson ("B.V.")</u>. London: A. and H. B. Bonner, pp. 51, 139-140.
Quotes passages on Thomson's poems from Melville's letters to James Billson, 22 January 1885 and 1 December 1884 [<u>Letters</u>, pp. 276-277].

5 JAMES, HENRY. "American Letter." London <u>Literature</u>, 2 (11 June), 676-677.
Writing of the "charming <u>Putnam</u> of...the early fifties," James refers to "a faint memory of very young pleasure in prose that was not <u>all</u> prose only when it was all poetry-- the prose, as mild and easy as an Indian summer in the woods, of Herman Melville, of George William Curtis and 'Ik Marvel.'" Reprinted in Edel, p. 235, and Monteiro (May 1977), p. 14.

1899 A BOOKS - NONE

1899 B SHORTER WRITINGS

1 GARNETT, RICHARD, LEON VALLÉE, and ALOIS BRANDL. "On the Track of the White Whale," in <u>The Universal Anthology: A Collection of the Best Literature, Ancient, Mediaeval and Modern</u>. Vol. 25. Eds. Richard Garnett, Leon Vallée, and Alois Brandl. London: Clarke Co., p. 117.
One paragraph headnote to extracts from chapters 12, 14, 15, and 16 of <u>Moby-Dick</u>; biographical, with list of

1899

Melville's works (giving <u>Mardi</u> as "Mardi Gras"). <u>Moby-Dick</u>
is perhaps his greatest work. <u>Israel Potter</u> is a genuine
and most curious biography, extracting romance out of very
squalid materials.

2   MITCHELL, DONALD G. <u>American Lands and Letters</u>. <u>Vol. 2:
    Leather-Stocking to Poe's "Raven."</u> New York: Charles
    Scribner's Sons, pp. ix, 235, 269.
        Melville gave "a lively Munchausen relish" to his South
    Sea stories. <u>Typee</u> and <u>Omoo</u> delighted Hawthorne as well as
    a world of readers. At the time he was Hawthorne's neigh-
    bor, Melville, "distrained of earlier simplicities--was
    torturing himself with the metaphysic subtleties of <u>Moby
    Dick</u> and whipping all the depths of his thought into turbu-
    lent and misty spray." Also refers to Hawthorne's "retreat
    to Lenox woods, where Sedgwick chirped and Herman Melville
    strode mystically on the scene." Reprinted in part in
    <u>Doubloon</u>, pp. 114-115.

3   PECK, HARRY THURSTON. "Herman Melville," in <u>Masterpieces of
    the World's Literature, Ancient and Modern</u>. Ed. Harry
    Thurston Peck. Vol. 15. New York: American Literary
    Society, p. 7853.
        One paragraph headnote to extracts from chapters 9, 31,
    and 32 of <u>Typee</u>. Biographical; no comment on works.

4   STEVENSON, ROBERT LOUIS. <u>The Letters of Robert Louis Stevenson</u>.
    Ed. Sidney Colvin. Vol. 2. London: Methuen and Co.; New
    York: Charles Scribner's Sons, pp. 115, 182.
        Letter to Charles Baxter, 6 September 1888: "...I shall
    have a fine book of travels, I feel sure; and will tell you
    more of the South Seas after very few months than any other
    writer has done--except Herman Melville perhaps, who is a
    howling cheese." Letter to E. L. Burlingame, February 1890:
    "...Our admirable friend Herman Melville, of whom, since I
    could judge, I have thought more than ever, had no ear for
    languages whatever; his Hapar tribe should be Hapaa, etc."

5   TOWNE, EDWARD C. "Melville, H.," in <u>Index-Guide to Library of
    the World's Best Literature, Ancient and Modern</u>. Vol. 46.
    New York: R. S. Peale and J. A. Hill, p. clxxxvi.
        Melville identified as "the author in 1846 of 'Typee,' a
    remarkably interesting book of adventure and travel in the
    South Seas."

6   WOLFE, THEODORE F. <u>Literary Haunts & Homes: American Authors</u>.
    Philadelphia: J. B. Lippincott Co., pp. 76, 93.

Notes that "the widow of the once famous romancer Herman
Melville" lives with her daughter in "delightful apartments
of the Florence"; and that "Hawthorne's friend Herman
Melville, whose tales 'Typee,' 'Omoo,' and 'Moby Dick' once
gave him wide reputation and were received by the critics
with paeans of praise, lived for many years and died at
No. 104 of the same street [E. 26th St.], in a pleasant
brick house which is now replaced by flats." Adds that he
wrote "Sheridan at Cedar Creek" there, other "Battle Pieces,"
and "volumes of now little-read verse."

7   ANON. "The Cruise of the 'Cachalot' round the World after
    Sperm Whales." London Athenaeum, No. 3718 (28 January),
    p. 107.
       Review of The Cruise of the Cachalot by Frank T. Bullen.
    Notes that Bullen was not the first to write of a South Sea
    whaler's cruise from the seaman's standpoint; nearly half a
    century previously, Melville, "who was every inch a sailor,"
    produced a work "unrivalled for accuracy" in its details of
    sperm whaling and of "enthralling interest" on account of
    its concluding tragedy. It is too little known in Britain.
    Reprinted in part in Doubloon, p. 115.

8   ANON. Review of The Cruise of the Cachalot by Frank T. Bullen.
    New York Times Saturday Review of Books (25 February),
    p. 125.
       Mention: "it was to an older generation that Herman
    Melville addressed his romances, and Moby Dick was impressed
    on its recollections."

9   ALDEN, WILLIAM LIVINGSTON. "London Literary Letter." New York
    Times Saturday Review of Books (22 April), p. 268.
       "Melville was perhaps the most original genius that
    America has produced, but he would have written much better
    than he wrote if he had been merely a man of talent. He
    never seemed to know when he was great and when he was
    merely tedious. I know nothing better than the two or
    three introductory chapters of 'Mardi,' and probably there
    is nothing more tedious than the rest of the book." Now
    that there is a sort of boom in books of the sea, perhaps
    the reprint of Melville's works will bring his proper
    recognition a step nearer. Reprinted in Monteiro (Spring
    1975), p. 70.

10 F., T. B. "Book News in London." New York Times Saturday
    Review of Books (22 July), p. 489.
       Reports "a conspicuous revival of interest in America's
    sea author," Melville, the revival having been brought about

1899

by Clark Russell's "repeated glowing tributes" to his
genius. Omoo and Typee especially are selling strongly in
the new Murray edition, "printed very badly from old plates."

11 ALDEN, WILLIAM LIVINGSTON. "London Literary Letter." New
York Times Saturday Review of Books (5 August), p. 518.
There is more true poetry in Melville's books than in
all of Ibsen's plays; they are full, too, of genuine realism. For all their defects, their occasional melodrama and
pathos and rank rubbish, Melville "is far and away the most
original genius that America has produced, and it is a
National reproach that he should be so completely neglected."
Moby-Dick is a masterpiece of sea lore and sea poetry. Like
Whitman, Melville needs to be studied with care. Advocates
a Melville society, devoted to securing Melville the reputation he deserves. Reprinted in Monteiro (Spring 1975),
pp. 70-71.

12 MacMECHAN, ARCHIBALD. "'The Best Sea Story Ever Written.'"
Kingston (Ont.) Queen's Quarterly, 7 (October), 120-130.
Melville's best work was written before the Civil War
and is cut off in taste and sympathy from literary fashions
of the present. None of his books is without distinct and
peculiar excellencies, but nearly all have some fatal fault.
Melville seems a case of arrested literary development; he
did not follow up the power and promise of his best work.
He is a man of one book, Moby-Dick. His three chief elements are Scottish thoughtfulness, love of literature, and
love of adventure. One part of Melville's triumph consists
in having made the complicated operations of whaling perfectly familiar to the reader, with the imagination, humor,
fancy, and reflection of a poet. Moby-Dick is at once the
epic and the encyclopaedia of whaling. It is undoubtedly
well-constructed. Melville is completely successful in
creating his atmosphere: granted the conditions, the men
and their words, emotions and actions are all consistent.
The book's theme is peculiarly American, whaling being
peculiarly an American industry. Melville's style is also
distinctly American: large in idea and expansive, with an
Elizabethan force and freshness; it is perhaps richer in
figures than any style but Emerson's and has above all a
free-flowing humor, the distinct cachet of American literature. It is not perfect; some mannerisms become tedious,
like the constant moral turn and the curiously coined ad-
verbs before the verb; there is more than a hint of bombast;
but on the whole the style is rich and clear, showing reading and full of thought and allusion; its chief charm is
its freedom from all scholastic rules and conventions.

Melville is a Walt Whitman of prose; like Browning he has a dialect of his own. His chief excellence is bringing to landsmen the salt of the sea breeze. Melville takes rank with Borrow, Jefferies, Thoreau, and Sir Richard Burton. Reprinted in 1901.B9; 1914.B3; Vincent, pp. 22-31; reprinted in part in Recognition, pp. 137-145, and Doubloon, pp. 115-118.

13 ANON. "Mr. F. T. Bullen." London Academy, No. 1440 (9 December), pp. 690-691.
    Review of Bullen's Log of a Sea Waif. Notes that Bullen is not another Melville--"he is without the dramatic force." Reprinted in Doubloon, pp. 118-119.

1900 A BOOKS - NONE

1900 B SHORTER WRITINGS

1 BEERS, H. A. "Melville, Herman," in The Universal Cyclopaedia. Vol. 8. New York: D. Appleton and Co.; A. J. Johnson Co., p. 22.
   Reprint of 1894.B2.

2 BRONSON, WALTER C. "Other Writers," in A Short History of American Literature. Boston: D. C. Heath & Co., pp. 148-149.
   Melville included as one of several "minor writers" of New York. Typee, Moby-Dick, The Piazza Tales, Battle-Pieces, and other poems and prose works all show "much strength and talent."

3 STEDMAN, EDMUND CLARENCE. "Biographical Notes," in An American Anthology, 1787-1900. Ed. Edmund Clarence Stedman. Boston: Houghton, Mifflin and Co., p. 809.
   One paragraph headnote to "The College Colonel," "The Eagle of the Blue," "Memorials: On the Slain at Chicka-mauga," "An Uninscribed Monument on One of the Battle-Fields of the Wilderness," "Crossing the Tropics," and "The Envi-able Isles." Melville's leading books are Typee, Omoo, White-Jacket, and Moby-Dick. Melville "now holds his sta-tion, both in Great Britain and America, as one of the most original romancers that this country has produced."

4 STEVENSON, ROBERT LOUIS. In the South Seas. London: Chatto and Windus, p. 26.
   First English edition. [See 1896.B4.]

1900

5   WENDELL, BARRETT. <u>A Literary History of America</u>. New York:
    Charles Scribner's Sons, p. 229.
        One sentence mention: "Hermann Melville, with his books
    about the South Seas, which Robert Louis Stevenson is said
    to have declared the best ever written, and with his novels
    of maritime adventure, began a career of literary promise,
    which never came to fruition." Reprinted in <u>Recognition</u>,
    p. 146.

6   TOFT, PETER. "In Praise of Herman Melville." [Letter to the
    Editor.] New York <u>Times Saturday Review of Books</u>
    (17 March), p. 176.
        Reports conversations with Melville in his last years.
    Though a delightful talker when in the mood, Melville had
    to be handled with care. He seemed to hold his works in
    small esteem and discouraged attempts to discuss them,
    telling Toft that he had forgotten them. Melville had a
    brother genius in Hawthorne; the two had no precursors,
    have had no successors, and stand unique in English litera-
    ture. Toft introduced Frank T. Bullen to <u>Moby-Dick</u>. Re-
    printed in part in <u>Log</u>, p. 799; reprinted in Monteiro
    (Spring 1975), pp. 71-72.

7   SACQUE, HAVRE. "Condensed Life of Herman Melville." Boston
    <u>National Magazine</u>, 12 (April), 804.
        Biographical sketch. Reprinted in Monteiro (Fourth
    Quarter 1976), p. 536.

8   ANON. "Novels of the Sea." New York <u>Times Saturday Review
    of Books</u> (5 May), pp. 296-297.
        The "sea novels of the realistic school" are in no way
    to be considered "better and purer literature than the im-
    aginative works of Marryat, Cooper, Melville, and Russell";
    the contrary is probably true. Moby Dick, "the vindicative
    leviathan was simply a splendid fancy, and he lives because
    he was a product of purely literary invention."

9   PLUNKETT, MRS. H. M. "Unveiling of a Great Genius. Melville
    and Hawthorne." Springfield (Mass.) <u>Sunday Republican</u>
    (1 July), pp. 14, 16.
        After many years of obscurity, Hawthorne (the "great
    genius") was unveiled in "Hawthorne and His Mosses" by the
    gifted Melville, a man of kindred but different type of
    mind and a worthy herald of Hawthorne. Sales of <u>Mosses</u>
    climbed straightaway to 4000. Lengthy quotation from
    "Hawthorne and His Mosses." Account of beginning of
    Melville's friendship with Hawthorne.

10 ALDEN, WILLIAM LIVINGSTON. "London Literary Letter." New
    York <u>Times Saturday Review of Books</u> (13 October), p. 702.

Alden would have substituted <u>White-Jacket</u> or <u>Redburn</u> for
<u>Moby-Dick</u> in a Sampson Low six-volume set of sea stories,
as better illustrating "Melville's power as a writer of sea
stories than does his prose epic." [<u>See</u> 1900.B11.]

11   ANON. "Novels of the Sea." London <u>Literature</u>, 7 (17 November),
386-387.
Review of a six-volume series, "Famous Novels of the
Sea," originally published in 1899 by Scribner in New York
and reissued in 1900 by Sampson Low, Marston in London.
[The books in the series were Marryat's <u>Mr. Midshipman Easy</u>,
Michael Scott's <u>Tom Cringle's Log</u>, Fenimore Cooper's <u>The
Two Admirals</u>, W. Clark Russell's <u>The Wreck of the Grosvenor</u>,
George Cupples' <u>The Green Hand</u>, and Melville's <u>Moby-Dick</u>.]
<u>Moby-Dick</u> is the only book in the series which is supremely
great and undoubtedly a work of genius. It is not a novel
and is hardly a story; it is a most astounding epic. It
is "half a nightmare"; it is natural history raised to the
highest power of tragedy. Ahab "hunts the whale that dis-
membered him through the seas of the earth as the Opium
Eater was hunted through the forests of Asia." The characters are types, human but superhuman; their talk is astounding. The "scheme of the book is no scheme, but it grows
Aeschylean and concludes inevitably upon an inexorable
vortex." A reprint of <u>Moby-Dick</u> has long been desired in
England by the few who knew its value. Melville is perhaps
America's greatest natural genius. [<u>See</u> 1900.B10.] Reprinted in Monteiro (November 1977), p. 9.

1901 A BOOKS - NONE

1901 B SHORTER WRITINGS

1   BECKE, LOUIS. "Introduction," in <u>Moby-Dick</u>. London:
G. P. Putnam's Sons, pp. ix-xii.
<u>Moby-Dick</u> is a strange, wild, and sad tale; one of the
best sea books ever written. Critics who see in it nothing
but the "mad rhetoric and bombast, the fantastic and unintelligible creation of a mind losing, or that had lost, its
balance," show "absolute ignorance of the strange conditions
and environment of the whaleman's life, as so truly portrayed by Herman Melville; the one man who knew his subject
and knew how to write about it, though much of his bril-
liancy of description is too often marred and obscured by
a headlong and purposeless dash away from his main theme
into the vague realms of weird and fantastic metaphysical
imagination."

1901

2   EGGLESTON, GEORGE CARY. The American Immortals. New York
      and London: G. P. Putnam's Sons, p. 313.
          Mention in section on Hawthorne: "Herman Melville
      lived at Pittsfield, not far away, and Hawthorne saw a
      good deal of him."

3   NEWCOMER, ALPHONSO G. American Literature. Chicago: Scott,
      Foresman & Co., p. 128.
          An occasional admirer can still be found who thinks
      Typee, Omoo, and Moby-Dick superior to Cooper's tales; they
      differ in portraying the life of the common sailor instead
      of the life of the officer. Dana's Two Years Before the
      Mast is superior in quality and scarcely inferior in roman-
      tic interest. Reprinted in Doubloon, p. 119.

4   STODART-WALKER, ARCHIBALD. Robert Buchanan the Poet of Modern
      Revolt: An Introduction to His Poetry. London: Grant
      Richards, p. 262.
          One sentence reference. Much of Canto II of Buchanan's
      The Outcast [1891.B2] owes its inspiration to Typee.

5   ANON. Notice of Putnam edition of Moby-Dick. London
      Daily Chronicle (6 February), p. 3.
          Some people think Moby-Dick is Melville's best work, but
      it would be hard to surpass Typee and Omoo.

6   ANON. "A Fine Book of the Sea." New York Times Saturday Re-
      view of Books (6 April), p. 239.
          Review of A Sack of Shakings by Frank T. Bullen. "Might
      we not call, in a certain way, Mr. Bullen the Gilbert White
      of the sea? We all have in mind Mobby Dick [sic], that
      champion of the whales. In his 'The Orphan' Mr. Bullen
      describes the cachalot and his prowess, and Herman Melville's
      masterpiece is recalled."

7   LA FARGE, JOHN. "Passages from a Diary in the Pacific:
      Tahiti." New York Scribner's Magazine, 30 (July), 70, 76-77.
          La Farge and his companions tried to find, "by the little
      river that ends our walk, on this side of the old French
      fort, the calaboose where Melville was shut up. There is
      no one to help us in our search; no one remembers anything.
      Buildings occupy the spaces of woodland that Melville saw
      about him. Nothing remains but the same charm of light and
      air which he, like all others, has tried to describe and to
      bring back home in words." Remembers "how Melville passed
      from those records of exterior life and scenery to a
      dwelling within his mind--a following out of metaphysical
      ideas, and a scheming of possible evolutions in the future
      of man." Reprinted in 1912.B3.

8   FERRIS, MARY L. D. "Herman Melville." New York Bulletin of
    the Society of American Authors, 6 (September), 289-293.
       Biographical, mainly drawing on material published in
    the early 1890s. On his mother's side Melville was de-
    scended from Wessel Gansevoort, Lux Mundi, of whom Erasmus
    said: "He was named, though certainly not with his consent,
    The Light of the World; for he was eminent for learning and
    Christian attainments." The revival of Melville's works is
    largely due to Arthur Stedman. [For letter by Melville's
    widow, Mrs. Elizabeth S. Melville, to Ferris in response to
    this article, see McNeilly, pp. 6-7; see also Sealts (1976),
    pp. 10-11.] Reprinted in McNeilly, pp. 2-3.

9   MacMECHAN, ARCHIBALD. "Herman Melville." London Humane Review,
    7 (October), 242-252.
       Reprint of 1899.B12.

10 ANON. "Herman Melville's Works." New York Times Saturday
    Review of Books and Art (5 October), pp. 706-707.
       Prints the list of Melville's works which the Times had
    sent to Mrs. Melville and which she had returned corrected
    and annotated. She noted: "Only the foreign editions of
    his works were issued in more than one volume, with the
    single exception of 'Clarel,' a long poem, a small edition
    of which was printed, and was withdrawn from circulation by
    Mr. Melville on finding that it commanded but a very limited
    sale, being in strong contrast to his previous popular works."
    Mrs. Melville supposed that all of the later books were out
    of print, though the principal sea stories, Typee, Omoo,
    Moby-Dick and White-Jacket, "which had always been in de-
    mand," had been reissued in 1892. [See 1892.B5.] Re-
    printed in part in Monteiro (September 1974), 11-12.

11 HAWTHORNE, JULIAN. "Hawthorne at Lenox." Philadelphia
    Booklover's Weekly, No. 10 (30 December), pp. 225-231.
       Account of visits by Melville to the Hawthornes at Lenox
    during the time he was writing Moby-Dick. Melville "would
    talk above our heads about metaphysical matters to my father
    and mother" but would also tell vivid stories. "He had led
    a strange, half wild life; but he had a keen and doubtful
    mind, always peering into the mysteries and riddles of crea-
    tion. The impression I had of him was of gloom, with rifts
    of fantastic gaiety coming through, and a sort of fascina-
    tion that attracted me against my will. In fact he was, at
    times, slightly unsettled in his mind." In 1883 he told
    Julian he "was convinced Hawthorne had all his life con-
    cealed some great secret, which would, were it known, ex-
    plain all the mysteries of his career." Reprinted in
    1902.B13.

1902

1902 A BOOKS - NONE

1902 B SHORTER WRITINGS

1   ABERNETHY, JULIAN W. "The Lesser Novelists," in American
    Literature. New York: Charles E. Merrill Co., p. 456.
       One sentence reference. "Another forgotten New York
    novelist is Herman Melville (1819-1891), whose 'Typee' and
    'Omoo'...were once the sensation of two continents." Re-
    printed in Recognition, pp. 146-147.

2   BACON, EDWIN M. "Among the Berkshire Hills," in Literary
    Pilgrimages in New England. New York: Silver, Burdett &
    Co., pp. 451-456.
       Biographical. Includes "October Mountain" in list of
    works written at Arrowhead. [See discussion in Sealts
    (1950), pp. 178-182.]

3   KEELER, CHARLES. Tahiti the Golden. San Francisco: Oceanic
    Steamship Co., p. 4.
       Brief reference: "lovers of Pierre Loti and Herman
    Melville, of Stevenson and Stoddard, have gleaned from their
    pages something of the glamor of tropic joy which invests
    the spot" [Tahiti].

4   LAWTON, WILLIAM CRANSTON. Introduction to the Study of American
    Literature. New York: Globe School Book Company, p. 246.
       Melville "holds his own beside Cooper and Marryat, and
    boy readers, at least, will need no introduction to him.
    Nor will their enjoyment ever be alloyed by a Puritanic
    moral, or mystic double meaning." Reprinted in 1907.B5
    and 1914.B2.

5   MALLARY, R. DeWITT. Lenox and the Berkshire Highlands.
    New York: G. P. Putnam's Sons, pp. 35, 62-63, 96, 142, 229.
       Mentions of Melville, "who appears often in the Hawthorne
    correspondence, and who was the author of Typee, Omoo, Mardi,
    Redburn, and other sea-tales, popular in their day, winning
    for their author two columns in Allibone, and still very
    much appreciated as first-rank stories of their kind."
    Hawthorne came to Lenox "obscure in a way," but it seems
    "a somewhat colossal joke to claim that Herman Melville, by
    his notice of The Scarlet Letter in the columns of a liter-
    ary journal, 'discovered' him!" The great among America's
    best minds had recognized Hawthorne's genius and "taken him
    into their innermost fellowship long before The Scarlet Let-
    ter, and long before any such person as Melville was known."
    [For discussion of Melville's alleged authorship of review
    of The Scarlet Letter, see Thorp (1942), pp. 302-305.]

242

6   PAYNE, WILLIAM MORTON. "A Century of American Fiction," in
    Editorial Echoes. Chicago: A. C. McClurg & Co., p. 109.
        One sentence reference: "The fifth decade was distin-
    guished by nothing more noteworthy than Herman Melville's
    stories of the southern seas, which appeared in rapid suc-
    cession during those years."

7   R[ICHARDSON], C[HARLES] F. "Melville, Herman," in Encyclopae-
    dia Britannica. 10th Edition. Vol. 6. London and
    Edinburgh: Adam and Charles Black; New York: The Encyclo-
    paedia Britannica Co., p. 631.
        Biographical and critical. Melville's verse is quite
    forgotten; his works of fiction and travel are of irregular
    execution. But few writers have been able so freely to
    introduce romantic personal experiences into their books.
    In Omoo, White-Jacket, and especially Moby-Dick, Melville
    portrayed seafaring life and character with vigor and
    originality, from a personal knowledge equal to Cooper's,
    Marryat's, or Clark Russell's. But he wrote other tales
    so turgid, eccentric, opiniative, and loosely written as to
    seem the work of another author. Melville was the product
    of a period in American literature when the fiction of
    writers below Irving, Poe, and Hawthorne was measured by
    humble artistic standards. Reprinted in part in Doubloon,
    pp. 120-121.

8   RICHARDSON, CHARLES F. "The Lesser Novelists," in American
    Literature, 1607-1885. Vol. 2. New York and London:
    G. P. Putnam's Sons, pp. 403-404.
        Reprint of 1889.B4.

9   SEARS, LORENZO. "A Reading List," in American Literature in
    the Colonial and National Periods. Boston: Little, Brown,
    and Co., p. 466.
        Lists Typee and Omoo. No discussion of Melville in the
    book.

10 TRENT, W. P. "Introduction," in Typee. Boston: D. C. Heath,
    pp. iii-v.
        Biographical and critical. Typee and Omoo are thoroughly
    in keeping with the romantic energy of adventurous Americans
    half a century ago. Their renewed popularity is owing
    partly to R. L. Stevenson's high praise and partly to the
    current interest in romantic adventure. Melville deserves
    a permanent place in American literature, with his fame
    probably resting chiefly on Typee and Moby-Dick, the latter
    one of the most interesting sea stories since Cooper. Typee
    is marked by sincerity and an absence of the mannerisms o

1902

> and straining after effect that somewhat mar the more
> powerful story of <u>Moby-Dick</u>. <u>White-Jacket</u> is perhaps
> Melville's only other work with any claim to popularity:
> all of his popular works are founded, more or less, on his
> own experiences. <u>Israel Potter</u> probably deserves to sur-
> vive because Franklin and John Paul Jones figure in it
> most interestingly.

11 WILSON, RUFUS ROCKWELL. <u>New York: Old and New. Its Story,
Streets, and Landmarks</u>. Vol. 2. Philadelphia: J. B.
Lippincott Co., p. 176.
    A more modern structure covers the site of the house
where Melville ended his days. Melville was a born romancer; the neglect he fell into is inexplicable to anyone
who has read his books.

12 WOODBERRY, GEORGE E. <u>Nathaniel Hawthorne</u>. Boston: Houghton
Mifflin Co., pp. 207, 221, 256.
    Mentions of Melville's visits to Hawthorne at Lenox; he
became "a welcome guest and companion, with his boisterous
genuine intellectual spirits and animal strength."

13 HAWTHORNE, JULIAN. "Tribute to Hawthorne." Pittsfield (Mass.)
<u>Berkshire Hills</u> (1 February), p. 6.
    Reprint of 1901.B11.

14 ANON. "Notes and News." New York <u>Times Saturday Review of
Books</u> (17 May), p. 328.
    Note that Frederick A. Stokes has added W. P. Trent's
edition of <u>Typee</u> to its Heath's Home Library. [<u>See</u>
1902.B10.]

1903 A BOOKS - NONE

1903 B SHORTER WRITINGS

1 ANON. "Melville, Herman," in <u>Lamb's Biographical Dictionary
of the United States</u>. Ed. John Howard Brown. Vol. 5.
Boston: Federal Book Company of Boston, p. 442.
    One paragraph biography; no comment on works. Reprinted
in 1904.B2.

2 ANON. "Melville, Herman," in <u>The New International Encyclopae-
dia</u>. Eds. Daniel Coit Gilman, Harry Thurston Peck, Frank
Moore Colby. Vol. 12. New York: Dodd, Mead and Co.,
pp. 93-94.
    One paragraph biography, with list of Melville's books.
The success of <u>Typee</u> was not undeserved; in <u>White-Jacket</u>

the horrors of flogging were so graphically portrayed that
the navy soon afterwards abolished the practice.

3   BAKER, ERNEST A.   A Descriptive Guide to the Best Fiction,
British and American.   London: Swan Sonnenschein and Co.;
New York: The Macmillan Co., p. 262.
Lists Typee, Omoo, White-Jacket, and Moby-Dick, with
brief comments. The vivid pictures in Typee and Omoo have
been often accepted as plain statements of fact; Moby-Dick
is a realistic story of whale fishing in the Pacific, inspired with all the fascination of nautical life and
adventure.

4   HAWTHORNE, JULIAN.   Hawthorne and His Circle.   New York:
Harper & Brothers, pp. 32-33.
Memories of Melville's visits to Lenox and his tremen-
dous stories of the South Sea Islands and the whale fishery.
There was vivid genius in Melville. Through all his wild
and reckless adventures he had been unable to rid himself
of a Puritan conscience; he afterwards tried to loosen its
grip by studying German metaphysics. He was restless and
disposed to dark hours; there is reason to suspect there
was a vein of insanity in him. His later writings were
incomprehensible. Melville visited the Hawthornes in
England "on one of his aimless, mysterious journeys round
the world." He told Julian he was convinced there was some
secret in Hawthorne's life which had never been revealed
and which accounted for the gloomy passages in his books
[cf. 1901.B11]. There were many secrets untold in Melville's
own career; but there were few more honest or more lovable
men.

5   HEMSTREET, CHARLES.   Literary New York: Its Landmarks and
Associations.   New York: G. P. Putnam's Sons, pp. 224-226.
Anecdote: Melville telling of his "life of trial and
adventure" at one of Alice and Phoebe Cary's Sunday night
receptions in New York at the time he was working on Battle-
Pieces.

6   PAYNE, JOHN.   "Herman Melville," in Vigil and Vision.   New
Sonnets.   London: The Villon Society, p. 62.
Sonnet, prizing The Whale above all Melville's writings.
Reprinted in Recognition, p. 148.

7   STODDARD, RICHARD HENRY.   Recollections Personal and Literary.
Ed. Ripley Hitchcock.   New York: A. S. Barnes & Co.,
pp. 142-144.
Memories of Melville in the Customs House. Next to
Emerson, Melville was the American mystic. He was also one

1903

of our great unrecognized poets, as he showed in his version of "Sheridan's Ride." Prints autograph transcript by
Melville of stanzas 2 and 3 of "Sheridan at Cedar Creek."

8   TRENT, WILLIAM P.   "The Romancers (1830-50)." A History of
     American Literature. New York: D. Appleton; London:
     William Heinemann, pp. 389-391.
         Survey. The quasi-speculative, chaotic Mardi gave pre-
     monition of aberration and the eventual frustration of a
     promising career. Melville's masterpiece, Moby-Dick, might
     be the greatest sea story in literature but for its inordi-
     nate length, frequently inartistic heaping up of details
     and obvious imitation of Carlylean tricks of style. None
     of his later books is comparable to his earlier. Israel
     Potter deserved Hawthorne's praise because of its spirited
     portraits of Franklin and Paul Jones, but no revival of
     Melville's fame will justify republication of these produc-
     tions of his decline. Reprinted in part in Norton Moby-
     Dick, p. 624.

9   ANON.   "Described by Herman Melville." Pittsfield (Mass.)
     Berkshire Hills: A Historic Monthly, 3 (1 August), 135.
         Melville was remembering an old elm tree in Pittsfield
     that had been struck by lightning, in describing Ahab's
     "slender rod-like mark" in chapter 28 of Moby-Dick.

1904 A BOOKS - NONE

1904 B SHORTER WRITINGS

1   ANON.   "Melville, Herman," in The Bibliophile Library of
     Literature, Art, and Rare Manuscripts. Comp. Nathan Haskell
     Dole, Forrest Morgan, and Caroline Ticknor. Vol. 30.
     New York and London: International Bibliophile Society,
     p. 10226.
         One paragraph biography; lists Melville's books, without
     comment. [Vol. 17, pp. 5806-5835, prints extract from Moby-
     Dick, under heading "On the Track of the White Whale."]

2   ANON.   "Melville, Herman," in The Twentieth Century Biograph-
     ical Dictionary of Notable Americans. Boston: The Biograph-
     ical Society, n.p.
         Reprint of 1903.B1.

3   BALFOUR, MARIE CLOTHILDE.   "Melville and the Marquesas: A
     Few Notes Upon his Facts and General Information," in
     Typee. Ed. W. Clark Russell. New Pocket Library. London:
     John Lane, pp. 429-451.

In all his main facts regarding the people of Typee, Melville is "minutely supported and confirmed by many other writers," though his Typees are "undeniably more respectable in their morals than Marquesans have ever tried--or desired--to be."

4   BALFOUR, MARIE CLOTHILDE. "Tahiti in 1842: as Melville Saw It," in Omoo. New Pocket Library. Ed. W. Clark Russell. London: John Lane, pp. 445-462.
No one will deny that Typee and Omoo contain Melville's finest work. The extravagances of his later style are as incredible as they are incomprehensible and concerned with much that can never have existed outside his own fantastic imagination. Moby-Dick contains much that is very fine; but in the midst of brilliant character sketches and a wealth of language and incident, the easy pen riots occasionally into mere wordiness, and the story recedes into the mists of symbolism. Yet in his greatest exaggerations Melville never allowed himself to falsify Nature; even in Mardi and Pierre his persistent truthfulness can be found. In Omoo Melville only told the truth about the Tahitians, though possibly the unfamiliar and unpopular side of it. But he does not do justice to the energy and devotion of the early missionaries, judging them by the results, by no means all of their making. Reprinted in part in Doubloon, p. 120.

*5   BORDEN, WILLIAM ALANSON. An Historical Sketch of the New Haven Young Men's Institute. New Haven, p. 10.
Mentions Melville among the eight or ten outstanding lecturers of the Institute lecture series. Cited in Hillway, p. 56.

6   BULLEN, FRANK T. Denizens of the Deep. New York: Fleming H. Revell Co., pp. 139-140.
Moby-Dick is, and must remain, the classic on whaling, both from the magic of its style and the accuracy of its descriptions.

7   RUSSELL, W. CLARK. "Editor's Preface," in Omoo. New Pocket Library. London: John Lane, pp. v-xii.
The descriptions of life on board a whaler in Omoo are wonderfully vivid and delightful. Neither Smollet nor Marryat has given a more remarkable picture of a sailor than that of John Jermin. The description of a dance in the valley is one of the famous things in literature.

1904

8   RUSSELL, W. CLARK. "Editor's Preface," in <u>Typee</u>. New Pocket
    Library. London: John Lane, pp. v-x.
        Melville has a two-fold claim on our admiration: first,
    as a man of fine and brilliant imagination, a humorist, and
    a poet; second, as a sailor, who, like Dana, interpreted
    the hidden parts of the merchant seaman's life. <u>Typee</u> is
    an accurate study rendered romantic by warm imagination.
    <u>Redburn</u> shows remarkable minuteness of observation. <u>Moby-
    Dick</u> is justifiably regarded as Melville's finest work; the
    opening chapters enchant the imagination and delight like
    a masterpiece of Dutch painting; some of the conversations
    among the sailors remind one of such dramatists as Dekker,
    Webster, Massinger, and Fletcher, for their strength, sweet-
    ness, and courage. Yet in parts it is too obscure, and the
    reader is frequently harassed by a transcendental mysticism
    which is often out of place in the mouths of sailors. Re-
    printed in part in Norton <u>Moby-Dick</u>, pp. 624-625, and
    <u>Doubloon</u>, p. 122.

9   TRENT, WILLIAM P. <u>A Brief History of American Literature</u>.
    New York: D. Appleton and Co., pp. 121, 138, 140-141.
        Only Kennedy, Bird, and Simms "need to be grouped with
    Melville as representing minor writers of fiction whose work
    deserves brief mention." <u>Typee</u>, <u>Omoo</u>, <u>White-Jacket</u>, and
    <u>Moby-Dick</u> constitute Melville's legacy to posterity. <u>Moby-
    Dick</u> "is in parts probably not exceeded in strength and
    general interest by any other romance of the sea. It is
    too long and too packed with details to suit some tastes,
    but these faults will scarcely be noticed by readers who
    once catch a portion of Captain Ahab's demoniacal eagerness
    to encounter the terrible monster." Melville's numerous
    later books "gave painful proofs of mental aberration."
    The really significant fiction of the period, so far as
    most readers are concerned, is to be found in the works of
    Hawthorne and Poe.

10 WILSON, RUFUS ROCKWELL. <u>New England in Letters</u>. New York:
    A. Wessels Co. pp. 324-326, 330.
        Mainly biographical. With the completion of <u>Moby-Dick</u>,
    Melville's important literary work came practically to an
    end. Though his gifts were great, he had never learned
    to control them; all his later writings were a puzzling
    mixture of philosophy and fantasy.

11 ALDEN, WILLIAM LIVINGSTON. "John Lane's Pocket Library."
    New York <u>Times Saturday Review of Books</u> (5 March), p. 150.
        Notes forthcoming publication of John Lane edition of
    <u>Typee</u> and <u>Omoo</u>.

12 ALDEN, WILLIAM LIVINGSTON. "Mr. Alden's Views." New York
    Times Saturday Review of Books (12 March), p. 172.
        Recommends that an English publisher bring out a complete
    edition of Melville's works--"surely there is enough genius
    in everything that Melville wrote to make it worth while."
    Melville has probably never been appreciated at his true
    worth, "and the fault was partly his own, for he did not
    seem to know when he was writing what deserved to live
    (and will live as long as the language lasts) and what was
    dull and trivial." The opening chapters of Mardi surpass
    anything written about the sea, but the greater part is
    unreadable. Reprinted in Monteiro (Spring 1975), pp. 73-74.

13 O., E. G. "Egomet." London Academy and Literature, No. 1666
    (9 April), p. 406.
        Typee is not a good "wander-book": "the writer is self-
    conscious, he ever has his reader in his mind's eye, and the
    author of a true wander-book has no one in his eye save him-
    self. I have never really liked Melville since I met him
    in 'Nathaniel Hawthorne and His Wife,' years ago." [See
    1884.B3.]

14 S., F. T. "Reprints and New Editions." London Academy and
    Literature, No. 1666 (9 April), p. 404.
        Review of John Lane edition of Typee. [See 1904.B8.]
    Typee is a fine bit of writing, but a little overrated.

15 ALDEN, WILLIAM LIVINGSTON. "Mr. Alden's Views." New York
    Times Saturday Review of Books (9 April), p. 246.
        Reply to praise of Norman Duncan by Frank T. Bullen.
    Before Conrad and Kipling, Michael Scott and Herman Melville
    had "some knowledge" of the sea's mysteries. Reprinted in
    Monteiro (Spring 1975), p. 74.

16 ALDEN, WILLIAM LIVINGSTON. "Mr. Alden's Views." New York
    Times Saturday Review of Books (30 April), p. 294.
        Reply to 1904.B13. Typee is probably one of the poorest
    of Melville's books. "Compared with such a work as 'Moby
    Dick,' or even 'White Jacket,' it reads very much like the
    work of a beginner, and not a very promising beginner at
    that." Reprinted in Monteiro (Spring 1975), p. 74.

17 ANON. "Nathaniel Hawthorne to E. A. Duyckinck on Herman
    Melville in 1850." New York Bulletin of the New York Public
    Library, 8 (June), 311.
        Prints Hawthorne's letter to Evert Duyckinck, 29 August
    1850, from the original manuscript in the New York Public
    Library. [See Log, p. 391.]

1905

1905 A BOOKS - NONE

1905 B SHORTER WRITINGS

1   MASEFIELD, JOHN. "Port of Many Ships," in <u>A Mainsail Haul</u>.
     London: Elkin Matthews, pp. 24-26.
          Writes of old sailor's prophecy that Moby Dick, "the
     King of all the whales," will lead a procession of whales
     and ships "into a grand anchorage in Kingdom Come" at the
     time when all the fishes in the sea die and every drowned
     sailor springs alive again.

2   MOULTON, CHARLES WELLS, ed. "Herman Melville," in <u>The Library</u>
     <u>of Literary Criticism of English and American Authors</u>.
     Vol. 8. Buffalo: The Moulton Publishing Co., pp. 62-64.
          Quotes from 1893.B3; 1891.B52; 1892.B14; 1847.B71;
     1852.B2; 1853.B8; 1889.B4; 1891.B26; 1891.B47; 1903.B8.
     [Vol. 6 (1904), pp. 356-357, quotes from Melville's letter
     to Hawthorne, 16? April? 1851 (<u>Letters</u>, pp. 123-125).]

3   ANON. New York <u>Times Saturday Review of Books</u> (20 May),
     p. 320.
          Notes that Sidney Low in the London <u>Standard</u> [unlocated]
     takes Rudyard Kipling and Frank Bullen to task for seeming
     to know nothing of Herman Melville and <u>Moby-Dick</u>. Reports
     that <u>Moby-Dick</u> is out of print in England and hopes for a
     new English edition soon. Reprinted in Monteiro (Spring
     1975), p. 75.

4   A., C. F. "Moby Dick." [Letter to the Editor.] New York
     <u>Times Saturday Review of Books</u> (15 July), p. 470.
          There is some unequalled character drawing in <u>Moby-Dick</u>;
     its whale fishing information is superior to Bullen's [in
     <u>The Cruise of the Cachalot</u>]. Reprinted in Monteiro (Spring
     1975), p. 75.

5   'COSMOPOLITAN.' "Herman Melville and Others." [Letter to the
     Editor.] New York <u>Times Saturday Review of Books</u> (22 July),
     p. 486.
          Delighted to have discovered Melville through the <u>Review</u>
     <u>of Books</u>. <u>Moby-Dick</u> "is one of those rare books which sug-
     gest tone poems"; it conveys "operatic strains far more
     grand than Wagner's 'Flying Dutchman.'" Reprinted in
     Monteiro (Spring 1975), pp. 75-76.

6   G., W. W. "Herman Melville." [Letter to the Editor.] New
     York <u>Times Saturday Review of Books</u> (29 July), p. 502.

Questions accuracy of statement about horse chestnuts in chapter 6 of Moby-Dick; wonders how much reliance can be placed on Melville's observations on whales and whaling. But Melville is the most interesting "of all our unjustly neglected writers." Reprinted in Monteiro (Spring 1975), pp. 76-77.

7   'MARQUESAS.' "Herman Melville." [Letter to the Editor.] New York Times Saturday Review of Books (12 August), p. 535.
    Mistakenly believes that 1905.B5 claims that Melville has only just been discovered; notes that Melville's sea tales were popular half a century ago and have never been out of print. Letter followed by editorial explanation that correspondent in 1905.B5 simply meant "that he had begun to read Melville and liked him." Reprinted in Monteiro (Spring 1975), pp. 77-78.

8   STEPHEN, GEORGE. "Melville and Bullen." [Letter to the Editor.] New York Times Saturday Review of Books (26 August), p. 562.
    Claims that Frank T. Bullen plagiarized from various writers, including Melville.

9   BULLEN, FRANK T. "Mr. Bullen and Melville." [Letter to the Editor.] New York Times Saturday Review of Books (30 September), p. 642.
    Denies plagiarism. [See 1905.B8.] Told Peter Toft [see 1900.B6]: "'Had I read "Moby Dick" first, I should never have dared to write "The Cruise of the Cachalot."' Mr. Toft thereupon asked me if I could account for the general neglect of Melville's masterpiece. I answered that perhaps it was partly on account of its length and partly because of the wonderfully transcendental and melodramatic story woven in with his splendid narrative of facts." Reprinted in Monteiro (Spring 1975), p. 78.

10 O[VERLAND], M. U. "Bullen and Melville." [Letter to the Editor.] New York Times Saturday Review of Books (7 October), p. 658.
    Reply to 1905.B9. "Melville's book simply carried me away. 'The Cruise of the Cachalot' I had read several times before I read 'Moby Dick,' and am ready to read it as many times again, after having read the older book. I think in these days everybody prefers a well-written narrative of facts to a poem as a steady diet." Reprinted in Monteiro (Spring 1975), p. 79.

1905

11   'GUARIONEX.' "Bullen and 'Moby Dick.'" [Letter to the Editor.]
     New York <u>Times Saturday Review of Books</u> (14 October), p. 698.
         Reply to 1905.B10. "Could it not have been that Bullen
     was prompted by Melville's 'Moby Dick'? M. U. O. seems to
     imply that much." Reprinted in Monteiro (Spring 1975),
     p. 79.

<u>1906 A BOOKS - NONE</u>

<u>1906 B SHORTER WRITINGS</u>

1   ANON. "Melville, Herman," in <u>The Harmsworth Encyclopaedia</u>.
        Vol. 7. London: The Amalgamated Press, p. 214.
            Short biographical paragraph; includes <u>Voyage round the</u>
        <u>World</u> (1860) in partial list of Melville's books.

2   ANON. "Melville, Herman," in <u>Herringshaw's Encyclopedia of</u>
        <u>American Biography of the Nineteenth Century</u>. Chicago:
        American Publishers' Association, p. 651.
            Short biographical paragraph; no comment on works.

3   ANON. "Melville,. Herman," in <u>Nelson's Encyclopaedia: Every-</u>
        <u>body's Book of Reference</u>. Eds. Frank Moore Colby and
        George Sandeman. Vol. 8. New York: Thomas Nelson & Sons,
        p. 77.
            Biographical sketch. <u>Typee</u>, <u>Omoo</u>, and <u>White-Jacket</u> con-
        tain an element of romance that makes them more interesting
        than any ordinary novel; <u>White-Jacket</u> did much to abolish
        flogging in the navy. <u>Moby-Dick</u> was probably Melville's
        most important effort. "Benito Cereno" and "The Bell Tower"
        have seldom been excelled by American writers of romantic
        fiction. <u>Battle-Pieces</u> contains some of the best lyrics
        inspired by the Civil War.

4   STEARNS, FRANK PRESTON. <u>The Life and Genius of Nathaniel</u>
        <u>Hawthorne</u>. Philadelphia and London: J. B. Lippincott Co.,
        pp. 244-245.
            Melville mentioned as Hawthorne's companion in the summer
        of 1851. "For older company he had Hermann Melville and
        G. P. R. James, whose society he may have found as inter-
        esting as that of more distinguished writers...."

5   ANON. "Literary Gossip." London <u>Athenaeum</u>, No. 4126
        (24 November), p. 658.
            Announcement that Melville's family is collecting material
        for a memoir and wishes persons with letters from Melville
        to send them to Miss Elizabeth Melville for copying.

1907 A BOOKS - NONE

1907 B SHORTER WRITINGS

1   ANON. "Melville, Herman," in The Americana: A Universal
      Reference Library. Ed. Frederick Converse Beach. New York:
      Scientific American Compiling Dep't, n.p.
          Identifies Melville as an American naval novelist.
      Typee, Omoo, White-Jacket, Moby-Dick, and Pierre were justly
      popular, but several "philosophical romances" met with lit-
      tle success. Battle-Pieces contains Melville's best verse.
      White-Jacket effected the abolition of flogging in the
      U.S. navy.

2   ANON. "Melville, Herman," in Chambers's Biographical Diction-
      ary. Eds. David Patrick and Francis Hindes Groome.
      London: W. & R. Chambers; Philadelphia: J. B.
      Lippincott Co., p. 649.
          Reprint of 1897.B2, omitting reference to the tales and
      poetry.

3   HAWTHORNE, NATHANIEL. Love Letters of Nathaniel Hawthorne,
      1839-1841; 1841-1863. Introduction by Roswell Field.
      Vol. 2. Chicago: Society of the Dofobs, p. 214.
          In letter to Sophia, 9 August 1851, Hawthorne mentions a
      fine ride with Julian, Melville, and two other gentlemen.

4   LATHERS, RICHARD. Reminiscences of Richard Lathers. Ed.
      Alvan F. Sanborn. New York: Grafton Press, pp. 51, 328-
      329, 407.
          Melville mentioned as one of the guests at the Saturday
      night supper parties of Evert Duyckinck in New York during
      the winter of 1855-1856. Lathers often visited Melville,
      one of his nearest neighbors in Pittsfield and "listened
      with intense pleasure to his highly individual views of
      society and politics. He always provided a bountiful
      supply of good cider--the product of his own orchard--and
      of tobacco, in the virtues of which he was a firm believer.
      Indeed, he prided himself on the inscription painted over
      his capacious fireplace. 'I and my chimney smoke together,'
      an inscription which I have seen strikingly verified more
      than once when the atmosphere was heavy and the wind was
      east." Melville and William Gilmore Simms listed among
      Lathers' guests at Abby Lodge.

5   LAWTON, WILLIAM CRANSTON. A Study of American Literature.
      New York and Chicago: Globe School Book Company, p. 246.
          Reprints Melville section in 1902.B4.

1907

6   MAHAN, A. T. <u>From Sail to Steam: Recollections of Naval Life</u>.
    New York and London: Harper & Brothers, pp. 62, 66, 107.
        Claims that a civil professor in the naval academy was
    the central figure of one of the most humorous scenes in
    <u>White-Jacket</u>; paraphrases chapter 83. Despite its preju-
    diced tone, <u>White-Jacket</u> has preserved many amusing and
    interesting inside recollections of a ship-of-war of the
    olden time.

7   RHYS, ERNEST. "Editor's Introduction," in <u>Typee</u>. Everyman's
    Library. London: J. M. Dent & Co.; New York: E. P. Dutton
    & Co., pp. vii-x.
        Mainly biographical. <u>Moby-Dick</u> is a highly transcenden-
    talized record of Melville's voyage on the <u>Acushnet</u>. But
    Melville included real people in his books; no one can
    doubt the reality of Jackson's portrait in chapter 12 of
    <u>Redburn</u>. <u>Battle-Pieces</u> contains four or five memorable
    songs and ballads but on the whole is less poetical in
    effect than some episodes of the sea stories; "A Dirge for
    McPherson" is perhaps the finest of Melville's war-poems.
    Melville's mysticism and love of philosophy hurt his art
    as a storyteller in the books of his later period, where
    the break with reality is complete; these books attempt a
    fantasy which is not justified by its result in narrative
    art. <u>Pierre</u> and <u>The Confidence-Man</u> are among Melville's
    failures. When Rhys visited E. C. Stedman in 1888,
    Melville had a hermit's reputation, and it was difficult
    to get more than a passing glimpse of his "tall, stalwart
    figure" and grave, preoccupied face. Frequent reprintings.

8   RHYS, ERNEST. "Editor's Note," in <u>Moby Dick</u>. Everyman's
    Library. London: J. M. Dent & Co.; New York: E. P. Dutton
    & Co., pp. vii-viii.
        The story of <u>Moby-Dick</u> is based on Melville's great
    adventures during his voyage on the <u>Acushnet</u>, after which
    he left the sea for good. His letter to Hawthorne of
    1? June 1851 shows his intellectual change between his
    first two books and <u>Moby-Dick</u>: he was not only a writer of
    sea tales but a transcendentalist in oilskins, who found a
    vaster ocean than the Pacific in his own mind and symbolized
    in the whale the forces of nature that produce and overpower
    man. <u>Moby-Dick</u> was the last of Melville's books in which he
    maintained a balance between transcendentalism and reality.
    Some of his books, such as <u>Pierre</u> and <u>The Confidence-Man</u>,
    are all but unreadable. Frequent reprintings. Reprinted
    in part in <u>Doubloon</u>, p. 123.

9   PERRY, BLISS. "The Editor Who Was Never the Editor." Boston
    Atlantic Monthly, 100 (November), 667.
        Melville invited (1857) to contribute to Atlantic Monthly.
    Prints Melville's response, 19 August 1857 [Letters,
    pp. 187–188]. Reprinted in 1908.B2.

10 COOK, ALBERT S. "Miscellaneous Notes." Modern Language Notes,
    22 (November), 207.
        In chapters 14 and 23 of Typee, the word "leafen" occurs
    in a sense not recognized by NED, namely "made of leaves."

1908 A BOOKS – NONE

1908 B SHORTER WRITINGS

1   JOHNSON, ROSSITER. "Melville, Herman," in A Dictionary of
    Biographies of Authors Represented in this Series. Vol. 19
    of Authors Digest. New York: Authors Press, pp. 315–316.
        Brief biographical sketch. Quotes from 1846.B67,
    1891.B52, 1892.B14.

2   PERRY, BLISS. Park-Street Papers. Boston: Houghton
    Mifflin Co., p. 239.
        Reprint of 1907.B9.

3   RHYS, ERNEST. "Editor's Note," in Omoo. Everyman's Library.
    London: J. M. Dent; New York: E. P. Dutton & Co., p. vii.
        Biographical sketch. Frequent reprintings.

4   SPEARS, JOHN R. The Story of the New England Whalers. New
    York: The Macmillan Co., pp. 157–158, 159, 185–186, 201,
    248, 257.
        Brief quotations from and references to Moby-Dick.
    Although Moby-Dick is a novel, Melville's descriptions of
    whales and whaling are accepted at New Bedford. The custom
    of the boat steerer striking the whale and then going aft,
    while the mate went forward to lance the whale seemed fool-
    ish and dangerous to Melville; but whalers thought the most
    experienced man was needed at the steering oar until the
    whale was struck and then he was needed at the lance.

1909 A BOOKS – NONE

1909

1909 B SHORTER WRITINGS

1 COOPER, LANE. "The Poets," in A Manual of American Literature.
Ed. Theodore Stanton. New York and London: G. P. Putnam's
Sons, p. 263.
In addition to the fascinating Typee, Melville published
Battle-Pieces and other poems. His verse is less objective
and sincere than his prose.

2 HUDSON, W. H. Afoot in England. London: Hutchinson & Co.,
p. 84.
"...this break in the history of the human race...
'shadows forth the heartless voids and immensities of the
universe, and thus stabs us from behind with the thought of
annihilation.' Here, in these words of Hermann Melville,
we are let all at once into the true meaning of those dis-
quieting and seemingly indefinable emotions so often experienced, even by the most ardent lovers of nature and of
solitude, in uninhabited deserts, on great mountains, and
on the sea."

3 MILLER, MARION MILLS. Manual of Ready Reference to The Authors'
Digest Containing Brief Analyses of the World's Great
Stories. New York: Authors Press, p. 86.
Indexes Typee ("1. Travel. 2. Adventure.") and Moby-
Dick ("1. Sea-Life. 2. Adventure. 3. Magic."); one sen-
tence summary of each.

4 NORTHUP, CLARK SUTHERLAND. "The Novelists," in A Manual of
American Literature. Ed. Theodore Stanton. New York and
London: G. P. Putnam's Sons, pp. 164-165, 169, 444.
Survey. Mardi's vagaries and lack of sobriety doomed
it to failure; Redburn includes some realistic horrors and
could hardly be popular. Melville's masterpiece was Moby-
Dick, an uneven work of excessive length, written partly
in a strained, Carlylesque style. The fierce contest of
Ahab with the whale is not unworthy of the pen of a greater
writer. Israel Potter listed among the more important early
contributions to Putnam's Monthly. Reprinted in part in
Doubloon, pp. 123-124.

5 SIMONDS, WILLIAM EDWARD. A Student's History of American
Literature. Boston: Houghton Mifflin Co., p. 304.
The fiction of adventure is represented at its best in
the novels of Melville, who was a master of a brilliant
style which gave his writings a distinction still retained.
His most successful books: Typee, Omoo, and Moby-Dick. Reprinted in Recognition, p. 149.

1910 A BOOKS - NONE

1910 B SHORTER WRITINGS

1   CHRISTIAN, F. W. Eastern Pacific Lands: Tahiti and the
     Marquesas Islands. London: Robert Scott, p. 155.
          Christian spent several weeks on Nukuhiva in 1894 and
     "visited on foot the famous valley of Tai-pi (Typee), the
     scene of Herman Melville's sojourn with the cannibals; a
     stirring tale, which every schoolboy worth his salt should
     know as well as his Robinson Crusoe." Typee was "practically
     a valley of the dead."

2   CLARKE, HELEN ARCHIBALD. Hawthorne's Country. New York:
     The Baker and Taylor Co., p. 258.
          Quotes 1852.B5. Reprinted Garden City, New York:
     Doubleday, Page & Co., 1913.

3   ERSKINE, JOHN. "Nathaniel Hawthorne." Leading American Novel-
     ists. New York: Henry Holt and Co., p. 253.
          "A few friends in the neighborhood visited the house-
     hold,--Herman Melville, the novelist, Fields, Holmes, and
     others...." Only Melville reference. [Chapters on Brown,
     Cooper, Simms, Hawthorne, Stowe, Harte.]

4   THOMSON, JAMES ("B-V"). Walt Whitman; The Man and The Poet.
     Introduction by Bertram Dobell. London: The Editor, p. 32.
     Reprint of 1874.B4.

5   LONDON, JACK. "Typee." Portland (Ore.) Pacific Monthly
     (March), 267-281.
          Reports the dying out of the Happar and Typee tribes.
     Frequent brief reference to and quotation from Typee. As
     a boy London dreamed many long hours over the pages of Typee.

1911 A BOOKS - NONE

1911 B SHORTER WRITINGS

1   HALLECK, REUBEN POST. "Supplementary List of Authors and Their
     Chief Works: Eastern Authors," in History of American Lit-
     erature. New York: American Book Co., p. 407.
          Lists Typee, Omoo, Mardi, White-Jacket, and Moby-Dick,
     which contain interesting accounts of Melville's wide
     travels.

1911

2   JACKSON, HOLBROOK. "Southward Ho!" in <u>Romance and Reality:</u>
<u>Essays and Studies</u>. London: Grant Richards, pp. 27-30.
Account of first reading of <u>Typee</u>, found on a secondhand
bookstall, and <u>Omoo</u>. "Doubtless there are people who,
having read 'Typee,' are not moved with an urgent desire
to take ship for the Marquesas, but I have yet to hear of
them. But there can be none in the early twenties who are
so tame.... I had barely got half through the book when
the South Seas filled my imagination with an overpowering
longing. I seemed to have known them all my life; Herman
Melville, most delightful and discursive of chroniclers,
simply relit my memory. He made it all quite clear and
revealed my destiny."

3   LONDON, JACK. "Typee," in <u>The Cruise of the Snark</u>. New York:
The Macmillan Co., pp. 154-177.
Reprint of 1910.B5.

4   REYNOLDS, CUYLER, ed. <u>Hudson-Mohawk Genealogical and Family</u>
<u>Memoirs</u>. Vol. 1. New York: Lewis Historical Publishing
Co., pp. 61-65.
Melville genealogy. Accounts of Melville's ancestors;
records only Melville's date of birth and date of marriage.
Melville listed with Longfellow, Hawthorne, and President
John Tyler as one of the guests at Broadhall when it was
kept as a boarding house.

5   [RICHARDSON, CHARLES F.]. "Melville, Herman," in <u>Encyclopaedia</u>
<u>Britannica</u>. 11th ed. Vol. 18. New York: <u>Encyclopaedia</u>
Britannica Co.; Cambridge, England: The University Press,
pp. 102-103.
Abbreviated version of 1902.B7.

6   [HOWELLS, W. D.]. "Editor's Easy Chair." New York <u>Harper's</u>
<u>Monthly Magazine</u>, 122 (February), 472.
Review of <u>Life and Letters of Edmund Clarence Stedman</u>
by Laura Stedman and George M. Gould. Mention. "...think
of them [the romancers of 1911] if you can, in the presence
of one such romancer as Herman Melville."

<u>1912 A BOOKS - NONE</u>

<u>1912 B SHORTER WRITINGS</u>

1   CAIRNS, WILLIAM B. <u>A History of American Literature</u>. New York:
Oxford University Press, pp. 304, 368-370.

Partial survey. Typee and Omoo are not fiction but sections of autobiography. Both are simple, straightforward
narratives, fascinating though wholly without plot interest.
The detail of many incidents in Moby-Dick suggests they were
Melville's own experiences. The conception of the story is
powerful but not adequately sustained. Melville's interest
in abstruse philosophy and Sir Thomas Browne led to a complete and disastrous change in style from the directness of
Typee and Omoo. Beginning in Moby-Dick, the change is more
marked in the later prose works, which are hardly readable.
The poems in Battle-Pieces are mostly crude and formless,
but written with much enthusiasm. As a writer of adventure
stories, Melville does not deserve to be classed with Cooper
or above Paulding. Reprinted in 1930.B4.

2   JACKSON, HOLBROOK. "Southward Ho!" in Southward Ho! And other
    Essays. The Wayfarer's Library. London: J. M. Dent & Sons
    pp. 6-9, 13, 16.
        Reprint of 1911.B2.

3   LA FARGE, JOHN. Reminiscences of the South Seas. Garden City,
    N.Y.: Doubleday, Page & Co., pp. 305, 317-318, 348.
        Reprints Melville references in 1901.B7. La Farge also
    refers to his pleasure in looking at his sketches of "that
    place where Melville last lived during his last days on
    Moorea, as he tells in 'Omoo.'"

4   TRENT, W. P. and JOHN ERSKINE. Great Writers of America.
    London: Williams & Norgate; New York: Henry Holt & Co.,
    pp. 51, 55-57.
        Moby-Dick is Melville's masterpiece. Not even Cooper
    could surpass the grandeur of its sea pictures; some of its
    adventurous episodes have an uncanny quality found nowhere
    else. In the fertility and excitement of his plots Simms
    excelled Cooper and in turn is rivalled by Melville. But
    Simms's work, in extent and contemporary importance, is far
    worthier of attention than all Melville's writing, with the
    exception of Moby-Dick. Cooper still keeps his secure
    place, above both Melville and Simms. Reprinted in part in
    Recognition, p. 150.

5   COURNOS, JOHN. "A Visit to John Masefield." New York
    Independent (5 September), p. 537.
        Quotes Masefield: "'You produced a great prose writer...
    in Herman Melville, who wrote about the sea. A noble and
    beautiful book is his "Moby Dick."'"

1913

1913 A BOOKS - NONE

1913 B SHORTER WRITINGS

    1   BAKER, ERNEST A. A Guide to the Best Fiction in English.
        London: George Routledge & Sons, p. 392.
            Revised edition of 1903.B3, with same comments on Typee,
        Omoo, and White-Jacket. Moby-Dick is by far Melville's
        finest book; it conveys the magic and beauty of the sea and
        the romance of nautical life better perhaps than any other
        story in the language.

    2   FRAZER, SIR JAMES GEORGE. "The Belief in Immortality Among
        the Marquesans," in The Belief in Immortality and the Wor-
        ship of the Dead. Vol. 2. London: Macmillan and Co.,
        pp. 328-374, passim.
            Frequent quotation from Typee. Notes that Melville
        "spent more than four months as a captive in the [Typee]
        tribe, and published an agreeable narrative of his captiv-
        ity; but never having mastered the language, he was not able
        to give much exact information concerning the customs and
        beliefs of the natives."

    3   JOHNSON, MARTIN. "In the Marquesas," in Through the South Seas
        with Jack London. London: T. Werner Laurie, pp. 161-163.
            Records visit to Typee. Melville told the truth in de-
        scribing it as a paradise.

    4   LONG, WILLIAM J. American Literature: A Study of the Men and
        the Books that in the Earlier and Later Times Reflect the
        American Spirit. Boston: Ginn and Co., p. 247.
            Melville identified as the author of "the stirring"
        Typee, White-Jacket, Moby-Dick, "and other stories of the
        deep." Dana's Two Years Before the Mast is better known.
        The tales of Irving, Cooper, and Poe are all the fiction of
        the period that seems destined to a permanent place in
        American literature. [Hawthorne is the major fiction writer
        of the following period.] Reprinted 1923; reprinted in
        Norton Moby-Dick, p. 625.

    5   MACY, JOHN. The Spirit of American Literature. Garden City,
        N.Y.: Doubleday, Page & Co., pp. 15-16.
            In American fiction the fine is weak and the strong is
        crude. Like Uncle Tom's Cabin, Moby-Dick, "a madly eloquent
        romance of the sea," fails in workmanship. Reprinted in
        Doubloon, p. 124.

1914 A BOOKS - NONE

1914 B SHORTER WRITINGS

1   CAIRNS, WILLIAM B. American Literature for Secondary Schools.
     New York: The Macmillan Co., p. 226.
          Moby-Dick is Melville's best novel of adventure. Both
     the autobiographical books and the novels are full of ex-
     citement, wholesome, and well told. Reprinted in Doubloon,
     pp. 124-125.

2   LAWTON, WILLIAM CRANSTON. Introduction to the Study of Amer-
     ican Literature. New Revised Edition. Yonkers-on-Hudson,
     N.Y.: World Book Co., p. 246.
          Reprints Melville section in 1902.B4.

3   MacMECHAN, ARCHIBALD. "The Best Sea Story Ever Told," in The
     Life of a Little College and Other Papers by Archibald
     MacMechan. Boston: Houghton Mifflin Co., pp. 181-197.
          Reprint of 1899.B12.

4   METCALF, JOHN CALVIN. American Literature. B. F. Johnson
     Publishing Co., pp. 389-391.
          Biographical and critical. Melville's fame rests almost
     entirely on Typee, Omoo, and Moby-Dick. Typee is part fact,
     part fiction. The more realistic Omoo has more action and
     more drama; parts of it amount to a satirical comedy of
     manners. Melville's great work is Moby-Dick, a strange
     mixture of adventure and philosophy, realism and fantasy,
     invested with the poetic coloring of romance. The white
     whale becomes a symbol of nature against which man is
     ultimately helpless. One of the greatest books of its kind,
     Moby-Dick links Melville with other masters of the sea story,
     from Defoe to Conrad. Because of the tributes of various
     writers and scholars and an increasing interest in South
     Sea explorations, Melville, long neglected, is again widely
     read at home and abroad.

1915 A BOOKS - NONE

1915 B SHORTER WRITINGS

1   KELLNER, LEON. "The Subjective Writers," in American Literature.
     Translated from the German by Julia Franklin. Garden City,
     N.Y.: Doubleday Page & Co., pp. 81, 116-117.
          Melville and Whitman are among the many who through their
     spiritual kinship belong to the circle of transcendentalists,

1915

though never mentioned in that connection. Typee, Omoo, Mardi, White-Jacket, and Moby-Dick are characterized by a realism which anticipates the Zolas and Goncourts "but surpasses them in verity, inasmuch as every particular was seen and experienced." Moby-Dick has considerable worldly-wise humor. But the influence of Carlyle and the spritualists proved very detrimental to Melville's delineation and style; and behind the most commonplace palpable events, the cosmic soul of things is constantly sought. Melville is almost unknown in Germany.

2 LONDON, CHARMIAN KITTREDGE. The Log of the Snark. New York: The Macmillan Co., passim.
   References to Typee.

3 ANON. "The Author of 'Two Years Before the Mast.'" New York Times (20 October).
   Mention of Melville, "forgotten or neglected in his last years, but since restored to something like his rightful place."

1916 A BOOKS - NONE

1916 B SHORTER WRITINGS

1 ANON. "Melville, Herman," in Encyclopaedia of Biography of New York. Ed. Charles Elliott Fitch. Vol. 3. New York: American Historical Society, p. 13.
   Biographical sketch; no comment on works.

1917 A BOOKS - NONE

1917 B SHORTER WRITINGS

1 LONG, WILLIAM J. Outlines of English and American Literature. New York: Ginn & Co., pp. 399, 500.
   In Melville, "we have an echo of Carlyle...who affected Melville so strongly that the latter soon lost his bluff, hearty, sailor fashion of writing, which everybody liked, and assumed a crotchety style that nobody cared to read."

2 MATTHEWS, BRANDER. These Many Years: Recollections of a New Yorker. New York: Charles Scribner's Sons, p. 221.
   Recalls that once or twice, around 1882, the "shy and elusive" Melville dropped in for an hour or two at the Authors Club.

3   VAN DOREN, CARL. "Contemporaries of Cooper," in The Cambridge
    History of American Literature. Ed. W. P. Trent et al.
    Vol. 1. New York: G. P. Putnam's Sons; Cambridge, England:
    University Press, pp. 320-323.
        Survey. Typee and Omoo are not as truthful as Dana's
    Two Years Before the Mast nor as crisp; Melville must be
    ranked less with Dana than with George Borrow. Typee is
    Melville at all but his best and must be classed with the
    most successful narrations of the exotic life. Omoo lacks
    its freshness and unity. Mardi is one of the strangest,
    maddest books ever composed by an American. Melville had
    shifted his interest from the actual to the abstruse and
    symbolical and never recovered from the dive into metaphysics
    which proved fatal to him as a novelist. Yet the peculiar
    mingling of speculation and experience lends Moby-Dick its
    special power; it is one of the best American romances and
    Melville's best, a work of immense originality, its theme
    the conflict between the forces of nature and man. Moby-
    Dick seems to have exhausted Melville; Pierre is hopelessly
    frantic; Israel Potter, The Piazza Tales, and The Confidence-
    Man are not markedly original; his verses are often jagged
    and harsh. Melville's earlier work should have taught him
    that he was lost without a solid basis in fact. Melville
    was one of American literature's most promising and most
    disappointing figures. Reprinted in part in Norton Moby-
    Dick, p. 626, and Recognition, pp. 153-154.

4   SLOSSON, EDWIN E. "A Number of Things." New York Independent
    (8 January), p. 84.
        The pamphlet on "Chronometricals and Horologicals" in
    Pierre advances a theory of ethics that would naturally
    occur to a sailor, visiting ports with different times and
    different codes of morality. Melville's conclusion in the
    pamphlet is as convenient as it is ingenious: it enables
    one to postpone to Heaven any precepts that prove impracti-
    cable on earth--"Which anyway is what we all do even with-
    out hearing of his justification."

1918 A BOOKS - NONE

1918 B SHORTER WRITINGS

1   CAIRNS, WILLIAM B. "Moby Dick." Encyclopaedia Americana.
        Vol. 19. New York: Americana Corporation, p. 281.
            Moby-Dick is "a strange, conglomerate book." It will
        prove disappointing to the reader impatient of delays and
        digressions but contains few pages not interesting in

1918

themselves. The effect produced by the mixture of erudi-
tion, speculation, poetical rhapsody, and narrative of real
and imagined occurrences is most impressive.

2   CHASE, FREDERIC HATHAWAY. Lemuel Shaw: Chief Justice of the
Supreme Judicial Court of Massachusetts, 1830-1860.
Boston: Houghton Mifflin Co., pp. 46-47, 70.
Relations of Shaw with the Melville family. Melville
was an author of considerable ability and note; his best
known works are Typee, Omoo, White-Jacket, and Moby-Dick.

3   HOWE, WILL D. "Poets of the Civil War I: The North," in The
Cambridge History of American Literature. Ed. William
Peterfield Trent et al. Vol. 2. New York: G. P. Putnam's
Sons; Cambridge, England: University Press, p. 279.
Melville "suffered in his verse as in his minor romances
from a fatal formlessness, but he had moments of contagious
enthusiasm" and "celebrated some of the most striking inci-
dents of the war."

4   QUILLER-COUCH, A. "Of Boys' Books." London Times Literary
Supplement, No. 847 (11 April), pp. 1-2.
The "average boy" reader struck a cache of gold in Typee,
Omoo, and Moby-Dick, loving Melville first for his mere
romance and later for having written, in patches, truly
magnificent prose.

1919 A BOOKS - NONE

1919 B SHORTER WRITINGS

1   BOYNTON, PERCY H. A History of American Literature. Boston:
Ginn and Co., pp. 304-309.
Melville was by nature a satirist, a master of irony,
and a speculative philosopher. The quest in Mardi is
annotated with passages in the mood of Swift and Rabelais
and passages in the manner of Sir Thomas Browne and Carlyle.
Moby-Dick is the story of Eve and of Prometheus, the perennial struggle of man for spiritual freedom in the midst of
an externally physical world--his attempt to make a conquest
of circumstance. It serves as a reminder that the greatest
stories in literature are never the most neatly constructed.
After Moby-Dick, Melville passed completely over from the
concrete material of narrative to the abstractions of metaphysics, depriving American literature of one of its most
brilliant novelists. He wrote some rather bewildering
verse. "The present 'Melville revival' can be accounted

for partly by the present-day vogue of South Sea literature
and partly by the post-war temper of skepticism, but more
because in Melville has been rediscovered one of the immensely energetic and original personalities of the last
hundred years."

2   BRONSON, WALTER C. A Short History of American Literature.
    Revised and Enlarged. Boston: D. C. Heath and Co.,
    pp. 148-149, 460.
       Melville was one of several minor writers resident in
    the city or state of New York. Typee, Moby-Dick, The Piazza
    Tales, Battle-Pieces, and other poems and prose works all
    show much strength and talent.

3   O'BRIEN, FREDERICK. White Shadows in the South Seas. New
    York: The Century Co., pp. 301-302.
       Brief reference: Melville lived many months among the
    Typees and heard no whisper of the havoc wrought by his
    countrymen (led by Captain David Porter in 1812) a little
    time before. The Typees had forgiven and forgotten it.

4   PATTEE, FRED LEWIS. "Herman Melville (1819-91)," in Century
    Readings for a Course in American Literature. New York:
    The Century Co., p. 407.
       Headnote to extracts from Typee (chapter 26) and Moby-
    Dick (chapter 42). Biographical sketch. Moby-Dick is a
    wild mélange of adventure and Gothic romance. As a novel-
    ist Melville was a failure; but he was strong in pictures
    of life on the ocean.

5   LAWRENCE, D. H. "Studies in Classic American Literature (viii):
    The Two Principles." London English Review, 28 (June), 477.
       Brief reference: "After Hawthorne come the books of the
    sea. In Dana and Herman Melville the human relationship is
    no longer the chief interest. The sea enters as the great
    protagonist." Reprinted in Lawrence, p. 175.

6   ANON. "A New Yorker's Centenary." New York Times Book Review
    (20 July), p. 376.
       Survey. Melville's first books are not solely chronicles
    of adventure, but are full of varied information, which
    makes them inimitable as travel books, and rich in excep-
    tionally vigorous character studies; their versimilitude is
    seldom found even in the best of our novels. In a superla-
    tive degree, Melville had the literary instinct and art to
    recognize the possibilities in fact that is stranger than
    fiction. Owing to some odd psychological experience,
    Melville changed from a writer of stirring, vivid fiction

1919

to a dreamer, wrapping himself up in a vague kind of mysticism that made his last few books, such as Pierre and The
Confidence-Man, quite incomprehensible; humor also disappeared. Moby-Dick was the last of his books belonging
to human literature--and even it is pervaded with a misty
sort of supernaturalism.

7   ANON. "Herman Melville." New York Times (27 July), p. 1.
Melville ranks among the famous writers of sea stories
and adventures, with perhaps four books that endure: Typee,
Omoo, Moby-Dick, and White-Jacket; his later books are unread and said to be unreadable. Melville was one of the
most tolerant of men; people of all colors and races are
one to his philosophic eye. Moby-Dick, his most famous
work, is "a rattling good book." Critics may complain
about its digressions, improbabilities, moralizing reflections, swollen talk, and imperfect art, but it has elemental
force and thrilling action.

8   JACKSON, HOLBROOK. "Herman Melville." London Anglo-French
Review, 2 (August), 59-64.
Melville had more energy than art and more thought than
imagination. He was only secondarily creative; his imagination needed the stimulus of experience. Left to invent,
"he moidered into metaphysics" and lost himself and his
readers. Turning experience into fiction, he was sure of a
hearing, though he could never hope to achieve the imaginative heights of the untravelled Defoe. Typee, Omoo, and
Moby-Dick are his three indisputable masterpieces; there
are notable passages in Mardi, Redburn, and White-Jacket,
but they are not numerous enough to rescue them from oblivion. Melville's method in Typee and Omoo is more that of
the old voyaging chroniclers than the modern storyteller;
they resemble Hakluyt's Voyages rather than Stevenson's
Island Nights Entertainment or Louis Becke's By Reef and
Palm. But at their best they are books apart, mingling
fact and fancy, adventures in thought and deed, and speculations in actions and ideas. Moby-Dick tastes and smells of
the sea and its very formlessness makes it more real. It
shows a bigger man and pen of greater strength than Typee
and Omoo, with which Melville is most commonly associated,
and will perhaps endure longer.

9   OWLETT, F. C. "Herman Melville (1819-1891): A Centenary
Tribute." London Bookman, 56 (August), 164-167.
Biographical and critical survey. Melville's great books
are Typee, Omoo, White-Jacket, and Moby-Dick. Mardi, Pierre,
Israel Potter, The Piazza Tales, and The Confidence-Man fail

because in them the transcendentalist and metaphysician too
often triumphed over the artist and poet. Melville and
Borrow both knew how to turn their vagabondizings to good
literary account; both had the poetic vision; both had
humor. But Melville was much more an idealist. Borrow's
robuster humor saved him from perpetrating a Pierre; his
greater matter-of-factness prevented him from writing a
Moby-Dick. Melville's humor is subtler, more intimate, and
permeates his work. His style is spontaneous, buoyant, and
has the richness of seventeenth century prose. Even in his
worst books, Melville never loses his sense of the force
and color of words; the badness of his worst work may be
due to an overdevelopment of this sense. Borrow occasionally achieves greater effects in spite of, or because of,
his terser statement of fact and the simplicity of his
style. But Melville had what Borrow lacked--the imagination that constructs. Reprinted in part in Recognition,
p. 170, and Doubloon, p. 126.

10   ANON. "Today's Centenary of Herman Melville." Boston Herald
     (1 August).
        Biographical; brief comments on works.

11   HALE, PHILIP. "As the World Wags." Boston Herald (1 August).
        Curiously, those now celebrating Melville have nothing
     to say about two of his books that are to be ranked with
     Typee and Moby-Dick: The Piazza Tales and Israel Potter
     alone would give Melville a high position in American and
     English literature. Hale wonders how Melville became im-
     bued with the mysticism that "crops out" even in Moby-Dick
     and what mental transformation led him to "unite" Pierre
     and The Confidence-Man, "which, to say the least, are queer,
     reminding one at times of a transcendentalist's ravings."
     There is no life of Melville, and the biographical sketches
     are inadequate.

*12 ANON. "Sailor Melville Still Read." New York Evening Sun
     (1 August), p. 16.
        Cited in Zimmerman, p. 117, and Ricks and Adams, p. 12.

13   CUDWORTH, WARREN, H. "Herman Melville." New York Times
     (1 August), p. 10.
        Centenary poem.

14   ANON. "An American Romancer: Centenary of Herman Melville,
     Writer of Sea Tales." New York Evening Post (2 August),
     pp. 1, 6.

1919

Stevenson had more literary art than Melville, but of
all the South Sea writers Melville has done the most mem-
orable work. He was not a writer of powerful imagination,
though he showed considerable invention. Yet in Moby-Dick
there is imagination enough: the wild tale has a bizarre,
overstrained quality that defies credulity; but we do not
care whether we can believe it or not. A certain interest
lies in the nightmare intensity of the tale, but interest
is captured far more by the pure exposition of fact. We
remember Melville primarily for scenes and incidents, not
characters; but there is vivid character depiction in his
books. Ahab stands out as his boldest and most original
creation. But the boldness was a little too great: he
impresses us as an utter abnormality. In porportion as we
see the whale typifying natural forces too powerful for
man, Ahab becomes less of a human being and more of a
philosophical abstraction. In style Melville regrettably
yielded at times to the influence of other strongly marked
writers; but his four great books (Typee, Omoo, White-Jacket,
Moby-Dick) have stylistic qualities of decided merit:
liveliness of manner, homely raciness of diction, and great
fertility of illustration. His quiet humor was a great
asset in all his books. A "morbid state of mind," clearly
encroaching on Moby-Dick, was Melville's literary ruin.
Pierre showed an evil French influence.

15   ANON. "Melville and Our Sea Literature." New York Evening
     Post (2 August).
          Melville's literary career was marked by three great
     exploits: he was the first to treat the South Seas as a
     romancer; he was the author of Moby-Dick; and in White-
     Jacket he has given the best picture of a sailor's life on
     a frigate. (Marryat with all his superiority at an imagina-
     tive yarn cannot teach us so much.) Redburn does nothing
     like justice to the merchant marine. Among Melville's
     books Moby-Dick has engaged the warmest affection of his
     readers. Chief among its rare merits, which greatly out-
     weigh its defects, is its unrivalled account of the natural
     history of whales, the business of catching them, cutting
     them up, and salvaging their oil--a marvel of lucidity and
     interest, achieved through a perfect command of subject and
     an enlivening play of fancy and illustration. Melville's
     "sun" rose early and brilliantly and disappeared midway
     under a heavy cloud of mental aberration.

16   WEAVER, RAYMOND. M. "The Centennial of Herman Melville."
     New York Nation, 109 (2 August), 145-146.

1919

Biographical and critical survey. For Melville litera-
tue was an adventure and escape after his return from his
South Sea voyages to the intolerable monotony of relatives
and friends. In <u>Mardi</u> he abandoned himself to the demon of
perversity. <u>Moby-Dick</u> reads like a great opium dream; to
analyze it logically is to be disgusted; to forget logic
and commonsense and abandon oneself to it is to acknowledge
a masterpiece. It contains some of the most finished comedy in the language. Melville's later novels mark a deep-
ening of despair. <u>Pierre</u> is comparable to Meredith's
<u>Egoist</u> in elaborate subtlety and mercilessness of psycho-
logical analysis and a prophetic parody of Hardy's most
poisonous pessimism; it is a book to send a Freudian into
ravishment. The unnecessary degradation of the hero at the
end of <u>Israel Potter</u> is inexcusable in art and probability.
<u>The Piazza Tales</u> gives proof that Melville had not yet
"buried his wand in a grave of metaphysical speculations";
but <u>The Confidence-Man</u> is a very melancholy performance,
not a novel at all. As a poet Melville is not distinguished.
Because of his multiplicity of personality, he eludes summary classification. Essentially he was a mystic, a delver
after hidden things spiritual and material, with the Comic
Spirit always at his elbow. His abiding craving was to
achieve some total and undivined possession of the very
heart of reality. Reprinted in part in Norton <u>Moby-Dick</u>,
pp. 626-627, and <u>Doubloon</u>, pp. 126-127.

17   ANON. "'Moby Dick' and the Years to Come." New York <u>Tribune</u>
     (4 August), p. 8.
        His books may or may not be classics, but however long-
     winded and confused Melville becomes (the strange, turgid
     disease of his later books was always close upon his mind),
     he never fails in his sure, authentic sense of the sea.
     The facts are there as in few other writers, and the whole
     vast sea mystery is in his writings--a real achievement
     which artists of greater technique have not paralleled and
     which promises Melville fame for long to come.

18   MATHER, FRANK JEWETT, JR. "Herman Melville." New York <u>Review</u>,
     1 (9 August), 276-278.
        Biographical and critical survey. Melville had three
     styles: (1) swift lucidity, picturesqueness, and sympathy
     (<u>Typee</u> and <u>Omoo</u>); (2) less colorful, straightforward, manly
     narrative (<u>Redburn</u> and <u>White-Jacket</u>); (3) a reflective,
     mystical, very personal style, probably influenced by
     Carlyle (<u>Mardi</u>, <u>Pierre</u>, and other later books). <u>Moby-Dick</u>,
     Melville's most characteristic and greatest book, is an
     extraordinary blend of 1 and 3, the pictorial and the orphic.

1919

For having saved a vanishing charm for posterity, Typee is
perhaps his most important book. The manly vigor of Omoo
(a book of straggling, picaresque vivacity, unlike the well-
proportioned Typee) recalls Borrow's masterpieces. Paragraphs 2 and 3 of chapter 60 in Redburn are purest Melville
in their combination of precise observation, felicity of
phrase, implications of mystery and immensity, and tinge of
conceitfulness. Melville's avowed program was to doubt
everything yet retain certain saving intuitions, a critical
destruction and reintegration typical of his times, the
Victorian mood. But few of his contemporaries had gone so
far in disillusion; Melville's process of reconstruction
lapsed into occasional strenuous gropings. His later and
forgotten work is not unreadable, but great in human interest. Continued in 1919.B19. Reprinted in part in Recognition, pp. 155-160.

19   MATHER, FRANK JEWETT, JR. "Herman Melville." New York Review,
      1 (16 August), 298-301.
          Continued from 1919.B18. Mardi and Moby-Dick are com-
      panion pieces: Mardi is a celestial adventure, Moby-Dick
      an infernal; Mardi is highly general, Moby-Dick is specific;
      the people of Mardi are all abstractions, those of Moby-Dick
      among the most vivid known to fiction. Mardi has a sane
      Rabelaisianism, wit and a rare pictorial quality; it is
      overwritten and too overtly satiric, but also full of wis-
      dom and fine thinking; Yoomy's songs often foreshadow modern
      free verse. Moby-Dick, Melville's greatest work, is an ex-
      traordinary work in morals and general comment. In the dis-
      cursive tradition of Fielding and Burton, Melville finds a
      suggestion or symbol in every event; the interplay of fact
      and application makes the unique character of the book.
      The effect of Moby-Dick rests on the blend of fact, fancy,
      and profound reflection. After Moby-Dick Melville never
      conceived a good book. (The cause was possibly poor health
      and brooding; possibly the lack of friendly, critical, un-
      derstanding companionship). But Pierre is powerful, if
      repellent and overwrought, and completely anticipates the
      leading motive of The Ordeal of Richard Feverel. Israel
      Potter contains the best account of a sea fight in American
      fiction. The Confidence-Man has numerous tidbits of irony
      and wit amid its somewhat dreary wastes. Battle-Pieces
      has striking anticipations of Kipling's terse, sententious
      method. Clarel has charming lyrics, sharp descriptions,
      humor, irony, and vigorous thinking; it is about the only
      American poetic treatment of Victorian theological concerns.
      John Marr and Timoleon have flashes of the old genius. In
      sheer capacity to feel, most American writers look pale

beside Melville. He combined in an extraordinary degree
impressionistic delicacy and precision, emotional and mental
vigor, and robust humor. Reprinted in <u>Recognition</u>, pp. 160–
169; reprinted in part in <u>Doubloon</u>, pp. 127–130.

20   ANON. "Centenary of Herman Melville, Who Lived in the Jungle
      of Literary Lions." Boston <u>Evening Transcript</u> (27 August),
      part 2, p. 5.
         Account of Melville at Arrowhead, with extracts from
      "The Piazza" and "My Chimney and I" [sic]. Claims that
      Melville wrote "a most appreciative and singularly sympa-
      thetic review" of <u>The Scarlet Letter</u> for the New York
      <u>Literary World</u>. [<u>See</u> discussion in Thorp (1942), pp. 302–
      305.] The friendship of Melville and Hawthorne "was that
      of kindred though diverse intellects; and in faith and
      feeling in which they were not diverse."

21   JOHNSON, ARTHUR. "A Comparison of Manners." New York <u>New
      Republic</u>, 20 (27 August), 113–115.
         "Bartleby" is not far from a short story in the early
      James manner, despite its occasional flatness; "Benito
      Cereno" might be compared with a Conrad tale. The style of
      Melville's sea tales is crystal clear; but Melville also
      wrote in a manner almost uniquely comparable to James's,
      though it falls short in beauty and revelation. Illustra-
      tion with six sentences from <u>Pierre</u> (which D. H. Lawrence
      has not exceeded "for mobid unhealthy pathology"); the
      technique and texture are essentially different from James's,
      but in the convolutions of both writers there is something
      that perhaps "savors of philosophers' painstakingness."

22   ANON. "Another Significant American Centenary." New York
      <u>Current Opinion</u>, 67 (September), 184–185.
         Quotes extensively from 1919.B7. Melville was a pre-
      cursor, by a good 50 years, of such masters of the sea as
      Kipling and Conrad. His realism was as vivid as Zola's or
      the Goncourts'. There are passages in <u>Typee</u> that recall
      some of the charm of W. H. Hudson's South America and de-
      scriptions that seem to antedate and suggest Gauguin and
      his <u>Noa-Noa</u>.

23   CHURCH, JOHN W. "A Vanishing People of the South Seas."
      Washington <u>National Geographic Magazine</u>, 36 (October), 285,
      306.
         Brief mentions. To Mendana, Stevenson, and Melville, the
      remarkable beauty of the Marquesan women was a source of
      surprise and admiration. The valley of Taipi, made famous
      by Melville's beautiful classic of the South Seas, is now
      given over to the silence of the jungle.

1919

24 CRAVEN, H. T. "Tahiti from Melville to Maugham." New York
    Bookman, 50 (November-December), 262-267.
        On literary treatments of Tahiti. Omoo is written
    rather in the manner of a first discoverer, despite refer-
    ences to Ellis. The impression that Melville wrote from
    his own fresh and vigorously individual point of view is
    indelible and one of the reasons the book has lived.
    Melville and Borrow have similarities; the Romany folk
    and the Polynesians, as contrasted with the routine social
    order of Anglo-Saxons, have points in common.

1920 A BOOKS - NONE

1920 B SHORTER WRITINGS

1   ANON. "Melville, Herman," in A Biographical Dictionary of
    Modern Rationalists. Compiled by Joseph McCabe. London:
    Watts & Co., p. 498.
        Brief biographical sketch; no comment on works. Records
    that Melville's rationalism is often noted in Hawthorne's
    diary and letters.

2   ANON. "Melville, Herman," in The New International Encyclopae-
    dia. 2nd ed. Vol. 15. New York: Dodd, Mead and Co.,
    pp. 378-379.
        Same entry as 1903.B2.

3   LEONARD, STERLING ANDRUS. "Introduction" and "Biographical
    Note," in Typee. New York: Harcourt, Brace and Co.,
    pp. v-viii.
        The most satisfactory second visit to the islands after
    a visit there with Melville is provided in Stevenson's The
    South Seas, which confirms all that Melville saw of the
    miserable results brought about by the coming of civiliza-
    tion. The text of Typee is "complete but for some minor
    omissions, chiefly philosophical discussions and diatribes
    against the French and the missionaries. Stevenson has
    treated these subjects more calmly and definitively; here
    they merely delay an excellent narrative."

4   MEYNELL, VIOLA. "Introduction," in Moby-Dick; or The Whale.
    The World's Classics, No. 225. London: Oxford University
    Press, v-viii.
        Melville is one of the greatest of all imaginative
    writers, as much for each page of scientifically accurate
    description in Moby-Dick as for any other part of it; there
    has never been such imaginative description of fact.

272

Moby-Dick is the high-water mark of Melville's achievement: its narrative and record of fact are superior to those of Typee and Omoo; its invention is superior to that of Mardi and Pierre. One is carried to the comprehensible limits of marvelous imagination. Melville has endowed human nature with writing absolutely unsurpassed; to read it and absorb it is the crown of one's reading life. It is the wildest farthest kind of genius. Melville is the master of all other sea writers. Barrie confessedly owes Captain Hook to him.

5   MEYNELL, VIOLA. "Herman Melville." London Dublin Review, 166 (January-March), 96-105.
      Moby-Dick is a work of wonderful and wild imagination, though it tells of the whale and its capture with detailed scientific accuracy. Melville has the quality, rare even in genius, "of wildness, imagination escaping out of bounds." His greatness is unsurpassed; even Conrad must own him as master among sea writers. In Moby-Dick trembling revelation awaits the reader. Ahab has a Shakespearean grandeur. The book is generally little known. Reprinted in 1920.B6; reprinted in part in Doubloon, pp. 130-131.

6   MEYNELL, VIOLA. "A Great Story Teller: Herman Melville." Boston Living Age, 304 (20 March), 715-720.
      Reprint of 1920.B5.

7   ANON. "The Best Books of the Sea." New York Yachting, 27 (May), 195.
      Report of the American Library Association's ballot on the best "books of the sea."--"Apparently the present generation has forgotten Melville for otherwise The Cruise of the Cachalot might not stand so high on the list [6th] while Moby Dick is in 24th place." [Stevenson's Treasure Island placed first.]

8   WATSON, E. L. GRANT. "'Moby Dick.'" London Mercury, 3 (December), 180-186.
      Moby-Dick is Melville's greatest and best-known work. Winding through the whole, giving cohesion and intensity, is the story of Melville's own fiercely vivid life-consciousness, the story of the soul's daring and the soul's dread. The reader is left aghast at the courage of one who dares with unflinching perception follow madness into the heart of its innermost ocean. Melville analyzes the stages of his own mentality: the Pequod is representative of his own genius, each character deliberately symbolic of a complete and separate element. The interplay and

1921

struggle between them are "portrayals of the vehement
impulsion and repercussion of a richly-endowed spirit that
draws inevitably, and yet of its own volition, towards the
limit of human sanity." Moby Dick is the symbol or mask
of that outer mystery which forever attracts and finally
overwhelms the imagination; he is the symbol of imaginative
life. Ahab is the incarnation of the active and courageous
madness that lies brooding within the man of genius. The
high quality of Moby-Dick as a piece of psychological synthesis has been neglected because of its richness of material; it "is indeed a book of adventure, but upon the
highest plane of spiritual daring." Reprinted in part in
Doubloon, pp. 134-137.

1921 A BOOKS

1   WEAVER, RAYMOND M. Herman Melville: Mariner and Mystic.
     New York: George H. Doran Co., 399 pp.
        The first book-length biography of Melville, drawing on
     hitherto unpublished material, including Melville's jour-
     nals, letters by Gansevoort Melville, Elizabeth Shaw
     Melville, and Lemuel Shaw, and Eleanor Melville Metcalf's
     recollections of Melville. Focuses mainly on Melville's
     first 33 years, treating his books as factual autobiograph-
     ical records; often derivative in critical comments.
     Melville's career is one of progressive disillusion: dis-
     illusion through early poverty and the coldness of his
     mother, later disillusion with civilization, romantic love,
     marriage, ultimately with idealism and writing itself;
     Hawthorne destroyed Melville's last illusion, his belief
     in the possibility of an all-solacing Utopian friendship.
     Throughout his life Melville was at odds with the stultify-
     ing influences of home, conventional society and conventional
     religion; his "whole history" was "the record of an attempt
     to escape from an inexorable and intolerable world of real-
     ity." His claim to distinction is three-fold: as the lit-
     erary discoverer of the South Seas; as the first, with Dana,
     to show what happens in a ship's forecastle; and as the
     author of Moby-Dick, remarkable for its intensity of imag-
     ination and harmonious synthesis of contradictory qualities.
     Pierre, a high achievement as a work of art, is an apologia
     of Melville's own defeat and despair; any further writing
     "was both an impertinence and an irrelevancy." Melville's
     last 40 years (to which Weaver devotes only one chapter)
     "are a record of a stoical--and sometimes frenzied--distaste
     for life." Billy Budd is not distinguished. Bibliography of
     Melville's works. Indexed. Reviewed in 1921.B28, B29, B30,

B31; 1922.B13, B14, B15, B16, B17, B18, B19, B20, B21, B26, B27, B29, B32, B34, B43; 1925.B21. [See also 1921.B12, B18, and 1922.B24.] Reprinted New York: Pageant Books, Inc., 1961.

1921 B SHORTER WRITINGS

1 DELLENBAUGH, FREDERICK S. "Travellers and Explorers, 1846–1900," in A History of American Literature. Eds. William Peterfield Trent et al. Vol. 3. New York: G. P. Putnam's Sons; Cambridge, England: Cambridge University Press, p. 156.
    Moby-Dick, Typee, and Omoo belong to our American classics.

2 MORISON, SAMUEL ELIOT. The Maritime History of Massachusetts, 1783–1860. Boston: Houghton Mifflin Co., pp. 227, 317, 323, 325–326.
    Brief mentions of, and quotations from, Moby-Dick. In all New England letters there is no genuine sea poetry. Maritime Massachusetts became articulate in Dana's Two Years Before the Mast and in Moby-Dick.

3 O'BRIEN, FREDERICK. Mystic Isles of the South Seas. New York: The Century Co., pp. 19, 76–77.
    Mentions his intense delight for years in Loti, Melville, Becke, and Stoddard. Quotes unhappy Russian resident of Tahiti: "'They have lied always, those writers about Tahiti.... Melville, Loti, Moerenhout, Pallander, your Stevenson...all are meretricious, with their pomp of words and no truth.'"

4 OVERTON, GRANT. The Answerer. New York: Harcourt, Brace and Co., pp. 79–90, 138, 277, 328.
    Imaginary meeting between Whitman and Melville, "a handsome young fellow, bronzed and earringed...heading for Sag Harbor to sign for a whaling cruise." The two discuss Emerson, Hawthorne, Poe, Burns, going to sea, success, and love. Later reference to the sensation caused by Typee.

5 SALT, HENRY S. Seventy Years Among Savages. New York: Thomas Seltzer, Inc.; London: Allen and Unwin, pp. 69, 110, 112.
    Melville's "extraordinary genius, shown in such masterpieces as Typee and The Whale, was so unaccountably ignored or undervalued that his name is still often confused with that of Whyte Melville or of Herman Merivale." Notes that Melville was a great admirer of James Thomson and quotes from his letter to Salt, 12 January 1890, and letter to

1921

James Billson, 22 January 1885, on the subject of Thomson [Letters, pp. 292-293, 277].

6 VAN DOREN, CARL. The American Novel. New York: The Macmillan Co., pp. 68-76; passim.
Reprints Melville section in 1917.B3, with some changes and additions. Melville "much surpassed Simms and Cooper in boldness and energy of speculation and in richness and beauty of style." Typee and Omoo are superior in charm to Redburn and White-Jacket. In Moby-Dick, the Pacific "seems less a fact than a truth, less a truth than an eternal symbol of the universe." The style is mannered but felicitous, pictorial, allusive, and witty. Clarel rivals Mardi in eccentricity.

7 ANON. "The Gossip Shop." New York Bookman, 52 (January), 371.
Announces "an authoritative life of Herman Melville" by Raymond Weaver, soon to be issued, and forthcoming Doran edition of Melville's novels with critical introductions by Weaver.

8 'A WAYFARER.' "A Testimonial for Moby-Dick." London Nation, 28 (22 January), 572.
Having read Moby-Dick, declares that "since letters began there never was such a book, and the mind of man is not constructed so as to produce such another"; puts its author with Rabelais, Swift, Shakespeare, "and other minor and disputable worthies." Reprinted in 1921.B19; Recognition, p. 171; Norton Moby-Dick, p. 628.

9 BIRRELL, AUGUSTINE. "The Great White Whale: A Rhapsody." London Athenaeum, No. 4735 (28 January), pp. 99-100.
Occasioned by publication of 1920.B4. The two striking features of Moby-Dick, "after allowing for the fact that it is a work of genius and therefore sui generis," are "its most amazing eloquence, and its mingling of an ever-present romanticism of style with an almost savage reality of narrative." Reprinted in 1921.B10; 1923.B1; Doubloon, pp. 137-140.

10 BIRRELL, AUGUSTINE. "The Immortal White Whale." Boston Living Age, 308 (12 March), 659-661.
Reprint of 1921.B9.

11 LOVETT, ROBERT MORSS. "The South Sea Style." New York Asia, 21 (April), 316-320, 366-368.
The interest of Melville's tales consists chiefly in his own adventures and those of his companions, but his pictures

of sea and mountains and native life have never been surpassed. The South Sea style is exotic, extravagant, hyper-
bolic; seeks to render the impossible. Melville originated
it, and Stoddard extended its resources. Stevenson,
La Farge, Grimshaw, and O'Brien succumbed to it. Notes
recurring themes in South Sea literature.

12 F., J. "What's What Among the Spring Books." New York Bookman,
53 (April), 155.
Notice of 1921.A1. Likes Weaver's clarity of style and
knows "there must be much that is thrilling in the doings
of that old chronicler of the South Seas for one who has
had access to much hitherto unpublished material."

13 HUDSON, HOYT H. "The Mystery of Herman Melville." New York
Freeman, 3 (27 April), 156-157.
Occasioned by publication of 1920.B3 and 1920.B4.
Melville has been neglected by critics and literary histo-
rians; little of his work has been reprinted in anthologies;
his stories and sketches remain uncollected; the larger part
of his work has never had a second printing; "Bartleby,"
with its Dickensian characters, is unread. Melville is
sometimes wild, sometimes crude and ranting, but he is also
great--though unfitted to be a philosophical thinker. His
defection as a writer after his first books was the result
of his coming to the philosophers a little late in life,
with little preparation and without humility. He gave up
the struggle for literary greatness to seek for abstract
truth. The sinister results of his thinking haunted him
and unfitted him for literary work. Melville needs a biographer and interpreter; the biographer cannot miss the
light shed from his four books of verse.

14 SWINNERTON, FRANK. "The Londoner." New York Bookman, 53
(May), 239.
Notes current London Melville vogue, following publication
of 1920.B4. Moby-Dick has been formally "found" and placed
as one of the masterpieces of all time. It can never again
be wholly forgotten, but may soon be half forgotten. It is
too fervid to be everybody's book. Hard to believe that
Melville's discoverers have done more than scratch the surface of Moby-Dick or that their enthusiasm will last.
Melville's later books are unreadable. Reprinted in
1928.B19; reprinted in part in Doubloon, pp. 140-141.

15 T[OMLINSON], H. M. "The World of Books." London Nation and
Athenaeum, 29 (4 June), 363.

277

1921

Chides Americans for neglecting Melville; calls for an American to produce a monograph on him. We need to know more about Melville, to understand how he could write Moby-Dick, one of the world's great works of art, having previously produced two merely lively and observant books of travel and White-Jacket, which does not call for any special attention. Reprinted in Doubloon, pp. 142-143.

16 BILLSON, JAMES. "Letters to the Editor. The Works of Herman Melville." London Nation and Athenaeum, 29 (11 June), 396-397.
Billson claims that he is perhaps the only man in England possessing all of Melville's "printed works." [His list of Melville's books excludes Timoleon.] Gives details of his correspondence with Melville. Surprised at neglect of Mardi, which develops into a curious, gigantic allegory, tremendously enlivened with humor and philosophy. No other author, except perhaps Jean Paul Richter, so thoroughly compels belief in his large-heartedness and has such a power of compelling affection.

17 SADLEIR, MICHAEL. "Letters to the Editor. The Works of Herman Melville." London Nation and Athenaeum, 29 (11 June), 396.
Objects to H. M. T.'s "bibliography" [1921.B15]; wishes to add a word in praise of "Benito Cereno," Pierre, The Confidence-Man, and even Redburn.

18 PAGE, FREDERICK. "Letters to the Editor. The Works of Herman Melville." London Nation and Athenaeum, 29 (18 June), 433.
Draws attention to forthcoming publication of 1921.A1, in reply to H. M. T.'s request for a monograph on Melville [1921.B15].

19 HALE, PHILIP. "As the World Wags." Boston Herald (22 June).
Reprints 1921.B8. The judicious Melville collector, already having Moby-Dick, would choose Typee, Omoo, White-Jacket, Israel Potter, The Piazza Tales, and probably Mardi; he would not be in a hurry to secure Redburn, The Confidence-Man, Pierre, or the volumes of verse. The sketches of the ship's captain and the surgeon in White-Jacket surpass the pages about the naval surgeon in Roderick Random. "The Bell-Tower" is the best known of The Piazza Tales, but "Bartleby" and "Benito Cereno" are even more worthy of attention.

20 ANON. "A Neglected American Classic." New York Literary Digest, 70 (16 July), 26.

Melville has come back "on the tidal wave raised by the
South Sea books of Frederick O'Brien, the art furor over
Gauguin, and all the smaller writers and painters who hurry
to adopt a new fashion." Quotes most of 1921.B15.

21   LAWRENCE, D. H. "Whitman." London Nation and Athenaeum, 29
      (23 July), 616-618.
          Notes Melville's "terrific cruise into universality."
      Dana and Melville set out "to conquer the last vast element,
      with the spirit." Melville, like all American authors, is
      guilty of a "provoking of mental reactions in the physical
      self, passions exploited by the mind." Reprinted in
      Lawrence, pp. 254-264.

22   BILLSON, JAMES. "Some Melville Letters." London Nation and
      Athenaeum, 29 (13 August), 712-713.
          Prints eight letters Melville wrote to Billson between
      10 October 1884 and 31 December 1888. [Letters, pp. 275-283;
      287-289.]

23   ANON. "The Mystery of Herman Melville." New York Current
      Opinion, 71 (October), 502-503.
          Quotes at length from 1921.B13 and 1921.B15. 1921.A1
      may help to clear up the mystery of Melville; English read-
      ers are eagerly awaiting its publication. The long enthusi-
      asm for Melville in England is leading to a revival of
      interest in one of the glories of American literature.

24   [BROOKS, VAN WYCK]. "A Reviewer's Notebook." New York
      Freeman, 4 (26 October), 166-167.
          Notes forthcoming biography of Melville [1921.A1], who
      has been justly appreciated only in England. Melville
      rises to his real height in Moby-Dick, but there are strange
      lapses that show the insecure control of the artistic ele-
      ment over the various parts of his mind. He was unable to
      keep his eye on his subject and was devoid of the sentiment
      of form; powerful in a phrase, a paragraph, an episode,
      wanders, in a large composition, like a garrulous old man.
      This weakness was his ultimate undoing as a writer. In
      Moby-Dick he forgets his story and loses himself in the
      details of cetology. But Melville was an American Borrow
      and one yields to the delight of the anomalous. Melville
      resembles Whitman in his mystical democratism and recalls
      Sartor Resartus in his soliloquizing; but one has to go
      back to The Anatomy of Melancholy and Religio Medici for
      the style and method of Moby-Dick. Ahab is a truly
      Shakespearean figure. Predicts Melville boom for the next
      six months. Reprinted in Doubloon, pp. 144-147.

1921

25   TOMLINSON, H. M. "A Clue to Moby Dick." New York <u>Literary</u>
     <u>Review</u>, 2 (5 November), 141-142.
        Survey. <u>Typee</u> and <u>Omoo</u> are not great literature, but
     <u>Moby-Dick</u> belongs in the small company of big, extravagant,
     generative books that have made other writers fertile in
     all ages: <u>Gargantua and Pantagruel</u>, <u>Don Quixote</u>, <u>Gulliver's</u>
     <u>Travels</u>, <u>Tristram Shandy</u>, and <u>Pickwick Papers</u>. <u>Moby-Dick</u>
     is as important a creative effort as America has made. If
     we could discover what happened to the author of the pedes-
     trian <u>White-Jacket</u> when he began <u>Moby-Dick</u>, we might go far
     towards learning the qualities of mind and character and
     the circumstances which produce great literature. Except
     for <u>Typee</u> and <u>Omoo</u>, the other books would be forgotten if
     the author of <u>Moby-Dick</u> had not written them. Melville
     lacked confidence in himself as a writer and became an un-
     conscious mimic of other artists he admired. <u>The Piazza</u>
     <u>Tales</u> come nearest to the Melville of <u>Moby-Dick</u>; the first-
     rate material of "Benito Cereno" is crudely handled, but
     the authentic Melville is found in "The Encantadas." Re-
     printed in part in 1926.B13 and <u>Doubloon</u>, p. 148.

26   TOMLINSON, H. M. "The Greatest Story of the Sea. The 'Moby
     Dick' Mystery." London <u>Review of Reviews</u>, 64 (December),
     432-436.
        Reprint of 1921.B25.

27   WEAVER, RAYMOND M. "Herman Melville." New York <u>Bookman</u>, 54
     (December), 318-326.
        Most of chapter 1 of 1921.A1.

28   EDGETT, EDWIN FRANCIS. "Herman Melville the Mariner-Author."
     Boston <u>Evening Transcript</u> (14 December), part 3, p. 4.
        Review of 1921.A1.--Discursive, with no apparent sense
     of the value of coherence in a biographical narrative; it
     is unfortunate that so little is told of Melville's last
     years. Recent writings about Melville have brought him
     before a wider public. Once for the few, he is now for the
     many. He is now the victim of extravagant praise.

29   [BROOKS, VAN WYCK]. "A Reviewer's Notebook." New York <u>Freeman</u>,
     4 (21 December), 358-359.
        Review of 1921.A1. America has never produced a more
     subjective mind than Melville's. The subject matter of his
     books is less important than the mind they reveal. Weaver
     does not see this; his biography is another "South Sea book,"
     presenting the romantic aspects of Melville. The eclipse
     of Melville's talent was perhaps not as complete as supposed;
     the later Melville, including the poetry, deserves to be
     examined.

30   MATTHEWS, BRANDER. "Tellers of Sea Tales." New York <u>Times</u>
     <u>Book Review</u> (25 December), p. 5.
         Review of Everyman reprints of <u>Typee</u>, <u>Omoo</u>, and <u>Moby-</u>
     <u>Dick</u>--which are judiciously introduced [<u>see</u> 1907.B7, 1907.B8,
     and 1908.B3]--and 1921.A1. Weaver is in the main successful;
     he would have done well to apply to the Hawthorne family for
     material and could have told his tale a little more directly;
     he is overemphatic in laudation. Melville "was not a clear,
     cool, consummate artist in story-telling, as Poe was; yet
     he was a born story-teller--affluent, varied and persuasive.
     He never achieved the artistic reserve and the architectonic
     harmony which Hawthorne attained in 'The Scarlet Letter';
     yet he had a faculty of observation and a creative force
     which almost, if not quite, lifted him to the level of
     Hawthorne. There is in Melville a volcanic fire as powerful
     in its way as the glacier-like movement of Hawthorne." His
     position among the giants is at last assured. <u>Moby-Dick</u> is
     first among Melville's books; the rest are nowhere. Neither
     Melville nor Conrad surpass Cooper in power of description,
     vigor, or variety. Remembers seeing Melville at the New
     York Authors Club, probably in 1883 or 1884; Melville was
     not known to the younger men.

31   VAN VECHTEN, CARL. "A Belated Biography." New York <u>Literary</u>
     <u>Review</u>, 2 (31 December), 316.
         Review of 1921.A1. Written with warmth, subtlety, and
     humor; but at times Weaver's treatment of his material seems
     arbitrary. He does not produce sufficient evidence for his
     claim that Mr. and Mrs. Glendinning are portraits of
     Melville's own father and mother. He seems to have missed
     the relation of <u>Israel Potter</u> to Melville's loss of fame,
     omits all mention of "Bartleby," and does not notice that
     <u>The Confidence-Man</u> is a sort of burlesque of Brook Farm.
     <u>The Confidence Man's</u> version of Transcendentalism and cari-
     cature of Emerson has escaped every other critic. <u>Mardi</u>,
     <u>Moby-Dick</u>, and <u>Pierre</u> form a kind of tragic trinity: <u>Mardi</u>
     is a tragedy of the intellect, <u>Moby-Dick</u> a tragedy of the
     spirit, and <u>Pierre</u> a tragedy of the flesh; <u>Mardi</u> a tragedy
     of heaven, <u>Moby-Dick</u> a tragedy of hell, and <u>Pierre</u> a tragedy
     of the world we live in. <u>Moby-Dick</u> far surpasses every
     American work from <u>The Scarlet Letter</u> to <u>The Golden Bowl</u> and
     stands with the great classics of all time--the Greek trag-
     edies, <u>Don Quixote</u>, the <u>Inferno</u>, and <u>Hamlet</u>.

<u>1922 A BOOKS</u>

1   MINNIGERODE, MEADE. <u>Some Personal Letters of Herman Melville</u>
    <u>and a Bibliography</u>. New York: The Brick Row Book Shop, Inc.,
    195 pp.

1922

       Part I: Extracts from letters written by Melville be-
tween 1846 and 1862, interspersed with biographical details
and frequent quotation from the novels and stories; three
letters from Elizabeth Melville to Evert Duyckinck (June
1860), concerning the proposed publication of a book of
Melville's verse. Letters are said to reveal an "utterly
different" Melville: "a lover of company, and of the good
things of life; a gay, ironical fellow, aiming his witty
shafts at the gods; a turbulent <u>enfant terrible</u> at times,
with his impudent personal pen, and yet a sensitive soul,
recoiling from criticism and abuse; a hot-headed proclaimer
of truth; a vivid, warm-hearted, gentle, friendly, impulsive
personality; and for several years a patient sufferer from
a great infirmity."
       Part II: Bibliography. While making "no claims to com-
pleteness," the bibliography attempts "a description of all
Melville first editions, both American and English, together
with a brief historical note, and also as full a list as
possible of subsequent reprintings." Lists differences
between revised edition of <u>Typee</u> (1846) and first edition.
Part of section on <u>Redburn</u> devoted to <u>Redburn or the School-
master of a Morning</u>, attributed to Melville by a cataloguer
for the New York Public Library. Quotes extracts from contemporary reviews. Reprints list of Melville's lecture
dates and fees from 1921.A1. Lists Melville's magazine
contributions. Reprinted in Select Bibliographies Reprint
Series. Fremont, New York: Books for Libraries Press, 1969.
Reviewed in 1923.B11, B16, B25, B26, B31.

1922 B SHORTER WRITINGS

1   CANBY, HENRY SEIDEL. "Conrad and Melville," in <u>Definitions:
    Essays in Contemporary Criticism</u> by Henry Seidel Canby.
    New York: Harcourt Brace and Co., pp. 257-268.
       Reprint of 1922.B23.

2   CHAPIN, HENRY. "Introductory Note," in <u>The Apple-Tree Table
    and Other Sketches</u>. Princeton, N.J.: Princeton University
    Press; London: Oxford University Press, Humphry Milford,
    p. 5.
       The previously uncollected sketches "cover a variety of
    homely subjects treated by Melville with a fresh humor,
    richly phrased and curiously personal." The volume responds
    to a growing demand for accessible reprints of Melville's
    works. Reviewed in 1923.B11, B12, B16, B17, B19, B31.

3   CHAPIN, HENRY. "Introductory Note," in <u>John Marr and Other
    Poems</u>. Ed. Henry Chapin. Princeton, N.J.: Princeton

University Press; London: Oxford University Press, Humphry
Milford, n.p.
   Melville's verse as a whole, is amateurish and uneven,
but his lovable freshness of personality is everywhere in
evidence. Through the mask of conventional verse, which
often falls into doggerel, the voice of a true poet is
heard. Reviewed in 1923.B11, B12, B16, B17, B19, B31.

4   HANDY, WILLOWDEAN CHATTERSON. Tattooing in the Marquesas.
      Honolulu: Bernice P. Bishop Museum [Bulletin 1], passim.
      Typee quoted on tattooing practices in the Marquesas.

5   HIND, C. LEWIS. "Herman Melville," in More Authors and I.
      New York: Dodd, Mead and Co.; London: John Lane,
      pp. 223-228.
         Enthusiastic account of recent first reading of Moby-
      Dick and Typee. Melville's eloquence is extraordinary:
      "he seems to have no desire but rapturously to express him-
      self, and to scatter his knowledge of everything that per-
      tains to the subjects engrossing him." His characters,
      "touched in with insight," are not the clear-cut individ-
      uals of our great novels; they sprawl; they come and go.
      These books have little in them of the "construction"
      learned from the French.

6   KELLER, HELEN REX. The Reader's Digest of Books. New York:
      The Macmillan Co., pp. 572-573, 866-867.
         Synopses of Moby-Dick, Typee, and Omoo, with brief crit-
      ical comment. Moby-Dick is of increasing value in litera-
      ture because it is a comprehensive handbook of the whaling
      industry at a time when individual courage and skill were
      prime factors. Typee is the forerunner of all South Sea
      romances, the most charming of all, and the source of many
      new words in our vocabulary, like taboo.

7   PHILLPOTTS, EDEN. The Red Redmaynes. New York: The Macmillan
      Co., pp. 127, 170-171, 230.
         The character Bendigo Redmayne's only book is an "ancient
      and well-thumbed" copy of Moby-Dick. Melville's "master-
      piece had long ago become for the old sailor the one piece
      of literature in the world. It comprised all that inter-
      ested him most in this life, and all that he needed to
      reconcile him to the approach of death and the thought of
      a future existence beyond the grave. 'Moby Dick' also
      afforded him that ceaseless companionship with great waters
      which was essential to content."

1922

8   RICHARDSON, WILLIAM L. and JESSE M. OWEN. <u>Literature of the World: An Introductory Study</u>. Boston: Ginn & Co., p. 484.
      In <u>Typee</u>, <u>Omoo</u>, and <u>Moby-Dick</u>, Melville has given expression to the spirit of the sea with masterly effectiveness. His real excellence has only recently begun to be properly appreciated.

9   SADLEIR, MICHAEL. "Herman Melville," in <u>Excursions in Victorian Bibliography</u>. London: Chaundy & Cox, pp. pp. 217-234.
      Bibliography of Melville first editions, with four-page introductory essay. If Melville belongs to any race or genealogy, he "is of the ageless, raceless family of the lonely giants"; he has "a quality of grandeur, a majesty of isolation" lacked by other writers of this volume [Trollope, Marryat, Disraeli, Wilkie Collins, Charles Reade, Whyte-Melville, and Gaskell], "and his very inchoate bitterness of spirit transcends by its datelessness their well-rounded friendliness and their complacent wit." But all except Whyte-Melville and perhaps Disraeli excell him in technique; Trollope excels him in humor, wisdom and depth of understanding. Melville's genius is more perfectly and skillfully revealed in <u>The Piazza Tales</u> than in <u>Moby-Dick</u>, which suffers from intolerable prolixity; in <u>The Piazza Tales</u> Melville improved in technical control.

10   SQUIRE, J. C. <u>Books Reviewed</u>. New York: George H. Doran Co., pp. 214-222.
      Biographical survey; appreciation of <u>Moby-Dick</u>. Impossible to describe Melville as anything but a pessimist, who habitually faced the harshest facts in the universe. <u>Moby-Dick</u> is an allegory of despair. Ahab is the innermost ego; the mates are the recurrent moods he must keep company with; the chase is the chase of life. Despairing and horrific, the book's darkest passages nonetheless exhilarate the reader; and the glory as well as the awfulness of life is celebrated; the book's moods are varied. In Melville there was a Conrad, a Stevenson, a Dickens, and a Defoe. The language of <u>Moby-Dick</u> is at best unsurpassed, though it lapses sometimes into excesses of rhetoric. Melville was a born poet; imagery pours out of him. There is no greater work of prose fiction in English than <u>Moby-Dick</u>.

11   STRACHEY, JOHN ST. LOE. <u>The Adventure of Living: A Subjective Autobiography (1860-1922)</u>. New York and London: G. P. Putnam's Sons, p. 213.
      Recalls discussing <u>Moby-Dick</u> with Frank T. Bullen and notes that "of late certain American and English writers

have become quite mystical" about the book, "or, as the
Elizabethans would have put it, 'fond.'"

12 VAN VECHTEN, CARL. "The Later Work of Herman Melville."
    New Orleans Double Dealer, 3 (January), 9-20.
        Typee, Omoo, Redburn, and White-Jacket sparkle with a
    sophisticated and cosmopolitan humor; but it is highly
    probable that some future readers will prefer the later
    Melville, the metaphysical and more self-revealing works,
    just as some prefer the later James. Mardi belongs with
    the later works, is sophisticated and full of fine humor.
    James Joyce or D. H. Lawrence might have conceived Pierre,
    with certain personal alterations; the subject would have
    delighted Henry James. A Freudian literature will grow up
    around the book, "the peripeteia of which occurs in a
    dream." The last chapter of Israel Potter symbolizes
    Melville's return to the field of literature, searching
    vainly for his fame. In The Confidence-Man Emerson is the
    confidence man; his essay on friendship is required prepar-
    atory reading for the book. Readers of Israel Potter and
    The Confidence-Man will get a clearer picture of
    Melville's bitterness and unhappy striving. Melville is
    the greatest writer America has yet produced, Moby-Dick
    one of the most significant achievements in the record of
    modern letters. Reprinted in 1926.B14; reprinted in part
    in Doubloon, pp. 148-149.

13 SABER, GAI. "New Books and the Seven Arts." New York Arts
    and Decoration, 16 (January), 205, 255.
        Review of 1921.A1--which possesses the great merit of
    thorough documentation and adequate preparation. Weaver
    was perhaps right to tell more about the mariner than the
    mystic. It should be profitable work for someone to un-
    ravel the mysteries of Melville's later books, such as
    Pierre.

14 ANON. "Rediscovering the Genius of Herman Melville." New
    York Current Opinion, 72 (January), 101-103.
        Review of 1921.A1. Mainly synopsis. Weaver brings out,
    above all, the tragedy of Melville's career.

15 HUDSON, HOYT H. "God's Plenty About Melville." New York
    Nation, 114 (4 January), 20.
        Review of 1921.A1. Weaver has ample materials; would
    have benefited from more time spent in assimilation. The
    extracts from Melville's work are particularly valuable.
    Melville can no longer be conveniently coupled with Dana,
    but is being ranked now with Poe, Hawthorne, Whitman, Twain,

1922

even with Rabelais, Swift and Cervantes. Long overdue,
a biography would never have been so timely as now.

16   MACY, JOHN. "Leviathan." New York <u>New Republic</u>, 29
        (11 January), 185.
            Review of 1921.A1--"a higgledy-piggledy of sound informa-
        tion and miscellaneous pedantry"; "hard navigating." Doubt-
        ful if Melville will ever be known to a large body of
        readers for he was not a storyteller; he did not know how,
        or perhaps care how, to make a tale for the tale's sake.
        He will remain a writer's writer, cherished by those who
        can enjoy amazing pages without much concern about the
        sequence of the pages or about how anything "comes out."

17   MORRIS, LLOYD R. "The Life of Herman Melville." New York
        <u>Outlook</u>, 130 (25 January), 149-150.
            Review of 1921.A1.--A "brilliant and vividly written
        biography," making "a substantial contribution to our
        knowledge of one of the most significant artists, and
        surely one of the most interesting figures, in American
        literature."

18   HALE, PHILIP. "The Atlantic's Bookshelf." Boston <u>Atlantic
        Monthly</u>, 129 (February), 6, 8.
            Review of 1921.A1. Engrossing and irritating; questions
        that have long been asked about Melville are not satisfac-
        torily answered. Better if fewer quotations from the books
        and more from the journals and letters.

19   ANON. "General Literature." Chicago <u>Booklist</u>, 18 (February),
        152.
            Review of 1921.A1. Weaver has succeeded in drawing a
        graphic picture, interesting and alive, of an old time
        American author.

20   ANON. "Biography and Memoirs." New York <u>American Review of
        Reviews</u>, 65 (February), 223.
            Review of 1921.A1; gives a full and authentic account
        of Melville's life and experiences.

21   ANON. "New Books." New York <u>Catholic World</u>, 114 (February),
        686-687.
            Review of 1921.A1. Admirers of Melville will be woe-
        fully disappointed. The biography is padded with long
        digressions and full of sophomoric finalisms that prove
        Weaver's inability to measure the character of his subject;
        Melville has found a biographer in perfect sympathy with
        his worst moods. Weaver does not fully understand the

allegory of <u>Moby-Dick</u>: the white whale is the heart of
humanity; he who turns on it in disdainful hate will be
destroyed by it.

22 ANON. "The Men That Found the South Seas." New York <u>Mentor</u>,
10 (1 February), 18-19.
Biographical; Melville in the South Seas.

23 CANBY, HENRY SEIDEL. "Conrad and Melville." New York
<u>Literary Review</u>, 2 (4 February), 393-394.
Melville writes at the beginning of the age of science;
he sees nature as greater and more terrible than man; sees
the will of man trying to control the universe but failing.
Conrad comes at the height of the age of science; he broods
over man in a world where nature has been conquered, but
the mind remains inexplicable. Melville is a moral philosopher, reasoning of God and nature; Conrad is a speculative
psychologist. Melville was a wilder soul, a greater man,
probably a greater artist, but a lesser craftsman. Both
authors write not so much of the seas they sailed as what
they dream when they remember their experiences. Reprinted
in 1922.B1 and 1924.B4.

24 HAWTHORNE, HILDEGARDE. "Hawthorne and Melville." [Letter to
the Editor.] New York <u>Literary Review</u>, 2 (4 February), 406.
Defense of Nathaniel Hawthorne and Sophia Hawthorne, in
reply to 1921.A1.

25 FAIRFAX, LEE. "Revival of 'Moby Dick.'" [Letter to the
Editor.] New York <u>Evening Post</u> (9 February).
Article by Christopher Morley in the <u>Evening Post</u> some
18 months previously [unlocated] deserves much of the credit
for the revival of interest in Melville. At the time of
Fairfax's apprenticeship at sea, <u>Moby-Dick</u> "was read as a
part of the curriculum of every marine school and training
ship in this country"; according to hearsay, "every appren-
tice aboard British ships was compelled or expected to
read it." [Fairfax "left the sea thirty-two years ago."]
Now younger seamen are reading it again.

26 R., J. C. "Reviews." New York <u>America</u>, 26 (18 February), 427.
Review of 1921.A1. The centenary salvaged Melville's
memory from oblivion three years ago. Weaver has at last
given Melville his rightfully won position in the history
of American letters and invested his biography with rare
charm. His documentation is authentic, and if not over-
abundant, at least sufficient for the understanding of the
man Melville and his work.

1922

27   McFEE, WILLIAM. "Blubber and Mysticism." New York <u>Bookman</u>,
      55 (March), 69–70.
          Review of 1921.A1.––A very complete biography and critical
      estimate; everything anyone can conceivably desire to know
      of Melville. It was Melville's misfortune "to imagine that
      he was unkindly used by fate, when he was only encountering
      the usual and inevitable agonies of the artist when his own
      personality is the raw material of his art."

28   COLUM, PADRAIC. "Moby Dick as an Epic: A Note." New York
      <u>Measure</u>, 2 (March), 16–18.
          In <u>Moby-Dick</u> Melville proposes the theme for an epic
      rather than a novel and so uses a rhythmic prose that at
      times resembles the language of MacPherson's <u>Ossian</u> and at
      times becomes blank verse, or free verse, or polyphonic
      prose. Examples. Reprinted in Colum, pp. 175–179.

29   ANON. "Herman Melville." London <u>Times Literary Supplement</u>,
      No. 1051 (9 March), p. 151.
          Review of 1921.A1. Melville "was more than a descriptive
      writer of the first rank, for he looked into the heart of
      things, albeit with a vision warped by bitterness and
      pessimism." But in the ordinary sense he was not a mystic.

30   LUCAS, F. L. "Herman Melville." London <u>New Statesman</u>, 18
      (1 April), 730–731.
          Mainly biographical. Finds in both Melville's life and
      style the same spacious Elizabethan carelessness. <u>Moby-
      Dick</u> is an epic of the sea and of human life, sublime in
      the sense of Longinus; it has a digressive unity to have
      delighted Aristotle, a gift of characterization more strong
      than subtle, but strangely real; the handling of the super-
      natural can compare with the "Ancient Mariner" or <u>Macbeth</u>.
      Reprinted in 1926.B7.

31   [BROOKS, VAN WYCK]. "A Reviewer's Notebook." New York <u>Freeman</u>,
      5 (12 April), 118–119.
          Something about the recent flurry of interest in Melville
      seems to bear out the notion that it is impossible to estab-
      lish his position for good and all.

32   HEWLETT, MAURICE. "Biography and Memoirs." <u>London Mercury</u>, 6
      (May), 106.
          Review of 1921.A1. Melville's life is told with great
      pains, a good deal of learning, and some weariness to the
      reader. "Melville, it seems, did everything under a goad.
      His will did not direct him. It emerged to meet the case,
      met it with energy, even with zest; then obscured itself
      again."

33 SALT, HENRY S. "Herman Melville." London Literary Guide,
NS 311 (May), 70.
Occasioned by publication of 1921.A1. Brief comments on
Melville's first six books. The Whale is among the very
greatest books of the nineteenth century. Salt (who first
heard of Melville from Bertram Dobell) brought The Whale
to the notice of William Morris and "a week or two afterwards" heard him "quoting it with huge gusto and delight."

34 STRACHEY, J. ST. LOE. "Herman Melville: Mariner and Mystic."
London Spectator, 128 (6 May), 559-560.
Review of 1921.A1.--Not a great book or even a satisfactory one; it might easily tell us more. Balzac exerted a
strong spiritual influence on Melville; the influence is
shown in the structure of the novels. The portrait of
Jackson and the account of the Liverpool boardinghouse in
Redburn are reminiscent of Balzac. Weaver does not realize
the continuous strong feeling about Melville in England. If
Melville were writing in 1922 he would be one of the world's
greatest sellers. Reprinted in part in Norton Moby-Dick,
pp. 628-629, and Recognition, p. 174.

35 ANON. "Barrie's Magic Island." London Times (27 May), p. 13.
Report of speech by J. M. Barrie to the Critic's Circle
at the Savoy Hotel. "'At present I am residing on an island.
It is called Typee, and so you will not be surprised to hear
that my companion's name is Fyaway. She is a dusky maid,
composed of abstractions but not in the least elusive. She
is just little bits of the golden girls who have acted for
me and saved my plays.'"

36 ANON. "There Melville Wrote and Hawthorne Dreamed." Boston
Evening Globe (7 June), p. 13.
Pittsfield literary associations; biographical details
of Melville.

37 [VAN DOREN, CARL]. "Mocha Dick." New York Nation, 115
(19 July), 60.
Tells story of Mocha Dick, material for Moby-Dick that
"underwent a great alchemy in Melville's imagination."
Reprinted in 1923.B10.

38 COLCORD, LINCOLN. "Notes on 'Moby Dick.'" New York Freeman,
5 (23 August), 559-562.
Moby-Dick gives off the aura of sublime and tragic greatness. Its art lies in the element of purposeful suspense
and in the accumulating grandeur and terror evoked by the
whale-motif. Its high point of inspiration is the dialogue

between Ahab and the carpenter (the equal of Shakespeare's best dialogue); its finest piece of descriptive characterization the sketch of the carpenter; its ablest piece of sustained writing the chapter on "The Whiteness of the Whale." Melville's treatment of the whaling industry is classic; it alone rescues from oblivion one of the most extraordinary episodes of human enterprise. But Moby-Dick has little of real nautical substance; it lacks the final touch of nautical verisimilitude, is full of nautical ineptitudes. Melville was not interested in becoming a true sailor; the psychology of the quarter-deck, of handling a vessel was foreign to him. Moby-Dick moves back and forth between first and third person narrative, and contains other technical irregularities; it is a striking commentary on the rigidity of present literary technique. Continued in 1922.B39. Reprinted in Recognition, pp. 174-182, and Vincent, pp. 32-39.

39   COLCORD, LINCOLN. "Notes on 'Moby Dick.'" New York Freeman, 5 (30 August), 585-587.
        Continued from 1922.B38. Melville's exhaustion is apparent in the latter part of the book. Moby Dick's final attack on the Pequod and its sinking are inadequate to the point of anti-climax. Melville chose to end the book on a note of transcendentalism; he does not seem to have visualized the scene at all. The influence of Hawthorne was probably the main cause of this grave error; Hawthorne's influence is painfully evident throughout the last two-thirds of Moby-Dick--it is incongruous with Melville's natural manner of narrative realism. (Melville's natural power of characterization is in description or analysis.) The book represents a struggle between realism and mysticism, between a natural and an artificial manner; it begins. naturally and ends artificially. But as a piece of pure realism the book would not have been such an inspired achievement. Melville's creative struggle at the time of composition was the intensifying medium through which the work rose to superlative heights; the inner battle caused him to produce what actually are gigantic fragments. Moby-Dick is the story of Melville's struggle with art and life. Reprinted in Recognition, pp. 182-186, and Vincent, pp. 39-43.

40   TURTLE, HERBERT E. "The Literature of Whaling." [Letter to the Editors.] New York Freeman, 6 (20 September), 41.
        Reply to 1922.B38-39. Colcord has apparently never heard of Frank T. Bullen's Cruise of the Cachalot, "which contains the most wonderful descriptions of the

1922

whaling-industry, written, too, by a man who knew ships
and the sea as Melville never did."

41   PEASE, Z. W. "Initial Production of Whaling Film 'Down to
      the Sea in Ships.'" New Bedford Morning Mercury
      (26 September), pp. 8-9.
          Brief mentions of Moby-Dick.

42   ANON. "The Vogue of Herman Melville." London Nation and
      Athenaeum, 31 (30 September), 857-858.
          Notice of Typee and Omoo, first two volumes of Constable
      edition. Recent cheap edition [see 1920.B4] has caused
      Moby-Dick to be generally acknowledged as a masterpiece.
      The book "indeed, appears to have been a wonder treasured
      as a sort of secret for years by some select readers who
      had chanced upon it. They said little about it. We gather
      that they had been in the habit of hinting the book to
      friends they could trust, so that 'Moby Dick' became a
      sort of cunning test by which the genuineness of another
      man's response to literature could be proved. If he was
      not startled by 'Moby Dick,' then his opinion on literature
      was of little account." Some of Melville's novels and
      narratives are pedestrian, others are flamboyant and wild,
      "and there are others so congested and tough that it is
      only the drive of one's desire to find a clue to the mind
      of so extraordinary a man which gets one through them."
      Reprinted in Doubloon, pp. 149-151.

43   QUINN, ARTHUR HOBSON. "The Creator of Moby Dick." New Haven
      Yale Review, NS 12 (October), 205-209.
          Review of 1921.A1 (on the whole Weaver has done his work
      admirably), but mainly about Melville. Revival of interest
      in Melville attributed to recent literature on the South
      Seas and the admiration of John Masefield and other British
      critics. Melville lacked the imagination of Hawthorne and
      the sense of formal artistry of Bret Harte. He rose to
      greatness only in Moby-Dick, where the introductory chap-
      ters and tiresome lectures on the structure and classifica-
      tion of whales illustrate his besetting weakness, his lack
      of humor and inability to distinguish fact from fiction.
      The book is so episodic that even the great passion of Ahab
      cannot make it an artistic unit. The chronic disorderliness
      of style is even more irritating. The incompleteness of
      Moby-Dick explains the periodic necessity for Melville's
      revivals. Reprinted in part in Doubloon, p. 151.

44   TOMLINSON, H. M. "An Estimate of Herman Melville's Prose."
      Boston Christian Science Monitor (14 October), p. 8.

1922

> Notice of the first two volumes of the Constable edition
> Hopes it will eventually include Melville's poetry. It
> may not be great poetry--and it would be silly to pretend
> that The Confidence-Man is really fascinating prose--but
> Melville's significance is too great for any of his writ-
> ings to be allowed to remain almost inaccessible. Moby-
> Dick sends one through all his work hoping for a clue to
> his mind. For years Moby-Dick was "a semi-secret wonder"
> to choice readers and a test by which they proved the qual-
> ity of another man's response to literature.

45   ANON. "The Perpetual Appeal of 'Moby Dick.'" Detroit Saturday
     Night (11 November), Review of Children's Books, p. 3.
        Notice of Dodd, Mead edition, illustrated by Mead
     Schaeffer. A great deal of the book should appeal to red-
     blooded boys of 14 years and over.

46   MINNIGERODE, MEADE. "Herman Melville, 1819-1891." New York
     Publishers' Weekly, 102 (18 November), 1866.
        Checklist of American first editions.

1923 A BOOKS - NONE

1923 B SHORTER WRITINGS

1   BIRRELL, AUGUSTINE. "The Immortal White Whale," in Fact,
    Fancy and Opinion. Ed. Robert M. Gay. Boston: Atlantic
    Monthly Press, pp. 47-51.
       Reprint of 1921.B9.

2   HOLT, HENRY. Garrulities of an Octogenarian Editor.
    Boston: Houghton Mifflin Co., p. 189.
       Anecdote. "The recently revived interest in Herman
    Melville may justify my recounting that late one night
    about 1870 he was one of a cheerful group of four who walked
    up Fourth Avenue from the Century Club, which was then in
    Fifteenth Street. I have often recalled that walk with
    peculiar pleasure: for notwithstanding the hermit-like
    character I have since known ascribed to Melville, tho it
    was over fifty years ago, I often recall him as one of the
    very most agreeable men I ever met. I've just read some-
    where some woman's expression, that his glance seemed to
    absorb one into himself."

3   LAWRENCE, D. H. "Herman Melville's Moby Dick," in Studies in
    Classic American Literature. New York: Thomas Seltzer,
    pp. 214-240.

Melville was a deep, great artist, even if he was a
sententious man, a solemn ass even in humor, hopelessly
au grand sérieux. Melville hardly reacts to human con-
tacts, or only ideally; he is abstract, self-analytical,
abstracted, more spellbound, like Dana, by "the strange
slidings and collidings of Matter" than by the things men
do. With physical, vibrational sensitiveness he registers
the effects of the outer world and records the extreme
transitions of the isolated, far-driven soul, the soul
which is alone, without any real human contact. The mad
ship, under a mad captain, in a mad fanatic's hunt--the
whole thing eminently practical--is American industry.
Moby Dick is the deepest blood-being of the white race, our
deepest blood-nature, hunted by the maniacal fanaticism of
our white mental consciousness, a ghastly maniacal hunt
which is our doom and suicide. Melville is a master of
violent, chaotic physical motion--and is as perfect at
creating stillness. The accounts of whale-hunts, killing,
and cutting up are magnificent records of "actual happening."
Moby-Dick is one of the strangest and most wonderful books
in the world, a book of exoteric symbolism of profound significance, and of considerable tiresomeness. Reprinted in
part in Vincent, pp. 44-50.

4 LAWRENCE, D. H. "Herman Melville's 'Typee' and 'Omoo,'" in
    Studies in Classic American Literature. New York: Thomas
    Seltzer, pp. 193-213.
    Melville is the greatest seer and poet of the sea: his
vision is more real than Swinburne's, because he doesn't
personify the sea, and far sounder than Joseph Conrad's
because he doesn't sentimentalize the ocean and the sea's
unfortunates. Melville cannot accept humanity, cannot
belong to it; no man "instinctly" hated human life more;
no man was so passionately filled with the sense of the
vastness and mystery of life which is non-human. Melville
at his best invariably wrote from a sort of dream-self, so
that events he relates as actual fact have a far deeper
reference to his own soul, his own inner life. His emergence
into the green Eden of the cannibals in Typee is an unconscious re-birth myth. But he could not be happy in his
Paradise: a white man cannot go back to savage life; the
South Sea islander is "uncreate," centuries behind in the
consciousness struggle, the struggle of the soul into fullness. Melville did not really want Eden--but wanted to
fight, like every American, with weapons of the spirit.
He is at his best, his happiest, perhaps in Omoo: for once
he is really reckless, taking life as it comes, though he

would never abandon himself, like Dr. Long Ghost, to despair
or indifference--he always cared. Melville refused life,
but to the end he pined for a perfect relationship--a
vicious, unmanly craving. Reprinted in Chase, pp. 11-20;
reprinted in part in Rountree, p. 39.

5 LINDSAY, VACHEL. "So Much the Worse for Boston," in Going-To-
The-Sun. New York: D. Appleton and Co., p. 60.
  Mention: "'Higher than the Back Bay whales, that spout
and leap, and bite their friends,/Higher than those Moby-
Dicks, the Boston Lover's trail ascends.'"

6 MORLEY, CHRISTOPHER. "Iota Subscript," in Parson's Pleasure.
New York: George H. Doran Co., p. 40.
  Reference to "the sand/Of our old Moby-Dick-shaped land,/
Our sea-rubbed Paumanok."

7 O'BRIEN, EDWARD J. The Advance of the American Short Story.
New York: Dodd, Mead and Co., pp. 58, 62-63, 86.
  Melville ranks with Hawthorne and Whitman, if indeed he
is not the greatest writer America has yet produced; he is
one of the greatest visionary artists the world has had
since William Blake. Hawthorne "established a kind of
harmony between himself and the sterile complacency of
New England at the expense of foregoing the richer experiences" which made Melville the greater, though less popular,
writer. The epic story of Moby Dick symbolizes the adventure of Poe and every sincere American artist during the
past century.

8 PATTEE, FRED LEWIS. The Development of the American Short
Story: An Historical Survey. New York and London: Harper
& Brothers, pp. 153-154.
  The Piazza Tales are peculiarly typical of the 1850s,
being literary rather than real, ornamented rather than
natural. Only in "Benito Cereno" is there anything convincing. "Despite its occasional prolixity and its sprawly
ending, it is told with real power, its background is
realistically sketched, and its strangeness and reality
are compelling. It is a prophecy of Jack London two decades
before he was born."

9 SADLEIR, MICHAEL. "Bibliography of the First Editions of the
Prose Works of Herman Melville," in The Works of Herman
Melville Standard Edition. Vol. 12. London: Constable
and Co., pp. 339-358.
  Expanded version of bibliography in 1922.B9.

10   VAN DOREN, CARL. "Mocha Dick," in The Roving Critic. New
       York: Alfred A. Knopf, pp. 97-99.
       Reprint of 1922.B37.

11   ANON. "Unknown Writings of Moby Dick's Biographer." New York
       Times Book Review (21 January), p. 3.
         Review of the Princeton edition of The Apple-Tree Table
       and Other Sketches [1922.B2] and John Marr and Other Poems
       [1922.B3] and Minnigerode [1922.A1]. The essays reveal
       Melville's essentially didactic and introspective nature.
       It becomes plainer that Melville was never really a man
       of action, but a dreamer, always noting the manifestations
       of the spirit, even in times of stress and hardship. Two
       of the sketches stand out especially: "The Apple-Tree
       Table" charms by its whimsical, occasionally broadly humor-
       ous prose, always distinguished in a grave way; "I and My
       Chimney" is more rambling in construction, but perhaps for
       that reason more delectable. Melville's kinship with
       Hawthorne, evident in the prose pieces, seems more a resem-
       blance of kindred natures than a conscious imitation of
       style. Melville's critical acumen is apparent in "Hawthorne
       and His Mosses" but the essay's quality of generous apprecia-
       tion is of greater importance. Melville is only occasion-
       ally a poet: his uncouthness and roughness in verse cannot
       be excused as ruggedness; but at times the voice of authen-
       tic poetry emerges from the doggerel, as in "Sheridan at
       Cedar Creek." The newly published letters are unimportant
       but interesting and indicative of Melville's nature.

12   EDGETT, EDWIN FRANCIS. "On the Trail of Herman Melville."
       Boston Transcript (27 January).
         Review of the Princeton edition of The Apple-Tree Table
       and Other Sketches [1922.B2] and John Marr and Other Poems
       [1922.B3]. There is little in the two volumes to enhance
       Melville's reputation; they do little more than increase
       the perhaps too rapidly increasing stock of Melvilleana.
       "Hawthorne and His Mosses" is more of a laudatory apprecia-
       tion by a friend than an unbiased literary judgment. The
       artifice of "The Apple-Tree Table" shows how much more at
       home Melville was with his tales of far-away regions. As
       a whole, the tales arouse more curiosity than admiration.

13   ANON. "Melville Again." New York Bookman, 56 (February), 753.
         Review of 1922.A1. "What a bellower and roarer old sea-
       dog Melville must have been!" Melville's refusal to review
       a book [see Letters, pp. 73-75] sounds like "our very
       Mencken." His analysis of madness is poetry [see Letters,
       p. 83].

1923

14   WELLS, WHITNEY HASTINGS. "Moby Dick and Rabelais." Modern
      Language Notes, 38 (February), 123.
          Draws attention to parallels between chapter 42, "The
      Whiteness of the Whale," in Moby-Dick and Book I, chapter
      10, "Of That Which is Signified by the Colours White and
      Blue," in Rabelais' Gargantua et Pantagruel--"the literary
      provenience of Melville's chapter."

15   BOYNTON, PERCY H. "Pessimism and Criticism." New York
      Literary Review, 3 (10 February), 446.
          Notes the moral tendency of "the English writing and
      English reading world" in the mid-nineteenth century. "In
      this country Poe was almost alone in apostasy.... Melville
      escaped, though a little shamefacedly, on [sic] 'Typee'...
      and had his fling at the contemporary reviewers in what he
      made them say of Pierre's writings: 'This writer is unques-
      tionably a highly respectable youth'; 'He is blameless in
      morals and harmless throughout.'" Reprinted in 1924.B3.

16   [BROOKS, VAN WYCK]. "A Reviewer's Notebook." New York
      Freeman, 6 (14 February), 550-551.
          Review of the Princeton edition of The Apple-Tree Table
      and Other Sketches [1922.B2] and John Marr and Other Poems
      [1922.B3] and Minnigerode [1922.A1]. It becomes more and
      more clear that Melville was a man who dived only on two or
      three occasions. The sketches and stories scarcely rise
      above the level of Ik Marvel's prose; the poems have even
      less of the personal accent, except in sea pieces where
      Melville succeeds in breaking away from the refractory meta-
      physics and wooden rhetoric that had turned him into a sort
      of inferior Clough and writes with a kind of wild power
      that takes one back to Moby-Dick. But the sketches and
      letters are interesting for the traces they reveal of
      Melville's mind and character. His comments on Hawthorne
      and Emerson in his letters mark the gulf that separates
      him, as it separates Whitman, from the New England mind of
      his epoch. Such sketches as "I and My Chimney" and "Cock-
      A-Doodle-Doo!" show the abundant satisfaction he found in
      the farmer's life and the source of the despair that finally
      overwhelmed him. We can see from the sketches that observa-
      tion, the master-faculty of the novelist, had never been his
      forte, that he had at best a feeble hold on the external
      world, that his eye was an inward eye and his universe the
      universe of his own ego. That it should have become at
      last a metaphysical universe--dry and disorderly--was per-
      haps inevitable. The mind revealed in the sketches is
      already an autumnal mind, the mind of an elderly sea captain
      lingering over the past.

17   L[UCAS], F. L. "More Melville." London New Statesman, 20
      (17 March), 696.
          Review of the Princeton edition of The Apple-Tree Table
      and Other Sketches [1922.B2] and John Marr and Other Poems
      [1922.B3]. Melville's spirit slept or wandered in a barren
      wilderness for the 40 years between Moby-Dick and his death.
      Melville withered when he left the sea; his imagination was
      based on it. Except at rarest moments there is no echo in
      these tales of the far Pacific; in their strained humor and
      forced heartiness and cliché sentiment there is no whisper
      of the deep-stirred despairs and ironic laughters of old.
      In his poems Melville's imagination seems to have been
      cramped in the chains of meter, though the verse occasion-
      ally quickens into transitory life, as in "Sheridan at
      Cedar Creek" and "Far Off-shore." The "Supplement" to
      Battle-Pieces proves that Melville's sense and humanity
      remained as sound as ever. Reprinted in 1926.B7.

18   T[OMLINSON], H. M. "The World of Books." London Nation and
      Athenaeum, 33 (7 April), 17.
          Occasioned by publication of the Constable edition of
      Israel Potter and The Confidence-Man and the Princeton edi-
      tion of The Apple-Tree Table and Other Sketches [1922.B2] and
      John Marr and Other Poems [1922.B3]. Enthusiastic account
      of reading Moby-Dick. Melville was not properly acclaimed
      until publication of the Oxford Moby-Dick [1920.B4]. Not
      a little of his verse "is a trifle embarrassing to post-
      Victorians; it reads as if the margins of the pages should
      be decorated with floral emblems and lovely females." Re-
      printed in part in Doubloon, pp. 151-153.

19   ANON. "More Herman Melville." London Saturday Review, 135
      (7 April), 466-467.
          Review of the Princeton edition of The Apple-Tree Table
      and Other Sketches [1922.B2] and John Marr and Other Poems
      [1922.B3]. The two volumes will not add to Melville's
      reputation, though the prose one will not detract from it.
      The most interesting of the sketches is "I and My Chimney,"
      a description in Melville's familiar exaggerated manner.
      "The Apple-Tree Table," an extravaganza, full of oddity and
      picturesqueness, shows the influence of Poe. "Hawthorne
      and His Mosses" shows a just and intelligent appreciation
      of Hawthorne's style. Melville was ambitious to be a poet,
      but the gift was not in him. Melville was not a poet, but
      at his best was a very great prose writer.

20   [BROOKS, VAN WYCK]. "A Reviewer's Notebook." New York
      Freeman, 7 (9 May), 214-215.

1923

   Notice of the Constable edition. It becomes clearer
than ever that Moby-Dick is Melville's one masterpiece,
but all his books throw some light on his history and
peculiar quality of mind. The whole tendency of his
work was an implicit assault on the whole doctrine of
progress as the nineteenth century conceived it. Harder
to forgive, in a hopeful age, was the note of tragic skepticism that reverberated through his work. His speculations,
too, were increasingly incomprehensible. Melville had a
furious development and passed while still young, to the
confusion of himself and his readers, into a long night of
the soul. Moby-Dick is his one supreme achievement because
only there do the subjective and objective elements in his
mind approach some sort of equilibrium. (Typee, Omoo,
Redburn, White-Jacket, Israel Potter, The Piazza Tales are
objective works; Mardi, Pierre, The Confidence-Man metaphysical works.) A handful of readers will always delight
in Mardi and Pierre; still more will be obliged to examine
them, from generation to generation, because they help to
explain a mind that had its moments of supreme greatness.
The Confidence-Man, singularly interesting in conception,
is an abortion; Melville had lost control of his medium;
the book is the product of premature artistic senility.
The delight in health and physical beauty, in the animal
man, is one of the bonds between Melville and Whitman.
Reprinted in 1927.B4.

21 [BROOKS, VAN WYCK]. "A Reviewer's Notebook." New York
    Freeman, 7 (16 May), 238-239.
       Surprised to find at a third reading of Moby-Dick how
    conscious Melville was of what he was doing [see 1921.B24];
    important to note "careful" in "There are some enterprises
    in which a careful disorderliness is the true method." The
    cetological material is necessary; the book is an epic and
    an epic requires ballast—like the catalogue of ships in
    Homer, the mass of purely historical information in the
    Aeneid, the long descriptions in Paradise Lost. It is only
    when we have grasped the nature of the book that we begin
    to perceive its cunning craftsmanship throughout. Melville
    invests the mates and harpooners "with a semblance as of
    Homer's minor heroes." The constant mythological allusions,
    the sweep of the style, and the bold splendor of the similes
    support the impression that we are living in a world by one
    degree larger than life—till at last the battles with the
    whales begin. The white whale torments the imagination;
    until just before the chase we see Moby Dick solely through
    the consequences of his actions and the eyes of superstitious
    men. The character of Ahab is developed and sustained with

uncanny adroitness. Moby-Dick revives the theme of Beowulf,
where Grendel is almost the prototype of the white whale,
the symbol of "all that most maddens and torments...all the
subtle demonisms of life and thought, all evil--visibly
personified." Reprinted in 1927.B4; reprinted in part in
Doubloon, pp. 153-158.

22   [BROOKS, VAN WYCK]. "A Reviewer's Notebook." New York
      Freeman, 7 (23 May), 262-263.
          Tries to trace to their sources certain features of
      Melville's character and certain aspects of his mental
      development. He received some mortal hurt at the thresh-
      old of life and felt that every man's hand was against him.
      Conjecturably, in Ahab's vindictive hatred of the whale,
      Melville vented the accumulated fund of bitterness that had
      rankled in the depths of his own heart. Considering that
      his knowledge of life and the world was derived almost en-
      tirely from his shipboard experiences in later adolescence,
      we can better understand the profound sense of the evil of
      the universe which marks all his later writings. In the
      solitude of the sea, too, we seem to find an explanation
      of his subsequent development; far from drawing him out,
      his companions at sea and his surroundings conspired to
      direct his eyes inward; he turned to metaphysics. With
      virtually no formal education, no intellectual discipline,
      inevitably he fell "into Plato's honey head, and sweetly
      perished there." If Melville had encountered other men he
      could respect and discuss writing with, had been able to
      count on a handful of understanding readers, he might have
      remained a man of this world and an artist; we cease to
      believe in our talent when no one shares our belief.
      Melville at 35 had come to despise the written word. He
      touched the uttermost note of pathetic irony when, for
      lack of a sole articulate companion, he dedicated Pierre
      to Greylock and Israel Potter to the Bunker Hill Monument.
      Reprinted in 1927.B4.

23   STRACHEY, J. ST. LOE. "The Complete Works of Herman Melville."
      London Spectator, 130 (26 May), 887-888.
          Review of the Constable edition, but mainly on the poems,
      with frequent quotation. In his prose Melville was not an
      imitator--he was always a most original man--but he was
      heavily influenced by other writers (Sir Thomas Browne,
      Burton, Charles Lamb, Carlyle, Borrow, Balzac). In his
      verse you are not haunted by references to past or contem-
      porary literature; instead the poems often forecast certain
      moods of quite modern poetry. Melville seems a rather
      clumsy imitator of Hardy, Meredith, Robert Graves ("The

1923

Figure-Head" seems strangely Gravesian), the Sitwells,
J. C. Squire, and a hundred others, including A. E. Housman
and Masefield. In his poetic moods Melville was always a
confirmed and irrational ironist, a real taster and enjoyer
of the irony of circumstances for its own sake. Melville
is always at his best when inspired by the freemasonry of
the sea. In its way the "Supplement" to Battle-Pieces is
as great as Wordsworth's letter to Captain Pasley.

24 [BROOKS, VAN WYCK]. "A Reviewer's Notebook." New York
    Freeman, 7 (30 May), 286-287.
        Mardi and Pierre seem the product of Melville's reading
    rather than of any intense personal experience. In Mardi
    neither the ostensible nor the concealed meaning hold our
    attention very long. In form the work is a more or less
    direct imitation of the fourth and fifth books of Rabelais.
    Thomas Moore seems to have influenced the etherealized back-
    ground and the conception of Yillah, who belongs to the
    same family as Poe's heroines, the Lenores, the Eulalies,
    and the Ligeias. In Pierre another set of influences is
    at work: Maturin, Mrs. Radcliffe, Monk Lewis, Vathek, and
    The Castle of Otranto. The last chapters of Pierre are
    transparently autobiographical; we are confronted with a
    scene of the most convincing reality. Melville's memory
    of "Hudibras" undoubtedly caused him to choose its meter
    for Clarel, an unhappy choice, for the jingling rhymes and
    the velocity of the style redouble the unpalatability of
    the subject. Reprinted in 1927.B4.

25 PALTSITS, VICTOR HUGO. "A Bibliography." New York Literary
    Review, 3 (9 June), 752.
        Review of 1922.A1. Melville's memory will not need
    so soon another bibliography as another biography,
    where the surface has only been scratched. Notes errors
    and omissions in the text of the letters and in the
    bibliography.

26 HIBBARD, C. A. "Recent Studies in American Literature."
    Studies in Philology, 20 (July), 375-376.
        Review of 1922.A1--perhaps the clearest evidence of the
    growing popularity of the Melville cult and definitely ex-
    tending "the limits of knowledge reached in previous dis-
    cussions of the mystic of Pittsfield." The letters to
    Evert Duyckinck are probably the most interesting parts of
    the new Melville material. His letter refusing to review
    a book [Letters, pp. 75-77] shows that in literary criticism
    Melville "had scarcely advanced beyond his contemporaries:
    what he writes is of a piece with the bias and vituperation
    which filled so many of the 'reviews' by Poe, Griswold, and

others of the period." The last half of the book is the most valuable to the Melville student. Minnigerode is in error in at least two of his bibliographical citations; but he corrects errors in Weaver [1921.A1].

27   [SULLIVAN, J. W. N.]. "Herman Melville." London Times Literary Supplement, No. 1123 (26 July), pp. 493-494.
        Moby-Dick is "an account of the mighty, mysterious, and troubled soul" of Melville. He is trying to say things which are not fully to be said. He sees the world differently from others, is trying to say something language was not invented to say; he can communicate with us only in so far as the world affords symbols for what he has to say. The recent acceptance of his work indicates a change taking place in the general mind. Melville's lack of popularity in his own time was due to the great dissimilarity between his personal vision and the vision of the Victorians, for whom the material world was a perfectly clear-cut and comprehensible affair. Lack of public understanding led to a recklessness in fantasy and a diminishing sense of proportion in Melville's later works; he made less and less effort to communicate to others the profundities of his inner life. Moby Dick is the evil principle of the universe; the horror to Melville is that the whale will be victorious. But Ahab's Lucifer-like pride, as much as the power of the whale, foredooms him to destruction. Moby-Dick has foreshadowings of Melville's later perception of the confusing beauty of evil, a beauty which can lead one to doubt the distinction between evil and good. Pierre is a book of despair and much bitter wisdom, in which the whole context of things is seen to be at enmity with the soul of man, entangling him with ambiguities, leaving him with nothing indubitable, no loyalties and no aspirations. Reprinted in Doubloon, pp. 158-165.

28   OWLETT, F. C. "Herman Melville." London Bookman, 64 (September), 282-283.
        Notice of Jonathan Cape edition of Typee, Omoo, Mardi, White-Jacket, and Moby-Dick. "To Melville was vouchsafed sudden visions of infinite things, and a power of expression that carries us in his great moments to the verge of the Incommunicable." He "saw and felt with the intensity of a poet and delivered himself with the energy of an Elizabethan dramatist, though he had neither the mental discipline nor the technical equipment that go to the making of a great poem or play."

1923

29   ANON. New York <u>Mentor</u>, 11 (September), 30.
      Item beneath photograph captioned "The Waterfront at
      New Bedford, As Seen By 'Moby Dick'" notes the recent
      revival of interest in Melville's "classic of the whaler's
      life." Identifies narrator as "Moby Dick, an Ishmael bent
      on seeing 'the watery part of the world.'" Reprinted (with
      photograph) in <u>Extracts</u>, No. 25 (February 1976), p. 10.

30   WOOLF, LEONARD. "Herman Melville." London <u>Nation and
      Athenaeum</u>, 33 (1 September), 688.
      Notice of Jonathan Cape edition of <u>Typee</u>, <u>Omoo</u>,
      <u>Mardi</u>, <u>White-Jacket</u>, and <u>Moby-Dick</u>. Melville is a very
      remarkable writer, but his rescuers and their followers
      have loaded him with a good deal of indiscriminate praise.
      Between <u>Omoo</u> and <u>Mardi</u> Dickens had a deep, and in some re-
      spects disastrous, influence on him. From Dickens he de-
      rived the exaggerated humor which disfigures so many pages
      of <u>Moby-Dick</u>, some marked features in the form of the con-
      versations and interminable soliloquies, and the repetitive
      style of his unending sentences. Melville writes the most
      execrable English; his next great vice is rant or rhetoric.
      But he is undoubtedly one of those strange geniuses, pecul-
      iar to English literature, who perversely produce master-
      pieces out of their most glaring vices. Both <u>Mardi</u> and
      <u>Moby-Dick</u> suffer a sea change and are lifted at a certain
      moment to a higher plane of fantastic grandeur and poetry
      where even the intolerable rantings and ravings find a
      proper place. The same happens once or twice in Joyce's
      <u>Ulysses</u>, which in style and conception continually recalls
      <u>Moby-Dick</u>. Reprinted in part in Norton <u>Moby-Dick</u>,
      pp. 629-631.

31   PARTINGTON, W. G. "With Herman Melville by His Whale of a
      Chimney." London <u>Bookman's Journal</u>, 9 (October), 8-10.
      Review of the Princeton edition of <u>The Apple-Tree Table
      and Other Sketches</u> [1922.B2] and <u>John Marr and Other Poems</u>
      [1922.B3] and Minnigerode [1922.A1]. Finds in the sketches
      the "tender philosophy and delightful whimsicality which
      suggest with extraordinary sincerity the personality of the
      man." The magic of Melville's style and the personal note
      lure the reader with increasing intimacy into themes, which,
      seemingly slight at first, develop into tremendous affairs
      of domestic state. Apart from "Hawthorne and His Mosses,"
      the most successful work is "I and My Chimney," though in
      "The Apple-Tree Table" Melville builds up his tale with
      masterly skill and humor. Much of Melville's verse is
      irregular and lacking in finish, yet there is a fine spirit
      in it, which often echoes, without rising to the standard
      of, his prose.

1924 A BOOKS

1 ROSENBACH, A. S. W. An Introduction to Herman Melville's
   MOBY-DICK: OR THE WHALE [1851]. New York: Mitchell
   Kennerley, 9 pp.
      Melville invests Moby Dick with a personality as rich in
   individuality as Hamlet. He represents the white whale as
   the Unattainable, the precious Desire that can never be
   fully realized. All of Melville's books to 1851 show a
   steady and remarkable advance in wisdom, power, imagination,
   and poetic spirit. In Moby-Dick Melville reached a point
   from which it was impossible to advance; he had plumbed the
   depths of the soul as few other men; he had summed up all
   his philosophy, beliefs, and aspirations. Each of his later
   books shows evidence of great power, but his vision is obscured. Melville could write with equal lucidity of immortal things and homely, commonplace things; he was the
   greatest reporter of any time. His wit is not unlike
   Dickens's. Moby-Dick is a biblical narrative, not a
   Miltonic one: "It unfolds new vistas of life and of experience with a calmness, a fecundity and dignity that could
   only come with a reading and understanding of the Bible"--
   the book that influenced Melville most. Reprinted in
   1928.B17 and 1929.B16.

1924 B SHORTER WRITINGS

1 ANON. "Introduction," in Moby Dick. The Fairmount Classics.
   Philadelphia: George W. Jacobs & Co., pp. 3-4.
      Biographical sketch. Wonderful movement and suspense
   and passion in the dramatic portrayal of the pursuit of the
   great whale.

2 BEEBE, WILLIAM. Galapagos: World's End. New York and
   London: G. P. Putnam's Sons, pp. 415-417.
      Notes excellent account of the Galapagos in the little-
   known Piazza Tales; the descriptive powers that made Moby-
   Dick and Typee fascinating had suffered no diminution.
   "The Encantadas" can "hardly be classed as history, for
   Melville has not hesitated to draw upon his imagination to
   supply missing facts, or make a good story better.... But
   though his ineradicable desire to spin a good yarn makes
   some of his statements decidedly doubtful, no better description of these arid lands has ever been written than
   the opening paragraphs...." Quotes first five paragraphs
   of "The Encantadas."

1924

3   BOYNTON, PERCY H. Some Contemporary Americans. Chicago:
    University of Chicago Press, p. 275.
        Reprint of 1923.B15.

4   CANBY, HENRY SEIDEL. "Conrad and Melville," in Modern Essays.
    Second Series. Ed. Christopher Morley. New York:
    Harcourt, Brace and Co., pp. 201-214.
        Reprint of 1922.B23.

5   EARLY, PRESTON HUSSEY. "Introduction," in Redburn. London:
    Jonathan Cape, pp. v-vi.
        The reader cannot help but feel that Redburn can be none
    other than the story of Melville's own experiences. Redburn
    is one of the foremost stories of the sea.

6   GRAHAM, BESSIE. The Bookman's Manual: A Guide to Literature.
    Revised and Enlarged. New York: R. R. Bowker Co.,
    pp. 445-446.
        Melville's masterpiece, Moby-Dick, " is an exciting and
    informing tale about Mocha Dick, a real whale of history....
    Melville was a man of great peculiarities. His books are
    filled with allegory and moralistic monologues." Revised
    in fourth edition, 1935.

7   HAWES, CHARLES BOARDMAN. Whaling. Garden City, N.Y.:
    Doubleday, Page & Co.; London: William Heinemann,
    pp. 102-106, 155-156.
        Has found no picture of the formalities of a whaler's
    cabin to equal that in chapter 34, "The Cabin-Table," in
    Moby-Dick: quotes paragraphs 1-8. Quotes Melville's
    record of what became of the Acushnet's ship's company.

8   HAWLEY, HATTIE L. "Foreword," "Introduction," and "Notes," in
    Melville's Moby Dick or The White Whale. New York: The
    Macmillan Co., pp. vii, xi-xiv, 399-430.
        Abridged, with biographical introduction and explanatory
    notes. "Foreword" explains that the book is "particularly
    well adapted for use in junior and senior high school read-
    ing courses."

9   HUTT, FRANK WALCOTT, ed. "New Bedford in Melville's Time,"
    in A History of Bristol County, Massachusetts. Vol. 2.
    New York and Chicago: Lewis Historical Publishing Co.,
    pp. 523-526.
        References to and quotations from early chapters in
    Moby-Dick. "The fascinating picture of New Bedford which
    Melville presented has caused many a boy and man to make a
    pilgrimage here." Reprinted in part in Kaplan (1975), p. 9.

10   LAWRENCE, D. H. "Herman Melville's 'Typee' and 'Omoo'" and
      "Herman Melville's 'Moby Dick,'" in Studies in Classic Amer-
      ican Literature. London: M. Secker, pp. 132-144, 145-161.
         First English edition. [See 1923.B3 and 1923.B4.]

11   MINNIGERODE, MEADE. The Fabulous Forties, 1840-1850: A Presen-
      tation of Private Life. New York: G. P. Putnam's Sons,
      pp. 113-114.
         Notes that there was "plenty to read in the Forties,"
      and that Melville "had produced his extraordinarily popular
      South Sea books, Typee and Omoo, and had not yet scandalised
      his public with Pierre."

12   MITCHELL, EDWARD P. Memoirs of an Editor: Fifty Years of
      American Journalism. New York and London: Charles
      Scribner's Sons, pp. 97, 185-186, 422.
         Brief references to Melville's obscurity in his last 30
      years and to Moby-Dick.

13   MUMFORD, LEWIS. Sticks and Stones. New York: Horace Liveright,
      p. 95.
         Mention: "By 1860 the halcyon day of American civiliza-
      tion was over; the spirit had lingered in letters and schol-
      arship, in the work of Parkman and Motley and Emerson and
      Melville and Thoreau, but the sun had already sunk below
      the horizon, and what seemed a promise was in reality an
      afterglow."

14   ROBERTS, MORLEY. W. H. Hudson: A Portrait. New York:
      E. P. Dutton and Co., p. 131.
         "...it was to Hudson that I owed my first knowledge of
      Herman Melville and his magnificent achievement, Moby-Dick.
      Often Hudson and I wondered how it was that the Americans
      still looked forward to some great American book when all
      they had to do was to cast their eyes backward and find it.
      Some day they will turn upon their path and see that in the
      cloud and mist which covered their passage they have missed
      one of their two great monuments of literature. It is ob-
      vious, of course, that Moby Dick is not flawless. There
      are pages of it in that fatal style which is not prose and
      yet has not the majesty of poetry, but when we contemplate
      it as a whole it has a strange unequalled power, an insight
      into character hardly to be surpassed by its grasp of great
      natural phenomena, and with all its terror there is also
      laughter. It is said to be a book of the whale. It is
      also a book of the ship and of the sea and of man, and
      Hudson knew it and learnt from it and spread its name."

1924

15 TUCKER, GEORGE F. <u>The Boy Whaleman</u>. Boston: Little, Brown, and Co., p. 8.
    As a boy, the narrator read with particular delight Dana's <u>Two Years Before the Mast</u> and Melville's <u>Moby-Dick</u>.

16 VAN DOREN, CARL. "Introduction," in <u>White Jacket</u>. The World's Classics, No. 253. London: Oxford University Press, pp. v-xiv.
    <u>White-Jacket</u> has less charm than <u>Typee</u>, less poetry than <u>Moby-Dick</u>; it is heavily weighted with blocks of disquisition which often crush the story. It stands, like <u>Omoo</u>, by virtue of its comic energy in the representation of character; it contains some of the wittiest and jolliest writing in all Melville. As a document it is inferior to <u>Two Years Before the Mast</u>; but in the force of the characters and situations, in eloquence and passion, in wit and poetry, Melville surpasses Dana. "The striking thing about <u>White Jacket</u>, as about Melville's work in general, is that traits so rarely seen together should here be so naturally joined without confusion; that there should be a single writer who touches Smollett in his character-drawing, Lamb in his playfulness, Ruskin in his splendour of prose, Hawthorne in his sense of allegory, the Restoration dramatists in his wit, and who yet communicates a personality which is powerful and distinctive." Reprinted in 1924.B24.

17 VAN DOREN, CARL. <u>Many Minds</u>. New York: Alfred A. Knopf, p. 215.
    Claims to have been "nearly the first to lift a voice in the revival of Herman Melville."

18 VAN DOREN, CARL. "Melville," in <u>A Short History of American Literature</u>. Eds. William Peterfield Trent et al. Cambridge, England: The University Press; New York: G. P. Putnam's Sons, pp. 198-201.
    Reprint of 1917.B3, with minor revision.

19 WEAVER, RAYMOND M. "Introduction," in <u>Israel Potter</u>. New York: Albert & Charles Boni, pp. v-ix.
    <u>Israel Potter</u> is Melville's own life allegorized. About half the book closely follows <u>Life and Remarkable Adventures of Israel Potter</u>; the more splendid half is all Melville's own. Melville's kinship was with tumultuous and uncharted souls, and upon Ethan Allen and John Paul Jones he lavished his best art. The chapters concerning Jones, who is presented as a young and gallant Ahab, are the book's signal achievement. Reprinted in 1925.B9.

20   WEAVER, RAYMOND M.   "Introduction," in Redburn.   New York:
       Albert & Charles Boni, pp. v-vii.
           "A sensitive and impetuous child of undisciplined imag-
       ination," the young Melville was, "both by temperament and
       training, at odds with himself and reality."   He made his
       first sea voyage stirred "by motives of desperation, and
       by the delusion that some stupendous discovery of happiness
       lay just over the world's rim."   With Redburn, Melville
       annexed a new literary kingdom: the commercial ship's
       forecastle.   Reprinted in 1925.B12.

21   [BROOKS, VAN WYCK].   "A Reviewer's Notebook."   New York
       Freeman, 8 (27 February), 599.
           Mention: Joel Barlow "witnessed the marriage of Thomas
       Melville to the niece of Madame Recamier—the same Thomas
       who, with scythe in hand on his Pittsfield farm, was to
       retain for his nephew Herman 'the shadowy aspect of a
       courtier of Louis XVI, reduced as a refugee to humble
       employment in a region far from gilded Versailles.'"

22   VAN DOREN, CARL.   "Mr. Melville's 'Moby Dick.'"   New York
       Bookman, 59 (April), 154-157.
           [One of a series of articles "in which various of our
       younger critics will attempt to express the reactions which
       well known books of an earlier generation would arouse in
       them, were those classics newly published today."]   Ahab
       has a hundred symbolical or allegorical implications.   The
       variety of Moby-Dick is one measure of its greatness, as is
       also that profound vitality which will make it long capable
       of being wrangled over by rival critics.   Better than any
       other novel it reproduces the works and days of the old
       whalers.   A more artful writer could have produced the "air
       of threatening postponement in the catastrophe" without
       ransacking so many encyclopaedias.   A more artful writer
       would have known better than to fall so often into blank
       verse in his elevated passages.   But there is evidence of
       powerful control in the book, and Melville writes with the
       energy of a man who is tirelessly alert.

23   PATTEE, FRED LEWIS.   "Call for a Literary Historian."   New
       York American Mercury, 2 (June), 135.
           Notes the recent sudden change in the estimate of
       Melville and wonders "which valuation is right, the old or
       the new?"

24   VAN DOREN, CARL.   "Melville before the Mast."   New York
       Century Magazine, 108 (June), 272-277.
           Reprint of 1924.B16.

1924

25   [MURRY, JOHN MIDDLETON]. "Herman Melville's Silence."
       London Times Literary Supplement, No. 1173 (10 July),
       p. 433.
          Those who feel the greatest novels are something quite
       different from a good story should seek out Pierre; they
       will understand why its outward semblance is clumsy and
       puerile. Melville is trying to reveal a mystery, trying
       to show that the completely good man is doomed to complete
       disaster on earth and that this must be so and ought to be
       so: horologically the disaster of the good ought to be so
       because there is no room for unearthly perfection on earth;
       chronologically it ought to be so because it is a working
       out, a manifestation of the absolute, though hidden, har-
       mony of the ideal and the real.--"In other words, Melville
       was trying to reveal anew the central mystery of the Chris-
       tian religion." Billy Budd is the last will and spiritual
       testament of a man of genius; it is startlingly like Pierre.
       Once more Melville is telling the story of the inevitable
       and utter disaster of the good and trying to convey to us
       that this must be so and ought to be so--chronologically
       and horologically. Billy Budd passes indisputably beyond
       the nihilism of Moby-Dick. In between Pierre and Billy Budd
       there was silence--occupied by poetry. The theme of Clarel
       once more is the essential mystery of the Christian religion,
       which is the mystery of the universe. Melville the poet is
       clumsy, but his matter is tremendous. Reprinted in
       1924.B27; 1930.B18; Murry (1950), pp. 208-212.

26   MURRY, JOHN MIDDLETON. "Quo Warranto?" London Adelphi, 2
       (August), 193-195.
          When great spirits touch a certain depth of knowledge of
       human life, they follow the path that leads to a new com-
       prehension of the mystery of Christ. From such a profound
       depth of knowledge in Moby-Dick--knowledge of the same order
       as that in King Lear and Macbeth--Murry confidently expected
       what he finally found on the publication of Billy Budd,
       Melville's "final word" and "spiritual testament": "a
       deliberate effort to restate the mystery of Christ--the
       catastrophe of the utterly pure and good, and its complete
       triumph in the very moment of death."

27   MURRY, JOHN MIDDLETON. "Herman Melville, Who Could Not Sur-
       pass Himself." New York Times Book Review (10 August),
       p. 7.
          Slightly revised and shortened version of 1924.B25.

28   MARSHALL, H. P. "Herman Melville." London Mercury, 11
       (November), 56-70.

The reason for Melville's obscurity after his early fame "lies not so much in his personal aloofness as has been supposed, but in the aggressive, bitter loneliness which permeated his later writings." Melville's prose work can be divided into three classes: that having literary value: (Typee, Omoo, Redburn, and some of The Piazza Tales); that which is badly written but interesting (Mardi and Pierre); and that which is simply dull (White-Jacket and the "monstrously constructed" The Confidence-Man). Moby-Dick is impossible to class in any list, being more than a book, a great experience. A few paragraphs of the sayings of Bardianna or the lecture of Plotinus Plinlimmon are worth more than the whole of Typee, Omoo, and White-Jacket. In Mardi Melville was conducting an experiment in introspection--an unusual and almost indelicate thing to do in his time. A deep consciousness of the soul's struggle against an almost visible evil power made him realize the need for religion as a weapon; his view of religion developed and shaped itself according to his mental explorations. Pierre is interesting for the diagnosis it gives us of Melville's mind, one wrestling incessantly with the ambiguities of life. "Benito Cereno" is very good indeed, with an unusual plot and sustained tension. "The Lightning-Rod Man" is Melville at his worst. "Bartleby" has an emotional undercurrent like that in Gogol's "The Overcoat." After Moby-Dick Melville's mind was still striking in new directions, but he ceased to produce important work. The Confidence-Man only confirms the suspicion aroused by Pierre that his desire for real expression had passed with his acknowledgment of the vanity of human endeavor.

29   MUMFORD, LEWIS. "Aesthetics: A Palaver." New York American Mercury, 3 (November), 363.
"...When either the critic or the writer aims at form alone he becomes empty and meretricious. People have criticized 'Moby Dick' because it is formless and full of irrelevancies; but the truth is that the irrelevancies are an essential part of its form, and had Melville attempted to reduce the bounds of his universe to the scene required for a slick story of the sea, that universe would not have been the multitudinous and terrible thing he sought to create." Reprinted in 1925.B6.

30   SMYTH, CLIFFORD. "A Letter from Herman Melville." New York Literary Digest International Book Review, 3 (December), 22, 65.
Looks forward to publication of an adequate Melville biography, one dealing satisfactorily with the years

1924

1855-1891. The latest development among recent studies of Moby-Dick is the recognition of its possible symbolism. Quotes from Melville's letter to Sophia Hawthorne, 8 January 1852, recently discovered and as yet unpublished [Letters, pp. 145-147].

31   MORLEY, F. V. "The Sea in Literature." New York Saturday Review of Literature, 1 (27 December), 410.
      Tomlinson's Tide Marks "is a real book. There is no drama, no artistic device. Unlike Conrad with his ship-- which is man's thing, not the sea's--or Melville with his whale--which is the symbol of the sea--Tomlinson is neither cunning and subtle, nor tempestuous and angry about his tale. He is too honest, and too much in earnest. Less of a detached artist than these two, though with power and capability as great, he is throughout the book closer to us as a friend."

1925 A BOOKS - NONE

1925 B SHORTER WRITINGS

1   BUCHMAN, S. R. "Moby Dick--the Book and The Sea Beast--the Picture: An Appreciation," in Moby Dick. New York: Grosset & Dunlap, pp. ix-xi.
      Defense of The Sea Beast. The construction of Ahab's early history, "which shows that the loss of his leg had cost Ahab the woman he loved because an envious brother had suggested that her love for Ahab would thenceforth be mere pity, is not presumptuous meddling" but "a laudable act of critical explanation." By these facts, "madness is more honestly incited, and the grief that leads to distraction, inhumanity, and sacrilege, can be understood." It is "a relief and satisfaction that the picture version allows Ahab to live,--with mind restored, and with some of earth's possessions and happiness." The Sea Beast is true to the essentials of Melville's chronicle--capricious seas, fearless men, and bold assaults on whales.

2   FOERSTER, NORMAN. "Herman Melville (1819-1891)," in American Poetry and Prose. Boston: Houghton Mifflin Co., pp. 1038-1039.
      Biographical sketch; quotation from 1917.B3. [Extract from Moby-Dick (chapters 132-135), at pp. 716-732.]

3   GOSSE, SIR EDMUND. "Herman Melville," in Silhouettes. London: Heinemann; New York: Charles Scribner's Sons, pp. 355-362.

Reprinted from London <u>Sunday Times</u> [unlocated]. Review
of the Princeton edition of <u>The Apple-Tree Table and Other
Sketches</u> [1922.B2]. The influence of Melville on Hawthorne
is not difficult to detect in what is audacious in <u>The
Scarlet Letter</u>, but not nearly so obvious as the influence
of Hawthorne in such a story as "The Apple-Tree Table."
Melville owed much to Poe; "The Apple-Tree Tale" is a "tale
of the Grotesque." The whole description of the garret is
characteristic of Melville's perfervid and tortured imagination and eloquent verbosity. The tale is told in the curious breathless air of being in a terrible hurry yet
magically rooted to the spot which is one of Melville's
peculiarities as a narrator. Melville's description of the
cock in "Cock-A-Doodle-Doo!" exemplifies the extreme difficulty of estimating the real value of his style, with its
vividness, exultation, and unfortunate tendency to repetition and over-emphasis.

4   HUXLEY, ALDOUS. <u>Those Barren Leaves</u>. London: Chatto &
     Windus, pp. 207-208.
          Mr. Cardan, in conversation with Miss Thriplow: "Styles
     that protest too much are not fit for serious, tragical use.
     They are by nature suited to comedy, whose essence is exag-
     geration.... And what prevents Herman Melville's <u>Moby Dick</u>
     from being a really great book is precisely the pseudo-
     Shakespearean idiom in which what are meant to be the most
     tragical passages are couched--an idiom to whose essential
     suitability to comedy the exceptional tragic successes of
     Shakespeare himself, of Marlowe and a few others has un-
     fortunately blinded all their imitators."

5   MACAULEY, ROSE. <u>Orphan Island</u>. New York: Boni and Liveright,
     p. 43.
          Conversation about Melville between small group of char-
     acters. Captain Paul (owner of the schooner <u>Typee</u>) used to
     read him as a boy. Mr. Thinkwell considers him overrated--
     "A clumsy and undistinguished style. In my generation we
     had got through Melville by the time we left school. He
     seems now to be better thought of." Charles, "who knew
     what was what in literature" thinks Melville "uncommonly
     good."

6   MUMFORD, LEWIS. <u>Aesthetics, A Dialogue</u>. Troutbeck Leaflets,
     No. 3. Amenia, N.Y.: Troutbeck Press.
     Reprint of 1924.B29.

7   PAGE, C. A. "Introduction," in <u>Israel Potter</u>. Boston: The
     St. Botolph Society, pp. v-xi.

1925

In Israel Potter Melville turns "from his philosophy of
pessimism to a philosophy of optimistic striving, from in-
tolerance of all human relations to a study and a sympathy
with his fellows." Bliss Perry and Brander Matthews, cham-
pions of Melville for years, are probably the "final causa-
tion" of the recent sudden interest in Melville in the
United States; the English have always had a high regard
for Melville.

8   PAGE, C. A.   "Introduction," in Israel Potter.   London:
    Jonathan Cape, pp. v-xi.
        Reprint of 1925.B7.

9   WEAVER, RAYMOND M.   "Introduction," in Israel Potter.   London:
    Jarrolds, pp. v-ix.
        Reprint of 1924.B19.

10 WEAVER, RAYMOND M.   "Introduction," in Mardi.   New York:
    Albert and Charles Boni, pp. v-viii.
        Mainly summary. The creation of Annatoo is an amazing
    feat of sardonic mirth, perfect in zest and cruelty; she is
    a kind of Zuleika Dobson "gone native." Mardi has a cer-
    tain kinship with L'Ile des Pingouins, Figures of Earth,
    Gulliver's Travels, Erewhon, Candide, The New Republic, and
    Alice in Wonderland; to most of them it can claim precedence.

11 WEAVER, RAYMOND M.   "Introduction," in Moby Dick.   New York:
    Albert & Charles Boni, pp. v-xi.
        Mainly derivative critical commentary. Moby-Dick is an
    allegory of the demonism at the cankered heart of nature.
    It is a book of adventure, but on the highest plane of
    spiritual daring [cf. 1920.B8]. The chapter "Pierre at
    his Book" in Pierre [Book 25, chapter 3] is an account of
    Melville's agony in writing Moby-Dick.

12 WEAVER, RAYMOND M.   "Introduction," in Redburn.   London:
    Jarrolds, pp. v-vii.
        Reprint of 1924.B20.

13 HOPKINS, FREDERICK M.   "The World of Rare Books."   New York
    Saturday Review of Literature, 1 (14 February), 535.
        Review of 1924.A1. Mainly quotation from Rosenbach's
    "delightful essay."

14 ANON.   "A Melville Novel."   New York Times Book Review
    (22 February), p. 23.
        Review of St. Botolph edition of Israel Potter [see
    1925.B7]. The novel has always been considered chiefly

important for its pen pictures of Franklin, Jones, Allen,
and George III, "which are realistic, vital, unsqueamish
portraits."

15   MORLEY, F. V. "Whaling Days." New York Saturday Review of
       Literature, 1 (14 March), 593-594.
           On the growth and decline of whale myths. Moby-Dick
       "is the apotheosis of whaling days; once more it has
       created the legendary monster of the past."

16   RUSSELL, SIR HERBERT. "When the Sea Came into Literature."
       New York Literary Digest International Book Review, 3
       (May), 373.
           Reminiscences of the author's father, Clark Russell.
       "...Herman Melville and Clark Russell maintained an inti-
       mate friendship for many years, altho, curiously enough,
       the two never met. But they were drawn together, not only
       by the freemasonry of the sea, but by a mutual generosity
       of recognition which was profound in its sincerity. I
       remember Melville writing to him: 'Where do you get your
       wonderful wealth of description?' and his answering: 'From
       the same place that you get yours.' I think that the in-
       fluence of Herman Melville is very clear in Clark Russell's
       story, 'The Little Loo.'"

17   S., O. "Herman Melville in the Berkshire Hills." Boston
       Christian Science Monitor (28 May).
           No writer has ever had a nobler landscape before him
       while he worked than Melville had at Arrowhead while he
       "wrought out the weird, compelling story and the magical
       rhythms" of Moby-Dick. As one looks out today "across the
       twenty miles of azure" to Greylock, "the depth and wonder
       of the book seem more comprehensible."

18   MABBOTT, THOMAS OLLIVE. "Poem by Herman Melville." Notes
       and Queries, 149 (18 July), 42-43.
           Prints uncollected poem by Melville, "Inscription For
       the Slain At Fredericksburgh," published in Autograph
       Leaves of our Country's Authors, eds. Alexander Bliss and
       John P. Kennedy (Cushings and Bailey, 1864).

19   GARNETT, R. S. "Mocha Dick, Or the White Whale of the
       Pacific." London Times Literary Supplement, No. 1228
       (30 July), p. 509.
           Quotes from "Mocha Dick, or the White Whale of the
       Pacific: a Leaf from a Journal" by J. N. Reynolds. Con-
       cludes that Melville wrote from first-hand knowledge of the
       real Leviathan; he did not wish to localize his whale, so
       changed "Mocha" into "Moby."

1925

20   VAN DOREN, CARL. "Lucifer from Nantucket: An Introduction
      to 'Moby Dick.'" New York <u>Century Magazine</u>, 110 (August),
      494-501.
          In Ahab, the Yankee Faust, the Yankee Lucifer, Melville
      found an opportunity to project his own drama. Ahab is
      created with such passion because Melville was nearly, or
      felt that he might have become, another Ahab. Christianity
      and transcendentalism had taught him that the cosmos had a
      simple and good meaning; but Melville found in the world a
      thousand malevolent contradictions, the apparent rule of
      blind chance, which could only come from the activity of
      the devil. The conflict between Melville's knowledge and
      his inherited formulas gave birth to Ahab. Reprinted in
      1926.B15.

21   RAUSHENBUSH, WINIFRED. "Reviews." <u>American Journal of
      Sociology</u>, 31 (November), 409.
          Notice of 1921.A1. The life of Melville will appeal to
      the sociologist because it is the life of a man who could
      not establish communication with his fellows.

22   SHEPPARD, ALFRED TRESIDDER. "Herman Melville." London
      <u>Bookman</u>, 69 (December), 156-158.
          Brief survey and notice of Hodder edition of <u>Omoo</u>;
      Jarrolds edition of <u>Redburn</u> and <u>Israel Potter</u> [<u>see</u> 1925.B12
      and 1925.B9]; and Jonathan Cape edition of <u>Israel Potter</u>
      [<u>see</u> 1925.B8]. Page's introduction (to <u>Israel Potter</u>) is
      "rather crudely written, and not always accurate."
      Melville's supreme gift is his capacity for seeing through
      the commonplace and material.

<u>1926 A BOOKS</u>

1   FREEMAN, JOHN. <u>Herman Melville</u>. London: Macmillan and Co.,
      200 pp.
          Biographical (three chapters on 1819-1851, one chapter
      on 1852-1891) and critical (mainly on the fiction, one
      chapter on the poems). During the first half of his life
      Melville was investing himself with illusions and discover-
      ing them to be illusions; during the second half he was
      "trying to make terms with the bareness that remained and
      avoid an exhausting, cynical conclusion." He instinctively
      repressed strong passions; except in <u>Moby-Dick</u>, he seldom
      broke through his powerful involuntary suppressions to re-
      veal the profound, dark depth of his nature. He withdrew
      into himself in his last 35 years because the world had de-
      feated him; his isolation was the isolation of renunciation,

not of sterility, as is shown by <u>Billy Budd</u>, which equals
<u>Moby-Dick</u> in loftiness of imagination. Melville is the
most powerful of all the great American writers. His ex-
cellencies--lucid, easy narrative, faithful description,
use of rich resources of experience, strangely modern
psychology, skill in portraiture, volubility in dialogue--
are offset by his comparative failure in invention, his
"disdain of a particular range of emotions," his extravagance and unresisted tendency to philosophize. But his
grand faculty was myth-making. Melville followed the full
romantic tradition: he disdained every curbing and extrav-
agated with absolute willfulness, being tempted by the richness and wildness of life rather than by its order and
discipline. <u>Mardi's</u> intellectual riotings and spiritual
musings match the aboundingness of Rabelais; all its wisdom
and poetry do not unite in a complete creation, but few
writers are vigorous enough to achieve such a failure. In
<u>Moby-Dick</u>, Melville achieved a simple and final felicity,
and its subject drew forth a humor which most of his writing
lacks and forbids. His theme is Milton's in <u>Paradise Lost</u>;
Ahab, a Miltonic figure, and the Whale are prototypes of an
eternal strife between opposites. Melville's whole apprehension of the world is mystical; in <u>Moby-Dick</u>, with Blake's
"cleansed" perception, he sees everything as infinite.
<u>Pierre</u>, written out of an exhausted imagination and an in-
flamed nervous system, shows an enormous and perverse sadness declining to mere madness. Melville seems an apostate
of the imagination, lacking faith in himself and his calling;
he is satirizing his soul, himself. The book's psychology
is intolerably followed; nothing outside the Russians could
be more subtle or less scrupulous. With his subject,
Melville could only have succeeded in a verse drama, where
he would have achieved the remoteness he needed. Except for
<u>Pierre</u>, <u>Israel Potter</u>, though far from being valuably and
typically Melville's, is the chief of his works published in
his lifetime after <u>Moby-Dick</u>. "Benito Cereno," Conradian
in its characters and method of broken and oblique narration,
is the greatest of the stories in <u>The Piazza Tales</u>. The
satire in <u>The Confidence-Man</u> fails completely through a
failure in intelligence; Melville's basis for satire is not
philosophical but a sense of personal failure: consciousness
that he could not live by producing masterpieces dictated
the mood of the book--the true meaning of which is hopelessly obscure. The chief value of the poems, many of them
Hardy-like, is in their matter, the manner being inadequate
to the nobility of the themes; Melville labored too little
at the technique of verse. "After the Pleasure Party" hints
at what Melville all his life had sternly repressed. <u>Clarel</u>

is marked by dull precision and contains less imagination
than any other of his verse. Billy Budd, Melville's "everlasting yea," shows his imaginative faculty and his inward
peace both secure. Melville did not always write greatly;
but he was among the greatest of modern imaginative writers
of prose, one of his chief gifts being his ear for rhythm.
He adheres to the English tradition of prose written for
the ear rather than the eye; he depends less on picture
than on music, on rhythms that stimulate our feelings.
Analysis of Melville's developing prose style through Typee,
Mardi, Redburn, and Moby-Dick. "Appendix" reprints anonymous account of "Mocha Dick" from the Detroit Free Press
published "a few months after Melville's death." Bibliography of Melville first editions. Indexed. Reviewed in
1926.B19, B21, B22, B23, B24, B25, B26, B27, B29, B30, B31,
B32, B33, B35, B36, B37, B38, B39, B41, B44, B46; 1927.B20.

1926 B SHORTER WRITINGS

1   ASHLEY, CLIFFORD W. The Yankee Whaler. Boston: Houghton
     Mifflin Co., pp. 106, 112, 113.
         "There is one writer of whaling fiction whose book may
     be taken seriously and unquestioningly. There could be no
     truer picture of whaling or finer story of the sea than
     Herman Melville's 'Moby Dick.' Melville knew his subject,
     and if he occasionally borrowed an English term, his was
     obviously the virtuosity of the scholar and not the ignor-
     ance of the novice." Quotes from Moby-Dick on
     scrimshandering.

2   BARRYMORE, JOHN. Confessions of an Actor. Indianapolis:
     The Bobbs Merrill Publishing Co., n.p.
         Writing while making The Sea Beast: Moby-Dick "appeals
     to me and always has.... I revel in the rough and almost
     demoniacal character, such as Captain Ahab becomes in the
     last half of the picture after his leg has been amputated
     by Moby Dick, the white whale. What we are going to do for
     a love interest, I don't quite know. He might fall in love
     with the whale. I am sure, however, Hollywood will find a
     way."

3   BEACH, JOSEPH WARREN. The Outlook for American Prose.
     Chicago: University of Chicago Press, p. 183.
         Mention: "In giving us something to awake our imagina-
     tions and to make his South Seas live for us, he [O'Brien]
     has shown some of the artistic sense of a Herman Melville,
     and has made it less probable that this realm of romance
     shall soon go out of the memory of men."

4 BEER, THOMAS. The Mauve Decade. New York: Alfred A. Knopf,
   p. 66.
        Melville included in list of eminent people "dying in
   groups" in 1891-1892. They all "vanished to appropriate
   music of the journals."

5 BRADDY, NELLA. "Melville, Herman," in The Guide to Literature.
   Vol. 25 of The University Library. Ed. John Finley.
   Garden City, N.Y.: Doubleday, Page & Co., p. 142.
        One of the greatest services of the recent interest in
   the South Seas has been to bring Melville's excellent
   novels back into prominence. His best titles: Typee, Omoo,
   and Moby-Dick.

6 COPELAND, CHARLES TOWNSEND. The Copeland Reader: An Anthology
   of English Poetry and Prose. New York and London: Charles
   Scribner's Sons, p. 1249.
        Plot summary precedes extract from Moby-Dick (chapter
   135 and "Epilogue").

7 LUCAS, F. L. "Herman Melville," in Authors Dead & Living.
   London: Chatto and Windus; New York: The Macmillan Co.,
   pp. 104-115.
        Reprint of 1922.B30 and 1923.B17.

8 MUMFORD, LEWIS. The Golden Day. New York: Boni and Liveright,
   pp. 142-153.
        Moby-Dick was unappreciated in the Victorian age because
   it is poetry. In all of Poe's poetry there is scarcely a
   line as good as pages of the best of Melville's prose, which
   has the richness of the early seventeenth century. Moby-
   Dick is not merely poetry but the product of that deep medi-
   tation on the world, life, and time which makes philosophy.
   The Whale is the Nature man hunts and subdues, the White
   Whale is the Nature that threatens man, calls forth his
   heroic powers, and in the end defeats him. To appreciate
   the reality of the White Whale "is to see more deeply into
   the expedience of all our intermediate institutions, all
   the spiritual shelters man puts between himself and the
   uncertain cosmic weather." In Moby-Dick Melville confronted
   the "blank" of the universe. Reprinted in part in Doubloon,
   p. 169.

9 PHELPS, WILLIAM LYON. As I Like It. Third Series. New York
   and London: Charles Scribner's Sons, pp. 77, 188.
        Mentions. Under Sail, by Felix Riesenberg, "deserves to
   stand on the same shelf with Two Years Before the Mast, with
   Moby Dick, with The Nigger of the Narcissus, with The Wreck

1926

of the Grosvenor, with The Ebb Tide, and with the other
classics of the sea." The fidelity to fact of F. T. Bullen's
The Cruise of the Cachalot "increases its value without de-
creasing its charm; and it has none of the tiresome metaphysics of Herman Melville."

10 SHAFER, ROBERT. "Herman Melville (1819-1891)," in American
Literature. Vol. 2. New York: Doubleday, Page & Co.;
New York: The Odyssey Press, pp. 1-2.
Introduction to extracts from Moby-Dick (chapters 36-41,
85, 96, 132-135, and "Epilogue"). Biographical sketch.
Melville's fierce integrity has given enduring substance to
Moby-Dick and "Bartleby" and perhaps also to Mardi and
cloudy Pierre.

*11 SULLIVAN, J. W. N. "Herman Melville," in Aspects of Science.
Second Series. New York: Alfred A. Knopf, pp. 190-205.
Reprint of 1923.B27. Cited in Ricks and Adams, p. 355.

12 TATE, ALLEN. "Foreword," in White Buildings: Poems by Hart
Crane. New York: Boni & Liveright, p. xiv.
Crane's sonorous rhetoric takes the reader to Marlowe
and the Elizabethans. "But his spiritual allegiances are
outside the English tradition. Melville and Whitman are
his avowed masters. In his sea poems, Voyages, in Emblems
of Conduct, in allusions to the sea throughout his work,
there is something of Melville's intense, transcendental
brooding on the mystery of the 'high interiors of the sea.'"

13 TOMLINSON, H. M. Gifts of Fortune. London: William Heinemann,
pp. 105-109.
Reprints part of 1921.B25. Moby-Dick is beyond criticism. The reader feels that Melville is possessed, that he
is on the point of flaring into a mania. Moby-Dick is
accepted now because our thoughts and our world have changed
in recent years. Reprinted in part in Doubloon, pp. 169-170.

14 VAN VECHTEN, CARL. "The Later Work of Herman Melville," in
Excavations: A Book of Advocacies. New York: Alfred A.
Knopf, pp. 65-88.
Reprint of 1922.B12, somewhat revised, with a small
amount of additional material.

15 VAN DOREN, CARL. "Lucifer from Nantucket: An Introduction
to 'Moby Dick,'" in American Criticism 1926. Ed. William A.
Drake. New York: Harcourt, Brace and Co., pp. 308-325.
Reprint of 1925.B20.

16   WILLIAMS, STANLEY THOMAS. The American Spirit in Letters.
      Volume 11 of The Pageant of America. New Haven: Yale
      University Press, pp. 213-215.
          Melville "has been too long undervalued, though he is by
      no means the union of Plato and Smollett, with an admixture
      of intervening writers, that some modern critics consider
      him.... Melville was a mystic. He suffered, besides pov-
      erty and grief, disillusionment, and a very pretty primer
      of misanthropy may be culled from his fifteen volumes."

17   WINTERICH, JOHN T. A Primer of Book Collecting. New York:
      Greenberg, pp. 44-46.
          References to the copy of Moby-Dick, "presumably not a
      first edition," owned by Bendigo Redmayne in Eden Phillpott's
      The Red Redmaynes. [See 1922.B7.]

18   TOMLINSON, H. M. "Two Americans and a Whale: Some Fruits of
      a London Luncheon." New York Harpers Magazine, 152
      (April), 618-621.
          The reason for the recent appreciation of Moby-Dick:
      "There has been such a change, in ten years, in the public
      consciousness that things in which once only odd men and
      women delighted have acquired a significance for the general.
      ...Melville, in his own day, was addressing an intelligence
      which was hardly awake." Moby-Dick is a book to put with
      the world's greatest.

19   ANON. "New Books at a Glance." New York Saturday Review, 141
      (24 April), 542.
          Notice of 1926.A1. Difficult not to feel a preliminary
      objection to Melville being included in the "English Men
      of Letters" series.

20   MORLEY, CHRISTOPHER. "The Bowling Green." New York Saturday
      Review of Literature, 2 (1 May), 755.
          Prints part of a letter from "a correspondent abroad":
      "Melville, it is supposed, has been re-discovered recently.
      Actually, folk here rave hysterically about 'Moby Dick,'
      principally, and apparently lack the wit to know that
      'Pierre' is one of the most important books in the world,
      profound beyond description in its metaphysic...a philo-
      sophic novel, reaching to heaven and down to hell in its
      march to a tragic culmination, a consummation....'"

21   ANON. "Herman Melville." Springfield (Mass.) Sunday Union
      and Republican (2 May).
          Review of 1926.A1.--A compact and discerning portrayal.

1926

22 COURNOS, JOHN. "Crowning a Hero of the Pen." New York
   Literary Review, 6 (8 May), 1-2.
   　　　Review of 1926.A1. Finds Moby-Dick more revealing bio-
   graphically than Freeman. Suggests that the White Whale is
   Melville's "confession of his own transcendent illusion, of
   his own quest of the unattainable, driving him to his ultimate despair, his ultimate doom."

23 EDGETT, EDWIN FRANCIS. "The Makers of Moby Dick and Atalanta."
   Boston Evening Transcript (15 May).
   　　　Review of 1926.A1--"a compact, well-knit and authorita-
   tive work that is both a chronicle and a study."

24 KELLETT, E. E. "Herman Melville." London New Statesman, 27
   (15 May), 121-122.
   　　　Review of 1926.A1. Great as Melville is as a writer, he
   was greater as a man, and at times the man was too great to
   write well. "Things were contending in his mind for utter-
   ance--conflicts, agonies, obstinate questionings--which
   strove in vain to emerge: and he has often given us the
   scattered attempts at the solution of his problem rather
   than the solution itself." Freeman has thrown light on
   one of the greatest but most intangible figures of modern
   times.

25 BROOKS, VAN WYCK. "Herman Melville." New York Herald Tribune
   Books (16 May), pp. 1-2.
   　　　Review of 1926.A1. Few critics now would not rank
   Melville among the two or three pre-eminent American men
   of letters. Melville is more powerful even than Whitman,
   for his depth of thought is equal to his depth of feeling.
   Weaver's book [1921.A1] remains the permanent sourcebook
   for all future biographers, but it indulged too much in
   conjecture; the theme was not reduced to a clear pattern.
   Abstaining from all conjecture, Freeman supplies this
   theme; if his insight is seldom profound, he satisfies by
   presenting a lucid, consistent story. The Confidence-Man
   is an obscure abortion, but Melville came to life again in
   some of his poems and in Billy Budd. Mardi and Pierre remain the great problems for every student of Melville. The
   allegory of Mardi is impossible to untwist, but the book
   reveals a great imagination, is filled with superb passages,
   and proves Melville's vigor even in its failure, as does the
   mad Pierre, which has passages of lovely prose but is even
   less effectual. In their love of complicated rhymes, their
   hesitation and roughness, their solemn movement and reminiscent sadness, the poems of Melville and Hardy have much in
   common.

26 SALPETER, HARRY. "Knighting Melville." New York <u>World</u>
    (16 May).
        Review of 1926.A1. Melville is one of America's greatest
    creative minds. The erratic and violent fancies displayed
    in such books as <u>Pierre</u> and <u>Mardi</u> excuse Julian Hawthorne's
    suspicion that he was somewhat insane, even if they do not
    justify it.

27 ANON. "Herman Melville." London <u>Times Literary Supplement</u>,
    No. 1268 (20 May), p. 337.
        Review of 1926.A1. In his maturity Melville produced two
    great prose tragedies, <u>Moby-Dick</u> and <u>Pierre</u>, and a short
    one, "Bartleby." Freeman generally does well, but fails to
    see a trilogy and crescendo in <u>Mardi</u>, <u>Moby-Dick</u>, and <u>Pierre</u>,
    and does not cope fully with "Bartleby." A key to <u>Pierre</u>
    perhaps lies in Schopenhauer and Hegel. Melville's pessi-
    mism, contrary to Freeman, cannot simply be ascribed to a
    reaction against the task of incessant composition; it was
    an inborn and developed habit of mind, a predisposition of
    temperament, diffused throughout his big works, and affining
    him spiritually to Dante, Shakespeare, Ecclesiastes,
    Schopenhauer, Hartmann and the like masters of a profound
    and unflinching philosophy of life. Freeman does not draw
    attention to the slight though intensely tragic story of
    the sea captain--Ahab, even a Melville, in miniature--which
    is one of the few redemptive passages in <u>Clarel</u>.

28 MILFORD, H. S. "The Text of 'Typee.'" London <u>Times Literary
    Supplement</u>, No. 1269 (27 May), p. 355.
        Corrects detail in 1926.B27: "The World's Classics"
    edition reproduces the unabridged text of <u>Typee</u>.

29 CAREW, DUDLEY. "Literary History and Criticism--I." <u>London
    Mercury</u>, 14 (June), 214-215.
        Review of 1926.A1. Freeman is sound and interesting in
    his analysis of the novels but fails rather badly to give
    any idea of Melville the man. The first name that leaps to
    mind in connection with Melville is Conrad, though Conrad's
    prose is more disciplined and self-conscious than Melville's
    and his creed of "the few simple things" would never satisfy
    the grander but less subtle imagination of Melville.
    Melville was a one-book author, the book <u>Moby-Dick</u>. What-
    ever Melville intended, it is impossible not to see a sym-
    bolic significance in Ahab's hatred for the whale.

30 ANON. "How Melville Got Lost in His Own Involuted Prose."
    New York <u>Times Book Review</u> (13 June), p. 11.

1926

Review of 1926.A1. Melville's literary ancestry is English--William Blake, Sir Thomas Browne, and the Elizabethan playwrights. Melville could not flourish in a restrained and unimaginative era; there had to be a little madness in the air before he could be brought back to life. Melville never satisfied himself with any single literary, moral or philosophical point of view; he was never quite sure who he was or what he had come into the world to do. After Moby-Dick he lost himself in the realm of symbols; he could no longer speak the American language, but developed a new, strange, often incomprehensible language of his own. Freeman has not probed to the depths of Melville's being; possibly only a psychoanalyst would venture that.

31 MUIR, EDWIN. "Herman Melville." London Nation and Athenaeum, 39 (19 June), 324.
    Review of 1926.A1. Melville was born out of his time; there is hardly an indication that he experienced at all his life in America and as a citizen of the nineteenth century; except in Pierre and The Confidence-Man he never treated his life as an American. The Confidence-Man is an almost inconceivable failure, with all the awkwardness of style which results from Melville's complete inability to get into communication with his theme, the American civilization of his time. Freeman is correct that Melville was a writer full of obscure repressions, but wrong in his assessment of Melville's last 40 years, which give an appalling sense of sterility and unhappiness. Freeman's study is admirable as far as it goes, but any criticism written now which does not make some use of the apparatus of psychology seems incomplete, off the mark.

32 MOULT, THOMAS. "Discovering 'Moby Dick.'" Boston Christian Science Monitor (26 June), p. 11.
    Review of 1926.A1. Freeman's estimate is precise, comprehensive, true, analytically conscientious; but still leaves room for an appreciation by someone less careful about biographical veracity. America has never produced an author of bigger vision than Melville; he is not to be comprehended or measured by the literary analyst. A true appreciation of Melville in his Moby-Dick period would betray continually a tendency to break the bonds of criticism and intellectual appreciation and soar into the plane of rhapsody.

33 ANON. "General Literature." Chicago Booklist, 22 (July), 416-417.

322

Notice of 1926.A1--which discusses, "besides the more familiar novels," Redburn, White-Jacket, Mardi, Billy Budd, and miscellaneous prose and poems.

34 CRANE, HART. "At Melville's Tomb." London Calendar, 3 (July), 105.
   Poem. [See 1926.B42.]

35 ANON. "New Books in Brief Review." New York Independent (24 July), p. 108.
   Review of 1926.A1. Freeman will help to dispel the air of mystery, misrepresentation, and ignorance which still clings to Melville's career.

36 ANON. "Our Own Bookshelf." Boston Living Age, 330 (31 July), 216.
   Review of 1926.A1.--A provocative and smoothly written account.

37 FAUSSET, HUGH I'A. "Herman Melville." London Bookman, 70 (August), 237-238.
   Review of 1926.A1. The history of nineteenth-century creative writers supports the theory that the artistic impulse originates in a neurosis caused by a failure of adaptability, and that a writer seeks through expression to relieve himself of a sense of conflict with his environment. Melville's work displays a wrestling between the finite and the infinite, a frenzied search for a harmony which life denied. Melville is supreme, as all great writers are, by his combination of a physical with a metaphysical consciousness; for Melville, man's physical struggle with the elements is but the shadow of his battle as a free spirit with hard necessity. As a comprehensive introduction to Melville, Freeman's book is admirable. His treatment of Pierre (superficially morbid but essentially cosmic) is perhaps the least satisfactory part; though to draw an entirely adequate portrait of Melville requires more imaginative daring.

38 HAWTHORNE, JULIAN. "When Herman Melville was 'Mr. Omoo.'" New York Literary Digest International Book Review, 4 (August), 561-562, 564.
   Review of 1926.A1, with personal reminiscences of Melville. Melville could not see that his proper function was description of things known and seen; he wanted to probe and solve the nature of the universe; for that he was equipped neither by nature nor education. He had already begun to succumb to insanity in the last chapters of Moby-Dick; in Pierre it became rampant. The poems are disordered doggerel; Israel

1926

Potter might have been written by any publisher's hack;
Clarel is depressing rubbish. Melville's own era appraised
him justly enough. In 1883 Melville told Julian that the
letters he had received from Hawthorne were all long since
destroyed. Freeman is at fault in assuming that characters
and incidents in Melville's books may be revelations, more
or less veiled, of his actual personal experiences.

39 PEARSON, EDMUND. "Essays and Criticism." New York Outlook,
143 (18 August), 547-548.
Review of 1926.A1.--Just what had been needed for the
general reader, though Freeman does the cause of Melville
no service by vaunting power, beauty, and artistic merit
where they least appear--as in Israel Potter. The conditions facing men of letters in the American forties and
fifties silenced Melville, snuffed him out as a literary
artist.

40 NELSON, JOHN HERBERT. The Negro Character in American Literature. Humanistic Studies, 4, No. 1. Bulletin of the University of Kansas, 27 (1 September), 29.
Rose-Water in White-Jacket cited as an example of the
Negro appearing in "unexpected places" in literature.

41 MUMFORD, LEWIS. "The New Men of Letters." New York New
Republic, 48 (29 September), 166-167.
Review of 1926.A1. The cast of Melville's mind brought
him closer to dramatists like Webster and Marlowe, with
their black and powerful imaginations, than it did to the
novelists of his own century. Time, fate, eternity,
destiny, "and what it is to be a man, afloat in solitude,
and an outcast from the miniature works of the shop and
the drawing room," were the things Melville faced. Freeman
comes near to doing justice to his large subject; his appreciation of Melville's lesser writings is particularly good.
Billy Budd shows Melville still with the same gesture and
grasp (if no longer with the reach of Moby-Dick), meditating
on man's tragic destiny.

42 M[ONROE], H[ARRIET]. "A Discussion With Hart Crane." Chicago
Poetry, 29 (October), 34-41.
Two letters from Monroe, criticizing Crane's poem "At
Melville's Tomb," and Crane's reply to the first. [Same
issue prints poem (p. 25).]

*43 BONE, DAVID. New York Saturday Review of Literature, 3
(2 October).
Cited in 1926.B45.

44 ANON. "Briefer Mention." Chicago Dial, 81 (November), 444.
    Review of 1926.A1. The biography is ordinary and adds
    little to previous accounts; the criticism, though unexcep-
    tionable, lacks the penetration which Melville's imagina-
    tive and emotional depths evidently require.

45 SPRAGUE, ROGER. "Melville and the Sea." [Letter to the
    Editor.] New York Saturday Review of Literature, 3
    (6 November), 280.
    Refutes statement in 1926.B43 that Melville wrote uncon-
    vincingly of the sea. White-Jacket is probably the finest
    account we have of life in the old-fashioned sailing frig-
    ate, though Moby-Dick is tinged with insanity and Melville's
    last stories are nothing but insanity.

46 VAN DOORN, WILLEM. Review of Herman Melville by John Freeman.
    [1926.A1.] Amsterdam English Studies, 8 (December), 194-195.
    Whitman specialized, of set purpose, in things vicarious;
    Melville dealt in nothing vicarious--even his most extrava-
    gant structures are raised on firm foundations of personal,
    first-hand experience. Freeman's is an excellent "first
    guide."

47 NASH, J. V. "Herman Melville, 'Ishmael' of American Litera-
    ture." Chicago Open Court, 40 (December), 734-741.
    Cursory general survey.

1927 A BOOKS - NONE

1927 B SHORTER WRITINGS

1   BEARD, CHARLES A. and MARY R. BEARD. The Rise of American
    Civilization. Vol. 1. New York: The Macmillan Co.,
    pp. 789-790.
    Out of wider and deeper experiences than Dana's, out of
    a more playful and mystic nature, Melville evolved still
    more powerful tales of ocean life. Moby-Dick seems to
    symbolize an eternal enmity between man and nature.
    Melville is one of the noteworthy figures of universal
    literature.

2   BELL, MACKENZIE. "Herman Melville," in Representative Novel-
    ists of the Nineteenth Century. Vol. 3. New York: Dial
    Press, p. 6.
    Headnote to extract from chapter 7 of Omoo. For many
    years previous to his death Melville "lived in seclusion
    owing to the gradual decay of his mind." He was a prolific

but very unequal writer. R. L. Stevenson awakened renewed interest in his supremely fine stories of the ocean.

3   BOYNTON, PERCY H. "Herman Melville," in More Contemporary Americans. Chicago: University of Chicago Press, pp. 29-50.
    Survey. Moby-Dick is as didactic in its sustained metaphors as in its chapters on cetology. The ocean is the boundless truth; the land is the reef of human error; the whale is the symbol of all property and all privilege. Pierre is not a good story for it does not contain a single thoroughly human major character. Billy Budd is full of the sweep and vigor of Melville's greatest work. Reprinted in part in Doubloon, pp. 170-171.

4   BROOKS, VAN WYCK. "Notes on Herman Melville," in Emerson and Others. New York: E. P. Dutton & Co., pp. 171-205.
    Reprint of 1923.B20, 1923.B24, 1923.B22, and 1923.B21, with minor revisions.

5   FORSTER, E. M. "Prophecy," in Aspects of the Novel. London: Edward Arnold & Co., pp. 178-184; New York: Harcourt, Brace & Co., pp. 199-206.
    The essential in Moby-Dick is its "prophetic song," which "flows athwart the action and the surface morality like an undercurrent" and "lies outside words." Nothing can be stated about Moby-Dick except that it is a contest. The rest is song. In Billy Budd the contest between Billy and Claggart is the contest between Ahab and Moby Dick, though the parts are more clearly assigned, and we are further from prophecy and nearer to morality and common sense--but not much nearer.

6   GARWOOD, IRVING. Questions and Problems in American Literature. New York: Century Co., pp. 100-101.
    Questions on Typee and chapter 48, "The First Lowering," of Moby-Dick.

7   GORMAN, HERBERT. Hawthorne: A Study in Solitude. New York: George H. Doran Co., pp. 92-93.
    In the "curious friendship" between Hawthorne and Melville the emotional exertion seems to have been on Melville's side, though it is apparent that Hawthorne responded in a friendly-enough fashion. The two discussed many things, including the existence of God.

8   GUNN, SIDNEY. The Story of Literature. New York: J. H. Sears & Co., p. 337.

Melville's life was a failure. Today he is enjoying a considerable popularity, but he is not able to profit by it.

9 HIND, C. LEWIS. "Herman Melville," in 100 Best Books. London: A. M. Philpot, p. 72.
Introduction to extracts from Moby-Dick, which "has bounded into a tardy and well-deserved fame" in America and Great Britain, mainly because of Viola Meynell's enthusiastic article [1920.B5].

10 LOWES, JOHN LIVINGSTON. The Road to Xanadu: A Study in the Ways of the Imagination. Boston: Houghton Mifflin Co., passim.
Brief mentions. Moby-Dick the titanic and unrivalled epic of the sea. Superb apotheosis of the albatross in Moby-Dick, chapter 42, "The Whiteness of the Whale."

11 MORRIS, LLOYD. The Rebellious Puritan: Portrait of Mr. Hawthorne. New York: Harcourt, Brace and Co., pp. 243-251; passim.
Hawthorne's friendship with Melville. Melville's agonized skepticism was probably only the symptom of his malady--an intolerable loneliness, a hopeless awareness of the necessity for a companionship so intimate and so understanding that it could have been satisfied only by love. Melville's marriage was scarcely happy; he was probably unsuited to marriage, and likely he was incapable of being physically attracted to women. In conversation and letters he was prolific in confidences. Hawthorne must have been frequently embarrassed by Melville's impulsive abandonment of reticence. Reviewed in 1928.B24.

12 PARRINGTON, VERNON LOUIS. "Herman Melville: Pessimist," in The Romantic Revolution in America. Vol. 2 of Main Currents in American Thought: An Interpretation of American Literature From the Beginnings to 1920. New York: Harcourt, Brace and Co., pp. 258-267; passim.
Survey, indebted to Weaver [1921.A1] who "has perhaps done all that the critic can to light up the darkness" of Melville's mystery. Melville's pessimism was a natural outcome of his transcendental speculations once they had come in intimate contact with life, given his passionate nature and large demands on life. For all his immersion in Plato, Melville was no Greek; rather he was Hebraic, out of Ecclesiastes, Solomon, and Jesus. His democracy was learned from Ecclesiastes rather than from Emerson. Reprinted in part in Rountree, pp. 37-38.

1927

13 ROSENBACH, A. S. W. <u>Books and Bidders: The Adventures of a</u>
<u>Bibliophile</u>. Boston: Little, Brown, and Co., pp. 26-27.
Remembers buying a first edition of <u>Moby-Dick</u>, worth
$150, for two dollars in Salem, Mass. Bought from English
poet and dramatist John Drinkwater Melville's presentation
copy to Hawthorne of <u>Moby-Dick</u> with Hawthorne's signature
on the dedication leaf, which Drinkwater had bought in a
New York bookstore for a few dollars.

14 SQUIRE, J. C. "Preface," in <u>The Cambridge Book of Lesser</u>
<u>Poets</u>. Cambridge: University Press, p. vii.
Lists Melville as one of the "giants" in the book.
[Prints "Marlena," "Crossing the Tropics," "Pipe Song,"
and "The Temeraire," pp. 398-401.]

15 PATTEE, FRED LEWIS. "Herman Melville." New York <u>American</u>
<u>Mercury</u>, 10 (January), 33-43.
Revived interest in Melville was a result of the interest in the South Seas exploited by London, O'Brien, and
others. Melville, a Titan in Soul, surpasses Lowell in
originality and daring, surpasses Whitman (whom he star-
tlingly resembles) in imagination and intellect; he surpasses both in epic sweep and superhuman force. Melville
blended the heritages of puritan New England and cosmopolitan New York. <u>Typee</u> is a product of New York; like
<u>Knickerbocker's History</u>, Cooper's novels, and <u>Leaves of</u>
<u>Grass</u> it could not have come from New England. But the
Knickerbocker romancer is interrupted by the Puritan;
<u>Typee</u> is a Carlylean sermon. All of Melville's major char-
acters are Byronic, Titans in rebellion; and in all his
characters we see only Melville: Melville is Taji, Jack
Chase, Jackson, Ahab, Paul Jones, Ethan Allen, and Israel
Potter. <u>Mardi</u> is not an insane jumble but a book of power,
in which Melville discovered Whitman's "poetic instrument"
years before Whitman himself, a book to live with and study
long. <u>Pierre</u>, also a book of real power, is not autobiography but Hawthorne-like romance in major key. Melville's
genius was like that of Coleridge: sudden lyric outbursts
rather than finished wholes. Reprinted in 1930.B21.

16 METCALF, ELEANOR MELVILLE. "A Pilgrim by Land and Sea."
Boston <u>Horn Book</u>, 3 (February), 3-11.
Brief accounts of Melville's books, for children. Reminiscences of Melville "forty odd years ago" in his "rather
dark" room, with walls "lined with tall book-cases, from
the tops of which peered dusty plaster heads of ancient
deities and mighty men of thought.... Here he lived in
company with the sages, poets, devils, giants, warriors,

heroes, saints and wits of all the ages. Yet he was lonely.
To the people of his day he seemed not altogether sociable."
Prints Melville's letter to Bessie Melville, 2 September
1860, and letter to Malcolm Melville, 16 September 1860
[Letters, pp. 203-205].

17 H., F. "Great Elements of Melville's Prose." Boston
    Christian Science Monitor (4 February), p. 7.
        Examples of Melville's excellence in alliteration,
    biblical and classical allusion, simile, metaphor, person-
    ification, and rhythm. His wavelike sentences afford an
    excellent study of balanced structure. Melville is to be
    ranked with Lamb, Ruskin, De Quincey, Stevenson, Pater,
    and other acknowledged masters of prose. As a nation we
    have not learned to place Melville above Poe and Hawthorne
    as "the most powerful of all the great American writers"
    [see 1926.A1].

18 ANON. "Benito Cereno." London Times Literary Supplement,
    No. 1309 (3 March), p. 140.
        Review of Nonesuch edition of Benito Cereno. Melville
    never became a master of the technique of fiction; of all
    the great nineteenth century storytellers he was the clum-
    siest. In Benito Cereno the reader is acutely conscious
    of the opportunities Melville missed. He lets his mysteri-
    ous atmosphere dissipate; indulges in a bewildering luxuri-
    ance of detail; and forgets that a ship's captain who is
    the terrified instrument of his apparent servants could not
    have failed to arouse the suspicions of so experienced a
    sailor as Delano.

19 'AFFABLE HAWK.' "Books in General." London New Statesman, 28
    (5 March), 635.
        Review of Nonesuch edition of Benito Cereno. Next to
    Moby-Dick this is the most impressive of Melville's stories,
    told in his best grand manner. From the start it leaves
    reality for the intensity of nightmare. Not even Conrad
    could have presented the mystery of the ship and its master
    more vividly to the imagination.

20 CHEW, SAMUEL C. "Men of Letters." New Haven Yale Review,
    NS 16 (April), 614-616.
        Review of 1926.A1. Parts of Freeman's book are stodgy,
    but his tone is judicious; while the astonishing merits of
    Billy Budd are clearly recognized, there is no tendency to
    overestimate the importance of the mysticism of Melville's
    other later books.

1927

21 OVERTON, GRANT. "America's Ancient Mariner." New York
   Mentor, 15 (April), 14–15.
       Biographical sketch. Moby-Dick is only beginning to be
   read. "Parts of it Victor Hugo might have written—-and
   they are not the best parts." Many passages are as sublime
   as the finest poetry.

22 MATTHEWS, HERBERT L. "Another Melville Tale Is Rescued From
   Oblivion." New York Times Book Review (15 May), p. 6.
       Review of Nonesuch edition of Benito Cereno. A
   story of breathtaking interest, flawless technique, unadul-
   terated by the introspection and mysticism that baffle the
   reader of Mardi and Pierre; an example of Melville's ripest
   genius and incomparable flair for telling a straight
   unadorned story.

23 CANBY, HENRY SEIDEL. "A Fragment of Genius." New York
   Saturday Review of Literature, 3 (28 May), 864.
       Review of Nonesuch edition of Benito Cereno. The story
   forecasts Conrad's method: by mere description Melville
   raises emotional intensity until with no real happening a
   ghastly situation is felt though not understood. But the
   conclusion shows that Melville has not yet learned the art
   of narrative development. He never learned it, as even
   Moby-Dick shows.

24 FAULKNER, WILLIAM. "Confessions." Chicago Tribune (16 July),
   "Books," p. 12.
       "...I think that the book which I put down with the un-
   qualified thought 'I wish I had written that' is Moby Dick.
   The Greek-like simplicity of it: a man of forceful character driven by his sombre nature and his bleak heritage,
   bent on his own destruction and dragging his immediate
   world down with him with a despotic and utter disregard of
   them as individuals.... There's magic in the very word.
   A White Whale. White is a grand word, like a crash of
   massed trumpets; and leviathan himself has a kind of placid
   blundering majesty in his name...." Reprinted in part in
   Burgert, p. 373, and Vincent, p. 162; reprinted in Doubloon,
   p. 172.

25 SALVIDGE, STANLEY. "Herman Melville and Liverpool." London
   Spectator, 139 (16 July), 88–89.
       On the growth of the Liverpool docks; quotation from
   Redburn. The opening of the Gladstone Dock (19 July) by
   King George V would appeal strongly to Melville. Redburn
   shows that if there was a thing that thrilled Melville more
   than the sight of the Liverpool docks, it was the chance of
   rubbing shoulders with royalty.

26 ANON. "'Moby Dick' House Sold." New York <u>Times</u> (30 July),
    p. 6.
        Notes sale of "the historic Melville place," in
    Pittsfield, Mass., which buyer, Colonel Robert E. Kimball,
    will maintain as a literary shrine.

27 HAWTHORNE, JULIAN. "Herman Melville and His Dog." Dearborn,
    Mich. <u>Dearborn Independent</u>, 27 (24 September), 3, 26.
        Reminiscences of Melville's visits to the Hawthornes
    during the composition of <u>Moby-Dick</u>; wishes that some of
    the careless felicity of those days could have found a way
    into the pages of "that appalling and inchoate work." <u>Moby-</u>
    <u>Dick</u> has many fine passages, but much can be found in the
    earlier books nearly or quite as good; as wholes they are
    superior. Melville was unable to assimilate his self-
    acquired knowledge; the dry rot of moral metaphysics got
    hold of him. He was perplexed by Hawthorne's knowledge
    of the human heart and seemed finally to think that
    Hawthorne had committed at least one of the seven deadly
    sins in his youth. When Julian visited him in his sixties,
    Melville's mind was sinking into a "dark region."

28 GALLAND, RENÉ. "Herman Melville et 'Moby-Dick.'" Paris <u>Revue</u>
    <u>Anglo-Américaine</u>, 5 (October), 1-9.
        Survey. Melville's books are irregular, and some of
    them are a little mad; but they are alive with an intense
    life. Conrad, who alone can be compared with Melville, has
    greater artistic force; but Melville has greater youth of
    spirit and vitality. In <u>Moby-Dick</u>, Melville's enormous
    humor is everywhere; but humor is not the dominant note.
    Imagination and symbol are what fill the book. The <u>Pequod</u>
    becomes humanity, Ahab (almost superman) its consciousness.

1928 A BOOKS - NONE

1928 B SHORTER WRITINGS

1   AMENT, WILLIAM S. "Preface," "Introduction," "Questions and
    Topics for the Study of 'Moby-Dick,'" "Notes," in <u>Moby-Dick</u>.
    Boston: Ginn and Co., pp. vii-viii; xiii-xxxvii; 437-443;
    445-474.
        Biographical introduction, with summaries of Melville's
    books; also includes "Selected List of Sea Stories" and
    list of "The Best Books of the Sea." Melville is almost
    unique among American writers in his powerful pictures of
    suffering and death, in which he rivals the greatest of the
    Russians. Only Dostoevski can equal the macabre naturalism

of Miguel Saveda's death in <u>Redburn</u>. Moby Dick becomes
the symbol of a malevolent nature, "the wall which closes
all the vistas to our lands of heart's desire, the immovable
object or fate which conquers the almost irresistible force
of the will of mortal man." "Preface" explains editor's
principles of abridgment.

2   ANDERSON, JOHANNES C. <u>Myths & Legends of the Polynesians</u>.
London: George G. Harrap & Co., p. 458.
Notes that although "no remains of pyramids have been
seen in the Marquesas, Melville has described stepped plat-
forms built against a hillside, the ruins, like those in
the Friendly Islands, being buried in tangled forests."

3   ANON. "Preface," in <u>Romances of Herman Melville</u>. New York:
The Pickwick Publishers, pp. v-vi.
Biographical sketch; brief comments on works. <u>Moby-Dick</u>
marked the end of Melville's powerful creation.

4   BATES, SYLVIA CHATFIELD. "Introduction" and "Appendix," in
<u>Moby Dick</u>, adapted by Sylvia Chatfield Bates. New York:
Charles Scribner's Sons, pp. v-vi, 117-133.
Melville dramatizes the immortal conflict between the
indomitable soul of man and the inscrutable evil in the
world which only he dares to assail. The weakness which
undoes him is the very pride in his own power and resentment
that anything should curtail it, which is also his strength.
The book may be read for the adventure alone. "Appendix"
consists of explanatory notes and "Topics to Talk About."

5   BENNETT, ARNOLD. <u>The Savour of Life: Essays in Gusto</u>.
London: Cassell & Co., pp. 248-259; Garden City, N.Y.:
Doubleday, Doran & Co., pp. 305-307.
Melville may become famous as the author of <u>Pierre</u>,
which contains superb writing and also grotesque writing,
which Melville mistakenly thought to be superb. It is full
of lyrical beauty, is conceived in an heroical, epical vein,
and executed (faultily) in the grand manner. In it Melville
essays feats which the most advanced novelists of today
imagine to be quite new. Reprinted in <u>Recognition</u>, p. 187.

6   BENSON, EARL MALTBY. "Foreword" and "Appendix," in <u>Moby Dick</u>.
Boston: Allyn and Bacon, pp. iii-iv, 439-493.
A school text issued in response to the "rapidly increas-
ing interest in the history of whaling." The text omits
"many long, uninteresting, philosophical digressions which
would not be appreciated even by the majority of adult
readers." "Appendix" contains a biographical sketch, a

brief history of the whaling industry, a bibliography of
whaling fiction and non-fiction, questions and topics for
discussion, explanatory notes, and a glossary.

7   CLARK, HARRY HAYDEN. "American Literary History and American
     Literature," in The Reinterpretation of American Literature.
     Ed. Norman Foerster. New York: Harcourt, Brace and Co.,
     pp. 207-212.
         Ahab was born out of the conflict in Melville's mind
     between his ingrained transcendental optimism, with its
     serene faith in a beneficent nature, and his first-hand
     knowledge of a nature "red in tooth and claw." If Melville
     had not gone to sea "in precisely this brilliant and pic-
     turesque period" he would have written a book of metaphysics
     instead of Moby-Dick.

8   COURNOS, JOHN. "The Comparison of Melville with Rimbaud and
     Doughty," in A Modern Plutarch. Indianapolis: The Bobbs-
     Merrill Co., pp. 127-134; London: T. Butterworth,
     pp. 113-118.
         Melville had too much heart, Rimbaud too much mind; they
     were both men of extremes and so lacked Doughty's virtue of
     endurance. The White Whale is Melville's "confession of his
     own transcendent illusion, of his own quest of the unattain-
     able, driving him to his ultimate despair, his ultimate
     doom." Melville is a symbol and a reflection of a country
     "whose spiritual self lies prostrate before its material
     power."

9   COURNOS, JOHN. "Herman Melville--The Seeker," in A Modern
     Plutarch. Indianapolis: The Bobbs-Merrill Co., pp. 78-95;
     London: T. Butterworth, pp. 77-89.
         Biographical. Focuses on Melville's need for friendship
     with Hawthorne.

10   ERSKINE, JOHN. "Moby Dick," in The Delight of Great Books.
     Indianapolis: The Bobbs-Merrill Co., pp. 223-240.
         Moby-Dick is not a novel but a poem, with the power of a
     great epic, gathering our emotions around a central figure,
     a central incident, and one central mood. Its art consists
     not in reproducing pictures of the outside of life but in
     preparing our minds for an effect of emotion, so that at
     the end there will be a powerful catharsis, or release of
     feeling. No detail is lost in the ultimate effect. Father
     Mapple's sermon introduces the fanatic note which is essen-
     tial to the final effect of the story, which becomes a
     parable of man's agony to unite himself with the universal,
     the infinite. The central theme of the book is the sea and

1928

all the vast aspects of nature; Melville's success in conveying the awful grandeur of the sea and space is what sets
him apart from other writers. In <u>Moby-Dick</u> he makes a kind
of circle out of three ideas: the sea, Ahab's madness, and
the whale. At the end Ahab is no longer a divided or incom-
plete personality but united within himself; Ishmael is a
symbol for the reader's own soul, which Melville has trans-
ported through a voyage of beauty and terror. Reprinted in
1929.B67.

11 FINLEY, JOHN H. "Foreword," in <u>Moby Dick</u>, adapted by Sylvia
Chatfield Bates. New York: Charles Scribner's Sons,
p. iii.
This book might well be called the American Odyssey, for
it tells in Homeric fashion of wanderings beyond "the paths
of all the Western stars."

12 HOHMAN, ELMO PAUL. <u>The American Whaleman</u>. New York:
Longmans, Green and Co., pp. 134-135, 173-176, 205-210,
214n, 346.
Illustrative quotation from <u>Moby-Dick</u>, where "the very
soul of whaling is laid bare," and where many descriptive
passages "combine accuracy of detail with a graphic portrayal of the spirit of the fishery far more successfully
than any piece of historical scholarship."

13 KAUFMAN, PAUL. "The Romantic Movement," in <u>The Reinterpretation of American Literature</u>. Ed. Norman Foerster. New
York: Harcourt, Brace and Co., pp. 115, 125, 128.
Hawthorne and Melville "were romancers par excellence,
both voyaging into strange seas of thought alone, the one
exploring intensively the inner realms of the soul, the
other ranging extensively over the earth and in his most
important work finding a certain cosmic meaning in man's
deeds of daring adventure."

14 MURDOCK, KENNETH B. "The Puritan Tradition in American
Literature," in <u>The Reinterpretation of American Literature</u>.
Ed. Norman Foerster. New York: Harcourt, Brace and Co.,
p. 113.
When we come to understand the Puritan literary tradition
and its implications, Emerson, Melville, Hawthorne,
Longfellow, Whitman, Dickinson, Thoreau, and other writers
will be seen in new lights and take on new meanings.

15 NEWTON, A. EDWARD. <u>This Book-Collecting Game</u>. Boston:
Little, Brown and Co., pp. 275, 379; passim.

Brief references to the greatness of <u>Moby-Dick</u>--"America's supreme contribution to world literature. For years we have been looking for the great American novel, not knowing or not remembering that it appeared in 1851." Knows of no uglier looking book than the 1851 edition of <u>Moby-Dick</u>, with the possible exception of <u>The Education of Henry Adams</u>.

16   OVERTON, GRANT. <u>The Philosophy of Fiction</u>. New York and
       London: D. Appleton & Co., pp. 88, 228-244, 251-252,
       295-296.
          Extends E. M. Forster's discussion of prophecy in fic-
       tion [<u>see</u> 1927.B5], distinguishing Dostoevski and Melville
       from Emily Brontë and D. H. Lawrence. Dostoevski and
       Melville have nothing to do with realism; they use the
       materials of ordinary life distorted by pressures of extra-
       ordinary experience. All their fiction moves toward an
       apotheosis of the Divine Will. <u>Moby-Dick</u> has affinities
       with Greek drama: when plot served great ends it was often
       loose and formless. <u>Moby-Dick</u> creates the emotion of an-
       cient fiction, in part the purge of Greek drama, in part
       "an emotion more ancient still, that of 'truth to the won-
       der,' an exertion to be worthy of the great creativeness
       going on all about us." Like other animists, Melville does
       not teach us how to live but teaches us how to be, shows us
       the wealth of being. Melville shares with Hardy a view of
       the universe as enactment.

17   ROSENBACH, A. S. W. "Introduction," in <u>Moby Dick</u>. Garden City,
       N.Y.: Doubleday, Doran and Co., pp. v-ix.
          Reprint of 1924.A1.

18   STARR, NATHAN COMFORT. "The Sea in the English Novel from
       Defoe to Melville." Ph.D. dissertation, Harvard University,
       pp. 315-362.
          Discusses Melville's sea fiction; relates <u>Moby-Dick</u> to
       earlier whaling narratives.

19   SWINNERTON, FRANK. "Herman Melville," in <u>A London Bookman</u>.
       London: Martin Secker, pp. 8-9.
          Reprint of 1921.B14.

20   WEAVER, RAYMOND. "Introduction," in <u>Shorter Novels of Herman
       Melville</u>. New York: Liveright Publishing Corp.,
       pp. vii-li.
          Biographical survey. The stories in this volume
       ("Benito Cereno," "Bartleby," "The Encantadas," and <u>Billy
       Budd</u>) are of prime importance for their inherent qualities
       as works of art and for their peculiar position in Melville's

development as artist and man. Melville's most enthusiastic
readers have been primarily interested in him as a tortured
and cryptic personality, not as a first-rate creative artist. But "Benito Cereno" and "The Encantadas" are slowly
coming to be seen as Melville's supreme technical achievements as an artist. The unqualified failures among
Melville's stories and sketches are those in which he tries
to imitate Hawthorne. Hawthorne and Melville were both
pessimists, but Hawthorne's pessimism was an expression of
lack of ardor and illusion; the ardor of his illusions was
at the basis of Melville's embittered defeat. Hawthorne
is portrayed as Plotinus Plinlimmon in Pierre, where most
of the characters are "unmistakably idealizations of actual
people." Among the many "parallels of contrast" between
Pierre and Billy Budd, each is a tragedy; but through the
tragedy of Billy Budd Melville affirms his everlasting yea,
justifies the ways of God to man. As a study in abnormal
psychology, Billy Budd is remarkably detached, subtle, and
profound. [See 1921.A1.] The whole known record of
Melville's life seems to indicate that "veiled and deep-
seated impulses from his nether-consciousness resolutely
blocked the way to singleness of purpose and whole-
heartedness of surrender; suppressions the more eloquently
betrayed by his efforts both in his writings and in his
life, to conceal them from himself." Melville's "most
relentless craving" was to discover and dissolve himself
into his other Platonic half. But, "disintegrated by the
New England contamination from Saint Paul," he viewed any
such dissolution as a surrender to iniquity.

21   WINTERICH, JOHN T. Collector's Choice. New York: Greenberg,
     p. 65.
        The Melville collector "must have" Moby-Dick (New York,
     1851).

22   BROOKS, VAN WYCK. "Book Reviews." New England Quarterly, 1
     (January), 84-88.
        Review of The Golden Day by Lewis Mumford. [See 1926.B8].
     Emerson, Thoreau, Whitman, Hawthorne, and Melville lived
     in an age that nourished a heroic conception of life. In
     Hawthorne and Melville, "the image of humanity still remains
     magnified, even, in Melville, colossal, however distorted."

23   McCUTCHEON, ROGER P. "The Technique of Melville's Israel
     Potter." South Atlantic Quarterly, 27 (April), 161-174.
        Examination of Melville's indebtedness in Israel Potter
     to his source, the autobiographical Life and Remarkable
     Adventures of Israel R. Potter (Providence, 1824), and his
     departures from it.

24   [READ, HERBERT]. "Nathaniel Hawthorne." London <u>Times Literary</u>
     <u>Supplement</u>, No. 1370 (3 May), p. 321.
          Review of <u>The Rebellious Puritan</u> by Lloyd Morris. [See
     1927.B11.] We cannot be sure of the rightness of Hawthorne's
     attitude in his rejection of Melville. Hawthorne was the
     greater artist, but not necessarily the greater man;
     Melville's "divine magnanimities" encompassed far more than
     Hawthorne's equanimity. Reprinted in 1929.B15.

25   O'BRIEN, EDWARD J. "The Fifteen Finest Short Stories." New
     York <u>Forum</u>, 79 (June), 909.
          Includes "Benito Cereno"--the noblest short story in
     American literature. "The balance of forces is complete,
     the atmosphere one of epic significance, the light cast
     upon the hero intense to the highest degree, the realiza-
     tion of the human soul profound, and the telling of the
     story orchestrated like a great symphony.... All Conrad's
     strivings reach fulfillment in this story, and its music
     lingers in the memory long after Conrad's music is
     forgotten."

26   SCUDDER, HAROLD H. "Melville's <u>Benito Cereno</u> and Captain
     Delano's Voyages." <u>PMLA</u>, 43 (June), 502-532.
          Reprints chapter 18 of <u>A Narrative of Voyages and</u>
     <u>Travels in the Northern and Southern Hemispheres</u> by Amasa
     Delano (Boston, 1817), Melville's source for "Benito Cereno."
     Notes departures from the original, which "very materially
     alter the tone of the narrative." Melville saw in Benito
     Cereno a parallel with his own fate: Benito Cereno is
     Melville; Babo is the personification of malicious criticism.

27   WEAVER, RAYMOND. "New England Gentlemen." New York <u>Herald</u>
     <u>Tribune Books</u> (16 September), pp. 1, 6.
          Account of Melville from Hawthorne's point of view.
     Hollingsworth in <u>The Blithedale Romance</u> is a portrait of
     Melville--"not a flattering portrait, though it is executed
     without satire, without any evident malice. It is a kind
     of post-mortem, undertaken with clinical precision, and at
     the same time a kind of self-justification, from Hawthorne's
     point of view, for the failure of friendship between him and
     Melville--an absolution by public confession." Plinlimmon
     in <u>Pierre</u> is based on Hawthorne. Quotes from Melville's
     letter of 17? November 1851 to Hawthorne [<u>Letters</u>,
     pp. 141-144] (which Hawthorne read with "fascinated and
     incredulous repugnance").

28   JOSEPHSON, MATTHEW. "The Transfiguration of Herman Melville."
     New York <u>Outlook</u>, 150 (19 September), 809-811, 832, 836.

1928

Survey. In his "revival," Melville is familiar as the
author of Typee, Omoo, and Moby-Dick. Less known or favored
is the other Melville, who as much as Poe was a psychological "case" of derailed genius, a dark temperament, steeped
in skepticism and despair. Profoundly changed inwardly
after Moby-Dick, Melville thenceforth suggests "one of
those solitary and 'dangerous' characters of literary history, Blake, Poe, Baudelaire, Rimbaud." His later "fragments" reveal a mystic who shares Schopenhauer's belief in
man's destiny of suffering, "escape from which lies only in
the intellectual rapture of the fakir seeking Nirvana."

29   MUMFORD, LEWIS. "The Significance of Herman Melville." New
       York New Republic, 56 (10 October), 212-214.
          Corresponds to "Epilogue" of 1929.A1, with minor
       differences.

30   DE VOTO, BERNARD. "Editions of 'Typee.'" [Letter to the
       Editor.] New York Saturday Review of Literature, 5
       (24 November), 406.
          Notes errors in Minnigerode's description of the first
       American edition of Typee and the revised edition [in
       1922.A1]; describes a "variant" of the first American edition.

31   MUMFORD, LEWIS. "The Writing of 'Moby-Dick.'" New York
       American Mercury, 15 (December), 482-490.
          Corresponds to chapter 6 of 1929.A1, with minor
       differences.

32   VAN DOREN, CARL. "A Note of Confession." New York Nation,
       127 (5 December), 622.
          Review of Shorter Novels of Herman Melville, ed. Raymond
       Weaver. [See 1928.B20.] These shorter novels belong with
       the most original and distinguished fiction yet produced on
       this continent. "Benito Cereno" equals the best of Conrad
       in the weight of its drama and the skill of its unfolding.
       Billy Budd surpasses the best of Conrad in the music of its
       language, as in the profundity and serenity of its reflec-
       tions. Billy Budd is particularly important because there
       alone Melville rises above the dark problems of his later
       years; he no longer asks why evil should exist but asks how
       it moves on its errands and what is to be done about it.
       Van Doren regrets his earlier dismissal of The Piazza Tales
       as "not markedly original" [see 1917.B3].

33   MUMFORD, LEWIS. "The Younger Olympian." New York Saturday
       Review of Literature, 5 (15 December), 514-515.
          Corresponds to the first four sections of chapter 3 of
       1929.A1, minus a few paragraphs.

34 GRATTAN, C. HARTLEY. "Melville's Shorter Novels...." New
    York World (16 December).
        Review of The Shorter Novels of Herman Melville. [See
    1928.B20.] "Benito Cereno" is a piece of psychological
    analysis of quite astonishing depth. It presents a typical
    Melvillean situation: purity juxtaposed in dramatic con-
    trast with evil. Melville's working out of this problem is
    as subtle and powerful as in any of his longer works. No
    faltering of his touch is discernible. "Bartleby" strongly
    suggests Sherwood Anderson. The Shorter Novels is a book
    of extreme importance, providing material for a deeper
    understanding of Melville, one of the truly extraordinary
    American writers, who wrestled with problems that have en-
    gaged the masters of literature, such as Dostoevski.
    Grattan is repulsed by Weaver's "hieratic manner" in his
    preface and thinks his theory of Melville's "sexual con-
    stitution" is wrong.

1929 A BOOKS

1 MUMFORD, LEWIS. Herman Melville. New York: Harcourt, Brace
   & Co., 377 pp.
        Biographical (often relying on the fiction as autobiog-
   raphy), historical, and critical. With Whitman, Melville
   is America's greatest imaginative writer--not a writer of
   romances, but a thinker, his thought and vision being "one
   of the most important things the century produced." Grap-
   pling with great spiritual dilemmas and seeking to answer
   them, he "sounded bottom." Not a romantic but a realist in
   the sense that the great religious teachers are realists, he
   brought back to the age the one element it completely lacked:
   the tragic sense of life. In depth of experience and religious insight there is scarcely anyone in the nineteenth
   century, except Dostoevski, who can be placed beside him.
   His triumph, like that of his contemporaries in the
   Golden Day, was the last expression of a provincial society,
   and the first prophetic achievement in a new and deeper
   culture, which received neither nourishment nor protection
   from the narrow, mechanistic, money-bent society that succeeded the provincial one after the Civil War.
        In Typee and Omoo Melville had superb aplomb, the result
   of an inner poise based on physical well-being and mental
   serenity. In Mardi the poise and completeness is gone;
   but such wit, humor, intelligence, wide knowledge, and
   resolute diving had not been known in American literature.
   From Azzageddi, working out of the depts of Melville's
   unconscious, come Melville's deepest perceptions.

White-Jacket shows greater art and control than any of his
earlier books; his power of invention appears only a few
times, but when it does it is magnificent; the prose is an
advance on all Melville's previous writing. Apart from
Moby-Dick, White-Jacket is Melville's fullest achievement.
    Melville's genius followed two separate lines of growth,
which joined in Moby-Dick: (i) that of Marlowe and Webster--
untrammelled emotions, stertorous vitality, keen transposition of dream into reality and reality into dream; and
(ii) that of Knox's Captivity, direct, honest, well-
ballasted. Moby-Dick is one of the supreme monuments of
the English language, belonging with the Divine Comedy,
Hamlet, The Brothers Karamazov, and War and Peace. Not a
novel but a poetic epic, with many meanings, it is funda-
mentally a parable on the mystery of evil and the accidental
malice of the universe. Neither Ishmael nor Ahab is the
hero: the central figure is the white whale, which stands
for the universe, for the demonic energies of existence,
which harass, frustrate, and extinguish the spirit of man;
Ahab is the spirit of man pitting its puniness against that
might. Ahab, however, becomes the image of the thing he
hates, losing his humanity in the very act of vindicating
it, not recognizing that the way of growth is not to become
more powerful but to become more human. In his refusal to
accept evil lies his heroism and his virtue; in fighting
evil with its own weapons lies his madness. Everything Ahab
despises when he is about to attack the whale, the love of
Pip, memory of wife and child, inner sense of calm, would
make him victorious. Ahab represents an heroic power that
misconceives its mission and misapplies itself; but he also
represents human purpose in its highest expression. Moby-
Dick is one of the first great mythologies to be created in
the modern world, created out of its science, exploration,
daring, and concentration on power over nature--not out of
ancient symbols. It "brings together the two dissevered
halves of the modern world and the modern self--its positive,
practical, scientific, externalized self, bent on conquest
and knowledge, and its imaginative, ideal half, bent on the
transposition of conflict into art, and power into humanity."
    Moby-Dick disintegrated Melville. The perfervid, mawk-
ishly poetical style of Pierre is itself witness to his
psychal disruption; the book is crude melodrama. Not concerned to portray "real life," Melville sought in Pierre to
arrive at the same sort of psychological truth he had
achieved in metaphysics in Moby-Dick; the book's supreme
quality is its candor. But Melville identified himself with
Pierre and defended his immaturity. All the values of the
book are distorted, its purpose is deflected, by Melville's

unconscious assumption that the romantic purity of adoles-
cence is central to all the other values. A much younger
Melville is in _Pierre_ than in _Typee_, a self erotically im-
mature, expressing itself in unconscious incest fantasies.
"Censorship" of _Typee_ kept Melville from maturing with reflection and experience; sex was taboo, until it suddenly
erupted in _Pierre_ with the violence of long repression.
Wherever sex is mentioned in Melville's other books it is
referred to in a mood of disillusion; he does not speak of
the experiences of husband and father as a mature man, but
as an adolescent. He associated his career with adolescent
purity, instead of with maturity. Lucy may signify the
naive writings of his youth and Isabel his darker consciousness, goading him to all his most heroic efforts--and possibly an impostor. Having abandoned everything to espouse
his inner life, he anticipated defeat: Lucy dies of shock,
Pierre and Isabel poison themselves, for Melville saw no
way to go on with his deepest self and still observe social
conventions and the responsibilities of a married man.

The last 40 years of Melville's life have been misinter-
preted as a time of insanity and silence. Melville became
"Timonized" during and after the writing of _Pierre_ and was
physically weakened; but not the least of his literary
achievements date from these years of debilitation and infirmity, and insanity is too loose a word to use about
Melville's mental illness. His superb craftsmanship in
"Bartleby," "The Encantadas," and "Benito Cereno" is objective proof: not wild, turgid, these stories are told with
delicacy, restraint, and great concentration. Melville's
blackness and spiritual desolation recalls that of
Shakespeare--their vision of life went through similar
stages. Every evidence in Melville's work points to the
restoration of his poise, intermittently during the fifties,
and steadily during the years that followed.

Melville's powers of invention were not small, but only
with difficulty could he escape the actual world and create
a world sustained by his own fantasy. The dwindling of his
first-hand sources was a great handicap to him; books helped
to form and crystallize experience but were not substitutes
for it. _Israel Potter_ is Melville manqué; Melville transformed Potter's bald story, but if he had made it wholly
his own, John Paul Jones would have been the central character. "Benito Cereno" marks the culmination of Melville's
power as a short story writer. Benito Cereno's fate parallels Melville's own life, his own dilemma, and his own bowed
and wounded spirit. _The Confidence-Man_ (unfinished) should
be seen not as a novel but as a companion volume to
Gulliver's Travels, containing dangerous and exhilarating

satire. The Confidence Man represents all the sweetness
and morality of the race, which, for Melville, had become
the greatest of frauds. The Confidence-Man can be seen as
Melville's own masquerade, his own bitter plea for support,
money, and confidence; savage, relentless humor took the
place of his earlier passionate defiance. Below the level
of the great eighteenth century satires, The Confidence-Man
is still far more deeply corrosive than anything in Bierce
or Twain as an indictment of humanity. Independent evidence shows that by 1858 Melville had regained possession
of himself.

In Clarel, a failure as poetry, Melville's skepticisms
are as thorough-going as in The Confidence-Man, but there
is a difference in mood, the beginnings of a new faith,
keeping Melville from slipping into hopeless indifference
or more hopeless despair. At the end of Clarel he found
life not good or bad, true or false, but livable; in the
Epilogue one sees the Melville who was slowly finding peace.
His last poems and Billy Budd contain the earlier themes of
his life transformed and resolved. Melville rarely achieved
form as a poet; he permitted himself to be conquered by the
external form of line and stanza. But in the last poems
there is a simplicity and directness which shows greater
control of his medium. Billy Budd is not a full-bodied
story: there is just statement, wise commentary, and apt
illustration; lacking is an independent and living creation,
the fecundity and energy of White-Jacket. The principal
characters are not primarily men but actors and symbols.
In Billy Budd Melville was reconciled to the paradoxes of
Pierre, accepted them as tragic necessity, and found the
ultimate peace of resignation. Indexed. Reviewed in
1929.B27, B28, B29, B30, B31, B32, B33, B34, B36, B37, B38,
B39, B41, B42, B43, B44, B45, B46, B51, B53, B54, B55, B59,
B60, B61, B66; 1930.B29. [See also 1929.B24, B26, B40,
B69; 1930.B42, B46.] Revised edition, Herman Melville:
A Study of His Life and Vision (New York: Harcourt Brace,
and World), 1962.

1929 B SHORTER WRITINGS

1   ARVIN, NEWTON. Hawthorne. Boston: Little, Brown and Co.,
     pp. 166-173, 233.
     On the friendship between Melville and Hawthorne. Only
external had their experiences been incongruous. Through
all his adventurous life, Melville's solitariness was no
less bleak than Hawthorne's; his sense of incurable isolation from his kind was as acute. In Ahab, Melville created
a symbol of the lonely intellect as monumental as any of

Hawthorne's. Probably the awareness of Hawthorne's understanding presence in the neighborhood helped Melville more
than anything else through the struggles of composing Moby-
Dick. There is reason to believe that in Ethan Brand
Hawthorne made a kind of portrait of Melville.

2   BEER, THOMAS. Hanna. New York: Alfred A. Knopf, pp. 47, 209,
    232-233.
       "The disaster to America caused by machinery was inscruta-
    ble to young Hanna. But the machine clattered under the
    prelude of the Civil War so certainly that Herman Melville
    caught the sound and wrote it down in The Confidence Man...."
    References to Senator Cushman Davis's knowledge of Moby-Dick.
    Reprinted in Beer, Hanna, Crane, and The Mauve Decade. New
    York: Alfred A. Knopf, 1941.

3   DOW, RALPH. "Introduction," in Moby Dick. New York: The
    Macmillan Co., pp. vii-xx. New York: Book League of
    America, pp. vii-xx.
       Biographical sketch and commentary on one of the great
    books of all time, "in which all life becomes clear in out-
    line and comprehensible in significance." The final combat
    between Ahab and the whale is as momentous a struggle as
    history ever recorded or poetry ever dreamed; their enmity
    is "in reality a microcosmical view of the struggle between
    man and his last enemy, between light and darkness, between
    God and the angels and Satan and the princes of hell."
    Melville continues the long tradition of English rhythmical
    prose, which appeals as much to the ear as the eye. The
    Confidence-Man is the nadir of Melville's writing. Clarel
    and the shorter poems are suggestive of the poetic manner of
    Meredith and Hardy. Billy Budd is written with much skill
    and care, but lacks the verve, zest, and fire of Melville's
    earlier writings.

4   FRANK, WALDO. The Re-discovery of America: An Introduction to
    a Philosophy of American Life. New York: Charles Scribner's
    Sons, pp. 140, 157-158, 196, 218n, 220-221.
       Brief references. Whitman, and less directly, Melville,
    naturalised within our world the project of an art created
    from, and not in spite of, chaos. Hawthorne and Melville
    were thwarted mystics on the fringe of the mystic tradition
    (which spoke through Emerson, Poe, Thoreau, and Whitman),
    trying to live and work in this tradition and failing.

5   HAWTHORNE, NATHANIEL. The Heart of Hawthorne's Journals.
    Ed. Newton Arvin. Boston: Houghton Mifflin Co., Riverside
    Press, pp. 143, 147, 148, 177, 229-232.

Entries for 5 August 1850; 31 July 1851; 5 August 1851; 28 December 1854; and 20 November 1856. Encounters with Melville.

6 JOHNSON, MERLE. High Spots of American Literature. New York: Bennett Book Studies, pp. 57, 107.

Bibliographical entry for Moby-Dick notes that the "mystic quality of the pursuit differentiates this from the conventional adventure story." Rejects prediction by A. S. W. Rosenbach that "the greatest value for American manuscripts" will be in the writings of Melville and Eugene O'Neill; Melville and O'Neill "have created no characters that live in the popular mind."

7 KREYMBORG, ALFRED. Our Singing Strength: An Outline of American Poetry (1630-1930). New York: Coward-McCann, pp. 603-605; passim.

Agrees with Tate [1926.B12] that Hart Crane's "real forebears" are Whitman and Melville. Sees Melville as misanthropic, an "epic hater."

8 LEISY, ERNEST ERWIN. American Literature: An Interpretative Survey. New York: Thomas Y. Crowell, pp. 102-105.

Brief survey. Only in recent years, with a revival of interest in the sea by men like Conrad, Masefield, and Kipling, has Melville received proper consideration. Moby-Dick is an epic of the human spirit and its eternal feud with the sheer brute energy of the universe. Excrescent chapters that seem to belong in an appendix give the epic its ballast. This powerful allegory will soon take its rightful place beside the Faerie Queene, Pilgrim's Progress, and Paradise Lost. Examples of Melville's use of alliteration, metaphor, biblical allusion, forceful adjectives, and rhythm.

9 MINNIGERODE, MEADE. "Herman Melville, 1819-1891," in American First Editions: Bibliographic Check Lists of the Works of One Hundred and Five American Authors. Ed. Merle Johnson. New York: R. R. Bowker Co., pp. 147-148.

Checklist of first editions of Melville's books; also lists 1921.A1 and 1922.A1.

10 MOORE, JOHN BROOKS. "Introduction," in Pierre. New York: E. P. Dutton & Co., pp. xxi-xxvii.

The chief interest of Melville's books derives from their account of the evolution of a remarkable man of the nineteenth century. They present a crescendo of protest, rebellion, disillusion, and quiescence. Pierre, the second

in power and personal significance of Melville's works,
is one of his lost novels; it is unread, unknown, like a
newly discovered manuscript; it has utterly disappeared
from libraries. It was condemned in 1852 because Melville
dared to write about incest and to portray a good young man
suffering appallingly because he was trying to do ideal
justice. The book is far from being metaphysically foggy,
as reviewers claimed: the theme and development, the mood
and the whole intent of the story are so powerfully en-
forced that no mistake would seem possible. Pierre is the
most powerful denunciation of mid-nineteenth century American society yet written. Expressing the desperation of the
noble individual surrounded by a world of comfortable com-
promises and snobberies, it deals with one of the greatest
and most insistent themes of nineteenth-century literature;
it belongs with Balzac's Lost Illusions, Tolstoi's two great
novels, Gorky's Foma Gordeev, and Hardy's Jude the Ob-
scure--not the first of the group but not the last either.
[See 1929.B17.]

11   MUNSON, GORHAM B. "Prose for Fiction: Herman Melville," in
     Style and Form in American Prose. New York: Doubleday,
     Doran & Co., pp. 135-149.
          Remarks on style in Mardi and analysis of Melville's
     "expert manipulations" of the reader in chapter 84, "Taji
     Sits Down to Dinner with Five-and-Twenty Kings, and a Royal
     Time They Have," where the Rabelaisian humor depends on the
     narrative of the banquet "being set to the form of a battle
     piece." Reprints (pp. 150-158) most of chapter 181, "They
     Sup," as further proof of Melville's "astounding powers of
     variation." Taken as a whole, Mardi is a failure--but a
     failure on a lofty level and an extraordinary exercise in
     virtuosity.

12   OVERTON, GRANT. An Hour of the American Novel. Philadelphia
     and London: J. B. Lippincott Co., pp. 30-33.
          Melville's fate was "to think too deeply on what he had
     seen and to be unable to throw off the unsolvable." He
     had a grasp of the sublime as profound as Hawthorne's, an
     exuberance, an imaginative power, a prophetic voice that
     Hawthorne never possessed. But Hawthorne was an artist, as
     Melville was not. The Scarlet Letter is a miracle of con-
     sidered workmanship; Moby-Dick is a miracle of nature.
     Billy Budd is Melville's only other triumph; Hawthorne
     could never have handled its theme, for conscience has no
     place in it.

1929

13 QUINN, ARTHUR HOBSON, ALBERT CROLL BAUGH, and WILL DAVID HOWE.
    "Herman Melville," in The Literature of America. Vol. 1.
    New York: Charles Scribner's Sons, p. N28.
        Brief biographical and bibliographical note. Moby-Dick
    is Melville's one great book.

14 RANKIN, THOMAS ERNEST, CLARENCE DEWITT THORPE, and MELVIN
    THEODOR SOLVE. College Composition. New York and London:
    Harper & Brothers, p. 278.
        Cites Melville's "sledge-hammering sea" and "sea-crashing
    boat" and Spenser's "sea-shouldering whales" as excellent
    examples of "compound adjective epithets."

15 READ, HERBERT. The Sense of Glory: Essays in Criticism.
    London: Cambridge University Press, pp. 155-156.
        Reprint of 1928.B24.

16 ROSENBACH, A. S. W. "Introduction," in Moby Dick. London and
    New York: Mitchell Kennerley, pp. v-ix.
        Reprint of 1924.A1.

17 TOMLINSON, H. M. "Preface," in Pierre. New York: E. P.
    Dutton & Co., pp. vii-xvii.
        In Pierre Melville was overcome by the terror of a shadow
    much more ominous than the quarry Ahab hunted--the ambiguity
    of both good and evil referred to in the subtitle. It is
    impossible for any reader to keep within soundings when
    reading Pierre, which is bottomless, out of soundings; the
    reader "is poised over an abyss of darkness most of the
    time, to the ultimate depth by which no sounding by man will
    ever be made." Some of Pierre is badly written, even ridic-
    ulous; in writing it Melville appears to have been too dour
    and congested, too scornful of his fellow creatures to allow
    him a little humor, with which he could have considered the
    proportions of his growing work. As a novel, Pierre is a
    failure, but a tragic and noteworthy failure; it "compels
    a reader, repels him, draws him to it again, shocks and
    disturbs in a way we never expect of the latest of our
    literary successes." The passages on "Chronometricals and
    Horologicals" and Enceladus show that Melville "must take
    his place with the masters." [See 1929.B10.]

*18 TRENT, W. P. A History of American Literature, 1607-1865.
    Revised and Enlarged. New York: D. Appleton & Co., passim.
        Cited in Ricks and Adams, p. 365.

19 TURNER, LORENZO DOW. Anti-Slavery Sentiment in American Lit-
    erature Prior to 1865. Washington, D.C.: The Association
    for the Study of Negro Life and History, pp. 50-51.

Notes that <u>Mardi</u> contains one of the most effective anti-slavery arguments.

20   EFFINGER, ELIZABETH. "Arrowhead." Boston <u>Atlantic Monthly</u>,
      143 (January), 136–138.
         Recounts two visits to Arrowhead. Claims that before
      their friendship began Hawthorne knew Melville was the author
      of a very appreciative review of <u>The Scarlet Letter</u>. [See
      Thorp (1942), pp. 302–305.] Melville's understanding of
      symbolism was too advanced for the age. Reprinted in part
      in 1929.B25.

21   ANON. "Journal of Melville's Voyage in a Clipper Ship." <u>New
      England Quarterly</u>, 2 (January), 120–125.
         Reprints fragment of Melville's journal of his voyage on
      the <u>Meteor</u> in 1860, by permission of his granddaughter,
      Mrs. Henry K. Metcalf. Brief introductory note.

22   DAMON, S. FOSTER. "Pierre the Ambiguous." Cambridge <u>Hound &
      Horn</u>, 2 (January–March), 107–118.
         Relates <u>Pierre</u> to other literary treatments of incest:
      <u>Pierre</u> was the first attempt to analyze incest and takes
      its place in literary history as the first novel based on
      morbid sex. In <u>The Marble Faun</u> Hawthorne used incest for
      theological dramatics only; <u>Pierre</u> is not drama but psychol-
      ogy. The gap between Hawthorne and Melville is the gap that
      separates Calvin and Freud. Pierre is the victim of the
      profound psychosis known today as the "Oedipus complex."
      Melville demonstrates in <u>Pierre</u> the impossibility of the
      pagan and Christian schemes of salvation: "Know Thyself"
      and the Golden Rule. The book's style points back to Sir
      Thomas Browne and forward to Henry James, but finds a con-
      temporary source in Sylvester Judd's <u>Margaret</u>. <u>Pierre</u> also
      has notable similarities with <u>Hamlet</u>. Reprinted in part in
      Willett, p. 4.

23   ANON. "Bibliography." New York <u>Wings</u>, 3 (March), 11.
         A "list of the works of Herman Melville, in the various
      editions in which they may be obtained."

24   ANON. "Happy Birthday." New York <u>Wings</u>, 3 (March), 10.
         Notes that the Literary Guild (now two years old) shipped
      copies of 1929.A1 to nearly 70,000 members.

25   EFFINGER, ELIZABETH. "In Herman Melville's Home." New York
      <u>Wings</u>, 3 (March), 6–7.
         Partial reprint of 1929.B20.

1929

26   VAN DOREN, CARL. "Why the Editorial Board Selected <u>Herman Melville</u>." New York <u>Wings</u>, 3 (March), 4-5.
"The time has finally come...for a study which, making use of the investigations lately carried out, can go further than any studies yet produced in defining Melville's genius, setting it in relation to the age and surroundings in which he lived, and throwing light, through him, upon various universal problems of character and fate." Mumford's biography [1929.A1] fulfills these requirements and is a moving account of Melville's "great power frustrated by lack of craft in directing it to its natural channels."

27   WEAVER, RAYMOND. "Mumford Sees New Cultural Synthesis in Melville." New York <u>Evening Post</u> (9 March).
Review of 1929.A1.--Among Melville studies "the most readable, the most comprehensive and the most superlative in its claims for Melville's greatness." Account of beginnings of Weaver's own studies of Melville.

28   BEER, THOMAS. "Good Friday Spell." New York <u>Herald Tribune Books</u> (10 March), pp. 1-2.
Review of 1929.A1.--A distinguished biography, in which Mumford fills out the one weak passage of <u>The Golden Day</u>: the Civil War is admirably treated at last. Melville's weakness is that he had been too long in perceiving that good and evil exist in the nature of things. He had not, somehow, been able to accept his own parables. Much of his best later work, "Benito Cereno," "Bartleby," and <u>The Confidence-Man</u>, is a protest against what he had superbly announced in <u>Moby-Dick</u>. In these tales his identity is paraded as the victim of human politics.

29   GORMAN, HERBERT. "That Strange Genius, Melville." New York <u>Times Book Review</u> (10 March), pp. 1, 14.
Review of 1929.A1.--The best book on Melville that we have, though Mumford does not sufficiently stress the tragic aspect of Melville's spiritual development. Contrary to Mumford's view, <u>Moby-Dick</u> is flawed: Melville succumbed to a certain degree to the "moralistic implications" of the narrow-minded civilization he was resisting. Mumford tends to overvalue Melville's lesser work.

30   GRATTAN, HARTLEY C. "Melville's Life and Work Clearly Reported and Explained." New York <u>World</u> (10 March).
Review of 1929.A1.--Clearly the best of the attempts to elucidate Melville's life and work; a comprehensive life, a clear, profound interpretation of Melville's thought and a

rational explanation of "the pass to which his thinking
brought him." The hardest problem for a Melville student
is to develop some explanation for Melville's relative
silence after Moby-Dick; Mumford's is the most satisfactory
yet advanced. Melville's tragedy may be reduced to this:
he was superb "in his pursuit of investigations of the
power of the intellect." He "could follow any search for
ultimate intellectual power to its logical conclusion, but
he failed when he saw the isolation this sort of adventure
brought, and sought to achieve an integration that would
bring him into life-giving contact with his fellow human
beings."

31 JOSEPHSON, MATTHEW. New York Outlook and Independent, 151
    (20 March), 467-468.
        Review of 1929.A1. Mumford interprets the drama of mar-
    tyrization by Yankee morality and materialism which composes
    Melville's career. Melville has come to be seen as a soli-
    tary and heroic enemy of his age, a rebellious protagonist
    of the imagination.

32 HALE, PHILIP. "Writer of 'Moby Dick.'" Boston Herald
    (23 March), pp. 19-20.
        Review of 1929.A1.--Adds little factually, but a book
    no lover of Melville can afford to ignore.

33 C., S. C. "Looking Back at Melville." Boston Christian
    Science Monitor (27 March), p. 10.
        Review of 1929.A1. Reviewer finds the causes of the
    Melville revival in the popularity of Conrad, the centenary,
    and "something in Melville's outlook upon life to which the
    present age responded." Mumford is to be commended as
    biographer (filling in many of the gaps in our knowledge
    of Melville's later years) rather than critic. Nothing he
    says will dispel memory of the longueurs of Typee and Omoo;
    the "ill-planned, ill-digested, rococo decoration and struc-
    ture" of that "impossible extravaganza" Pierre; the uncouth-
    ness of many of the short stories; the unending dreariness
    of The Confidence-Man; and despite its superb merits, the
    verbosity, extravagance, frequent tediousness, flaws in
    composition, mannerisms, and pedantry of Moby-Dick.

34 HICKS, GRANVILLE. "Study of Herman Melville." Springfield
    (Mass.) Republican (31 March).
        Review of 1929.A1.--Unquestionably the best recent crit-
    ical biography of an American writer, literature in its own
    right, a work to be experienced rather than merely read.
    Its chief beauty is its successful fusion of four types of

approach: the biographical, the critical, the sociological, and the philosophical. All four are essential to an adequate understanding of Melville's significance. Mumford gives admirable restatement of Melville's humanism, which is not fearful of "admitting the possibility of the great negations."

35   M[ORISON], S. E. "Melville's 'Agatha' Letter to Hawthorne." New England Quarterly, 2 (April), 296-307.
       Prints Melville's letter of 13 August 1852 to Hawthorne [Letters, pp. 153-161], with brief introduction.

36   MacLEISH, ARCHIBALD. "A New Life of Melville." New York Bookman, 69 (April), 183-185.
       Review of 1929.A1.--A good book, but dull, offering an economic and new-psychology explanation of Melville's "blackness." Mumford is magnificent on the meaning of Moby-Dick, though it is not a poem. Melville as an American of his time is Mumford's real contribution.

37   BRICKELL, HERSCHEL. "Herman Melville." New York New Republic, 58 (3 April), 205-206.
       Review of 1929.A1.--A full, rich combination of biography and critical analysis, a companion-volume to The Golden Day. Mumford has never written anything more deeply moving than his discussion of Moby-Dick. His enthusiasm for Moby-Dick makes him overzealous for Melville's lesser writings.

38   CROWLEY, PAUL. "Melville's New Halo." New York Commonweal, 9 (17 April), 687-688.
       Review of 1929.A1.--Has nobility of intention and an intelligent point of view but never comes alive, with its Paterian pose. Mumford is a preacher and reformer and Melville is his text. The dimensions of Melville for Mumford are the dimensions of his doctrine. Mumford is incapable of the necessary just critical appreciation of Melville through his age; he can only write down the age.

39   MATHER, FRANK JEWETT, JR. "Herman Melville." New York Saturday Review of Literature, 5 (27 April), 945-946.
       Review of 1929.A1. There has been some exaggeration in the general view of Melville as a lonely Prometheus. Mumford offers the first complete and integrated interpretation of Melville the man; a chief merit of the book is to dispel the legend of misanthropy and insanity that has gathered about his last years. Pierre and The Confidence-Man were and are unreadable, though Pierre has beautiful and profound passages. Twenty-five years previously Mather

had written to "the American publishers whose list is
heaviest with our classics" and proposed a modest one-
volume biography of Melville: their answer was that
Melville "was a hopelessly bad risk, and one that no
prudent publisher could undertake even to the extent of a
few hundred dollars."

40   STEWART, RANDALL.   "'Ethan Brand.'"   [Letter to the Editor.]
      New York Saturday Review of Literature, 5 (27 April), 967.
          Mumford [1929.A1] errs in assuming that Hawthorne had
      Melville in mind when he wrote "Ethan Brand." The story
      was first published in the Boston Museum, 5 January 1850.
      It existed in embryo in Hawthorne's journal some two years
      before the publication of Melville's first book. The story
      was conceived, developed, and brought to a final form with-
      out reference to either Melville or his writings.

41   MOORE, JOHN BROOKS.   "Book Reviews."   American Literature, 1
      (May), 215-217.
          Review of 1929.A1.--A gallant and strenuous attempt to
      Mumfordize Melville's mystery. Melville's last 30 or 40
      years suggest not psychical rehabilitation, as Mumford
      claims, but reluctant resignation to living out a somewhat
      weary and devitalized existence. Clarel and Billy Budd
      indicate a general flagging of physical and spiritual vigor
      rather than energetic spiritual re-integration. Mumford's
      chapters on Moby-Dick and Pierre constitute the most com-
      plete writing on Melville to date.

42   ANON.   "Biography."   Chicago Booklist, 25 (May), 319.
          Review of 1929.A1. Mumford succeeds admirably in evok-
      ing the rounded image of Melville and in interpreting the
      thought of his novels.

43   MORRIS, LAWRENCE S.   "The White Whale."   New York Forum, 81
      (May), xiv-xvi.
          Review of 1929.A1.--The finest study of Melville to date.
      Melville was one of the giants, a maimed, one-armed giant,
      fighting alone and striking out blindly into the dark, but
      still a giant. He started into depths Emerson could think
      about but not feel, that Whitman was incapable of thinking
      about and had no desire to feel. Mumford might have carried
      his interpretation of the White Whale still further, into
      the inner life of every individual, where the White Whale
      is the inexhaustible, blind inertia of unconsciousness,
      against which consciousness struggles for a time before
      being drowned. Mumford's faith in culture is a weakness
      in his program for a life of realization.

1929

44   BRICKELL, HERSCHEL. "The Symbolical Melville." New York
      North American Review, 227 (May), n.p. [Front Advertising
      Section.]
         Review of 1929.A1.--Quite as much about American culture
      as about Melville and a further exposition of the optimistic
      philosophy of The Golden Day; its high spot is Mumford's
      stirring interpretation of the symbolism of Moby-Dick.

45   KRUTCH, JOSEPH WOOD. "Taming Leviathan." New York Nation,
      128 (8 May), 561.
         Review of 1929.A1.--Full of penetrating comments, but
      Mumford overstresses Melville as a social misfit. Melville
      was more concerned with the immensities and eternities than
      with society; he was impatient of everything except the
      absolute. Mumford prefers to turn away from Melville's
      depths and blacknesses, perhaps because he is determined to
      make Melville more a part of the Golden Day of New England
      than he really was.

46   ANON. "Briefer Mention." Chicago Dial, 86 (June), 529.
         Review of 1929.A1.--As critical biography, admirable in
      rhythm, balance and proportion; as appraisal of Melville's
      disheartening era, brilliant in keenness of perception.

47   WOOLF, VIRGINIA. "Phases of Fiction." New York Bookman, 69
      (June), 408-410.
         Comparisons of Moby-Dick and Wuthering Heights. In both
      "we get a vision of presence outside the human beings, of a
      meaning that they stand for, without ceasing to be them-
      selves." Both Bronte and Melville simplify their characters,
      till only the great contours are visible, and allow nature
      at her wildest to take part in the scene. There is poetry
      in novels both where the poetry is expressed through the
      characters and again where the poetry is expressed not so
      much by the particular character in a particular situation,
      but rather by the whole mood and temper of the book, like
      the mood and temper of Wuthering Heights or Moby-Dick to
      which the characters of Catherine or Heathcliff or Ahab
      give expression.

48   BENSON, E. M. New York Outlook and Independent, 152
      (19 June), 311.
         Review of Dutton edition of Pierre. [See 1929.B10 and
      1929.B17.] Pierre contains some of Melville's best writing
      and some of his worst. His subject ran away with him. He
      was so completely in sympathy with Pierre's moral disinte-
      gration that he approached his subject with the same ulcer-
      ous contempt with which his protagonist approached life.

Pierre's defeat was Melville's defeat; symbolically, it was the defeat of America.

49 MUMFORD, LEWIS. "Catnip and Amaranth." New York Saturday
    Review of Literature, 5 (29 June), 1141.
        Notice of Dutton edition of Pierre. [See 1929.B10
    and 1929.B17.] Pierre is Melville's "most ambiguous
    achievement--so good that it cannot be neglected, and so
    verbose, high-flown, hectic, weakly theatrical, that one is
    at loss to pick out a romantic work, from Byron onward, that
    can rival it in loud ineptitude." Pierre is a complicated
    symbol of Melville's dilemmas as a man and his explorations
    as an imaginative writer and a philosophic thinker. (Accord-
    ing to Dr. Henry Murray, Jr., there is evidence which might
    link Isabel with Melville's sister who had made fair copies
    of his manuscripts.) Melville's mental health was shattered
    when he finished Pierre; the story is plainly autobiograph-
    ical even in its fantastic melodramatic conclusion. Its
    chief importance lies not in the adolescent revolt of
    Pierre, which discloses Melville's failure to achieve com-
    plete sexual maturity, but in the insight into certain
    truths that had come forth as byproducts of his personal
    dilemma. The principal moral of Pierre, perhaps, is the
    relativity of vice and virtue: "The appetite for God might
    usurp the place that should be open to other appetites, and
    in becoming a philosopher or seer one might become something
    less than a man. Thought that displaced all other form of
    experience was sterile, as blackly ineffectual as those
    incestuous wishes that spoiled one's married love. Was not
    Melville's own mind, particularly his unconscious, his dark
    half-sister Isabel?" If in Pierre Melville often seems one
    of the last and weakest of the Romantics, he is also one of
    the first, and one of the most profound, of the moderns.

50 GLEIM, WILLIAM S. "A Theory of Moby Dick." New England
    Quarterly, 2 (July), 402-419.
        Highly schematized, allegorical reading, in which the
    Whale represents fate and Ahab is "a composite of all the
    historical and mythical rebels against Destiny." Water
    represents truth and life. The Pequod is a symbol of the
    world; its crew personify the "virtues, vices, passions, and
    and other qualities of mind and heart." Starbuck personi-
    fies Platonism; Stubb, epicureanism; Flask, stoicism;
    Queequeg, religion; Tashtego, sin; Dagoo, ignorance;
    Bulkington, reason; Fedallah, the future. Passages in the
    book embody the teachings of Swedenborg. Moby-Dick is "a
    treasure of hidden meanings." As a great artist, Melville
    understood the relation of mystery and obscurity to the

sublime; his method "was indirect and ambiguous, for his
purpose was to convey ideas, without definite expression;
to present the great enigma of life, in an enigmatic manner, and to emphasize the mystery of the ineffable myster-
ies." Reprinted in part in Doubloon, pp. 174-175.

51   MURRAY, HENRY A. "Book Reviews." New England Quarterly, 2
     (July), 523-526.
          Review of 1929.A1.--Full of enlightened sanity. Mumford
     telescopes Melville's South Sea adventures and expands his
     later period, with a significant gain in understanding over
     Weaver [1921.A1]. The central problem of the Melville
     biographer is to "explain" the writing of Moby-Dick; here
     Mumford's psychological intuitions are rather vague and
     sublimated, but his literary judgments are eloquently de-
     finitive. At times Mumford's attitude seems too rational,
     too consciously elaborated. In 1848 Melville discovered
     the unconscious and proceeded to lose himself in his ex-
     ploration of it. Melville has been resurrected but has
     not been generally admitted into academic circles. Re-
     printed in part in Doubloon, pp. 175-176.

52   PALTSITS, VICTOR HUGO, ed. "Family Correspondence of Herman
     Melville, 1830-1904." Bulletin of the New York Public
     Library, 33 (July), 507-525.
          Prints and annotates letters by Melville, his brothers
     Gansevoort and Allan, George Griggs, Peter Gansevoort,
     Henry Sanford Gansevoort, and Elizabeth Shaw Melville in
     the Gansevoort-Lansing Collection of the New York Public
     Library. Brief introduction characterizes the letters as
     "human, unrestrained, intimate, social, and often jolly"
     and describes Melville's handwriting. (Reproduces por-
     traits, photographs, and a sketch from the collection.)
     Continued in 1929.B58.

53   MURRAY, H. A. "Timon of America." Cambridge (Mass.) Hound &
     Horn, 2 (July-September), 430-432.
          Review of 1929.A1.--More than a biography, an essay on
     the nature of the creative spirit in art and in life.
     Mumford follows Weaver in his facts but makes more magic
     out of them; his most notable contribution to Melville's
     factual existence is a complete account of the later days.
     Mumford's literary criticisms are acute, his general com-
     ments permeated by humane wisdom. Moby-Dick marks an
     eternal Himalayan moment in the history of the human mind
     when soul and substance were unequivocally fused.

54   PLOMER, WILLIAM. "Herman Melville." London Nation and
     Athenaeum, 45 (27 July), 570.
          Review of 1929.A1. Mumford not only sticks to the facts
     but throws light on them. His analysis of Moby-Dick forms
     one of his best chapters.

55   ANON. "More Books of the Week." London Spectator, 143
     (27 July), 138.
          Review of 1929.A1.--A rather wordy study of a curious
     and interestingly eccentric mind. Many English readers
     still read Typee and Omoo; many more greatly admire, and
     are puzzled over, Moby-Dick, but not perhaps to the extent
     of thinking it, as Mumford does somewhat uncritically, "one
     of the supreme poetic monuments of the English language."

56   ANON. "Melvilliana." New York Times (28 July), section 3,
     p. 4.
          Review of 1929.B52. One is grateful for anything about
     Melville; he and his career are stranger than his most
     orphic works. The description of the boarding house keeper
     in his letter to Peter Gansevoort [Letters, pp. 5-6] gives
     an early glimpse of the later Melville. His "restorers,
     exalting the book by which he is best remembered, hardly
     succeed in getting at the man and take their revenge by
     elaborate theories to explain him."

57   CORT, DAVID. "Rock Rodondo: A Memory of Paris, 19--." New
     York Bookman, 69 (August), 596-608.
          Notes that the Galapagos Islands have been "surveyed
     imaginatively in former times by Melville and more recently
     and less imaginatively by William Beebe"; quotes from "The
     Encantadas."

58   PALTSITS, VICTOR HUGO, ed. "Family Correspondence of Herman
     Melville, 1830-1904." Bulletin of the New York Public
     Library, 33 (August), 575-625.
          Continued from 1929.B52. Prints and annotates letters
     by Melville, Elizabeth Shaw Melville, Catherine Gansevoort
     Lansing, Abraham Lansing, Melville's "Receipt for Inherit-
     ance" from the estate of Priscilla F. Melville, 16 March
     1889, and extracts from Mrs. Lansing's diary, 28 September-
     1 October 1891.

59   MILTON, MARY MOORE. "Herman Melville." New York Letters,
     2 (August), 45.
          Review of 1929.A1.--A vivid, readable, and intriguing
     biography. Melville will live, not because of his adven-
     tures, but because of his great emotional, spiritual, and

mental experiences. Not afraid of undressing his soul, he laid bare the stupendous evolution of a man's ego.

60 ANON. "Herman Melville." London Times Literary Supplement, No. 1436 (8 August), p. 621.
    Review of 1929.A1.--A careful, thoroughly sympathetic study, but does not clear up the mystery of the inner development that transformed the writer of Typee into the writer of Moby-Dick. Mumford's subtle analysis of Moby-Dick is perhaps more ingenious than convincing; Melville was never a complete artist. No other artist of equal importance has shown so little sustained power. Melville's expression of his really valuable perceptions and reflections in Clarel is so inept that the work is practically unreadable. Mumford's study reinforces the conviction that Melville was essentially a man of one book. It is doubtful that he found the solution of his spiritual problems which Mumford credits him with.

61 ANON. "Melville." London Saturday Review, 148 (10 August), 161-162.
    Review of 1929.A1. Mumford needed more "plain facts," overpraises Melville, and fails most clearly in dealing with his intellectual life.

62 LITTMANN, MINNA. "Edgartown Finds New Link with Melville." New Bedford Sunday Standard (11 August), section 4, pp. 31, 39.
    Report that Mrs. Henry B. Thomas, Melville's daughter (Frances), is living in the former home of Valentine Pease, captain of the Acushnet at the time of Melville's voyage on her. Reminiscences of Melville by Henry Thomas and daughter Eleanor Melville Metcalf. Mrs. Thomas "does not reminisce of her distinguished father. He had the failings of genius, and her memories of him are not wholly happy ones."

63 QUENNELL, PETER. "The Author of Moby Dick." London New Statesman, 33 (24 August), 604.
    Notice of Mitchell Kennerly edition. [See 1929.B16.] Moby-Dick is among the most delightful books ever written and among the most tedious. Melville is equally the seeker and the object of his own absorbing quest; he is Ahab and he is Moby Dick. With its muddied speculation, the story of Ahab and Moby Dick may be regarded as the least valuable part of the book. Its supreme beauties appear to be a kind of incidental product--fifteen to twenty passages which compose a sort of internal poem or intricate dreamy figure.

In "the centre of self-centred tornadoes," Melville can
always distinguish "a zone of sweet quiescence." In Moby-
Dick, a spirit of lyrical hedonism is imprisoned within a
body of ponderous speculation.

64 PALTSITS, VICTOR HUGO. "Melvilliana." [Letter to the Editor.]
New York Times (25 August), section 3, p. 5.
Response to 1929.B56. Melville has been resurrected on
the wave of the disease of psychoanalysis afflicting American biography. His words are seized on "as indubitable
autobiographical allusions, which are set forth with a
cocksureness incubated either in illusion or in the twists
of a pseudo science."

65 ANON. "One Minute Biographies." Boston Christian Science
Monitor (28 August), p. 17.
Brief biographical sketch. Beneath the surface of Moby-
Dick lies a mighty allegory applicable to all human
experience.

66 WILLIAMS, STANLEY T. "Victorian Americans." Yale Review,
NS 19 (September), 191-193.
Review of 1929.A1. Factual inaccuracies, imaginative
use of fiction as sources, and silence about authorities
for important statements injure the work as a judicial pro-
nouncement on the life of Melville. But the book is penetrating criticism and displays Mumford's powers of
psychological dissection. Mumford is at his best in the
chapter on Moby-Dick.

67 ERSKINE, JOHN. "A Whale of a Story." New York Delineator,
115 (October), 15, 68, 71, 72.
Reprint of 1928.B10.

68 REDMAN, BEN RAY. "Old Wine in New Bottles." New York Herald
Tribune Books (20 October), p. 12.
Review of Dutton edition of Pierre. [See 1929.B10 and
1929.B17.] Since it is by the author of Moby-Dick, Pierre
now has its apologists and eulogists, "along with other
Melville rubbish that has solemnly and proudly been dragged
forth into the light by undiscriminating but fervent brothers of the Melville cult." Pierre is an absurd tale ab-
surdly told. The actions of its characters are insanely
motivated, its sentiments are maudlin, its transcendental
philosophy is hysterical, and its style is a pompous,
strutting horror.

69   STARKE, A. H.   "A Note on Lewis Mumford's Life of Herman
       Melville."   American Literature, 1 (November), 304-305.
           Mumford errs in his account of Melville's parting from
       Hawthorne in Liverpool, neglects account in Hawthorne's
       journal. This "grave error" reveals Mumford's inability
       to do justice to Hawthorne and raises the question of his
       fitness for the role of scholar and biographer.

70   WINTERICH, JOHN T.   "Romantic Stories of Books. Second
       Series IV. Moby Dick." New York Publishers' Weekly,
       116 (16 November), 2391-2394.
           Biographical sketch; details of the 1853 fire at
       Harper & Brothers.

71   GARNETT, R. S.   "Moby-Dick and Mocha-Dick. A Literary Find."
       Edinburgh Blackwood's Magazine, 226 (December), 841-858.
           Reprints part of "Mocha-Dick or The White Whale of the
       Pacific," by J. N. Reynolds, which motivated Melville to
       go whaling and furnished him with the grand idea for
       Moby-Dick.

1930 A BOOKS - NONE

1930 B SHORTER WRITINGS

1   ADAMS, HENRY.   Letters of Henry Adams (1858-91).   Ed.
       Worthington Chauncey Ford. Boston: Houghton Mifflin Co.,
       pp. 463, 483.
           Letter to Elizabeth Cameron from Papeete, 6 February 1891:
       "Tahiti! does the word mean anything to you? To me it has
       a perfume of its own, made up of utterly inconsequent asso-
       ciations; essence of the South Seas mixed with imaginations
       of at least forty years ago; Herman Melville and Captain
       Cook head and heels with the French opera and Pierre
       Loti...." Letter to Elizabeth Cameron from Papeete,
       3 May 1891: "Like Robinson Crusoe and Herman Melville, I
       have been able to turn my mind to nothing except escape
       from my island...."

2   BAKER, ERNEST A.   Intellectual Realism: From Richardson to
       Sterne. Vol. 4 of The History of the English Novel.
       London: H. F. & G. Witherby, p. 206.
           Melville included in list of sea novelists (Marryat,
       Cooper, Michael Scott, Dana, Clark Russell, Conrad, W. W.
       Jacobs) all "indebted in one way or another" to Smollett.

3   BARNES, HOMER F. <u>Charles Fenno Hoffman</u>. New York: Columbia
    University Press, pp. 111, 185.
       Lists Melville among signers of petition for an inter-
    national copyright law presented before the House of Repre-
    sentatives 19 July 1852. In his 5 April 1849 letter to
    Duyckinck [<u>Letters</u>, pp. 82-84], Melville writes of Hoffman
    "in something of a prophetic tone."

4   CAIRNS, WILLIAM B. <u>A History of American Literature</u>.
    Revised Edition. New York and London: Oxford University
    Press, pp. 304, 368-370.
       Reprints the partial survey in 1912.B1.

5   CLARK, HARRY HAYDEN. "Pandora's Box in American Fiction," in
    <u>Humanism and America</u>. Ed. Norman Foerster. New York:
    Farrar and Rinehart, pp. 175-176.
       Melville is perhaps the most vigorous and passionate
    Arcadian in American literature. In the frankly idyllic
    and nympholeptic <u>Mardi</u>, his nostalgic idealism and hatred
    of reality become intensified. The allegorical quest for
    Yillah "follows Unitarianism and Transcendentalism, with
    their hope for the infinite perfectibility of men."
    Melville's first-hand experience of the reality of the sea
    and "the mystery of iniquity" tended to clash with his
    dreams of Utopia. <u>Moby-Dick</u> was born of this clash between
    the hope of a paradise of supernal beauty and the sight of
    a malignant reality from the deck of a whaler.

6   COURNOS, JOHN. "Introduction," in <u>American Short Stories of</u>
    <u>the Nineteenth Century</u>. Everyman's Library. London:
    J. M. Dent & Sons; New York: E. P. Dutton & Co., pp. v-ix.
       Hawthorne, Melville, and Henry James alone, among the
    great American fiction writers, wrote what they wanted and
    how they wanted, unaffected by economics. Melville's daemon-
    ism and metaphysics could not appeal to a democratic public
    at any time.

7   CRAWFORD, MARY CAROLINE. <u>Famous Families of Massachusetts</u>.
    Vol. 1. Boston: Little, Brown, and Co., p. 253.
       Biographical details of Lemuel Shaw, his daughter
    Elizabeth, and Melville.

8   CURLE, RICHARD. <u>Collecting American First Editions: Its Pit-</u>
    <u>falls and Pleasures</u>. Indianapolis: The Bobbs-Merrill Co.,
    passim.
       Comments on Melville's books from a collector's point of
    view.

1930

9   DAMON, S. FOSTER. Thomas Holley Chivers, Friend of Poe.
    New York and London: Harper & Brothers, pp. 17-20, 266.
        When Thoreau issued his call to self-discovery in Walden,
    there were already those who had come to grief on just such
    voyages, including Poe and Melville. One of the dominant
    impulses of American literature has been exploration of
    the mental frontier: from Jonathan Edwards to Hawthorne is
    but one step, from Hawthorne to Melville but one more, and
    but one more from Melville to Freud; from Edwards to
    Channing, Judd, and the other Unitarians is but one step,
    and from Judd we step directly to Melville.

10 FLETCHER, JOHN GOULD. The Two Frontiers: A Study in Histor-
    ical Psychology. New York: Coward-McCann, pp. 255-266.
        Melville was the first man to ask himself and others the
    question: "If savage life is so much more rational and
    sensible than Christianity, why pretend to be Christian?"
    He affirms the sole achievement Christianity has to its
    credit, the conquest of the world by democracy, while at
    the same time his eyes are open to all the evil done daily
    in the world in the name of democracy. Each of the major
    novels, Mardi, Redburn, White-Jacket, and Moby-Dick, is
    less the description of an actual voyage than a terrible
    allegoric record of spiritual defeat and despair. Dostoevski
    and Melville both attempted the complete, candid, and ter-
    ribly disillusioned revelation of the workings of the naked
    and helplessly-entangled human spirit. Both carried
    character-creation further than any other writer has
    attempted, except perhaps Shakespeare in Hamlet; both, like
    Shakespeare in Hamlet, were obsessed by their characters,
    and obsessed above all by the "mystery of iniquity," the
    infinite perversion and moral deformity of humankind. In
    Moby-Dick, which recalls the Shakespeare of Macbeth and
    King Lear, the Whale is nothing but a symbol--of the un-
    earthly, unconquerable, superhuman, and strangely beautiful
    power of evil. Before Melville concluded that the world
    was more evil than good, he had striven to portray the
    ideal human type of his dreams in Jack Chase.

11 FLITCROFT, JOHN E. Outline Studies in American Literature.
    New York: Prentice-Hall, pp. 78-79, 189.
        Brief biographical sketch. "Melville's fame has increased
    since 1920 with the growing recognition of Moby Dick as a
    major American classic, but much of the present enthusiasm
    for Melville is apparently an extreme reaction against
    earlier neglect."

12 FOERSTER, NORMAN. Towards Standards: A Study of the Present
    Critical Movement in American Letters. New York: Farrar &
    Rinehart, pp. 117, 124, 125n.
        Understanding the obstacles met by our writers in the
    past, such as Melville, might link us in brotherhood with
    those writers and thus offer a basis for "a national
    culture."

13 FORSYTHE, ROBERT S. "Preface" and "Introduction," in Pierre.
    New York: Alfred A. Knopf, pp. ix-xi, xix-xxxviii.
        Largely in reply to "amateur psychologizing" critics who
    have interpreted Pierre as autobiography. Pierre is not
    the work of a diseased mind but an experiment by a mentally
    sound and healthy Melville in the problem novel. Not a
    mere confession of its author's despair and soul sickness,
    the book presents an invented situation objectively, the
    story of Pierre Glendinning, not of Herman Melville. Many
    of its details are based on events in Melville's life or
    the lives of his relations; but they are twisted and dis-
    torted to suit his purpose as a novelist. They are almost
    always mere details used in heightening character or render-
    ing settings more vivid; hardly ever do they enter into plot.
    The plot, sensational and unconvincing, is only a necessary
    structure based on Melville's ideas of life--the most valu-
    able part of the novel for readers today. Pierre has a
    multiplicity of themes and wealth of symbols but is first
    a study in disillusionment; it is also the presentation of
    a fundamental human problem: whether to do right, regard-
    less of consequences, or to compromise. The unhappy type
    of prose in the narrative and the dialogue of the principal
    characters (the language of the lower class characters and
    Charlie Millthorpe is usually realistic) is probably an
    experiment, like the plot. Pierre is modelled on a verse
    tragedy (Hamlet) and its essentials do not necessarily call
    for ordinary prose expression. Important influences on
    style were probably Carlyle's Sartor Resartus and French
    Revolution, De Quincey's Suspiria de Profundis, and possibly
    Longfellow's Hyperion. Carlyle's Teufelsdröckh probably in-
    fluenced the portrayal of Plinlimmon, who does not represent
    Hawthorne [see 1928.B20 and 1928.B27]. Pierre has grave de-
    fects of structure, characterization, and style, and is fur-
    ther weakened by overemphasis of the role of Fate, but
    demands attention as a serious and thoughtful work, as a
    literary experiment, and as a novel by Herman Melville.

14 HEARN, LAFCADIO. Letter to Charles Warren Stoddard. Word
    Shadows of the Great: The Lure of Autograph Collecting by
    Thomas F. Madigan. New York: Frederick A. Stokes Co.,
    p. 179.

1930

Hearn writes that Stoddard's <u>South Sea Idyls</u> "bewitched" him before he heard of Melville.

15   JOSEPHSON, MATTHEW. <u>Portrait of the Artist as American</u>. New York: Harcourt, Brace and Co., pp. 27-36.
        Incorporates parts of 1928.B28. In <u>Typee</u>, Melville is a "young and early neophyte of Rousseau and eighteenth century Naturism"; spirited passages curiously match the "anarchism" of Thoreau. Later a sense of desperate alienation from the life about him weighed on Melville; <u>Moby-Dick</u> is a book of anger, a narrative of Promethean struggle. <u>Pierre</u> attacks existing institutions and offers the case of a moral con-science in arms against the proprieties of the Philistines. But Melville recoiled from the gesture of revolt; the "veri-table problem of his soul" was a paralyzing introspection, and he reveals in <u>Pierre</u> his own temporizings, falterings, and regrets. His revolt is deflected and takes a midway course between that of two other "rebels": Poe moved toward self-destruction; Whitman detached himself serenely from the Philistines. Melville schooled himself to silence, but this was a mask. In <u>Clarel</u> one reads the reflections of his defeat. Melville longed for freedom and liberty of conscience but foresaw democracy, under mechanism, preparing its own degraded level. The great alterations of the whole surface of life in America he experienced as a personal disaster.

16   MADIGAN, THOMAS F. <u>Word Shadows of the Great: The Lure of Autograph Collecting</u>. New York: Frederick A. Stokes, p. 178.
        Notes the rarity of Melville's autograph, few of his manuscripts and letters having survived and fewer still having "come into the market."

17   MOTT, FRANK LUTHER. <u>A History of American Magazines, 1741-1850</u>. New York and London: D. Appleton and Co., pp. 416, 587.
        Claims that among the early novels <u>Mardi</u> called forth the most understanding notice, by the unknown critic for the <u>Democratic Review</u>, "who, in spite of a rather theologic cast of mind, or possibly because of it, saw something fine in Melville." [<u>See</u> 1849.B77.] Includes Melville in a list of brilliant contributors to <u>Godey's Magazine and Lady's Book</u> in the 1840s.

18   MURRY, J. MIDDLETON. "The End of Herman Melville," in <u>Discoveries</u>. The Travellers' Library. London: Jonathan Cape, pp. 257-263.
        Partial reprint of 1924.B25.

19   NOLIE, MUMEY. "Moby-Dick," in A Study of Rare Books. Denver:
      The Clason Publishing Co., pp. 374-375.
          Description of first edition of Moby-Dick and reproduc-
      tion of title page; brief biographical note.

20   PARRINGTON, VERNON LOUIS. The Beginnings of Critical Realism
      in America, 1860-1920. Volume 3 of Main Currents in Amer-
      ican Thought. New York: Harcourt, Brace and Co., pp. 14,
      252, 403.
          Reference to Melville as colossal and dynamic beyond
      Whitman and Twain, looking out sardonically "from his tomb
      in the Custom House where he was consuming his own heart"
      and as a "turbulent soul" unlike W. D. Howells. Melville
      included (with Paine, Jefferson, Emerson, Thoreau, and
      Whitman) in list of the few American intellectuals who
      were democrats.

21   PATTEE, FRED LEWIS. "Revaluations," in The New American Liter-
      ature. New York: The Century Co., pp. 359-384.
          Reprint of 1927.B15, somewhat revised.

22   SALT, HENRY S. Company I Have Kept. London: George Allen &
      Unwin, pp. 108-110, 126.
          Mainly reminiscences. Remembers bringing Moby-Dick to
      the notice of William Morris, and a week or two afterwards
      hearing him quoting it "with huge gusto and delight."
      [Cf. 1922.B33.] The appreciation of Melville which W. H.
      Hudson liked best was Salt's article in the Gentleman's
      Magazine [1892.B14]. Melville's genius is in no way more
      clearly shown than in the slow culmination of the interest
      of Moby-Dick.

23   SHURCLIFF, SIDNEY NICHOLS. Jungle Islands: The "Illyria" in
      the South Seas. New York and London: G. P. Putnam's Sons,
      Knickerbocker Press, p. 114.
          Brief reference. Visits "Typee Valley, Herman Melville's
      famous vale." (Photograph opposite of "Melville's Vale of
      Typee.")

24   SCHWEIKERT, H. C., REWEY BELLE INGLIS, and JOHN GEHLMANN, eds.
      Adventures in American Literature. New York: Harcourt,
      Brace and Co., pp. 12, 346-347, 935-936.
          In introduction to short story section, Melville is
      listed among "Minor Writers Following Poe"; his short tales
      are not well known, though he is now considered a genius of
      the longer story. Headnote to "Herman Melville Writes
      'Moby-Dick'" (an extract from chapter 6 of 1929.A1) acknowl-
      edges that at the turn of the first quarter of the twentieth

century much of Melville's work seems almost contemporary. Biographical sketch in "History of American Literature: A Review and Re-Interpretation."

25 [TARG, WILLIAM]. <u>Targ's American First Editions & Their Prices</u>. Chicago: William Targ, p. 79.
Lists prices of first editions of Melville's first nine books.

26 TOMLINSON, H. M. <u>Between the Lines</u>. Cambridge, Mass.: Harvard University Press, pp. 4, 31.
Brief references. "I put him [Thoreau] with Melville and Whitman, and I could hardly say more than that..."; "Once you have been moved by it, once you have been changed by <u>Moby Dick</u>, or by a passage of great music, you will find it hard and even dangerous to venture upon a survey of modern life and its native literature. Neither editors nor publishers would like it. We have to lower the standard, and judge contemporary letters on an easier plane."

27 STONE, WELDON. "Book Reviews." <u>American Literature</u>, 1 (January), 462-464.
Review of Dutton edition of <u>Pierre</u>. [<u>See</u> 1929.B10 and 1929.B17.] <u>Pierre</u> is not a great novel, nor even a good one; Melville took his idea (of the ambiguity of good and evil) too seriously and forgot, or refused, to be an artist. But <u>Pierre</u> is worth something to every student of American literature, as an autobiography of an American who failed tragically because he dared to think and write as he pleased in the middle of the nineteenth century. It is the most significant and most valuable of Melville's books except <u>Moby-Dick</u>, and worth more as an index to Melville's character than all three of the books about him. Moore's "Introduction" should be illuminating to any first reader of <u>Pierre</u>, but Tomlinson's "Preface" can only confuse and alarm him.

28 ANON. "In Aid of Moby Dick." New York <u>Outlook and Independent</u>, 154 (1 January), 17-18.
Announcement of a British scientific expedition en route to the Antartic "to gather data on Moby Dick's habits and migrations." Romance and adventure glossed the industry Melville studied on his voyage with Ahab, but modern whaling is solely commercial. Modern whale-hunting methods have spelled wholesale slaughter; unless active effort is made, the picturesque mammal may vanish. A month's catch by a modern steam trawler equals the four years' catch of a New Bedford whaler.

29   BLAIR, E. A.   "Herman Melville."   London <u>New Adelphi</u>, 3
     (March-May), 206-208.
          Review of 1929.A1. Mumford is excellent when interpret-
     ing Melville himself, analyzing his philosophy, psychology,
     religion, and sexual life; for the first time Melville's
     strange and conflicting qualities are disentangled. Mumford
     is less successful in interpreting his works, least happy
     in dealing with <u>Moby-Dick</u>. Justly appreciative and nobly
     enthusiastic, he has altogether too keen an eye for the
     inner meaning; he should have simply discussed the form
     and left the "meaning" alone. The best chapters are those
     in which Mumford relates Melville to his times and shows
     how the changing spirit of the century made and marred him.
     Melville was a kind of ascetic voluptuary, a man who felt
     more vividly than common men.

30   ANON. "New Names for the Hall of Fame?" New York <u>Publishers'</u>
     <u>Weekly</u>, 117 (8 March), 336.
          "Of the authors who are likely to be considered...there
     immediately come to mind the names of Walt Whitman...,
     Herman Melville, Henry David Thoreau, Bret Harte, Emily
     Dickinson and John Hay."

31   WATSON, E. L. GRANT. "Melville's <u>Pierre</u>."   <u>New England</u>
     <u>Quarterly</u>, 3 (April), 195-234.
          A study of the book's symbolism, or "inner reality," in
     which characters are seen as "representing tendencies or
     complexes within the <u>psyche</u>." Finds <u>Pierre</u> a "uniquely
     penetrating and profound book," a "work of surprising love-
     liness, of most accurate and delicate perception," the
     greatest of Melville's books, in which the imaginative
     quality is as fine as the best in <u>Moby-Dick</u> and the style
     less flamboyant, a far better artistic whole than <u>Moby-Dick</u>,
     with less matter irrelevant to the main theme. <u>Pierre</u> is
     the center of Melville: to understand him one must under-
     stand this book before all others; he is even profounder
     here than when he created Ahab, Fedallah, and Moby Dick.
     His greatness as a psychologist is unsurpassed by any other
     writer. With the exception of the inserted satirical chap-
     ters on American literature, <u>Pierre</u> is all symbolism and no
     realism. Placed initially in a deliberately artificial set-
     ting, it is "the story of the coming of the knowledge of
     good and evil, of the fall from innocence and the
     paradisaical, unconscious spell of childhood," which brings
     "a soul-shaking increase of consciousness." Mrs. Glendinning
     represents the complex of the social instinct and those ele-
     ments of Pierre's environment that have fashioned his life,
     filling him with artificial values. Lucy symbolizes those

conscious elements of his soul that appear all purity and
goodness. Isabel is the manifestation of the dark half of
his soul, the symbol of the consciousness of the tragic
aspect of life to which he must awaken; through her he must
descend into the depths of the underworld. Her asylum experience portrays the awakening consciousness of the soul
"closely and dangerously beset, in its lonely infancy, by
the undifferentiated and demented-seeming forms of the
collective unconscious." In the city, Pierre the thinker
is at variance with the mystic acceptance of both Isabel
and Lucy: he will not accept the child-like wisdom of
either and does not rest from thinking. At critical moments he hesitates between "the polite, non-benevolent and
aloof masterliness of Plinlimmon" and "the tragic acceptance of the Untergang that embracing of the religious
principle involves." Isabel becomes the symbol of the
seductive power of the unconscious; she hates Pierre's book
as a part of the realm of thought and thus opposed to her.
At first seeming to lead him to Truth, she contains qualities which will destroy in the mind the apprehension of
Truth. Pierre seems to discover an outlet for growth and
freedom in Isabel; but espousing her as his wife is a dis-
guised incest tendency toward his mother. His is the history and tragedy of a soul seeking to free itself from the
psychic world-material in which mankind is unconsciously
always enfolded. Isabel "is of the same world-substance
(mother-substance) as Moby Dick"; their mystery, attractive-
ness, and destructiveness are the same. Pierre renounces
both Isabel and Lucy and with them the complete erotic experience in order that he may remain a child. At the end
he murders that part of himself which Glen symbolizes, and
after this act of inner violence falls into a self-shut-in
state of despondency symbolized by the prison. Pierre's
is the tragedy of a divided nature and in this book Melville
has set down a large portion of his own psychic history. He
seems to be primarily a thinker, who by accident of deep
experience has become a mystic; he is never quite content
to be led solely by the inner light; even in his most mystic
moods conscious strivings are not far distant.

32   WATSON, ARTHUR C. "A Hundred Years Since the First 'Father
       Mapple' Exhorted Whalemen." Boston Evening Transcript
       (17 May), p. 2.
          References to and quotation from chapter 7 of Moby-Dick.
       Notes absence in the New Bedford Seamen's Bethel of Father
       Mapple's curious pulpit, which probably never existed out-
       side of Melville's imagination. Rev. Enoch Mudge cited as
       the original for Mapple.

33   ANON. "One Hundredth Anniversary of the New Bedford Port
     Society." New Bedford Morning Mercury (19 May), pp. 5-6.
        References to and quotation from Moby-Dick, in address
     by Zephaniah W. Pease. In describing the Seamen's Bethel
     at New Bedford (chapters 7 and 8) Melville was improvising
     from memory. It is remarkable that he came so close to the
     reality.

34   ANON. "Reprints and Renewals." New York Times Book Review,
     (20 July), p. 10.
        Review of Knopf edition of Pierre. [See 1930.B13.]
     Forsythe aligns himself with those who seem to think that
     "amateur psychologizing" about the relations of an author's
     life to his work is not quite nice. Yet Forsythe does de-
     tective work into the literary influences on Pierre. Logic
     seems to indicate that if one sort of sleuth work is per-
     missible then so is the other. Forsythe's essay is, however,
     valuable for its array of facts. The story of Pierre sags,
     but even its unsuccessful passages have an archaic flavor
     that gives amusement, if nothing else.

35   ANON. "Barrymore Chases the Whale Again." New York Literary
     Digest, 106 (30 August), 15-16.
        Mainly quotation from (unlocated) favorable reviews of
     the movie Moby Dick, with John Barrymore as Ahab, in the
     New York Herald Tribune, New York Times, and New York World.

*36 HUNT, LIVINGSTON. "Herman Melville as a Naval Historian."
     Harvard Graduates' Magazine, 39 (September), 22-30.
        Cited in Stern, p. 278, and Ricks and Adams, p. 163.

37   MacLEAN, MALCOLM S. "A Restoration." Quarterly Journal, 21
     (Fall), 76-78.
        Review of Knopf edition of Pierre. [See 1930.B13.]
     Forsythe's introduction offers for the first time a truly
     critical appreciation and balanced judgment of Pierre. He
     has shown how unreasonable it is to generalize the autobio-
     graphical element in the novel to cover all its incidents,
     characters, and especially the workings of the hero's mind.
     He has drawn forth other important influences at work on
     Melville during the creation of the novel, using documentary
     evidence, which has been notably lacking in the work of
     recent critics and biographers who have found a Freudian
     significance in the darker phases of plot and character.
     Forsythe has restored to us Pierre for exactly what it is,
     an experiment of a great American writer; not a great book,
     but one worth reading.

1930

38   ANON. "Moby Dick." New York <u>Theatre Magazine</u>, 52 (October),
      47.
          Review of Warner Brothers movie <u>Moby Dick</u>, starring John
      Barrymore--altogether "a highly creditable, moving record
      of Melville's stirring tale."

39   ANON. "Herman Melville's <u>Pierre</u>." London <u>Times Literary
      Supplement</u>, No. 1500 (30 October), p. 884.
          Review of Knopf edition of <u>Pierre</u>. [<u>See</u> 1930.B13.]
      Whether or not it is so perfect a masterpiece as Grant
      Watson would persuade [<u>see</u> 1930.B31], <u>Pierre</u> is a deeply
      interesting book. What the author of <u>Moby-Dick</u> did next,
      even if it seemed pure nonsense, is bound to be significant;
      and <u>Pierre</u> is a very long way from looking like nonsense.
      It is uncouth, cumbersome, poised uneasily between realism
      and symbolism; it is melodramatic, as <u>Hamlet</u> is melodramatic,
      but the melodrama strikes more violently because the lan-
      guage lacks the pregnant subtlety of Shakespeare's. Yet
      <u>Pierre</u> contains profound and elusive thinking. Melville
      shows that the angelical quality of divine and universal
      love cannot be implicated in action, for purity and embodi-
      ment are mutually exclusive terms. <u>Pierre</u> is a book of a
      Titan among writers; its uncouthness is the uncouthness of
      the huge Enceladus. It seems to have had its origin in a
      meditation upon <u>Hamlet</u>, the influence of which seems appar-
      ent in the texture and rhythm of Melville's language.

40   DAMON, S. FOSTER. "Why Ishmael Went to Sea." <u>American Litera-
      ture</u>, 2 (November), 281-283.
          Boston <u>Museum</u> anecdote [<u>see</u> 1852.B24] of Melville's
      being driven out of school by two of his students helps
      explain his running away to sea: he had tried clerking,
      farming, teaching, and failed at everything. Going to sea
      was his "substitute for pistol and ball."

41   EBY, E. H. "Book Reviews." <u>American Literature</u>, 2 (November),
      319-321.
          Review of Knopf edition of <u>Pierre</u>. [<u>See</u> 1930.B13.]
      Forsythe takes a sane middle course, as opposed to the
      elaborate conjectures which have been offered in explana-
      tion of <u>Pierre</u>. That it is an autobiographical novel is an
      assumption not proven by ascertainable facts; Melville al-
      tered personal facts to suit his artistic intentions. Yet
      <u>Pierre</u> is still the key to a knowledge of Melville's inner
      biography; his problems and feelings about life are recorded
      in these pages. Forsythe has been unduly reticent on this
      most important aspect of the novel. His suggestions on
      literary influences, however, are so valuable that they

need further investigation. "Melville, as did many of the
romantics, felt the need of a new prose style more fluid,
more rhythmical, an intermediary between blank verse and
ordinary prose. With Hamlet so strongly in mind, Melville
carried this experiment farther than he did previously.
This accounts for the curiously inflated style, for the
stilted dialogue of the 'high' characters, for the contrast-
ing realism of the 'low.'" Sylvester Judd's Margaret reveals "the same effort to enrich the prose with poetic
feeling and rhythm, the same desire to reveal the symbolism
which inheres in every object and event, the same careless-
ness of plot structure that comes from a shift in attention
from the outer to the inner world." The chief importance of
Pierre is in Melville's attempt to show the "ambiguities" of
motive which underlie the conventional and the conscious.
The destruction of certainties alienated Melville from his
generation and brought him close to the moderns.

42   FORSYTHE, ROBERT S. "Mr. Lewis Mumford and Melville's Pierre."
     American Literature, 2 (November), 286-289.
         Points out errors in Mumford's summary of Pierre in
     1929.A1. Mumford has twisted the plot badly.

43   REDMAN, BEN RAY. "White Whale." New York Herald Tribune
     Books (30 November).
         Notice of Random House edition of Moby-Dick, illus-
     trated by Rockwell Kent. Considers Moby-Dick the greatest
     single work of American fiction. The narrative has a surge
     and sweep, a mad pulsing poetry, a sustained irresistible
     drive found nowhere else in our literature. Moby-Dick is
     the creative debauch of a great storyteller intoxicated by
     his own unleashed powers.

44   ANON. "New & Special Editions." New York Times Book Review
     (14 December), p. 15.
         Review of Random House edition of Moby-Dick, illustrated
     by Rockwell Kent. The task was perfectly suited to Kent's
     power. Moby-Dick is now secure in its place not only as an
     American classic, but as one of the great books of its
     period.

45   ANON. "Pays $3,750 for Barrie Manuscript." New York Times
     (18 December), p. 6.
         A first edition of The Whale brought $850 at the same
     sale.

46   RITCHIE, MARY C. "Herman Melville." Kingston, Ont. Queen's
     Quarterly, 37 (Winter), 36-61.

Mainly biographical, drawing on 1929.A1. Summary of
Moby-Dick. Admires its generous and tolerant spirit, its
deep, religious thought and profound philosophy of life,
"the mighty sweep of a poetry surely unapproached in the
literature of this continent." Some readers will think
that Mumford [in 1929.A1] "has gone too far in his attempt
to compress Melville's wild and mighty genius into the
forms of any theory."

47   ROBERTS, MORLEY. "The Sea in Fiction." Kingston, Ont. Queen's
      Quarterly, 37 (Winter), 18-35.
          Roberts discovered Moby-Dick well over 40 years ago with
      W. H. Hudson. Americans who ask when the great American
      book is to come before the world do not know that it was
      written long ago--in Moby-Dick, "a great thing standing for
      ever without likeness or a peer." Melville "gave way too
      much to his lyrical spirit, and often confounded poetry
      with pure prose, so that he wrote neither, but terrible
      hybrid stuff that some ill-educated folks think poetic
      prose. And yet he could write prose of a high rhetorical
      order, or of the greatest simplicity, and he saw deep into
      the hearts of men." The last paragraph of chapter 26 ("If,
      then, to meanest mariners, and renegades and castaways, I
      shall hereafter ascribe high qualities, though dark..."),
      which is curious in over-wrought rhetoric but has peculiar
      power and the strangeness of some new beauty, owes its
      origin to the last writer in the world we might think
      Melville would have cared to read, Laurence Sterne.

Index

Note: Readers should also consult the
indexes in 1921.A1, 1926.A1, and 1929.A1

Ellis, William, 1849.B36;
1919.B24
Elwes, Robert, A Sketcher's Tour
Round the World, 1854.B1
Emerson, Ralph Waldo, 1849.B3,
B34; 1852.B31; 1853.B3, B9,
B19; 1859.B29; 1867.B2;
1899.B12; 1903.B7; 1921.B4,
B31; 1922.B12; 1923.B16;
1924.B13; 1927.B12; 1928.B14,
B22; 1929.B4, B43; 1930.B20
--"Friendship," 1922.B12
"Encantadas, The," 1854.B3, B5-6,
B8; 1856.B6-7, B11, B20, B22,
B26, B29, B32, B39; 1873.B4;
1921.B25; 1924.B2; 1928.B20;
1929.A1, B57
Encyclopaedia Americana, 1918.B1
Encyclopaedia Britannica,
1902.B7; 1911.B5
Encyclopaedia of Biography of New
York, 1916.B1
Erasmus, 1901.B8
Erskine, John, 1929.B67
--The Delight of Great Books,
1928.B10
--Leading American Novelists,
1910.B3
Essex, 1851.B68
Everett, Edward, 1889.B3
Evil, 1849.B77, B137; 1923.B22,
B27; 1924.B28; 1928.B4, B32,
B34; 1929.A1, B17, B28;
1930.B10, B27, B31

F

Fairfax, Lee, 1922.B25
Faulkner, William, 1927.B24
Fausset, Hugh I'A., 1926.B37
Faust, 1925.B20
Fayaway, 1847.B83; 1848.B3, B9;
1849.B2, B17, B94, B106;
1850.B63; 1851.B4, B7, B10;
1852.B6; 1856.B5; 1858.B22;
1868.B4; 1922.B35
Ferris, Mary L. D., 1901.B8
Field, Maunsell B., Memories of
Many Men and of Some Women,
1874.B1
Fielding, Henry, 1919.B19

Fields, James T., 1910.B3
--Yesterday with Authors, 1872.B4
Finley, John H., 1928.B11
Fisher, William, The Petrel,
1850.B28
Fletcher, John, 1904.B8
Fletcher, John Gould, The Two
Frontiers, 1930.B10
Flitcroft, John E., Outline
Studies in American Litera-
ture, 1930.B11
Foley, P. K., American Authors,
1795-1895: A Bibliography
of First and Notable Editions,
1897.B6
Foerster, Norman
--Towards Standards, 1930.B12
--ed., American Poetry and Prose,
1925.B2
--ed., Humanism and America,
1930.B5
--ed., The Reinterpretation of
American Literature, 1928.B7
Forgues, E.-D., 1853.B9, B11
Forster, E. M., Aspects of the
Novel, 1927.B5; 1928.B16
Forsythe, Robert S., 1930.B13,
B34, B37, B41-42
France, Anatole, L'Île des
Pingouins, 1925.B10
Francis, John Wakefield, 1852.B25,
B28; 1858.B1
Frank, Waldo, The Re-discovery of
America, 1929.B4
Franklin, Julia, 1915.B1
Franklin, S. R., Memories of a
Rear-Admiral, 1898.B2
Frazer, Sir James George, The
Belief in Immortality and the
Worship of the Dead, 1913.B2
Freeman, John, Herman Melville,
1926.A1
Freud, Sigmund, 1919.B16; 1922.B12;
1930.B9, B37

G

Galland, René, 1927.B28
Gansevoort, Henry Sanford,
1929.B52; 1875.B4

378

B48–49, B68; 1930.B13, B15,
B27, B31, B34, B37, B39,
B41–42
Plato, 1849.B50; 1858.B28;
1926.B16; 1927.B12
--Dialogues, 1857.B15
Plunkett, Mrs. H. M., 1900.B9
Plomer, William, 1929.B54
Poe, Edgar Allan, 1852.B31, B71;
1853.B3, B27; 1856.B7, B20,
B22, B38, B42; 1902.B7;
1904.B9; 1913.B4; 1921.B4,
B30; 1922.B15; 1923.B7, B15,
B19, B24, B26; 1925.B3;
1926.B8; 1927.B17; 1928.B28;
1929.B4; 1930.B9, B15, B24
Poems, 1888.B5; 1891.B1, B18,
B26; 1897.B2; 1899.B6;
1900.B2; 1902.B7; 1903.B7;
1909.B1; 1917.B3; 1918.B3;
1919.B1, B16, B19; 1921.B13,
B19, B29; 1922.B3, B44;
1923.B11, B16–19, B23, B31;
1926.A1, B25, B38; 1929.A1,
B3; see also Battle-Pieces,
Clarel, John Marr and ·Other
Sailors, Timoleon, and Uncollected Poems
"Poor Man's Pudding and Rich
Man's Crumbs," 1854.B11
Porter, Captain David, 1846.B33;
1919.B3
Potter, Israel, Life and Remarkable Adventures of Israel R.
Potter, 1855.B12, B26;
1924.B19; 1928.B23; 1929.A1
Prescott, William Hickling,
1850.B111
Prometheus, 1919.B1; 1929.B39;
1930.B15
Psychology, 1851.B72; 1852.B53,
B63, B71; 1920.B8; 1922.B38;
1926.A1, B31; 1928.B20, B34;
1929.A1, B22, B36, B51;
1930.B29, B31
Puritan literary tradition,
1928.B14

Q

Quarles, Philip, 1847.B59

Quarll, Adventures of Philip,
1846.B7
Quennell, Peter, 1929.B63
Quiller-Couch, A., 1918.B4
Quinn, Arthur Hobson, 1922.B43
Quinn, Arthur Hobson, Albert Croll
Baugh, and Will David Howe,
The Literature of America,
1929.B13

R

Rabelais, François, 1849.B7, B17,
B25, B59–60, B85; 1853.B19;
1856.B27; 1857.B3, B17;
1891.B18; 1919.B1, B19;
1921.B8; 1922.B15; 1926.A1;
1929.B11
--Gargantua et Pantagruel,
1849.B17, B138; 1921.B25;
1923.B14, B24
Radcliffe, Ann, 1852.B36;
1923.B24
Rankin, Thomas Ernest, Clarence
Dewitt Thorpe, and Melvin
Theodor Solve, College
Composition, 1929.B14
Raphael, 1849.B77
Rationalism, 1920.B1
Rauschenbush, Winifred, 1925.B21
Read, Herbert, 1928.B24
--The Sense of Glory, 1929.B15
Reade, Charles, 1922.B9
Récamier, Jeanne Françoise Julie
Adélaïde, 1924.B21
Redburn, 1849.B91, B101–104,
B107–111, B116–52; 1850.B6,
B8, B17–20, B27, B58, B73,
B82, B87; 1851.B21, B80;
1852.B7, B12, B19; 1855.B2;
1856.B1; 1857.B3; 1871.B1;
1873.B2; 1879.B3; 1883.B2;
1884.B1, B7; 1887.B2; 1889.B1,
B7; 1890.B1; 1892.B4–5;
1893.B13; 1900.B10; 1902.B5;
1904.B8; 1907.B7; 1909.B4;
1919.B8, B15, B18; 1921.B6,
B17, B19; 1922.A1, B12, B34;
1923.B20; 1924.B5, B20, B28;
1925.B12, B22; 1926.A1, B33;
1927.B25; 1928.B1; 1930.B10